EUROPEAN COMMISSION

The Single Market Review

IMPACT ON COMPETITION
AND SCALE EFFECTS

COMPETITION ISSUES

The Single Market Review

SUBSERIES V: VOLUME 3

OFFICE FOR OFFICIAL PUBLICATIONS
OF THE EUROPEAN COMMUNITIES

KOGAN PAGE . EARTHSCAN

This report is part of a series of 39 studies commissioned from independent consultants in the context of a major review of the Single Market. The 1996 Single Market Review responds to a 1992 Council of Ministers Resolution calling on the European Commission to present an overall analysis of the effectiveness of measures taken in creating the Single Market. This review, which assesses the progress made in implementing the Single Market Programme, was coordinated by the Directorate-General 'Internal Market and Financial Services' (DG XV) and the Directorate-General 'Economic and Financial Affairs' (DG II) of the European Commission.

This document was prepared for the European Commission

by

London Economics

It does not, however, express the Commission's official views. Whilst every reasonable effort has been made to provide accurate information in regard to the subject matter covered, the Consultants are not responsible for any remaining errors. All recommendations are made by the Consultants for the purpose of discussion. Neither the Commission nor the Consultants accept liability for the consequences of actions taken on the basis of the information contained herein.

The European Commission would like to express thanks to the external experts and representatives of firms and industry bodies for their contribution to the 1996 Single Market Review, and to this report in particular.

Office for Official Publications of the European Communities
2 rue Mercier, L-2985 Luxembourg
ISBN 92-827-8803-2   Catalogue number: C1-71-96-003-EN-C

Kogan Page . Earthscan
120 Pentonville Road, London N1 9JN
ISBN 0 7494 2336 6

Table of contents

List of tables

List of figures

List of abbreviations

BEUC	Bureau Européen des Unions de Consommateurs
CAA	Civil Aviation Authority
CCD	Concentrations with a Community dimension
CEPR	Centre for Economic Policy Research
CRS	Computerized reservation system
DoJ	Department of Justice [USA]
EAG	Economists Advisory Group
EC	European Communities
ECJ	European Court of Justice
ECSC	European Coal and Steel Community
EEA	European Economic Area
EEC	European Economic Community
EU	European Union
FFP	Frequent Flyer Programme
GAO	General Accounting Office (USA)
GATT	General Agreement on Tariffs and Trade
IATA	International Air Transport Association
IPR	Intellectual property rights
JV	Joint venture
M&A	Mergers and acquisitions
MEIP	Market Economy Investor Principle
MMC	Monopolies and Mergers Commission
MPV	Multi-purpose vehicle
MTF	Merger Task Force
NIC	Newly Industrialized Countries
OJ	Official Journal
R&D	Research and development
RHT	Reverse hooking tyre
SEA	Single European Act
SME	Small & medium-sized enterprises
TOs	Telecom operators
UBC	United Brands Corporation
VAT	Value added tax
VER	Voluntary Export Restraint

Acknowledgements

In preparation for the Intergovernmental Conference, the Commission commissioned a number of studies on the impact of the single market programme. Some studies focus on developments in specific industries, whereas others examine the wider economic impact. In this major study the Commission sought a wide-ranging examination of the competitive behaviour of firms faced with changes in market conditions, in particular those aspects of firm behaviour that may prevent the benefits arising from the single market being fully realized.

The research for this study was undertaken by three groups of consultants and academics based in London, Barcelona, Brussels and Berlin.

The project team consisted of a core group that was supported by two groups of advisers and collaborators:

London Economics: Cristina Caffarra, Robin Cohen, Pietro Crocioni, Tom Hoehn (project director), John Kay (main project adviser), Christian Koboldt, Aubrey Silberston (main project adviser);

Instituto de Análisis Económico/Fundación de Economía Analítica, Barcelona: Kai-Uwe Kühn, Carmen Matutes, Xavier Vives (main project adviser);

Fachhochschule für Wirtschaft, Berlin: Jürgen Müller, Georg Merdian;

Other collaborators: Daniel Maldoom, University College, Oxford; Robin Nuttall, Nuffield College, Oxford; Nick Owen, Department of Trade and Industry, London; Stefan Szymanski, Imperial College, London.

The final report was prepared by the editorial team consisting of Cristina Caffarra, Tom Hoehn, Kai-Uwe Kühn and Daniel Maldoom. The project director, Tom Hoehn, acted as general editor. Sub-editing and final collation of the document was done by Audrey Minton (London Economics).

A supplementary report, *Competition Issues in the Single Market: Case Studies*, London Economics [1996], contains the case studies that served as empirical background material for the analysis of various issues throughout this study. The case studies were the editorial responsibility of: Tom Hoehn (soda ash); Jürgen Müller (airlines); Nick Owen (cars); Stefan Szymanski (beer).

1. Summary

The 1985 White Paper, *Completing the internal market*, carried a great number of expectations with it. The Cecchini report, published in 1988, quantified these expectations and concluded that a substantial part (23%) of the benefits of completing the single market would derive from the effects of intensified competition.

These high expectations of the effect of increased competition in the single market are at the heart of this study, which is part of a series that the European Commission has initiated. In line with the terms of reference, this study, by London Economics, the Instituto de Análisis Económico (Barcelona) and the Fachhochschule für Wirtschaft (Berlin), comprises an economic analysis of the evolution of competitive conditions in European markets, and how these have been affected by measures to complete the single market. Our analysis includes an examination of aspects of firm behaviour which may be preventing the benefits of effective competition in the single market being fully realized, and leads to an assessment of the role of competition policy in achieving these aims.

1.1. Main findings

The study reviews trends in integration and competition across individual markets. We use a variety of statistical indicators and consider competition issues arising from European competition cases as well as individual market studies. The study aims specifically to test and evaluate the following effects expected to arise from the single market programme:

(a)   reductions in the cost of doing trade across national borders are expected to lead to increased trade and the entry of new competitors into national markets;

(b)   markets that were previously mainly delineated by national borders are expected to become larger and market boundaries to be determined by the economic fundamentals;

(c)   market power and hence profit margins would be reduced, and within these larger markets tougher cross-border competition would ensure that inefficient firms would either exit the market or improve their performance;

(d)   in larger markets firms would be able to exploit economies of scale, leading to changes in market structure;

(e)   integrated larger markets would act as a spur to designing new products and undertaking increased R&D.

Our study results in the following main conclusions:

(a)   There is strong evidence of the pro-competitive effects of integration. Integration in the EU has generally increased, when assessed against a variety of economic indicators derived from a large sample of sectors. Furthermore, our research provides econometric evidence of the significant impact of integration on price-cost margins, an important indicator of the intensity of competition in European markets. We also find significant evidence of a fall in cross-sector and cross-country differences in price-cost margins in the second half of the 1980s.

(b)   The full potential benefits have not yet been achieved. Although we find strong evidence that the single market programme has had beneficial pro-competitive effects, it seems to be the case that the full potential benefits of market integration are yet to be completely realized. Our econometric analysis confirms a fall in price-cost margins only for a subset of those sectors where the impact of the single market programme was expected to be high. Achievement of the full benefits may take longer and may require further specific intervention by the Commission (e.g. national deregulation initiatives or external trade liberalization).

(c)   There are multiple drivers of competition including external trade liberalization as well as major changes in technology. Our data is consistent with deepening market integration, but we cannot in general rule out the possibility that there are other causes for movement towards more competitive outcomes. For example, in the case of soda ash, external trade liberalization was found to have a more significant impact in constraining prices than the single market programme. In the case of cars, external trade policy and competition policy appear to have inhibited rather than promoted integration; and in the case of air travel, external and internal trade liberalization are working in parallel. External and intra-EU trade flows are generally correlated and it is difficult to establish the respective impact of external trade liberalization and the single market programme.

(d)   The limits to integration should not be ignored. Case study evidence suggests that the scope for increased market integration is often limited due to the importance of transport costs (e.g. soda ash, beer) or because markets are already integrated at a European or global level.

(e)   There is considerable scope for anti-competitive responses. Both theoretical and empirical analyses suggest that there are a wide variety of strategic responses of firms which could lead to the potential benefits of integration not being fully achieved. For example, access to essential facilities in a previously national market may not be forthcoming at a reasonable price and cross-border entry may be hampered; firms may collude and share markets across the EU along national borders; pro-competitive direct entry into foreign markets may be avoided by joint ventures or licensing agreements; mergers may lead to market power even in a broader post-integration market; and finally, firms may call on national governments to protect them from the necessary adjustments to a more competitive environment.

(f)   There is a continued role for competition policy. The role of competition policy in promoting integration and securing the benefits of increased competition in integrated markets is reinforced by our study. The need for competition policy in larger markets remains. The single market programme, with very few exceptions, is not a substitute for a vigorous enforcement of competition policy. Dominant firm behaviour and anti-competitive practices can arise irrespective of market size. However, if consistency is to be achieved, the conduct of national competition policy in integrated markets requires more coordination, particularly in areas where competition policy and industry regulation interact (e.g. access to essential infrastructure facilities).

(g)   The focus of competition policy in integrated markets needs to change. In many markets and industries, where integration has been substantially achieved, European competition policy, as reviewed across the case law of the last decade, could benefit from a clearer focus on the objective of competition as a means to promote economic efficiency rather than integration. Some types of cooperative behaviour of firms are possibly too easily exempted by the Commission (e.g. joint ventures and other cooperative agreements) because they are thought to facilitate integration, whereas others are too readily challenged as being incompatible with the single market (e.g. price discrimination and vertical agreements).

1.2. Supporting evidence

1.2.1. Sectoral indicators

The general evidence of positive trends in integration is derived from aggregate indicators of price convergence, trade flows, price-cost margins and changes in concentration, as well as extensive cross-sectoral data on trade flows and price-cost margins. The findings on the development of price-cost margins are to our knowledge unique and provide confirmation of the significant impact of the single market programme in two ways:

(a)   first, the data suggests a clear reduction in the variation of price-cost margins across sectors and countries after 1985;

(b)   second, the inclusion of a policy impact variable in our regression analysis confirms the significant cumulative effect on price-cost margins of policy measures implemented after 1986.

The five indicators listed in the table below are on the whole consistent with what we would expect to see if integration had had effects.

Table 1.1.   Trends in integration

Trade creation	yes
Price convergence	yes
Exploitation of economies of scale	yes
Reductions in price-cost margins	yes
Reduced variance of price-cost margins	yes

(a)   Trade between Member States has increased. External trade flows, however, also increased, suggesting perhaps that competition from outside has been an equally important factor in shaping the evolution of competition in the EU for these sectors.

(b)   Price differentials, particularly for consumer goods across the EUR-12, narrowed, in line with expected reductions in the costs of arbitrage across EU economies, with economic fundamentals becoming more similar.

(c)   We also expect market structure itself to be affected by integration, with firms exiting as a response to tougher competition even if the product differentiation potential allows additional players and niche suppliers to survive. Research in other studies in *The Single Market Review* appears to confirm these expectations.

(d)   The expectation that increased cross-border competition should lead to reduced market power and falling price-cost margins is generally confirmed. At the sectoral level this finding only applies to a subset of sectors, but not for some of those sectors for which EU internal trade barriers were considered to be relatively high (for example, public procurement sectors).

(e)   In addition, there is evidence that the dispersion of price-cost margins across countries has been substantially reduced. There appears to be a decisive downward trend in the late 1980s, since which time the variance has halved. The equalization of price-cost margins across the EU is consistent with increased competition.

1.2.2. Case study analysis

We have analysed a number of markets in detail (cars, beer, soda ash, airlines). These case studies are revealing because they show that the effects of market integration may be very different in different markets. Some markets, like soda ash, a key raw material for the production of glass, have limited scope for integration due to high transport costs. Other markets, like cars and beer, remain substantially segmented along national or regional borders for a number of reasons and have only been partly affected by the single market programme. National distribution patterns dominate for historical reasons, and have not been radically challenged by either the single market programme or the intervention of the Commission's Competition Policy Directorate. Table 1.2 summarizes key features of our analysis of the selected markets.

These case studies and the review of competition case law also illustrate some examples of what we have called 'anti-competitive responses' to integration. This confirms our general conclusion that achievement of the full potential benefits of integration may in some cases be hampered by the strategic behaviour of firms, despite on average there being consumer and efficiency benefits from integration.

Table 1.2. Summary of market studies

	Soda ash	Beer	Cars	Domestic appliances	Airlines
Initial market structure	Oligopolistic national markets	National or regional markets often oligopolistic	Oligopolistic with national champions	Fragmented national markets	Protected national monopolies/ international cartels
Single market measures	Negligible	Technical and physical measures	Important technical measures, continued block exemption for distribution arrangements	Reduction in cross-border transaction costs	Major liberalization pressures being implemented by 1997
Competition issues	Major collusion case and protection through trade policy measures	Cross-country licensing and vertical restraints	Distribution agreements, strategic alliances and R&D JVs, VERs	Mergers	Dominance, barriers to entry, joint ventures, mergers
Integration	High, but markets limited by transport costs	Moderate	Relatively high at manu-facturing level, low in distribution	High with remaining market segmentation limited by taste	Still low

1.3. Analysis of competition issues

Against this complex picture of the interaction of integration and competition, we have focused our attention on the analysis of behavioural obstacles to further integration. We believe that in many industries the remaining obstacles to integration are based on a combination of factors that can reinforce each other. For example, purchasing habits that are based on national preferences, or are due to environmental and cultural factors, can be exploited in conjunction with behaviour that may sometimes be anti-competitive. This behaviour then has the effect of maintaining some segmentation of markets along national borders.

Our analysis of the behaviour of firms in the single market has focused on those strategic responses that are most closely related to the single market programme. Where possible, we generalize about the likelihood of such responses by type of industry and draw policy conclusions.

(a)   Price discrimination and parallel import restrictions. This competition issue is intimately connected with market integration. A number of cases dealt with by the Commission, involving branded goods, indicate a desire to segment markets that have different demand elasticities across the EU. Our analysis demonstrates that price discrimination can have several pro-competitive effects (output expansion and market-opening effects; competition for marginal consumers), suggesting a case by case approach when considering the application of Art. 85 to measures facilitating price discrimination.

(b)   Access restrictions. Typically these apply to industries where access to infrastructure facilities and networks are essential for entering a new market. Our analysis emphasizes the need for a proper definition of an essential facility that takes into account the costs of duplication and the lack of substitutes.

(c)   Collusion. Homogeneous goods industries with high sunk costs that are exposed to demand fluctuations have been shown to have strong incentives to enter into collusive agreements. Integration can be expected to make within-country collusion more difficult to sustain and less attractive. There is, however, little reason to suppose that market integration will reduce the scope for cross-country collusion, such as market sharing by national boundaries. This implies a continued need for tough enforcement of competition policy towards EU-wide cartels. The only other effective instrument against national market sharing appears to be external trade liberalization.

(d)   Joint ventures. A general picture emerges of a decline in the need to establish collaborative agreements in order to enter new markets following market integration. Nevertheless, our analysis highlights concerns over the potential anti-competitive effects of those agreements that avoid direct entry into new markets and combine the substitutable activities of two potential competitors. We observe that current treatment of such agreements may in some cases be too permissive.

(e)   Mergers. Contrary to general expectations, no obvious trend or generalizations can be made regarding merger activity in the single market. Nevertheless, we note that, as a result of market integration, the costs of inappropriate EU-wide merger policy are higher, since a mistake affects more consumers while the administrative burden on firms from the one-stop shop is lessened.

(f)   State aid. Industries that are subject to major restructuring under the single market programme may be particularly prone to state aid cases. Even if the official statistics do not record an increase in the amount of state aid granted to individual companies, there are other Community programmes (Structural Funds) that are designed to support industries in lagging regions. Given that the distortive effect of state aid is felt more widely in larger, more integrated markets, great vigilance and careful analysis of their justification is required when adjudicating on the appropriateness of aid to specific companies.

1.4. Policy conclusions

Our main policy conclusion, that there is a continued role for a vigorous European competition policy, is borne out in the wide-ranging analysis of competition issues summarized above. Other policy conclusions relate to the relationship of competition policy with other Community policies and to the role of the Commission as a coordinator and facilitator of an effective competition policy across the EU.

1.4.1. Trade policy and competition policy

We reject the notion that trade policy and competition policy are substitutes in the sense that market integration should obviate the need for a vigorous competition policy.

(a)   Trade policy works differently from competition policy: the former enlarges markets and encourages competition by facilitating market access, while the latter is directed at the exercise of market power and other distortions of competition.

(b)   Trade policy and competition policy can either work in harmony or result in conflict (e.g. dumping policies undermining competition policy intervention). Similarly the single market programme, which is a form of internal trade policy, can work together with other policies or can create policy conflict.

1.4.2. Efficiency and integration objectives of competition policy

In our study we find that the execution of competition policy under Art. 85 in the EU appears to suffer from a perhaps excessive emphasis on behaviour that appears to inhibit integration rather than prevent or distort competition. Behavioural responses of firms to changes in the competitive environment are not easily found to be both anti-competitive and anti-integration, except for some well-defined situations such as explicit market sharing, cartels or price-fixing agreements across national markets. In many other instances, the objectives for increased integration and effective competition may clash.

(a)   Vertical restraints are generally not anti-competitive unless they are undertaken by dominant firms and serve to foreclose entry to new competitors; their effect on national market segmentation may be an undesirable by-product.

(b)   Licensing agreements by firms across Member States are considered a positive indicator of integration. Yet these agreements may or may not be anti-competitive depending on who agrees what, with whom and in what market environment. In other words, the identity of the parties to an agreement matters within the specific market context.

1.4.3. The role of the Commission

The final set of policy conclusions deals with the role of the Commission. Our assessment suggests, among other things, that in addition to the Commission's traditional task of direct enforcement of Community competition policy:

(a)   there is a residual role to act as a regulatory authority when dealing with access restrictions that are not subject to national regulation;

(b)   similarly, there is a coordinating role for the Commission to secure the consistent application of competition policy in Member States.

Furthermore, we consider that it is extremely valuable to make competition policy intervention contingent on market structure analysis. This is already done in the case of mergers where the analysis of dominance by the Merger Task Force is at the heart of the investigation. This structural approach does not replace a thorough analysis of the nature of competition in the relevant markets, but certainly helps to deal with certain types of behaviour quickly when, for example, concentration in the relevant market is low and allegations of anti-competitive behaviour cannot be sustained. Our conclusion on these issues is that market structure, monitoring and provision of market data by Eurostat would greatly facilitate the assessment of competition issues in the single market, whether undertaken by the Commission or by national competition authorities.

The resources that need to be expended on this role (residual regulation, coordination of national merger policy, monitoring market structure) can be at least partly found from savings made in resources that are currently used to vet and monitor vertical agreements with no serious negative consequences for competition in the single market.

2. Introduction

The single market programme, launched in 1985 with the White Paper, *Completing the internal market*, carried a great number of expectations with it. In the most wide-ranging study of its effects, the Cecchini report [1988] estimated the benefits of achieving the single market to be worth around 4.5% of European gross domestic product. These benefits were to be derived from the direct efficiency gains of eliminating non-tariff barriers, which impose costs on businesses doing trade across the EU. In addition, businesses were expected to take advantage of opportunities to sell across larger markets in the EU through the exploitation of economies of scale in production and distribution. The third major benefit would result from the effects of increased competition in integrated markets. While the Cecchini report associated most of the benefit of the completion of the single market with the direct efficiency gains resulting from the removal of trade barriers, and from exploiting economies of scale, 23% of all gains were expected to result from the effects of intensified competition.[1]

The competitive effects of internal trade liberalization are crucial not only for the benefits that arise from the improved allocation of resources, but also because competition is the chief mechanism through which efficiency gains are passed on to consumers. It is one thing to argue that the costs of doing business across Europe are coming down, but another matter to ask whether these cost reductions are passed on to consumers. Many obstacles to the operation of competitive markets exist, quite independently from those directly associated with the single market programme. The development of adequate policies to tackle these obstacles to competition can be expected to be of great benefit.

An assessment of the changes in competitive conditions in the EU, and an investigation of the scope for strategic responses by businesses and government to single market measures, is therefore essential for an evaluation of the success of the single market programme. Equally important is to recommend policies to remove any remaining obstacles to competition and integration in the EU.

2.1. Aim of the study

In line with the terms of reference, this study comprises an economic analysis of the evolution of competitive conditions in European markets, and how these have been affected by measures to complete the single market. The analysis has three key aims:

(a) to examine aspects of the competitive process which may be preventing the realization of the benefits of effective competition in the single market;

(b) to examine the interaction between competitive conditions, competition policy interventions and the single market programme;

(c) to reach conclusions about the role of competition policy and whether policy has to be adjusted once integration has substantially been achieved.

Dealing with the first of these aims helps to identify the extent of the potential problem presented by strategic responses by business to the single market programme. Addressing the second is intended to assess the extent to which competition policy plays a major role in

---

[1]   See also Silberston and Raymond [1996].

achieving or frustrating integration. The third aim reflects the need to provide recommendation on future policy. In particular, this study needs to consider whether completion of the single market changes the need for competition policy intervention, or whether (and, if so, how much and of what kind) further intervention is required to realize the full benefits of the single market programme.

2.2. Method of analysis

The method of analysis is based on interviews with businesses, expert reviews of industry and market studies, and analysis of market data.

The analysis has three elements. The first strand of analysis comprises a review of available statistics and the development of case study material to provide empirical foundations from which more generalized conclusions can be drawn. The second strand of analysis provides a rigorous theoretical evaluation of the main competition policy issues that arise as a consequence of the single market programme. These two elements of analysis need to be brought together in a third element. This integrates case studies and other case law with the theoretical analysis of competition issues, leading to a set of conclusions on the future direction of policy.

2.2.1. Indicators of trends in integration

The analysis of trends in integration reviewed aggregate statistical material across industrial sectors in the EU. We have also made use of the results of other studies and, where necessary, have undertaken our own research to update older studies. The principal indicators that we evaluate at the aggregate sectoral level include:

(a)   trade flows;
(b)   price differentials;
(c)   concentration;
(d)   price-cost margins.

The research on the impact of the single market programme on price-cost margins across sectors and countries is, to our knowledge, wholly original and provides valuable insight into the development of integration.

2.2.2. Case studies of the development of competition

Six market studies have been selected to provide an empirical basis for the assessment of the main themes of this study, namely the extent to which markets have become more integrated, and the extent to which the competitive strategies of European companies have changed in response to single market measures. In this way the market studies should exemplify how competitive conditions have evolved. At the same time, the studies have been selected so that they assist in the policy analysis by illustrating potential conflicts between the single market competition policy and other objectives. They should also facilitate generalization to other markets, with respect to possible adjustments to national and EU competition policy instruments.

The market studies we have selected cover soda ash, beer, cars and airlines. The main competition issues that these market studies address are as follows.

Soda ash. The anti-competitive behaviour of colluding, dominant firms may inhibit an enlargement of the economic market and result in market segmentation. Soda ash as a homogeneous, intermediate product may offer scope for generalization to other raw material, intermediate products, including cartonboard, cement, wood pulp and to some extent steel.

Beer. Vertical restraints and cross-country licensing can limit entry and potentially lessen competition. Vertical restraints may take a range of forms: the case of beer represents predominately exclusive dealing and offers scope for generalization to petrol and other consumer products.

Cars. Many European car makers pursue joint ventures and have some strategic alliances. Most of them organize their distribution at the national level in the form of selective distribution agreements. The car market raises issues of vertical restraint, market access and external trade policy.

Airlines. Firms controlling absolute advantages can prevent market entry, and inhibit the development of competition and integration. The air travel industry is a key service sector and offers considerable scope for competition at the level of an integrated EU market. It thus represents an obvious choice for a case study.

There are two other market overviews which cover interesting examples of industries that have changed radically over the last two decades. These market overviews are much less detailed than the four main market studies but offer useful background information. The market for telecommunication equipment has seen both technological changes and changes in the procurement of telecommunication operators, who themselves have been forced to operate in a more liberalized environment. The markets for domestic appliances on the other hand have been completely restructured through a series of mergers and acquisitions, and it is arguable that the market for washing machines, for example, no longer operates at a mainly national level.

2.2.3. Analysis of competition policy issues

The strategic responses of businesses to the single market programme raise a number of competition issues which are at the heart of this report. Firms will react to increased competitive pressures that result from trade liberalization in pro- as well as anti-competitive ways. We investigate the incentives for strategic behaviour that attempts to frustrate the aims of the single market. These competition issues are examined from a theoretical perspective and are illustrated with reference to our market studies, and further references to competition cases brought before EU competition authorities. There are six competition issues which are directly relevant to the theme of market integration.

(a)   Geographic price discrimination and parallel import restrictions are a major issue for policies towards integration. We examine in some detail the economic rationale for allowing or prohibiting these forms of vertical restraints, and we consider their validity in integrated markets.

(b)   Market access restrictions and entry barriers may be used by firms attempting to counter the pro-competitive effects of the single market. This may be through raising the costs of rivals' entry, foreclosure effects, horizontal pricing policies and, in particular, by limiting access to networks and other essential facilities.

(c)   Collusion: firms may agree to share markets and coordinate price setting through collusive agreements, which would undermine the prospects for increased competition arising from market integration. Incentives to collude, and the sustainability of collusion, are themselves affected by single market measures.

(d)   Cooperative agreements: joint ventures and licensing arrangements form a major element in business strategies aimed at gaining or blocking market entry, and exploiting or limiting market integration.

(e)   Mergers, like joint ventures, can be an appropriate way to enter new markets or to exploit a firm's competitive advantage. There are, however, other motives that need to be assessed which relate to the maintenance, creation or extension of market power.

(f)   State aids and other forms of government support for undertakings may distort the operation of the single EU market, and may represent a response by governments to protect firms from the impact of single market measures.

2.3. Structure of report

This report falls naturally into three parts.

Part 1 (Chapters 3–6) deals with the key concepts preceded by a short overview of the single market programme. The trends in integration and competitive conditions are reviewed at both an aggregate and sectoral level. In addition we summarize the results of selected case studies.

Part 2 pursues in a rigorous manner a number of competition policy issues. Our discussion of these issues draws not just on our own case study material, but also refers to various competition cases brought before EU and national competition authorities (Chapters 7–12).

Part 3 then draws out the main conclusions and provides policy recommendations which follow from our analysis (Chapters 13 and 14).

Part I Integration and competition

The concept of an integrated economic market in Europe is as old as the idea of a unified Europe. The Treaty of Rome, one of the founding Treaties of the European Communities, already highlighted integration as the primary goal of the Community and linked it to competition policy as one of the means of achieving it. A new impulse to the European policy towards economic integration was given in 1985 with the presentation of the Commission's White Paper, *Completing the internal market*, which culminated in the signing of the Single European Act (SEA) in 1986.

'Market integration' is a term which is often used but is seldom – if ever – clearly defined. In the political context of the Treaties of Rome and Maastricht, it has a highly normative content. European integration is what we are all supposed to be striving for. To some people, European integration is associated with freedom of movement of products, services, capital and labour across Europe. To others, European integration is often associated with the assumption of a European identity over and above a national identity. For the purposes of this study it is essential that we define this term more clearly. Market integration has to be given a precise meaning so that we can study its connection with competition, and draw conclusions as to the application of European competition policy with respect to the integration process. These conceptual issues are dealt with in Chapter 4. The mechanisms through which integration affects competition in product and input markets are also discussed, as are the types of anti- and pro-competitive behaviour to which the single market measures may give rise.

What has been the effect of the single market programme in practice? What are the trends in integration across selected industries? What can we observe about the way the nature of competition has changed in specific markets? These and other questions are addressed in parallel studies in the Commission's research programme. The programme covers a wide range of industries and deals with specific themes, such as the effect of the single market programme on the exploitation of economies of scale, trade flows and prices. The aim of our study is to focus on the interaction of competition and integration, with a particular emphasis on the role of competition policy in dealing with pro- and anti-competitive responses to single market measures. In Chapter 5 we explore the effects of the single market programme and review trends in market integration and competition at an aggregate as well as a sectoral level. We make use of the results provided by other studies, as well as by our own original research into the development of price-cost margins across sectors, in order to confirm some of the expectations associated with the single market. In Chapter 6 we summarize the findings of selected case studies. These studies are illustrative and are specifically selected to highlight some of the strategic responses that firms can be expected to make when confronted with increased competitive pressures in integrated markets. The focus of these case studies is on identifying changes in competitive conditions, and on typical behavioural responses to these changes in the affected industries.

3. The single market programme

What the single market programme seeks to achieve is the completion of the single market through a set of specific measures and policies that work alongside other existing policies. It is therefore important to set out the policy framework in which competition policy and integration policy interact.

This chapter first provides a brief description of Community policy on integration, and then presents a brief summary of the main categories of measures that aim to complete the single market. The chapter also lists the main expectations associated with the single market programme and its impact on competition.

3.1. The Treaty of Rome

The Treaty of Rome, signed in 1957, lays down firm principles to govern the European Economic Community. Article 2 states that the goal of the Community is the establishment of a common market and a progressive approximation of the economic policies of Member States. In Article 3 (f) the Treaty states how this task should be achieved. Competition policy is given a central role, to ensure 'that competition in the common market is not distorted'. Article 5 provides that Member States shall take all appropriate measures, whether general or particular, to ensure the fulfilment of the obligation arising out of the Treaty. Article 7 adds a general prohibition on Member States from discriminating on the ground of nationality.

Several provisions in the Treaty have a significant bearing on the nature of competition within the common market. In particular, the following articles set out the four fundamental liberties of movement of goods, services, labour and capital:

(a) Articles 9–37 allow for actions to be taken against Member States where national regulations discriminate against imports and impede the free movement of goods;
(b) Articles 48–58 govern the free movement of persons;
(c) Articles 59–66 relate to problems in the services sector and promote the free movement of services;
(d) Articles 67–73 concern the free movement of capital.

The rules on competition allow the Commission to intervene directly in the operation of the common market. Several Articles give the Commission power to prevent both firms and Member States from impeding the achievement of a common market:

(a) Articles 85 and 86 establish the principles for action to be taken against anti-competitive behaviour of firms in the common market;
(b) Article 90 relates to support by Member State governments of public undertakings;
(c) Articles 92–94 relate to firms which have been granted special or exclusive rights that have an effect on competition, or have been granted support in the form of state aids.

The achievement of a common market is the overriding aim of the founding treaty and it guides the implementation and execution of European competition policy.

3.2.   The role of European competition policy in promoting integration

Many commentators on European competition policy have noted the overriding influence of integration policy. The former commissioner with direct responsibility for competition policy, Sir Leon Brittan, emphasized the unusual nature of European competition policy right at the beginning of his series of lectures on European competition law, when he comments that:

> '... the promotion of competition as a process and an economic system is inextricably intertwined with the goal of market integration. The concept is evident from the Treaty itself and is again explained in greater detail in the Commission's Competition Reports.'[2]

and a few paragraphs later he comments that:

> 'The combined goals of achieving an internal market and promoting competition create a form of competition law which does not fit neatly with any particular school of economic analysis used in other jurisdictions. For example, the Chicago School approach currently in favour in the USA is not directly relevant to EC Competition Policy. Chicago does not need to worry about creating a single market. Rather, it presupposes the existence of an integrated market.'

Another leading textbook on UK and European competition law (Whish [1993]) talks of the multifaceted nature of European competition law. He underlines the fact that there are issues of particular importance, in addition to the primary objective of safeguarding individuals against the power of monopolists, or anti-competitive agreements made by independent firms.

> '... EEC competition law plays an important part in the overriding goal of achieving single market integration. The very idea of the common market is that internal barriers to trade within the EEC should be dismantled and that goods, services, workers and capital should have complete freedom of movement. Firms should be able to outgrow their national markets and operate on a more efficient scale throughout the Community. Competition law has both a negative and a positive role to play in this. The negative one is that it can prevent measures which attempt to maintain the isolation of one domestic market from another: for example national cartels, export bans and market sharing will be seriously punished. The positive role is that competition law can be moulded in such a way as to encourage inter-state trade, partly by levelling the playing fields of Europe as one catchphrase has it and partly by facilitating cross-border transactions and integration.' (Whish [1993, p. 14])

In practice this integration objective manifests itself in an emphasis on preventing measures taken by firms to divide up markets, and measures designed to prevent the commercial freedom to trade goods and services throughout the Community. The Commission has therefore pursued particularly vigorously the elimination of vertical restraints and territorial restrictions along national borders.

---

[2]   Brittan, L., 'European competition policy: keeping the playing field level', *CEPS*, 1992, p. 3.

A case which particularly highlights the tension between the competition objective and the integration objective of EU competition policy is Distillers[3] where the Commission challenged price discrimination supported by an export ban imposed by Distillers on its UK distributor. Distillers supplied a variety of whisky throughout Europe. For some brands Distillers was able to charge a premium price in some countries but not in others. UK consumers did not treat Red Label Whisky as a specially rare or premium brand whereas other countries did. The export ban was designed to market and promote Red Label on a country by country basis without arbitrage undermining the value of the product in high price countries. In the proceedings before the ECJ the Advocate General had been sympathetic to the case made by Distillers. However, the court ruled against Distillers without commenting on the merits of Distillers' arguments. It is arguable that without the ability of Distillers to market Red Label whisky profitably in some Member States, less efforts would be made to promote this particular brand, leading to a decrease in sales.

3.3. The single market programme and the Single European Act

European integration took a step forward with the launch of the single market programme. In the 1985 White Paper, the Commission expressed concern over the lack of substantial progress in achieving a single (previously called common) market. They proposed a series of measures to remove various non-tariff barriers on the free movement of goods, services, capital and labour within the EEC.

In 1986, the 12 Member States adopted the single market programme by signing the Single European Act and agreed to a completion date of 1992. By the end of 1992 most of the legislative measures proposed by the Commission had been adopted.[4]

The single market programme generated great political momentum and provided the impetus for the implementation of new as well as dormant policy initiatives, not least in the traditionally protected sectors, such as transport and telecommunications. It also led to further political integration in the form of the Maastricht Treaty in 1993, which established a framework for a common European foreign and security policy, as well as cooperative arrangements over home affairs and justice. In this study we focus on the impact of the single market programme, and it is to this that we now turn.

The 1985 White Paper identified around 300 measures – later reduced to 282 – which aimed to remove three broad categories of barriers: physical, technical and fiscal.

3.3.1. Physical barriers

Physical barriers to trade involve limits to the free movement of goods and people across borders.

Eleven measures aimed to remove physical barriers on goods, including VAT exemption for goods carried for personal consumption, and increases in tax-paid allowances for intra-Community travel. A further seven measures aimed to reduce physical barriers on the free

---

[3]   Competition vs. Distillers, Case 30/78[1980] ECR 2229, discussed for example in Whish [1993, p. 565].

[4]   As of 2 February 1993, 261 out of 282 measures had been adopted by the Council of Ministers. On 3 measures Member States had reached a common position, and the remaining 18 had been proposed.

movement of people, including VAT exemption for goods carried for personal consumption, and increases in tax-paid allowances for intra-Community travel.

3.3.2. Technical barriers

Technical barriers to trade involve differences in regulations, technical standards and specifications, public procurement, professional qualifications and financial rules, which obstruct companies trading their products across borders.

169 measures – the majority of the single market measures – involved removing technical barriers. These can be divided into six further subcategories:

(a)   free movement of goods;[5]
(b)   liberalization of public procurement;[6]
(c)   free movement of labour and the professions;[7]
(d)   creation of a common market for services (financial services, transport[8] and new technologies[9]);
(e)   measures to liberalize capital movements;
(f)   measures aimed at company mobility.[10]

3.3.3. Fiscal barriers

Fiscal barriers are elements of the government's tax and spending policies which make trade across borders more costly. Seventeen proposals were concerned with the removal of fiscal barriers, through the harmonization and approximation of indirect taxes and excise duties, as well as administrative cooperation in indirect taxation. These measures are not primarily aimed at eliminating distortions of trade between Member States but seek to bring about the equal treatment of consumers. For example, the harmonization of excise duties primarily affects the level of prices that consumers pay in the country of purchase. Excise duties are imposed equally on suppliers of imported goods and domestically produced goods, and are not distortive in the way that, for example, tariffs levied on cross-border transactions are. Nevertheless, they may have a distortive effect when they lead to arbitrage measures by consumers – or intermediaries – who want to take advantage of lower prices in third countries, and try to avoid payment of higher duties for domestic purchases.

---

[5]   Eighty proposals concerned technical barriers to trade in goods. Most related to specific sectors (food, pharmaceuticals, motor vehicles, chemicals, agricultural machines, construction); however some were more general: e.g. procedures for assessing whether technical standards were met, and measures relating to the indication of prices on products.

[6]   Seven measures.

[7]   A number of proposals (12 measures) were intended to encourage the free movement of labour, mostly through achieving comparability and mutual recognition of qualifications. Others were concerned with rights of residence in other Member States, and with the coordination of laws on self-employed people.

[8]   A number of measures were aimed at the liberalization of air, maritime and road transport, as well as leading to the application of EU competition rules to the transport sector.

[9]   These were intended to encourage a single market in mobile telephony, TV broadcasting, telecommunication services and equipment.

[10]   A number of other measures were aimed at making it easier for companies to operate across Europe, relating in particular to company law, intellectual and industrial property, including the approximation of trademark laws and tax barriers.

3.4. The expected impact of the single market programme

The single market programme carried with it a great number of expectations. The Commission launched a major study that set out to quantify the beneficial impact of the various measures across a large number of sectors.[11] In the Cecchini report [1988], the overall gains from the implementation of the single market programme were estimated to be the following:

(a) to trigger a major relaunch of economic activity, adding on average 4.5% to the Community's GDP;

(b) to simultaneously cool the economy, deflating consumer prices by an average of 6.1%;

(c) to relax budgetary and external constraints, improving the balance of public finances by an average equivalent to 2.2% of GDP and boosting the Community's external position by around 1% of GDP;

(d) to boost employment, creating 1.8 million new jobs, reducing the jobless rate by around 1.5%.

The 'technical' measures were seen as the most important for realizing the expected benefits from increased access to each market. The 1985 White Paper argued that while physical barriers impose a burden on industry, their significance is rather that they are 'the obvious manifestation of the continued division of the Community'.

> 'While the elimination of physical barriers provides benefits for traders, particularly through the disappearance of formalities and frontier delays, it is through the elimination of technical barriers that the Community will give the large market its economic and industrial dimension by enabling industries to make economies of scale and therefore to become more competitive.'

3.5. How does the single market programme affect competition?

The removal of barriers to trade leads to what Krugman and Venables [1993, p. 3] describe as 'a reduction in the cost of doing business across space', and Hoekman and Mavroidis [1994, p. 3] 'a decline in the cost of contesting markets for foreign producers'. Measures aimed at fostering competition and promoting market integration affect the cost of selling in foreign markets in several different ways.

(a) A reduction in firms' costs of entering foreign markets (which is a fixed cost). For example, one such fixed cost would be registering car models to check they comply with national technical and safety standards.[12]

(b) A reduction in the cost of supplying goods and services to other markets (which is equivalent to a reduction in the marginal cost of the delivered product).[13] Examples are

---

[11] See Cecchini, P. et al., *The European Challenge – 1992 – The Benefits of a Single Market*, Wildwood House, 1988.

[12] Although these barriers should have been removed, the practical impact is not yet very important: 'A uniform set of technical requirements was finally agreed upon in the EU and took effect in 1993. A car model that meets these requirements and has received type approval in one country can now, in principle but apparently not in practice, be sold in all EU countries without the need to fulfil any additional national requirement.' (Flam and Nordström [1995, p. 5])

[13] Most studies seeking to estimate *ex ante* the effects of integration tend to model the move towards completion of the single market as a reduction in the cost of intra-EU trade. For example, Smith and Venables [1988], and Gasiorek, Smith and Venables [1991] assume that trade liberalization takes the form of an equiproportionate reduction in all the implicit barriers to trade between EU countries. In their models, the size of the reduction is chosen so that the direct cost saving achieved by the policy is equivalent to 2.5% of the value of base-level intra-EU trade.

border costs which arise from the requirement that goods have to be checked at the border (for reasons of taxation, as well as to uphold national health regulations and trade policies against non-member countries). Other examples are the costs of different technical regulations on product packaging and marketing which mean that every unit that is sold into a foreign market has to carry additional costs of adjustments.

The distinction between these two effects on costs is not always clear-cut. While tariff barriers almost always relate to a per unit or per value charge on imports, most non-tariff barriers imply a mixture of fixed entry costs and variable per unit cost. For example, border costs can take the form of import-export paperwork; hiring specialized handling agents to deal with the procedures of intra-EU trade; delays at the border.

Both types of costs, fixed and variable, affect entry into a foreign market, although in different ways. The first type simply reduces entry costs regardless of the scale of entry. The second type affects decisions to supply foreign customers in much the same way as a reduction in transport costs. More specifically, they reduce the costs that must be incurred in supplying a foreign customer relative to the cost of supplying a domestic customer at the same distance. Where market integration is achieved, there should be no difference in the cost of supplying foreign and domestic customers who are at the same distance from the supplier. In other words, the labelling of one customer as 'foreign' and the other as 'domestic' should have no economically relevant effect.

In our terminology (see Chapter 4) the single market programme will have achieved its aim once firms and individuals consider their actions independent of national borders. In general, if cross-border trade between Member States becomes easier, differences in economic conditions between countries or regions within the EU will be eroded. Outcomes will become independent of borders as the range of available goods, the range of prices, the range of quality or employment opportunities become increasingly similar in all countries. For example, measures facilitating the free movement of labour will tend to erode differences in employment conditions that are due to national regulations.

Table 3.1 presents an overview of the effects of different integration measures on the entry of new suppliers, the aggregate trade volume between Member States, and the product quality and prices faced by consumers in individual Member States.

Table 3.1.   Effects of the single market programme

Measure related to	Entry	Trade volume	Economic conditions (prices and qualities)
Direct harmonization of economic conditions	Possibly induced by changes in demand and supply; exit possible	Possibly reduced by changes in demand and supply	Directly affected by the measures
Reduction in fixed costs of trade/entry	Increased entry	Increase due to higher number of suppliers	Change due to change in trade volume
Reduction in per unit cost of trade	Increased entry	Increase due to increase in quantity supplied by existing suppliers and entry of new suppliers	Change due to change in trade volume

Competitive conditions are changed in every case, either directly by harmonization measures which affect taxes, excise duties and general industry regulation, or indirectly through measures which increase entry and trade volumes.

3.6. Conclusions

This brief review of European competition and integration policy has provided the institutional background to our study. In particular, we sought to establish that the single market programme cannot be seen in isolation from the historical context and other Community policies. European competition policy itself is an instrument of Community integration policy, with the explicit remit in the Treaty of Rome to support the overall aim of establishing a common market. Furthermore, there is a rich history of intervention by the Commission's Competition Policy Directorate in pursuit of this aim.

The single market programme is a deliberate attempt to re-enforce the trend towards integration. It is arguable that the impact of single market measures depends very much on the specific actions taken in industries that have traditionally been highly protected from the entry of new competitors. The general impact of reductions in trade barriers only establishes more favourable conditions within which firms can exploit new opportunities provided by specific liberalization measures. The next chapter deals more explicitly with the economic concepts that underlie integration and competition policy. After this mainly theoretical exploration, we then examine the empirical evidence of trends in integration and competition.

4. Concepts of market integration and competition

4.1. Introduction

The aim of this chapter is to set out an overall framework for the assessment of the relationship between market integration and competition, leading to an evaluation of the possible implications for competition policy at the EU level.

We start in Section 4.2 by defining market integration as a state where the outcomes of economic decisions are independent of national frontiers – more succinctly, 'borders do not matter'. This is quite distinct from Europe comprising a single economic market. We then identify the potential economic benefits from market integration, including distributive effects and particularly the enhancement of economic efficiency through direct efficiency gains, economies of scale and competition effects. Subsequently, in Section 4.3, we develop the analysis of integration at a more disaggregated level, separating product markets, input markets, and the choice of product characteristics (product design). In Section 4.4 we examine the other main theme of this study, namely the notion of competition, and discuss in detail the ways in which competition may increase economic efficiency (also pointing out the main ambiguities and conflicts). Next, we consider a number of ways in which firms may take action to frustrate the pro-competitive effects of market integration (Section 4.5).

4.2. Integration and integration policy

4.2.1. What is 'market integration'?

The public debate on the economics of 'European integration' has been most often concerned with the macroeconomic side of integration. This encompasses issues such as the best way to accommodate macroeconomic shocks in the face of labour immobility (optimal currency area), and the international transmission of shocks (see for example Bean [1992]). The informal notion of macroeconomic integration is usually described as a process whereby country-dependent idiosyncrasies are lessened. According to this view, integration can be interpreted as a strengthening of the macroeconomic transmission mechanisms interlinking economies with each other. As a result, for example, changes in national GDPs would become more closely correlated. This means that country-specific shocks should affect all countries, and common shocks should impact upon all countries symmetrically.

This study on integration and competition is expected to examine the interaction of the single market programme with competitive conditions and the anti-competitive responses of firms to integration. This market focus requires a microeconomic perspective with reference to product (output) markets and input markets (i.e. components, raw materials, labour and capital markets). We are also concerned with firms' strategies in the area of product design (especially product variety, advertising, and R&D). The appropriate notion of 'integration' should therefore encompass all these aspects.

A suitably general definition, which we adopt in this study (and which is logically consistent with the macroeconomic notion of integration as given above), describes integration as a process whereby the outcomes of economic decisions become less dependent on the existence of borders. In integrated markets, firms will be able to consider entry into a product market ignoring the costs of selling across a national border. They will compete with other firms across geographic markets that are no longer determined by national borders, except where natural geographic features impose transport costs along borders (e.g. coastlines).

This general definition covers a number of outcomes of economic decisions such as purchasing of input or location of production facilities. For example, it may be argued that integration is already advanced in some respects in the car industry, where manufacturers generally operate their purchasing and sourcing of parts and components on a pan-European scale, leading to closer correlation of the prices of these across Member States. This is in contrast to the output market for passenger cars, where we still observe national price differentials and national distributional channels. Integration of the passenger car market cannot therefore be considered complete in terms of our general definition.

The above definition of integration does not imply the absence of cross-country differences. Geography will still be important even in perfectly integrated markets. Location affects economic decisions – and therefore outcomes and welfare – due to:

(a)   transport costs;
(b)   differences in consumers' preferences across regions (as explained by culture, tastes, etc.);
(c)   differences in factor endowments;
(d)   firm-specific economies of scale (and in particular their interaction with transport costs and/or consumers' preference for variety);
(e)   local productive externalities and returns to specialization.[14]

In conclusion, markets can be considered integrated where national characteristics do not exert an influence above and beyond that of the factors listed above.[15] The abolition of artificial border effects will lead to larger geographical markets across Europe, within which more firms are likely to compete. If markets are not integrated, due to barriers to trade and costs of entry, then national market segmentation and fragmentation of markets will remain.

4.2.2.   Why is market integration desirable?

There are two main reasons why the integration of markets may be a desirable objective: one is a distributional objective, the other is based on efficiency benefits. These are logically distinct, and may indeed give rise to conflicting goals in some circumstances.

First, market integration in the way defined ('borders do not matter') may have distributive effects which might be judged beneficial by public policy, in the sense that they should

---

[14]   See, for example, Caballero and Lyons [1990a], Romer [1986], and Krugman [1990].

[15]   It is perhaps useful to illustrate this notion by way of an econometric analogy. Suppose we were to model some economic outcome. After taking into account country-specific factors, such as cross-country differences in preferences, factor endowments, etc., integration, according to this definition, would mean that dummy variables for each individual country should be insignificant. Vice versa, country dummies should be significant in the absence of integration. In product markets, for example, this approach implies there is market integration if (properly correcting for preference and endowment differences between countries) the distribution of relative prices within any particular country was the same as the EU-wide distribution. Hence notions such as 'the law of one price', which should prevail as a result of integration, are only to be used in this sense. Even within one country, there are often differences in prices due to differences in search costs.

encourage a convergence to similar conditions in different parts of the EU. There are three main benefits of more equal distribution.

(a) Allocative efficiency requires that consumers who are similar (in the sense of having similar preferences and income levels – or else quasi-linear preferences) should receive similar allocations of goods and services.

(b) There may be an equity argument for similar consumers being treated similarly, though economic analysis often ignores this aspect because it involves interpersonal comparisons.

(c) Economic cohesion of different parts of the Union, in itself an objective of the EU, could be furthered by the integration process. If economic conditions become more similar across regions, there is less reason for socio-economic conflict, which should facilitate bargaining on issues of common interest. Moreover, increased economic interdependence between countries makes the disruption of cohesion more costly and therefore less likely to occur.

The second reason why market integration may be desirable is that it may enhance economic efficiency through a reduction in impediments to trade and the promotion of competition across the EU. In practice, it may be the case that the efficiency objectives are in conflict with the distributive goals of market integration, and we will seek to discuss the conflicts as they emerge.

We distinguish between three types of efficiency gains that may result from the single market programme.

Direct efficiency gains

The reduction of transport costs involved in eliminating trade barriers is *per se* a social benefit: resource allocation is improved, *ceteris paribus,* by a reduction in input costs. Resources can be saved by the ending of border controls and the abolition of administrative barriers on business. Lower cost producers can enter markets that were previously subject to extra costs associated with entry and cross-border trade. In addition, the removal of fiscal distortions and restrictions on procurement and other sectors should also deliver pure allocative efficiency gains, since economic decisions were previously distorted.

Economies of scale effects

Scale economies were the source of much of the Commission's estimated gains from integration. In the presence of economies of scale, integration which expands market boundaries may lead to efficiency gains. In other words, the increase in market size should create the opportunity and the incentive to exploit economies of scale (and scope). This should generate some efficiency gains regardless of the *ex post* market structure (even if integration were to lead to the unification of two previously separate markets into one monopoly, there could still be productive efficiency gains because of economies of scale effects).[16]

---

[16] These economies should be viewed cautiously, however, at least at the aggregate level: Kay [1989] argued that they should not be overestimated, as, for almost all products, the minimum efficient scale of production does not exceed 10% of the European market.

Economies of scale can be external to the firm as well as internal. This means that a firm's productivity may increase when the output of other firms rises. External economies arise essentially from the public good nature of some inputs. The most plausible source of external economies are due to technological spillovers as a result of the partial appropriability of knowledge (see Romer [1986]).

For example, Baldwin [1989] considers country-specific external economies (both in a static and a dynamic sense) as the main determinants of productivity gains and growth from '1992'. He estimates a medium-term growth bonus (from higher productivity and output raising the capital-labour ratio) leading to an output effect for '1992' about twice as large as the static gains estimated in the Cecchini report [1988]. Furthermore, there should be permanent (long-term) dynamic effects which would increase (adding between 0.2-0.9 percentage points) the EU's long-term growth rate, over and above the 2.5-6.5% one-off increase in EU income from static efficiency gains, as estimated in the Cecchini report. Notice that if external economies at the national level are indeed substantial, the implication is that some countries may benefit more than others: there might be thus a conflict between efficiency and distributive effects, in that efficiency might lead to decreasing equity. Caballero and Lyons [1990a] also find evidence of country-specific inter-industry effects in four European countries. They [1990b] seek for evidence of externalities at the EU level, proposing a means of discriminating between inter-industry and intra-industry effects. The empirical results obtained on industry-level data on manufacturing support the existence of inter-industry effects (estimated at around ECU 47 billion); however, support for cross-country intra-industry effects is weak. Internal economies are found to be already exploited to a significant degree – which casts some doubts on the Cecchini report's estimates of ECU 61 billion cost savings from economies of scale in manufacturing.

Competition effects

A reduction in trade barriers, which should imply both a reduction in transport costs and in fixed entry costs, should result in greater access to every sub-market. Competition is increased, and – to the extent that competition has positive efficiency effects (in the three dimensions we identified above) – this should improve economic outcomes. There might, however, be a conflict between the previous economies of scale effect and the competition effect, if the former leads to greater concentration.

The Cecchini report associated 41% of the benefit of the completion of the single market with the direct efficiency gains resulting from the removal of trade barriers, 30% from exploiting economies of scale, 23% from the effects of intensified competition, and another 5% from the removal of barriers affecting trade.[17]

This study does not primarily address distributive effects, direct efficiency gains, nor economies of scale (the latter forming the object of a separate study). It is specifically concerned with the efficiency gains realized through increased competition, induced by market integration and competition policy. Chapters 5 and 6 provide some empirical evidence of the benefits of increased competition, while the discussion of competition issues in Chapters 7-11 analyses the scope for frustrating the competition process. The overall welfare assessment will

---

[17]   See also Silberston and Raymond [1996].

depend heavily upon the effectiveness of competition, and efficiency gains may be frustrated by strategic actions taken by firms to protect themselves from increased competition.[18]

Before moving to a discussion of the impact of single market measures, it is important to acknowledge that convergence of economic conditions may also be induced by intensified trade with the outside world. A reduction in trade barriers between Europe and the rest of the world, in the context of the conclusions of the GATT Round on world trade, may introduce new incentives for EU firms (and individuals) to exploit scale economies and gain comparative advantages. It may also increase the number of competing suppliers on the European scene. These in turn can be expected to promote an internal adjustment process, leading to increased convergence and therefore also to integration in the way we have defined it.[19]

One of the main challenges for any study of the consequences of internal integration measures is thus to separate their effects from the impact of removing business to trade world-wide.

4.3. The dimensions of market integration

The single market measures may be expected to affect integration along three relevant dimensions:

(a) product markets (pricing, output);
(b) input markets (capital, labour, location);
(c) product design, and technology choices (horizontal and vertical product differentiation, advertising, R&D).

For example, the elimination/simplification of border procedures, which implies an effective reduction in transport costs across the EU, should directly concern product and input markets. The harmonization of technical standards, removing the requirement to adapt products for different markets, should lessen the extent of artificial diseconomies of scale and scope, and is significant for product design. The removal of restrictions on market access is obviously relevant to product markets, including the services sector (for example, entry may be easier in banking).

In this section we consider in greater detail the relationship between integration, distributional issues and competition across the three dimensions – product markets, input markets and product design/ technology.

---

[18] This is illustrated, for example, by the variety of welfare results obtained by Smith and Venables [1988]: for the cement industry, for example, they estimated that welfare could increase by 2.2% or fall by 1%, depending on the assumptions adopted on competition between firms.

[19] Several studies of the extent of integration across countries (Neven and Röller [1991], Jacquemin and Sapir [1991, 1988], but also Sleuwaegen and Yamawaki [1988], Yamawaki et al. [1989]) have examined the evolution of trade flows both within the EU and between the EU and the rest of the world. One result is that between 1975 and 1985, non-tariff barriers appeared to affect trade with the rest of the world more than intra-EU trade (the strength of non-tariff barriers was not a significant determinant of intra-EU trade flows). From these studies it appears, therefore, that competition from non-EU imports may have more of a pro-competitive effect on EU industry than increased imports from within the EU.

4.3.1. Economic integration in product markets

In Section 4.2.1, market integration was defined as a process whereby outcomes of economic decisions become less dependent on national borders. We need to interpret this idea in the context of product markets.

A common view of product market integration is that price distribution across countries should become more similar. Price dispersion is always limited by consumer arbitrage possibilities, therefore reduced costs of arbitrage will cause price distributions to become similar.

This concept does not exclude the persistence of differences in outcomes. Established differences in preferences across regions may mean that outcomes, e.g. consumption levels, are quite different in different countries; hence even when prices converge, this does not mean that outcomes are the same. What matters is that, given preferences, outcomes should not be dependent on the presence of borders.

Thus, as long as there are differences across regions, and there are some transport costs, there will be price dispersion. The degree of integration should then be correctly assessed on the basis of the correlation of prices, and transmission of shocks. That is, in a fully integrated market, local shocks should be transmitted into prices in other areas. For example, an increase in demand in country A should lead to a price increase in country B – and a reduction in consumption of that product in country B – if they are perfectly integrated. Similarly, a positive cost shock which raises the price in one country should be transmitted to other countries through arbitrage. Hence a high degree of integration means that prices are highly correlated.

In this sense, we should interpret as moves towards integration in product markets any measures that reduce transport costs or other costs of arbitrage, and which increase the correlation of prices. This will have both distributional and competitive effects.

Distributional effects

Integration measures have distributional effects if they encourage consumer arbitrage which reduces price discrimination across geographic regions. Since price discrimination across regions always involves redistribution from one region to another, there is a distributive effect in eliminating price discrimination through pure consumer arbitrage. From an efficiency point of view, eliminating price discrimination may be welfare-enhancing or welfare-reducing; indeed, this is one instance where the distributional goals of market integration may come into conflict with efficiency considerations.

To give a simple example, suppose that markets in all countries were served by a single monopolist. Before introducing integration measures, this firm was able to price-discriminate across different countries, and charge different prices. If market integration measures eliminate all costs of consumer arbitrage, this does not affect the market power of the monopolist, but forces him to set a single price in all countries. This means that the price rises in some countries, and falls in other countries. It may even mean that this 'average' price is prohibitively high in some regions, which as a result choose not to buy. It is possible that consumers in regions where the price was previously lower may lose so much more in benefits than those consumers that are gaining, that it may be judged that there is an overall reduction in welfare.[20]

Competitive effects

Integration may also have competitive effects. A reduction in the transport and arbitrage costs will reduce firms' marginal cost of supplying different markets, while any reduction in the fixed cost of market access should encourage new entry (both by domestic and foreign producers). This should lead to increased competition in the market place, with corresponding efficiency and concentration effects. The equilibrium configuration is difficult to predict: if domestic firms operate at different cost levels, then entry by foreign competitors should induce a shake-out of the domestic high-cost firms. As a result, EU-wide concentration might increase, particularly if the technology is such that foreign entrants may exploit economies of scale and come into the market with a lower cost.

4.3.2. Economic integration in input markets

Liberalization of factor markets (capital and labour) is one important aspect of integration, and has important distributional implications. Winters and Venables [1991] argue that consideration of factor markets is essential to addressing the issue of how the costs and benefits of 1992 are likely to be distributed across the EU.

Capital and labour market mobility

The single market programme contained several measures aimed at capital markets. These should imply lower costs of trading between different regions in Europe, which should increase the mobility of capital. This will facilitate direct investment, and as a consequence make it easier for investors to use arbitrage opportunities when economic conditions differ across countries.

Similarly, a number of single market measures are aimed at the integration of labour markets, particularly facilitating the mobility of individuals across borders. However, even if barriers to labour mobility are removed, this may not necessarily lead to increased labour mobility, because lack of mobility may be induced by preferences. Indeed, empirical research shows that there is a high degree of aversion to mobility in many regions of Europe. In such a situation, the liberalization of capital markets has a second important effect. According to traditional trade theory, capital mobility should tend to result in equalization of wage rates, under the assumptions of the 'factor price equalization' theorem (which includes sufficiently similar initial endowments). Significant wage dispersion would only persist in the long term in labour markets if capital arbitrage across labour markets is not effective.

There is an important caveat here, related to heterogeneity of skills in labour markets – and generally other endowments. If there is complementarity between high skills and capital investment in R&D, R&D investment will move out of regions with low-skilled labour, into regions with a higher proportion of high-skill labour, especially if there are relatively lower wages for higher-skilled workers in those regions. This may lead to a different proportion of high-skilled jobs in different regions, and to long-term differences in the wage distribution

---

[20]   See Chapter 6 for a discussion of price discrimination as a competition issue in the single market.

between regions. This might imply that these high-skill regions will have more spillovers between firms in R&D, resulting in more growth through external economies – see Baldwin [1989] – since these are areas in which R&D is concentrated. Hence it may be the case that integration of some sub-markets actually leads to less integration, in the distributive sense of less similarity in living conditions.[21]

Location decisions

Relative input costs may be expected to affect location decisions. However the effect of integration does not lead to an immediate decision to relocate to minimize the cost of reaching a particular market. This is because firms have already made investment decisions, and sunk costs in production capacity. Since all investment decisions are marginal decisions (adding to existing capacity), it may be a long time before location structure converges to an optimal structure. Location structure soon after integration may not therefore be very different, and location patterns not necessarily a reliable indicator of the degree of market integration.

Hence, location decisions depend partly upon historical decisions, and costs which are already sunk. Integration cannot be necessarily identified in the short term by location decisions that minimize the cost of getting the product to the customer.

4.3.3. Economic integration in product design and technology choices

Integration may have a further important effect on firms' decisions about the range (and quality) of products offered, the type of advertising and the way in which R&D is carried out. These choices, to do with degree of product differentiation, how products are advertised, and what technology is chosen, may be collectively described as the area of product design decisions by firms.

Product variety

A first important issue is the relationship between integration and product variety. How are firms' selection of product characteristics – e.g. models, versions – affected by integration? How does the availability of variety to consumers across Europe change with integration?

According to intra-industry trade theories, which explain international trade as a result of product differentiation and scale economies, integration should be expected to lead to increased trade within each industry across the EU. In this way, integration would generate benefits because consumers would be given access to a larger range of products in all countries. Integration could also bring about allocative efficiency gains because of the following.

(a)   Consumers would be more likely to be matched with their preferred product variety.

        Trade barriers that distort relative prices might imply, for example, that consumers are buying a domestic product when they would actually prefer a foreign make. If these

---

[21]   For an analysis of the analogous case in the US context, see Barro and Sala-i-Martin [1992].

barriers are eliminated, some marginal consumers, who were inefficiently buying the domestic product before, would be able to start buying their preferred product.

(b)   Consumers would be able to choose from a wider range of products.

The range of products will be determined as a trade-off between the economies of scale of producing any one product, and consumers' preferences for variety. We can interpret integration as an increase in market size, and a larger market will support more varieties of products for given levels of economies of scale and preferences for variety.

In addition, integration would encourage greater variety because the associated reduction in trade costs makes it profitable for firms to enter a market even with smaller quantities. Furthermore, there may be efficiency gains from exploiting previously unexploited economies of scale and scope, and thereby a wider product variety may be sustainable. (A possible analogy is the way in which technological improvements in packaging and transport have made it possible to buy tropical fruit anywhere in Europe at any time of the seasonal cycle.)

Of course, it must again be emphasized that integration may not necessarily mean that the same range of products would be offered everywhere in Europe. Indeed, differences may persist in product range and specifications, if these reflect underlying preferences, and particularly if it is not very costly for firms to adapt the product to cater for local tastes and preferences. Even so, we should expect integration measures to increase the similarity of varieties offered across countries, because they reduce artificial diseconomies of scope and scale resulting from differences in regulations and standards. In this framework, one important measure of integration would be the correlation of product availabilities across countries.

The alternative approach to intra-industry trade theory is the classical theory of increased exploitation of comparative advantage based on factor endowments, and 'specialization': inter-industry trade theory.[22] From this perspective, trade liberalization should lead to relocation of production to reflect comparative advantages and factor endowments. However, in a European context the benefits in terms of allocative efficiency could be expected to come more from increased variety (product differentiation) than from comparative advantage and specialization. This is because factor endowments may not be very different across the EU (with some exceptions). Furthermore, if there is integration in capital markets (i.e. capital mobility), then we may expect some equalization of labour costs across Europe (relative factor prices will tend to equalize, see Helpman and Krugman [1989]), and the long-run effects of greater variety should be more important than comparative advantage effects.

The evidence for this is that most of the observed trade growth in the EU has been intra-industry trade. Neven [1990] examines intra-industry trade flows in Europe in 1985 for 29 industries, and finds that – with the exception of Portugal and especially Greece – intra-

---

[22]   This is the traditional Heckscher-Ohlin explanation of international trade. Here, the existence of barriers to trade may prevent the exploitation of comparative advantages; if the elimination of such barriers through the single market programme makes it possible to exploit these advantages, prices may fall, which might foster allocative efficiency.

industry trade tends to prevail.[23] Flam [1992] observes that most intra-Community trade, as indeed most world trade, is not driven by comparative advantage.

Advertising

As a general point, there are no 'markets' for advertising (and to a lesser degree for R&D) which can be compared conceptually to the product and factor markets discussed above. That is, advertising and R&D are not 'traded' in the classical sense. Hence restrictions of trade affect advertising and R&D only indirectly, through their direct effects on product and factor markets. Therefore measures which liberalize products and factor markets affect the incentives for advertising and R&D activities, which may in turn affect the distribution of economic outcomes in the community.

In this framework, the 'globalization' of advertising (i.e. the adoption of a common advertising message across different countries) may or may not be a consequence of market integration. This will depend on the trade-off between economies of scale in advertising and the benefits of tailoring advertising to local culture. However, increasing returns to scale in advertising may also be exploited in segmented product markets.

An important additional benefit of integrating advertising is that it can establish a single 'global' reputation for quality. Reputation in one product market is tied to product quality in other markets, therefore a unified advertising strategy may give a stronger signal of a commitment to quality.

Overall, globalization of advertising is not a direct implication of market integration, but is a consequence of market integration only if integration increases market access. For example, an integration measure that standardized security design on cars would not be sufficient to make car producers advertise globally. However, global advertising might be adopted because of economies of scale in designing an advertising campaign. For this reason, we should not take globalization of advertising as an indicator of the degree of market integration.

Research and development (R&D)

Further important issues are the location of R&D activity, and the possible changes in the organization of R&D: how does integration affect the location of R&D? How does it affect the way in which firms carry out R&D, e.g. their incentives to internalize the problem of R&D spillovers, or the threat of being leap-frogged in a patent race, through joint ventures or strategic alliances?

On the first point (R&D location) it is not clear whether market integration should lead to a more or less even distribution of R&D activity across countries in Europe. With capital mobility (capital market integration), and in the absence of labour market mobility, R&D activity should follow the underlying endowments in skill levels, and this may lead to

---

[23]   The industries where intra-industry trade was found to be more significant were clothing, footwear, wood, electrical machinery and tobacco processing. 'On the whole, trade arising from the 'classical' factors is fairly limited between European countries, at least in terms of the product scope' (Neven [1990, p. 23]). Neven also evaluates possible deviations from the equality of factor prices across Europe, which could be an indicator that comparative advantage is not exploited because of non-tariff barriers. He finds that there is some scope for exploiting comparative advantage (low labour costs) in Portugal and Greece, and in the UK (human capital), once barriers were removed.

concentration of R&D activity in regional centres with a dense agglomeration of highly skilled labour. As a result, market integration may well lead to unequal distribution of R&D, and wage incomes of skilled labour across different countries.

In addition, R&D is an activity beset with productive spillovers. This may give strong local external economies of scale, and benefit the geographical concentration of particular R&D activities (e.g. Silicon Valley).

4.4. Competition and efficiency

Competition is the second major theme in this study. The aim of the study is to analyse the interaction between integration and competition and to examine the evolution of competition conditions in the single market. Earlier in this chapter we identified the efficiency gains associated with the single market programme, and emphasized that in this study we are particularly interested in assessing the benefit of increased competition in the single market.

It is therefore crucial to understand how competition provides efficiency in the economy. Economics distinguishes three dimensions of efficiency.

(a) Allocative efficiency. This means that:
(i)   prices reflect costs so that consumers make the right trade-offs;
(ii) there is efficient organization of production (i.e. appropriate combinations of inputs, and economies of scale and scope exploited).
(b) Productive (internal) efficiency, which means that, given output, production takes place in practice at minimum costs: hence productive efficiency implies that internal slack (X-inefficiency) is absent.
(c) Dynamic efficiency, which means that there is optimal trade-off between current consumption and investment in technological progress.

4.4.1. Competition and allocative efficiency

Traditionally, the economic literature has put particular emphasis on how competition might promote allocative efficiency (in layman's terms: how relatively more is produced of what people want and are willing to pay for). This mechanism is easier to understand and study empirically than other notions of efficiency. Quite simply, competitive pressures tend to push prices towards marginal costs by eroding market power. Given a certain number of firms in a market, the alignment of prices with marginal costs generates allocative efficiency.

However, in some circumstances marginal cost pricing may conflict with other objectives. In particular, in the presence of increasing returns to scale, increasing the competitive pressures on prices may not give the optimal incentive for market entry.[24] More competition (in the sense of more firms) causes prices to fall towards marginal costs, but at the same time less advantage is taken of scale economies related to fixed entry costs, and so average cost rises. Under fairly general conditions, the negative externality that an additional entrant imposes on existing firms, by taking business from them, may outweigh the positive externality to

---

[24] This point is illustrated by Mankiw and Whinston [1986], in a model of a symmetric, homogeneous goods, Cournot oligopoly, with fixed (and sunk) entry costs. Under these assumptions there is a trade-off between productive and allocative efficiency, resulting in too much entry from the point of view of welfare.

consumers in terms of lower price. Here more competition appears to be good for allocative efficiency, but bad for productive efficiency.

When firms' costs differ, competition will, however, play an important role in selecting firms with more efficient technologies, and forcing the less efficient ones to leave the market. That is, competition ultimately causes efficient organizations to prosper at the expense of inefficient ones, which will eventually drop out. This selection process is 'good' for allocative efficiency (see Vickers [1994]), and also for productive efficiency.

4.4.2. Competition and productive efficiency

The causality between competition and productive efficiency is deeply rooted in economic folklore: starting from Hicks' notion that 'the best of all monopoly profits is a quiet life', economists have always had a 'vague suspicion that competition is the enemy of sloth' (Caves [1980]). The theoretical literature is not in agreement on the exact nature of this relationship. However the empirical literature provides a relative wealth of evidence to support the notion that competition enhances productive efficiency.

The theory tends to explain the existence of technical (or productive) inefficiencies through the following mechanisms.

(a)   Contractual and organizational failures: inefficiencies may be induced by second-best bargains struck between principals (firms' owners) and agents (hired managers), or managers at any level and their work-force, which means that the latter will not pursue profit-maximizing goals. These may depend on the degree of competition in the product market. In other words, rents from market power may take the form not of profits, but may instead be dissipated in the form of managerial slack (and more generally X-inefficiency).

(b)   Strategic manipulation of cost levels to affect the nature of competition in the output market (see literature on strategic delegation, e.g. Vickers [1985], Fershtman and Judd [1987]; and others). The intuition here is that in oligopolistic settings firms have powerful incentives to soften price competition, and they may adopt devices which can support such an outcome. One option is to 'signal' to one's rival that one's costs are high. By committing itself to a course of action which increases its own costs, the firm is implicitly indicating that it is not going to follow an aggressive strategy on prices. The rival is better off conforming, and equilibrium prices are higher.

On the first point, it seems plausible that competition may promote productive efficiency by overcoming various agency/informational problems, improving monitoring and therefore sharpening incentives and reducing sloth and slack. Competition may influence not only managerial effort, but also the effort of workers (if product market rents are shared with them in some ways).

As the effects of competition on managerial slack can be modelled in different ways, and conclusions are sensitive to model specifications, there are still some ambiguities in the theoretical literature. For example, Hart [1983] proposes a model where inefficiency (slack) is explicitly the result of a conflict of incentives between owners and managers, and competition reduces inefficiency in 'good states'. In his model, an increase in competition ('captured' through an increase in the number of entrepreneurial firms) forces managers of managerial firms to work harder, because they cannot meet their profit targets – for example when an exogenous reduction in costs leads to output expansion by their competitors, and lower prices. However changing the assumptions on the incentive scheme for managers, Scharfstein [1988] reaches different conclusions.

Other models (e.g. Holmström [1982], Nalebuff and Stiglitz [1983], and Mookherjee [1984]) emphasize a different reason why competition may sharpen incentives. Because a larger number of players implies greater opportunities for comparative performance evaluation, explicit incentive schemes should improve incentives the greater the number of players involved. The positive effects of competition are also reinforced as a result of the bankruptcy constraint (Schmidt [1985]; Vickers and Yarrow [1988]), whereby firms/managers tend to work harder when they are faced by the threat of going bankrupt.

The second effect, i.e. the strategic manipulation of costs, is fairly clear-cut. It has been shown (Kühn [1994]), that increases in competition, due to a larger number of firms, reduce the effects of strategic manipulation. The idea is that as the number of competing firms increases, the marginal effects of their actions affect other firms less; and thus other firms will react less to commitments towards higher prices. Indeed, typically these strategic effects disappear faster than prices converge to marginal cost, as the number of firms increases.

Though to some extent ambiguous, the conclusion from these models appears positive with regard to the claim that competition increases productive efficiency.[25] The results from empirical literature are more clear-cut. To mention but a few, Caves and Barton [1990], and Caves et al. [1992] use frontier production function techniques to estimate technical efficiency indices in a number of industries, and relate these to concentration (as a proxy for competition). They find that increases in concentration beyond a certain threshold tend to reduce technical efficiency. Nickell et al. [1992] find that market concentration has an adverse effect on the level of total factor productivity. This means that (*ceteris paribus*) an increase in market concentration should be followed by a fall in productivity.[26]

Overall, academic work up to this point appears to support the contention that competition has positive effects on productive efficiency.

4.4.3. Competition and dynamic efficiency

Dynamic efficiency is defined as the optimal trade-off between current consumption and investment in technological progress. The intensity of competition may be expected to affect the incentive to undertake R&D, since it will condition the firm's rewards from innovation.[27]

---

[25]   In addition to problems of sensitivity to model specification, it must be mentioned that increased product market competition has been argued to increase X-inefficiency in some circumstances. For example, greater product market competition may lead to managers losing their jobs more frequently, and hence taking too short-term a view. A second very important point is that managers may divert their effort, from important but weakly monitored activities to unimportant but more visible activities, as a result of the improved monitoring from comparative performance evaluation in more competitive environments (Holmström and Milgrom [1987]).

[26]   At the same time, firms with high market share tend to have higher productivity growth. Nickell [1993] further investigates the impact of competition on the productivity performance of a panel of UK manufacturing companies. The hypothesis is that firms which operate in a more competitive environment have higher levels of productivity, and/or higher rates of productivity growth. The intensity of competition is measured by concentration, import penetration, and a survey-based dummy for competition. The evidence in favour of the base hypothesis is rather weak.

[27]   It is worth pointing out that there is in principle a trade-off between allocative and dynamic efficiency: costs might fall as a result of competition in technological innovation, yet this may actually lead to increased market concentration, and

These effects are potentially important for macroeconomic performance and ultimately for welfare, but are extremely difficult to unravel.

Early discussions of the relationship between product-market competition and innovation (e.g. Schumpeter) held that the driving force in the process were firms with *ex ante* market power, rather than just the prospect of market power. An argument in favour of this position is the so-called 'long purse' effect; due to capital market imperfections more monopolistic firms can more readily fund R&D expenditure out of retained profits (see Telser [1966]; Fudenberg and Tirole [1986]). In this Schumpeterian view, as the product market becomes more competitive, the pay-off to innovation would become lower, and the incentive for R&D would be blunted.

However this conjecture has been extensively challenged. More product-market competition could lead to stronger incentives to innovate, since a potential benefit of innovation is escape from tough competition, by earning a monopoly right to an invention protected by a patent (Arrow [1962]).

The more recent theoretical literature on the subject has treated innovation as a patent race between firms, where the 'prize' from being first (and thus being able to appropriate the profits from the innovation) is the incentive spurring firms along. These micro models of R&D investments actually suggest that competitive pressures typically boost, rather than dampen, innovation. The optimal innovation pace will accelerate under the threat that actual (or potential) competitors may register the patent first.

Overall, the welfare effects from this substantial literature are ambiguous, because there are always at least two effects at work: on the one hand, firms' private benefits from successful innovation are usually less than the social benefits. On the other hand, the result of R&D, i.e. knowledge, is a public good, and thus R&D expenditure by a number of firms may involve a wasteful duplication.

In addition to product-market competitiveness effects, it is worth noting that there may also be a 'market-size effect' to the pay-off from innovation. If integration (i.e. removal of barriers) leads to an increase in the size of the market, this may increase the pay-off to innovation, i.e. the expected reward for winning a patent race, and therefore the incentive for firms to compete to achieve an innovation ahead of their rivals.[28]

Overall, although theoretical results are – as often – ambiguous, it is likely that competition increases the amount of R&D. However, whether this conclusion holds is necessarily an empirical question.

The Schumpeterian hypothesis has been subject to extensive empirical testing, (Kamien and Schwarz [1975], Scherer [1967], Cohen and Levinthal [1989]). As Garcia Peñalosa [1996] remarks, the evidence is not strong because market concentration and R&D intensity may be

---

prices in excess of marginal costs might be necessary in order to give firms a suitable return on their R&D effort (see von Weizsäcker [1980]).

[28]   Notice, however, that integration may also increase the return to R&D through the impact of mergers of European firms, joint ventures, or less duplication of national research effort. Each of these would either increase the probability of a research project succeeding (or winning the patent race), or mean that a successful research effort would reach a larger share of the market. This may be expected to have an effect on the private return to innovation which is for some greater than the effect of growth of the EU market as a whole.

chiefly the result of industry characteristics rather than causally linked. Some recent empirical studies by Porter [1994], Nickell [1996], Geroski [1993] and Blundell et al. [1995] have all found that increased competition and market concentration promote innovative activity. This evidence seemingly contradicts the Schumpeterian view.

4.5. The behaviour of competing firms in the single market

Our previous discussion in this chapter leads us to characterize integration as a process of convergence of prices across borders (through arbitrage), increasing access to markets and therefore intensifying competition, increasing exploitation of economies of scale, leading to economic decisions that are independent of national borders. However, while some firms will be able to take advantage of the opportunities provided by the single market, others will want to resist the competitive threats that this development implies.

Overall, it can be expected that the loss of price discrimination possibilities and the intensification of competition will tend to reduce firms' profits, unless the increased intensity of competition leads to higher levels of concentration. In some sectors that are particularly exposed to the single market programme (air travel comes to mind here) firms might have an incentive to frustrate the process of integration. That is, market integration might give firms additional motives to behave in an anti-competitive way, where it has the effect of threatening their profits and entrenched positions in the market.

4.5.1. Pro-competitive responses: meeting the new competitive conditions

Before focusing on the behaviour of firms that poses obstacles to integration, it is useful to consider the converse – the potential pro-competitive responses to the single market programme. The process whereby prices reflect costs and firms seek to determine their strategies independently of national frontiers would be consistent with the following.

(a) Expansion and entry into foreign markets exploiting internal return to scale costs. The harmonization of technical standards should have enabled some firms to market their products not just in their domestic market but also in other geographical markets, without incurring additional costs to adapt their products to meet differing technical standards. This would then allow some firms to expand their production and exploit any available cost economies.

(b) Removal of X-inefficiency. The entry of firms into new markets would prompt incumbent firms to improve their efficiency in order to sustain their profitability in the face of new competition.

(c) Tougher price and service competition resulting from entry into foreign markets. Response to new entrants could also include increasing levels of competition on both price and quality of service, as incumbent firms seek to preserve market share and new entrants seek to establish a market position.

(d) Exit of weakest firms and growth of strongest firms. The breakdown in collusive behaviour and the increasing levels of competition, coupled with the ability of firms to exploit potential economies of scale across new geographical markets, could lead to the weakest firms being forced out of business altogether, and the more successful firms becoming both larger and stronger.

(e)   Search for process innovation to reduce costs. With the advent of increased rivalry, the pressure to reduce costs, either to be able to reduce prices or to increase profitability, intensifies and stimulates a search for new and more efficient processes.

(f)   Enhanced incentives for product innovation via two routes: market-size expansion, and more robust competition, implying an Arrow replacement effect and patent races. Increasing market opportunities, together with intensifying competition, serves both to stimulate further innovation in product development to win new customers and to fight off new competitors.

(g)   Improvement in the quality and variety of products. The enhanced incentives in product innovation should translate not just into new products but also into higher quality and greater variety of products.

(h)   Breakdown in collusive behaviour. With new entrants and changes in the size of potential markets, the 'pay-offs' to incumbent firms will change, and as a result any existing agreements may break down. Thus firms which had previously reached 'arrangements' to share a particular market, now begin to find that those market-sharing arrangements yield insufficient or uncertain profits, and so begin to compete for market share. It is also arguable that the increased activity of regulatory (especially competition) authorities at the EU level makes it more difficult to sustain the national regulatory relationships which often sustain collusive behaviour.

Anti-competitive responses

The pro-competitive effects of single market measures can be undermined by the strategic behaviour of private undertakings. Firms which feel threatened by the impending or actual entry of newcomers into their domestic market might seek ways of strengthening their position through taking action to:

(a)   exclude rivals from markets;
(b)   share markets with rivals;
(c)   prevent parallel trade between markets.

These various strategic responses of firms can be grouped under six headings. These headings form the structure within which the examination of the major competition issues in Part 2 of this report is undertaken. This classification does not directly correspond to the traditional framework under which European competition policy is usually evaluated. However, given the focus of this study on the interaction of integration and competition, it is felt that a perspective which gives particular prominence to strategic behaviour that relates to segmentation of national markets is most appropriate.

Preventing consumer arbitrage

If there are significant price differences between national markets, then consumers and intermediaries will be tempted to arbitrage between them. The single market programme makes it easier to exploit arbitrage opportunities as it removes some of the extra costs of purchasing goods in other Member States. We can therefore expect more cross-border shopping to occur, unless existing price differences are reduced.

Firms might try to prevent consumer arbitrage by measures that prevent resale by intermediaries (e.g. exclusive dealing with restrictions to resale). Since there are economies of scale in arbitrage (increasing returns to scale in terms of transport costs), if intermediaries are prevented from reselling in other markets arbitrage may not occur at all.

Notice, however, that while these restrictions to arbitrage may prevent integration with respect to a specific product, they may not be anti-competitive. Price discrimination supported by parallel import restrictions may actually be desirable (i.e. welfare-enhancing) if it implies that markets are served which were not served before, or that firms compete more intensely at the margin for low-valuation consumers. Further, limiting discrimination in some cases may facilitate collusion. This is essentially because it may be generally easier to monitor deviations from an agreement where there is a unique focal price for several sub-markets, than to monitor deviations from a vector of prices for a variety of consumers. In other words, restricting price discrimination is equivalent to a reduction in the dimensionality of the problem, in order to make it easier to sustain collusion. Thus allowing some discrimination may be preferable.

Erecting entry barriers and maintaining access restrictions

Increased entry into larger markets is one of the expected consequences of the single market programme. A larger number of competitors who actively compete with each other is one of the main mechanisms through which the benefits of integration are expected to occur. Firms, however, may take a number of actions to prevent the entry of other EU firms into their national markets, in particular by denying access to essential infrastructure or simply by raising rivals' costs[29] through vertical restraints and predatory pricing.

For example, firms might be able to raise rivals' entry costs through vertical integration, or a variety of vertical agreements. Other potential means of deterring entry are through predatory behaviour, and strategic investment in R&D or advertising which serves to raise the sunk costs of entry. Another way in which firms might be able to raise entry costs is, for example, through lobbying for the introduction of technical standards which are favourable to them.

It must be emphasized that the entry-deterrence problem is likely to be most significant where national concentration is already high and where the existence of national networks and essential facilities create access issues. Where this is not the case, entry-deterring strategies may be less effective, due to the difficulties of coordinating many firms in an attempt to exclude foreign rivals.

Collusive behaviour and market sharing along national boundaries

Market sharing along national boundaries is an effective form of collusion: since cross-border trade is particularly easy to monitor, collusive arrangements to share markets along national borders may be relatively easier to sustain than market-sharing arrangements within countries or across larger territories.

The question is whether and how integration can be expected to change the incentives to collude. In some instances it may well be that collusion may persist after integration, as historical market shares may serve as focal points for coordination, even after integration. In other circumstances, integration will lead to new entry into a national market and undermine a collusive agreement.

---

29   See Salop and Scheffman [1983].

Efficiency defences for cooperative agreements

There are many instances where firms cooperate to share facilities, or to coordinate their behaviour, in new markets that they want to enter jointly rather then separately.

Cooperative motives largely explain the joint ventures and strategic alliances being formed between firms. For example, joint ventures in R&D may be equivalent in effect to the parties 'merging' in the design of the next generation of products. (This is an area where competition policy may come into direct conflict with industrial policy, aimed at strengthening Europe's position as a whole in R&D, in relation to America and Japan.)

Firms may seek to reduce the competitive effect of direct market entry by entering into various forms of production or distribution agreements with established producers in other markets. The effect is that the entrant essentially defers all decisions on the relevant variables (such as prices, quantities, retailing format and advertising) to an established firm which is a direct competitor in the product market. While there may be efficiency justifications for this course of action (exploiting economies of scale in production/distribution, and avoiding duplication of networks), where the licensee is a competitor to the entrant the agreement may have a collusive purpose.

Mergers

Mergers may just be an 'equilibrium response' to integration measures, because stronger competition may not allow the same number of firms to remain in the market – even though the market size becomes larger. Thus stronger competition should imply a shake-out of firms (in the form of takeovers, mergers or outright exit), which means that concentration must tend to rise.

Apart from this selection effect, mergers across countries may also be used in an anti-competitive mode, to eliminate the competition that arises from additional market access.

Mergers within countries may in some circumstances be detrimental to competition at the EU level: this is the case of mergers which are 'defensive', in the sense that firms within a country merge to internalize externalities in entry deterrence, in order to be better placed to keep out potential foreign entrants.

Rent-seeking behaviour through lobbying

Firms might also seek to defend their position through various forms of lobbying. An example could be lobbying for specific regulations and standards to be adopted. Established firms in a market may exert pressures for certain standards to be set, in the knowledge that they will be consulted and may thereby influence the entire process. At the very least, they will then lobby for standards which are favourable to themselves, and less so to their competitors. This may be especially the case in the context of new developments in environmental protection: while the single market programme incorporated the elimination of certain differences in technical standards, new standards may be adopted and entry may be rendered more difficult. For example, the German recycling system effectively bars from entry certain products which do not confirm to strict environmental rules. Other examples include lobbying to obtain state aids.

4.5.2. The behaviour of national governments

The behaviour of firms may also be distorted by national governments which may take actions which maintain segmentation.

State aids and industrial policy

The economic rationale for granting state aids is the correction of market failures, with associated losses in economic efficiency and welfare. The justification for a European Community policy controlling state aids is to prevent such subsidies from affecting market behaviour and competition in a way which reduces efficiency and welfare. The potential problem is compounded by the fact that many EU Member governments have established industrial policies based on supporting their national producers – especially state-owned firms which in some cases still play a significant economic role. The integration process may have made it more difficult for firms that used to be partially protected from foreign competition to achieve sufficient levels of profitability. The incentive for these firms to rely on state support (and for the government to avoid liquidation and social costs) is certainly increased in a more competitive environment.

Procurement policies

Public procurement refers to contracts awarded by public authorities, semi-public bodies and public utilities for the supply of goods and services and for major works. In 1990 public procurement contracts amounted to 8% of the European Union gross domestic product. Their significance is such that any serious attempt to lift trade impediments between EU Member States must also include rules allowing firms from different countries to bid for public procurement contracts (until recently, as a rule, public procurement contracts in most Member States have been the exclusive domain of firms with the same nationality as the awarding public body).

5.   Trends in integration and competition

5.1. Introduction

How do we measure the progress of integration within the EU? How do we determine whether integration has had any significant effect on firm behaviour? Is there a single measure that captures integration? Do we need to employ a series of indicators? Are aggregate level statistics, on their own, sufficient? Who is realizing any gains from integration – firms or consumers?

In this chapter we address these key issues. It bridges the gap between these theoretical concepts of integration and the analysis of competition issues and integration trends in selected markets. Our starting point is the concept of integration developed in Chapter 4, where we defined integration as the process by which outcomes of economic decisions become independent of borders. More specifically, this process is brought about by a reduction in the costs of doing business across borders. Market integration should in most cases lead to greater similarity of outcomes across countries since economic fundamentals will be similar across countries. Notice, however, that this does not, according to our definition of integration, necessarily lead to location being unimportant, but rather that nationality should not determine outcomes. To the extent that integration leads to economies experiencing more closely correlated economic shocks, we may use increasing similarity and increasing correlation of economic variables, such as prices etc., as evidence consistent with the progress of integration. In particular, as integration progresses, one would expect to see the following developments:

(a)   Shifting trade patterns within the EU and a deepening of intra-EU trade. Trade flows are perhaps the most widely used indicator of the degree of economic integration.

(b)   The potential for cross-border arbitrage increase, and a convergence of prices within the EU to result.

(c)   The geographical market within which firms operate become wider as barriers to trade recede. The likely increase in competitive pressures should result in lower price-cost margins.

(d)   Integration lead to tougher product-market competition and hence lower profits for a given number of firms at the EU level. Thus we would expect firms to exit as a response to this leading to higher concentration.

(e)   Increased possibilities for exploitation of economies of scale – which in turn has implications for market structure and for concentration. This gives an additional reason why integration is likely to increase concentration.

In this chapter we trace these effects through a number of empirical studies and original research that makes use of selected indicators of integration. The breadth of this empirical review is largely determined by the number and by the sectoral coverage of the empirical indicators chosen.

Such studies entail practical difficulties as well as issues of interpretation. With the advent of the single market, statistical information about cross-border trade has become much more difficult to collect and prepare, which makes the analysis of intra-EU trade after 1992 much more arduous. When one turns to the interpretation of such data, some degree of caution is called for. Moreover, aggregate-level studies, whilst clearly important, are not on their own sufficient; they may obscure the quite significant impact of integration at the product-market level. We consider that the most useful evidence about the effects of integration is in fact gathered by looking comparatively at a number of different sectors.

Section 5.2 discusses how we might expect market integration to impact differently on different sectors, and how we might use this to help identify the impact of market integration. Sections 5.3, 5.4, 5.5 and 5.6 discuss the impact of integration on trade flows, prices, price-cost margins and concentration respectively. Section 5.7 pulls together this different evidence and concludes.

A set of annexes to this chapter provide additional information about the data we used in our own research, together with some details of the empirical analysis of price-cost margins.

5.2. The sectoral impact of integration

The single market programme will clearly impact upon different product markets in different ways. In some product markets, the market structure may be such that outcomes are already independent of borders – the impact of integration will therefore be negligible. In other markets, however, it may be that outcomes will never be independent of borders – for example, where transport costs are extremely high, local monopolies may be the only tenable market structure. Once more, in markets such as these, integration is likely to have little effect. However, in other markets, the effects of integration are likely to be considerable. Consideration of aggregate indicators alone will mask the impact of integration in this group of product markets.

As a result, we have carried out a sector-level empirical assessment of those areas where the potential gains from integration are considered to be substantial. Where possible, we will look for the impact of the single market programme not only using aggregate-level data, but also using sectoral data. In order to use sectoral-level data, we must clearly have some prior view about which sectors are likely to be most affected by integration and which least affected. Our starting point is a wide-ranging study by Buigues et al. [1990].[30]

In this study on the likely effects of the single market, Buigues et al. [1990] identified the 40 industrial sectors most likely to be affected by single market measures. These 40 sectors are industries which were most heavily protected by non-tariff barriers, such as frontier formalities, and in which these barriers led to persistent price differentials across Member States and/or little trade indicated a failure to exploit economies of scale within the EU. The study classified these 40 sectors into three sub-groups according to these two sets of criteria, namely the degree of price dispersion and the degree to which the sectors were open to intra-Community trade. The following three groups were identified.

(a) *High technology public procurement sectors (Group 1).* This group includes office and data processing equipment, telecommunications equipment and medical equipment. Non-trade barriers are considered high, but price dispersion is relatively low due to substantial extra-EU trade and the presence of large multinationals in Europe.

(b) *Traditional or regulated public procurement sectors (Groups 2 and 3).* This group covers two types of industries. The first type was, pre-single market, heavily protected

---

30   P. Buigues, F. Ilzkovitz and J.-F. Lebrun, 'The impact of the internal market by industrial sector: the challenge for the Member States', *European Economy, Social Europe*, special edition, 1990.

by, for example, national standards, and where as a consequence intra-Community trade was weak and price dispersion was considerable. This type of industry includes rolling stock and pharmaceutical products. The second type of industry that falls into this sector was also, before the launch of the single market programme, subject to significant non-tariff barriers and, as with the former group, was characterized by weak intra-Community trade. However, due to the presence of competition from newly industrialized countries (NICs), price dispersion within the Community was relatively low. This type of industry includes shipbuilding and electrical equipment.

(c)   *Sectors with moderate non-trade barriers (Group 4)*. This group is the largest of the three in terms of industrial value added. Before the launch of the single market programme, there was already a significant amount of intra-Community trade in these industries, but, due to various non-tariff barriers, the degree of price dispersion remained relatively high. This group includes a number of basic consumer products (including domestic appliances and motor cars).

Table 5.1 overleaf provides a summary of these three groups and describes their key characteristics. A detailed description of the sectors is provided in Appendix C.

In their study, the authors put forward the following arguments.

(a)   The impact of integration was likely to be greatest for Groups 1 and 2 (high technology public procurement sectors and traditional or regulated public procurements sectors where price dispersion is high). In Group 1, single market measures could be expected to encourage exploitation of economies of scale; in Group 2 sectors, the single market programme could be expected to boost intra-Community trade and lead to reductions in prices.

(b)   For Group 3 sectors, the impact of integration may be somewhat less significant, but is still likely to impact upon technical efficiency.

(c)   For Group 4 sectors, the primary effect of integration is likely to be a reduction in the degree of price variation between Member States.

We now turn to consideration of empirical indicators. In the case of trade flows and price-cost margins, we investigate the impact of integration at a sectoral level and use the classification of sectors described above.

Table 5.1.   The industrial sectors most affected by the single market

		Price differences between Member States	
		Weak	Strong
T r a d e i n t e n s i t y	Weak	**Traditional or regulated public procurement markets**	
		GROUP 3	**GROUP 2**
		Characteristics:	Characteristics:
		– sectors subject to competition from NICs	– sectors in which competition in intra- and extra-EC imports is weak
		– restructuring in progress	– high concentration and economies of scale
			– restructuring expected in 1992
		Example: electrical and electronic equipment, shipbuilding	Example: energy producing equipment, railway equipment, pharmaceutical products
	Strong	**High technology public-procurement sectors**	**Products with moderate non-tariff barriers**
		GROUP 1	**GROUP 4**
		Characteristics:	Characteristics:
		– sectors already partly open to competition	– sectors with fragmented distribution and/or marketing networks
		– degree of openness to extra-EC countries	– high levels of differentiation
		– high concentration and economies of scale	
		– relatively low European productivity, compared with American and Japanese producers	
		Example: telecommunications, data processing	Example: motor vehicles, textiles, clothing, footwear, domestic electrical appliances, television, video, toys

Source: Taken from *The impact of the internal market by industrial sector: the challenge for the Member States*, Buigues, Ilzkovitz and Lebrun [1990].

5.3. Trade flows

In this section we consider to what extent intra-Europe trade patterns have changed and support the assertion that European integration is progressing.

5.3.1. Aggregate trade flows

Following the approach of Neven and Röller [1991],[31] there are two separate ways in which trade flows may be used to analyse trends in European integration.

(a)   Intra-European trade may increase due to trade creation. Trends in trade creation may be measured by changes in the share of intra-EU imports in total demand over time.

---

[31]   See D.J. Neven and L.H. Röller, 'European Integration and trade flows', *European Economic Review* 35, 1991.

(b)   Changes in intra-European trade flows may also arise because of trade diversion, i.e. intra-EU trade may increase at the expense of trade previously carried out with third parties outside the EU. This latter effect is reflected in an increase in the share of intra-EU imports of total imports.

Original results of Neven and Röller

Neven and Röller used these measures to analyse empirically the extent to which EC integration had been deepening, and compared trends in integration within the EU with trends in integration between the EU and the rest of the world. They used trade and consumption data for 29 industries in 4 countries, covering the period 1975–85. Their results are reproduced in Tables 5.2 and 5.3.

Table 5.2.   **Average trade share in the four big EU countries (all sectors except foodstuff, wood, paper, mineral products, steel, non-ferrous metals)**

Period	EC imports as a % of apparent consumption	Non-EC imports as a % of apparent consumption	EC imports/total imports
1975–78	16.00	10.42	66.23
1979–82	17.02	12.00	63.95
1983–85	18.80	13.98	63.49

Source: Table 1 in D.J. Neven and L.H. Röller, *European integration and trade flows.*

Table 5.2 shows that, for most sectors, trade flows within the EU increased between 1975 and 1985. Trade with non-EU countries increased too, but at a faster rate.

Neven and Röller therefore concluded that:

(a)   European integration had been proceeding along with integration in the rest of the world;
(b)   for most of the sectors analysed, integration between the EU and the rest of the world had been happening faster than integration between European countries.

Update of Neven and Röller for 1980–93

For the purposes of our study we updated the analysis of Neven and Röller. Instead of 29 sectors, we used data on 46 NACE categories and calculated an analogous set of indicators. These show the evolution of intra-EU trade as a percentage of apparent EU domestic demand, the evolution of extra-EU trade as a percentage of the apparent EU domestic demand, and the increase in proportion of total imports represented by intra-EU imports.

Table 5.3 provides summary measures for these three indicators for the three periods 1980–84, 1985–88 and 1989–93.

Table 5.3.   Measures of trade penetration for the manufacturing sector

Period	Intra-EU imports as a % of demand	Extra-EU imports as a % of demand	Intra-EU imports as a % of total imports
1980–84	17.9	12.0	57.7
1985–88	20.8	12.8	60.0
1989–93	22.9	14.0	60.8

Source: Eurostat VISA database; data covers 46 NACE branches.

The data for the three periods analysed indicate that, as in Table 5.2 and Table 5.3 above, EU integration is proceeding alongside integration between the EU and the rest of the world. However, in contrast to the findings of Neven and Röller, our figures suggest that integration within the EU is proceeding faster than integration between the European and the world economies (illustrated by the rising share of intra-EU imports in total imports).

Table 5.3 also shows that changes between 1980 and 1984, and 1985 and 1988, are larger than between 1985 and 1988, and 1989 and 1993. The data seems to suggest that integration, as indicated by increasing intra-EU import penetration, proceeded at a faster rate immediately after the launch of the single market programme. As Neven and Röller note, the evolution of trade shares is only indicative of the extent to which integration has proceeded – it is impossible to isolate the impact of the single market programme. In addition, the single market programme did not occur at a precise point in time, but was gradually introduced over a number of years.

5.3.2.   Sectoral trade flows

We now consider whether there was any difference in how trade flows have changed for different sectors. In particular, we consider whether the Buigues sectors defined in Section 5.2 have a different experience of intra-EU trade deepening to other sectors.[32]

Table 5.4.   Intra-EU trade creation (intra-EU imports as a percentage of demand)

	1980–84	1985–88	1989–93
Group 1 average	24.8	25.8	26.0
Group 2 average	4.9	6.2	7.9
Group 4 average	26.1	29.9	31.0
14 Buigues sector average	24.4	27.6	28.7
46 sector average (Table 5.3)	17.9	20.8	22.9

[32]   The trade flow analysis in Section 4.3.2 was carried out for 46 NACE sectors; 14 of these were identified by Buigues et. al as most likely to be affected by integration. There were no Buigues Group 3 sectors amongst the 46 sectors in the data.

Table 5.3 and Table 5.4 illustrate the following trends.

(a)   The 14 sectors identified by Buigues et al. to be most affected by single market measures have seen a steady increase in intra-EU imports as a percentage of total demand over the last decade or so.

(b)   As with the aggregate analysis presented in Section 5.3.1, the impact on trade flows was greatest immediately following the introduction of the single market programme in the mid-1980s.

(c)   However, quite surprisingly, on average, trade flows increased less for the 14 Buigues sectors than for the 46 NACE sectors taken together. This may be because the majority of the Buigues sectors analysed belonged to Group 4, where trade intensity was already high, and where the primary impact of the single market was expected to be on price levels.

(d)   On average, for the 14 Buigues sectors, trade diversion rose immediately following the introduction of single market measures, but has fallen in recent years. This is in contrast to the average for the 46 NACE sectors, where trade diversion steadily rose throughout the time period. Table 5.4 shows that the share of extra-EU imports in total imports for the 14 Buigues sectors has risen relatively quickly over time. This suggests that, for these sectors, integration between the world economy and the EU is deepening at a more rapid pace than integration within the EU.

Table 5.5.   Trade diversion (intra-EU imports as a percentage of all imports)

	1980–84	1985–88	1989–93
Group 1 average	47.5	49.3	47.9
Group 2 average	79.9	84.6	84.8
Group 4 average	64.0	63.9	62.5
14 Buigues sector average	62.8	63.3	62.0
46 sector average (Table 5.3)	57.7	60.0	60.8

Table 5.6.   Extra-EU imports as a percentage of total demand

	1980–84	1985–88	1989–93
Group 1 average	25.5	24.5	26.4
Group 2 average	1.3	1.3	1.8
Group 4 average	14.5	16.7	19.4
14 Buigues sector average	15.1	16.7	19.2
46 sector average (Table 5.3)	12.0	12.8	14.0

5.3.3. Extra-EU and intra-EU trade effects

The data set of trade patterns across 46 sectors over the period 1980–93 also allows us to check for the interaction between intra-EU trade and extra-EU trade across the 46 NACE sectors. Are we merely observing that sectors that show high levels·of intra-EU trade flows are also those that have high levels of extra-EU trade? This question can be analysed by a simple correlation analysis of the two variables, EU imports as a percentage of apparent consumption. This analysis of trade flows in 46 sectors reveals that these two variables are indeed correlated across sectors.

Table 5.7.   Cross-sectoral correlation of trade flows intra-EU and extra-EU (%)

Variable	1980	1981	1982	1983	1984	1985	1986	1987	1988	1989	1990	1991	1992	1993
Corr. sector	34.9	36.4	33.6	32.8	33.4	33.0	34.4	34.7	35.0	37.8	38.6	38.7	38.5	45.2

Table 5.7 shows the cross-sectoral correlation coefficients for each year. What is immediately apparent is that the trend of the coefficient increases over time.

In 1980, intra and extra trade flows in the 46 sectors showed a correlation coefficient of 35%. By 1993 this coefficient had increased to 45%. The increase is particularly steep after 1988.

What does that statistic tell us? These correlation coefficients are not very high. This suggests that, at least in the 1980s, trade within Europe was to a certain degree divorced from that with non-EU countries. The changes that can be observed since the late 1980s suggest that intra- and extra-EU trade increasingly have common drivers. It may be that trade flows in a particular sector are now more determined by economic fundamentals such as transport costs rather than by trade barriers (internal or external).

5.4. Price dispersion

5.4.1. Trends in price convergence

In this section we briefly review the results presented in the DRI study[33] on changes in price disparities and assess the degree to which these support the existence of a distinctive trend in integration.

The single market programme carried with it expectations of a narrowing of price differentials for products sold across different national markets. As the Cecchini report [1988] put it: 'The removal of barriers and the freedom of supply which business will enjoy as a result should lead, through increased competitive pressure, to some downward convergence of prices of benefit to the customer'. Price convergence is thus one measure of the impact of integration. As geographical markets become increasingly independent of national borders, then we would expect to see some convergence of prices within these markets.

---

[33]   DRI, E. de Ghellinck, Horack, Adler & Associates, *Study on the emergence of panEuropean markets*, draft final report, February 1996.

To assume, however, that there will be a single European market in which each product is sold at a single price is erroneous. Even within national markets we see more than one price quoted for a good; there is a distribution of prices rather than a single price. Consumer arbitrage may not remove these price differentials due to costs of consumer search. In addition, there are many reasons why geographical markets remain smaller than the area defined by the boundaries of the European Union, for example transport costs and language barriers. The incremental amount of price convergence will also be limited, and, indeed, may well be negligible, in those markets where considerable integration has already taken place. For example, there are many markets, like foreign exchange markets, whose boundaries transcend those of the European Union and are already globally integrated.

The DRI study, which was commissioned in parallel with this report, has as its central task the analysis of changes in price disparities in the EU following the launch of the single market programme.[34] This study covers a large number of products and services for which price indices were collected for four years: 1980, 1985, 1990 and 1993. These indices are then used to calculate indicators of price dispersion to test the hypothesis that prices have indeed converged across the EU. The study does not address the issue of the level to which prices may be converging. The central question for competition policy is, of course, whether prices are converging towards cost (which we consider in our analysis of price-cost margins).

The analysis of price convergence has been undertaken at a relatively detailed level for 174 goods and services using price dispersion indices provided by Eurostat. The data covers the 12 Member States for the period 1980–93 and 15 Member States for the period starting from 1985.

The DRI report concludes that:

(a)   there has been a general trend towards price convergence in the 12 Member States over the period 1980–93;

(b)   this trend has been more pronounced for consumer and equipment goods than for energy, services and construction;

(c)   indeed, as illustrated in Figure 5.1, price dispersion has increased over time in energy and construction;

(d)   the convergence in consumer products and services has tended to accelerate following the launch of the single market programme.

Figure 5.1 summarizes some key results for the EUR-12.

---

[34]   We acknowledge that the DRI study [DRI, E. de Ghellinck and Horack, Adler and Associates, *Study on the emergence of panEuropean markets*, draft final report, February 1996] is, as yet, incomplete.

Figure 5.1.   Coefficients of price variation for the EUR-12

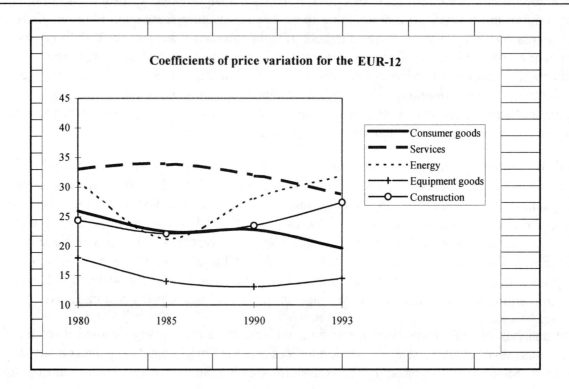

Source: DRI, E. de Ghellinck and Horack, Adler and Associates, *Study on the emergence of panEuropean markets*, draft final report, February 1996.

The report also concluded that the tendency for prices to converge has been more pronounced for the enlarged EU including the new Member States, Greece, Spain and Portugal, than in the EUR-9, as illustrated by Table 5.8 below. This is only to be expected given the initial greater differences of prices. Single market measures have sought to remove non-tariff barriers within the EUR-9. Within the EUR-12, however, recent years have seen the gradual removal of tariff as well as non-tariff barriers – hence, not surprisingly, the greater the degree of convergence within the EUR-12 than within the EUR-9.

These general results are based primarily on an analysis of final consumer prices (including tax) in the respective countries. The report states clearly that overall neither the different levels of, nor the changes in, VAT rates seem to have distorted general price trends (i.e. there is no significant difference in price convergence trends including or excluding VAT).

The report does underline, however, the important role played in some product categories by excise duties, notably for energy products, alcoholic beverages and tobacco products. In fact, for these goods, the study finds increasing price divergence compared to the underlying trend in prices net of taxes.[35]

---

[35]   This divergence has a bearing on our assessment of integration. For personal consumption post-tax prices are relevant. If these prices differ significantly across Member States, then this may create arbitrage opportunities. If pre-tax prices differ, then this matters for trade at the wholesale level; and raises the issue of the existence of any barriers to arbitrage.

Table 5.8.   Coefficients of price variation for selected groupings (prices incl. taxes)

	1980	1985	1990	1993
EUR-9				
Consumer goods	19.9	19.1	20.3	18.0
Services	25.2	25.6	24.6	23.4
Energy	22.1	16.1	24.7	30.6
Equipment goods	13.1	12.5	12.2	12.9
Construction	20.1	14.4	16.5	22.4
EUR-12				
Consumer goods	26.0	22.5	22.8	19.6
Services	33.0	33.7	31.8	28.6
Energy	30.8	21.1	28.0	31.7
Equipment goods	18.0	14.0	13.1	14.5
Construction	24.4	22.1	23.5	27.4

Source: DRI, E. de Ghellinck and Horack, Adler and Associates, *Study on the emergence of panEuropean markets*, draft final report, February 1996.

5.5. Price-cost margins

Through increased competition, the single market is expected to benefit consumers. Rather than the cost savings resulting from reductions in the cost of trade and exploitation of economies of scale being retained by firms, it is hoped that they get passed on to consumers in the form of lower prices.

The measurement of trends in relative prices across Member States is one set of indicators that can be used to assess the impact of integration on prices. Another, more direct, assessment is to analyse price-cost margins across sectors. The advantage of such a measure of gross profitability of an industry is that it can ignore issues of changes in prices that are due to changes in costs and identify changes in competitive conditions. This measure is frequently used in studies that seek to establish whether market concentration has any impact on profitability.[36] For the purpose of this study we have undertaken an analysis of price-cost margins to complement the analysis of other indicators of integration. We are not aware of any other study that has traced the trend in this primary measure of competition conditions.

If the single market programme has had a pro-competitive effect (bringing firms in different Member States into direct competition where previously non-tariff barriers prevented this), then we would expect price-cost margins to be reduced. Most theories of firm behaviour in oligopolies predict that cost-price margins are negatively related to the number of firms in a market; we can interpret market integration as the unification of previously distinct markets and so an increase in the number of competing firms, with a consequent reduction in margins.

5.5.1. Analysis of price-cost margins

The data for this exercise was drawn from the Eurostat Survey of Industrial Production for the EUR-12 for the period 1980–92. This was available at a highly disaggregated level; the 3-digit

---

[36]   See Geroski [1994] for an overview.

NACE classification has 115 sectors. This gave a data set of about 8,000 observations. Unfortunately, Spain and Portugal had to be dropped from the analysis due to insufficient data. Fuller details of the data and reports of relevant econometric results are given in annexes to this chapter.

Our analysis has been carried out for two definitions of price-cost margins:

$$M1 = (\text{value added - labour costs}) / \text{value added}$$

$$M2 = (\text{value added - labour costs}) / \text{sales}$$

The first definition is often used in empirical studies examining the link between profitability and concentration.[37] The second definition has also been used in empirical studies but less widely. However, it conforms more closely to the theoretical notion of a profit/sales ratio in the economic literature: (p-c) / p. In general, our results are not very sensitive to which definition is used.

5.5.2. Average margins

The average level of margins is shown in Figure 5.2 below.

Figure 5.2.   Average margins

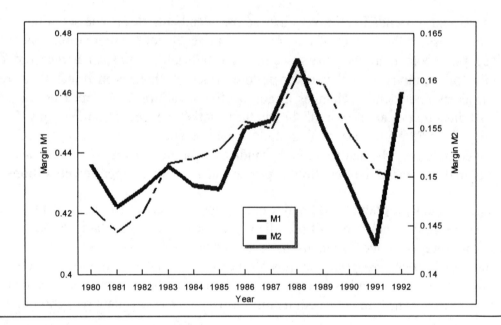

A table of summary statistics from which this is drawn is given in Appendix C. It may be seen that there appears to be a positive trend for the early 1980s, though average margins have

---

[37]   Dowrick, S., 'Wage pressure, bargaining and price-cost margins in UK manufacturing', *Journal of Industrial Economics*, Vol. 38, No 3, March 1990, pp. 239–67.

fallen relative to this trend in the late 1980s. However, margins move in response to the state of the economic cycle: there was a major upturn in the mid-1980s, preceded and followed by major recessions. We correct for this effect in Section 5.5.3.

The two different definitions of margins have rather different overall average levels: 44% for the measure M1 and 15% for M2. There is also significant cross country variation in average margins for the whole sample period. Table A3.1 in Appendix C shows that we can group the countries in the following way:

(a)   high margins: Italy, Belgium;
(b)   medium margins: France, Netherlands, UK, Ireland;
(c)   low margins: Germany, Luxembourg, Denmark, Greece.

Interestingly, there is evidence that the cross-country dispersion in margins reduced over the sample period. The following figure shows a plot of the cross-country variance in margins using the two measures for the period 1980–91. We do not show 1992 due to lack of data. The decline in cross-country dispersion happens from 1987.

Figure 5.3.   Cross-country variance of average margins

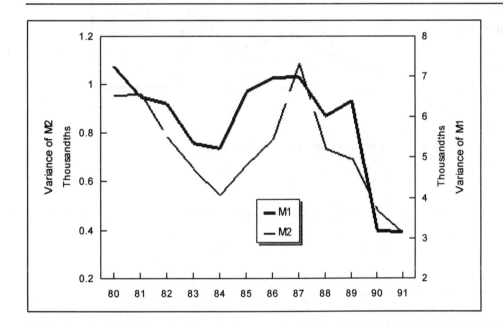

This would be consistent with the single market programme having an equalizing effect. Appendix C gives a formal statistical test of this decline in variance, and shows a statistically significant fall in variance at the end of the sample period. We take this as evidence of an impact of the single market programme (even if slightly lagged), which we would expect to lead to more similar economic outcomes across countries.

5.5.3. Evolution of margins

This section presents a summary of the way in which margins have changed over the period 1980–92 by typed sector. To make sense of the data it is necessary to correct it at least for the influence of the economic cycle and for country- and sector-specific effects. This was done using a random effects regression using time dummies; the details of this analysis are reported in Section C.5 of Appendix C. Separate time dummies were included for each of the Buigues sectors, so that the evolution of margins could be charted for each sector separately. The results are summarized in the following figures which show deviations from a trend that captures the effects of the economic cycle and certain country and sector specific effects.

Figure 5.4.   Evolution of margins (M1) (controlling for country- and sector-specific effects and cycle)

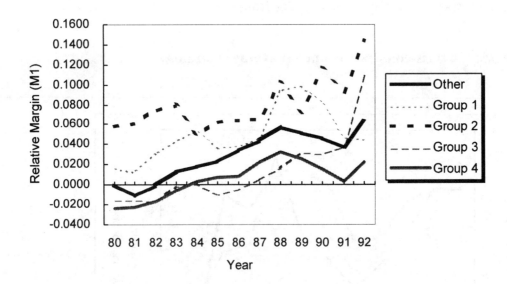

Figure 5.5. **Buigues sectors relative to other sectors**

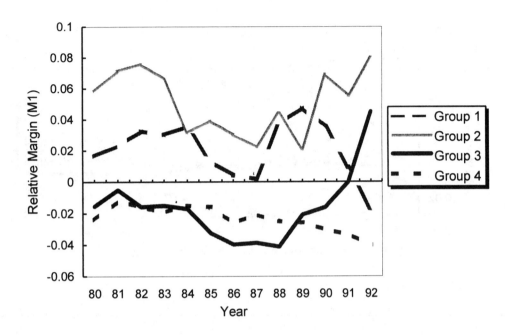

Figure 5.6. **Evolution of margins (M2)**
(controlling for country- and sector-specific effects and cycle)

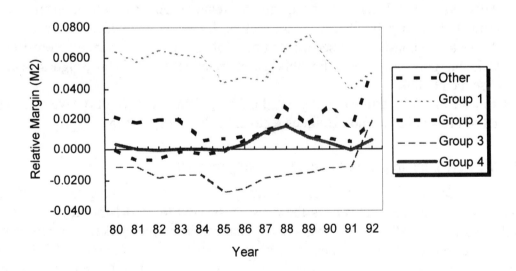

Figure 5.7.   Buigues sectors relative to other sectors

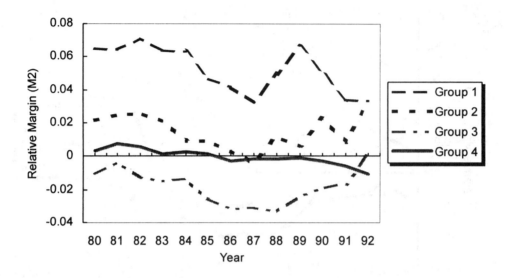

This preliminary analysis of the behaviour of margins over time suggests the following conclusions.

(a)   There has been a general trend upwards in margins for the non-Buigues sectors over the whole sample period, but there has been a decline from 1988 to 1991.

(b)   The behaviour of all sectors in 1992 seems rather anomalous. There is very little data for this year compared with previous years, so not too much should be read into this.

(c)   Group 4 (products with moderate non-tariff barriers) have margins which are falling relative to the non-Buigues sectors, with this relative decline accelerating since 1988.

(d)   Group 1 (hi-tech public procurement sectors) have margins which are generally falling relative to the non-Buigues sectors, but most of this decline occurred before 1987. Since 1987, margins have risen for this group relative to the non-Buigues sectors, but subsequently fallen.

(e)   Groups 2 and 3 (traditional or regulated public procurement sectors) have margins which first fell relative to the non-Buigues sectors, but have since risen.

5.5.4. Measuring the impact of the single market programme

We now consider whether it is possible to identify any impact of the single market programme on margins from the data. This begs the question of how to model the impact of the single market programme. Rather than being a 'step' change, the single market programme has been a rolling sequence of incremental measures throughout the period 1986–92. Without identifying the time at which a particular measure became effective and which sectors it affected, we must use a simple proxy.

We have investigated the use of two alternatives which are illustrated by:

(a)   a ramped policy variable with an impact starting in 1986;

(b)   a 'delayed impact' policy variable with an impact starting in 1987.

Figure 5.8.   Definition of policy variable

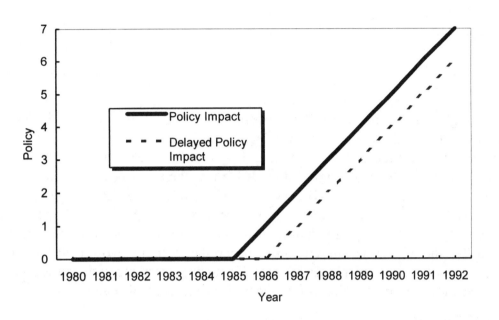

These policy variables were included in regressions along with variables for economic cycle, country-specific effects and trend. The policy variables were interacted with dummies for each Buigues group and for 'non-Buigues' sectors, allowing the total impact of the policy to be assessed for each group. Sector specific effects were modelled in a number of alternative ways as fixed and random effects. The details of these regressions are shown in Section C.8 of Appendix C. All the coefficient estimates are reported in the annex.

We find that we may draw the following conclusions from these regressions:

(a)   There is very significant evidence (from models 1 and 9) of the single market programme reducing margins in the non-Buigues sectors and Group 4 even if we assume that there was an impact of the policy from 1986.
(b)   There is even stronger evidence of a policy impact on the non-Buigues sectors and Group 4 if we suppose, as seems reasonable, that there was a short delay of one year before the single market programme affected firm behaviour (from models 5 and 13).
(c)   There is significant evidence that there was a larger policy impact on Group 4 than on the non-Bui gues sectors (see the relative effects tables for model 13) using the definition of margins M1, but not using M2.
(d)   We would estimate (using the delayed impact) the overall impact of the single market programme to be as given by the following table.

Table 5.9.   Impact on price-cost margins

	Average level of margin across EU in sample period (%)	Policy impact on non-Buigues sectors (% per annum)	Policy impact on Group 4 (% per annum)
Margin definition M1	44.1	-0.7	-0.9
Margin definition M2	15.2	-0.2	-0.2

(e)   The single market programme does not appear to have affected margins in Groups 2 and 3: they rose at the time of implementation of the programme. This may be understandable if the measures affecting these groups were adopted relatively later in the sample period. There is significant evidence that there has been less policy impact for these sectors than for the non-Buigues sectors (see relative effects tables).

(f)   The evidence for Group 1 is unfortunately lacking. The sign of the policy impact for this sector depends on the margin definition and is in neither case significantly different from zero. On the other hand there is no evidence that margins evolved differently for this group than for the non-Buigues sectors. We cannot determine with confidence what has happened to margins for Group 1 on the basis of the available data.

5.5.5.   Analysis of advertising and research intensive industries

The data allows the application of an alternative industry classification by Davies and Lyons [1996] which distinguishes between homogenous goods industries and those that are characterized by heavy expenditure on advertising and R&D. The regressions used the following dummy variables:

A = advertising intensive dummy

R = research intensive dummy

AR = both advertising and research intensive dummy

Section C.8.1 of Appendix C shows the results of random effects regressions using this classification of sectors.

These regressions show that advertising intensive sectors have had a significantly smaller impact from integration than those sectors which are neither advertising nor R&D intensive. This finding is consistent with the hypothesis that in enlarged markets for differentiated goods, such as branded consumer goods, advertising expenditure is a relatively more important strategic variable than in smaller more protected markets. In the sense that advertising spending can be considered endogenous sunk costs this requires increased margins. Alternatively this finding may indicate that markets served by advertising intensive industries have become more concentrated and sustain higher price-cost margins. With both explanations integration suggests a differential response in advertising intensive industries which is worth taking note of.

5.5.6. Summary

The analysis of price-cost margins presented here shows a significant impact of integration. This is of considerable interest since it shows a direct measure of competition being affected by integration, rather than looking at indirect measures (such as trade flows, price dispersion, etc.). Although we cannot ascribe the fall in margins for some sectors since 1986 to the effects of integration with certainty, the timing of this fall strongly suggests that integration measures are the cause: the response in margins followed with a short lag after the start of the single market programme.

Interestingly, not all sectors have been affected equally. The Buigues Group 4 sectors have been most affected by integration, the non-Buigues sectors have been affected, but somewhat less. Buigues Groups 2 and 3 appear not to have been significantly affected by integration. The data does not allow us to identify what has happened to the Buigues Group 1 sectors. This accords with some, but not all, of the original expectations of Buigues et al. Group 4 includes sectors which are traded and had moderate non-tariff barriers, so should have experienced an impact from integration. The lack of an impact for Groups 2 and 3 supports that the single market programme has not affected public procurement markets, despite the expectations of Buigues et al.

5.6. Concentration

One set of expectations of the impact of the single market programme centres on the opportunities provided by the creation of larger markets and the reduction in trade barriers to exploit economies of scale. As discussed in Chapter 4, the realization of economies of scale was widely considered to be one of the main gains of the completion of the single market. Other things being equal, greater exploitation of economies of scale will lead to increases in concentration – whether it be via organic growth or via merger. The other main effect – independent of economies of scale – is the exit of firms as a response to tougher competition. Hence, increases in concentration over time may indicate that single market measures are starting to take effect. Increases in concentration do not necessarily imply, however, that competition will be lessened. Fewer firms in larger markets may well start to compete more vigorously with each other. Shifts in the nature of competition may therefore bring greater benefits to European consumers, despite any concentration increases.

In one of the parallel studies reviewing the impact of single market legislation, the Economists Advisory Group in collaboration with the University of East Anglia[38] has evaluated changes in concentration for the period 1986–91 across a number of 3-digit NACE sectors. The study covers other market structure variables, such as firm size distribution, but also seeks to assess the extent to which economies of scale have been realized.

The EAG study analyses the changes that occurred in firm size (from 1986 to 1991) and market concentration (from 1987 to 1993) at both the EU and national level. Basing its analysis on Sutton [1991] and Davies and Lyon [1996, forthcoming], the EAG classifies the manufacturing sector into four categories.

---

[38]   European Commission [1997a], 'Economies of scale', *Single Market Review*, Subseries V: Volume 4.

Table 5.10.   Changes in size and concentration by industry type

	Industries	Growth in size		Concentration		
		% growth 1986–91 at national level		Mean national change (C4NÅT)	EU level (C4EU)	
	Industries	Firm	Industry	1986–92	1987	1993
Type 1	Homogenous goods	3.2	1.8	-0.3	12.3	16.5
Type 2a	High advertising intensity	14.3	3.5	1.3	21.1	23.5
Type 2r	High R&D intensity	-0.7	0.2	-1.9	31.6	38.9
Type 2ar	High R&D and advertising intensity	-3.9	2.3	1.3	34.8	37.2
All				-0.1	19.7	23.8

Notes:
1. All means are simple arithmetic averages.
2. 'Mean national' refers to the simple means of Belgium, France, Germany and the UK; for France the time period is 1985–92, for Germany it is 1987–93, and for Belgium it is 1986–91.
3. Changes in concentration ratios refer to percentage points.
4. C4NAT = four firm concentration ratio. C4EU = four firm concentration ratio, EU.
Source: European Commission, 1997a.

The study confirms that the EU market was not fully integrated at the start of the single market programme, and that there was the potential for further achievement of economies of scale. Overall, the study claims that the most interesting result is that the early effects of the single market programme have shown through in the R&D intensive industries. In these industries, firm size was found to be positively related to specialization in Member States with a comparative advantage.

The study further finds important differences between industries. Table 5.10 summarizes the main results in changes in the size of firms/industry at the national level and the development of concentration at both the EU and national levels.

(a) *Type 1 industries* (homogeneous goods). Typical national concentration declined on average. However, concentration at the EU level appears to have increased, although starting from a relatively low starting point. The implication is that there was either a substantial increase in the extent of the intra-EU multinationality and/or an increase in international specialization within the EU. Another indicator of the change in concentration is provided by the indicators of change in firm size and size of the industry. The average size of firms increased (3.2%) by more than the size of the industry (1.8%), suggesting an increase in concentration.

(b) *Type 2a industries* (high advertising intensity). The typical size of business units within Member States increased substantially. Because they easily outstripped the growth in overall national industry size, this implies increased national concentration. This finding is confirmed by the change in the four-firm concentration ratio at the national level (+1.3%) and the changes at the EU level (from 21.1% to 23.5%).

(c)   *Type 2r industries* (high R&D intensity). This group of industries had relatively high levels of concentration in 1987. In the period 1986–91 the mean business size has tended to decline very slightly, while industry size has virtually been static. This contrasts strikingly with the very rapid increase in EU concentration. Likely reasons given are increasing specialization and substantial increases in intra-EU multinationality.

(d)   *Type 2ar industries* (high R&D and advertising intensity). This group, like the previous group, exhibited relatively high levels of concentration in 1987. Over the period 1986–91, mean business size tended to decline, while industry size has slightly increased, suggesting a decentralizing trend at the national level. This finding contrasts the change in the four-firm concentration ratio at both the EU and national levels.

5.7. Conclusions

We have found a variety of independent pieces of evidence which are consistent with the hypothesis that integration has had pro-competitive effects. The indicators we have looked at show movements consistent with integration.

(a)   Trade patterns have shown trade creation with the EU as well as some degree of trade diversion away from external trade since 1985.
(b)   There has been convergence of post-tax prices, particularly for consumer goods.
(c)   Concentration has increased at the EU level (and particularly for advertising intensive industries), which is consistent with increased competition across borders and greater exploitation of economies of scale.
(d)   Price-cost margins have fallen for a large number of sectors as the single market programme has been implemented. The magnitude of this effect is large, in the order of 0.2% per annum on margins with an average level of 15% (using margin definition M2). Over a decade, for example, this is a fall of 2%.

The pattern of impact of integration is also of interest. Looking at the so-called Buigues sectors for which there was a strong prior expectation of an impact of integration we found the following.

(a)   Price-cost margins appear to have been most affected by integration in the Buigues Group 4 sectors (tradable products with moderate non-tariff barriers).
(b)   Price-cost margins appear not to have been affected by integration in public procurement markets.
(c)   There was trade creation in the Buigues sectors, but at a slightly slower rate than other sectors. The trade diversion measure fell for these sectors, suggesting that integration between the EU and the rest of the world may be proceeding at a faster rate than integration within the EU.

This final point demonstrates an unavoidable difficulty in the analysis: that intra-and extra-EU trade liberalization tend to move hand in hand and so separating the effects of the two measures is very difficult. Nevertheless, there is some evidence that the single market programme has in fact caused a change in margins. In particular, the timing of the fall in margins matches the single market programme having an effect with a short delay. Also, we find that the cross-country variance in margins fell at the same time. Of course, the timing of these effects on margins may just be a chance event, but the close association of these effects with the onset of the single market programme is in our view more than a coincidence.

Using the Davies/Lyon classifications of sectors, our main finding was that integration has had a significantly smaller impact on advertising intensive sectors. This accords with the economic reasoning that advertising intensive industries are likely to produce differentiated goods which can exploit economies of scale in larger markets and need to recover higher levels of sunk endogenous costs.

Therefore, we may conclude that integration has not affected all sectors equally, as would be expected. The sectors which are comparatively more affected are among those we would expect to be most affected by integration. This again provides a confirming check that what is being identified econometrically is indeed an integration, or at least a trade, effect.

There is certainly evidence of a major change in competitive conditions in the EU from 1986 to 1992, with a trend towards more competitive outcomes and changes in business strategies (advertising). This is consistent with the single market programme having a significant pro-competitive impact, although this positive impact may be restricted to some sectors and countries and may not apply throughout all sectors of the EU. Furthermore, these findings may mask the scope for anti-competitive responses as well as the lack of progress in implementing measures in heavily protected sectors.

6.   The evolution of competition in selected markets

6.1. Introduction

In Chapter 5, we used a series of empirical measures – trade flows, price dispersion, market concentration and price-cost margins – to assess whether the statistical picture both at the aggregate and at the sectoral level was consistent with deepening integration within the EU. We concluded that this was indeed the case, but noted that we had not established causality, merely consistency. In other words, our indicators do not prove that integration is occurring, but neither do they disprove it. In addition, changes in the nature of competition cannot be inferred from such statistics. It is for this reason that, in this chapter, we consider evidence from selected market studies to obtain a more informed picture of the evolution of competition in the single market. Of course, by being selective we forego the ability to make observations that apply more generally throughout the economy. So what we gain in selective insight into competitive processes we lose in terms of the general validity of our findings.

We begin, in Section 6.2, by reviewing changes in statistical indicators for selected market studies. In the remainder of the chapter, we turn to market fundamentals in order to explain what drives changes in competitive conditions. We focus on the following markets – soda ash, beer, cars, air travel, domestic appliances and telecommunications switching equipment[39] – using, in each case, the framework outlined below:

(a)   first, we provide a market overview;
(b)   next we discuss the expected impact of the single market programme on competition and industry structure;
(c)   finally, we discuss the interaction between integration and competition.

Our objective is to establish the key drivers of integration and of changes in the nature of competition, from which we can draw some clear-cut implications for competition policy.

Our market studies constitute a small but reasonably representative selection of sectors, with different degrees of exposure to single market measures. Volume II of this report contains these studies in full.

6.2. Trends in integration and competition in selected case studies

In this section we review changes in two of our statistical indicators discussed in Chapter 5 – trade flows and measures of price dispersion – for selected market studies.

6.2.1. Evolution of trade patterns

In Chapter 5, we updated the analysis of Neven and Röller [1991], which analyse͏   ͏͏es in trade flows in selected 3-digit NACE sectors, using two measures of d   ͏ᵗ͏ integration:

---

[39]   See Chapter 1 for selection criteria.

(a)   the share of intra-EU imports in total demand; this represents the degree of trade creation;

(b)   the share of intra-EU imports in all imports; this represents the degree of trade diversion.

We particularly focused on changes in these measures for the sectors identified by Buigues et al. [1990], as most likely to be affected by single market measures. Most of our market studies fall into one of these 40 industrial sectors.

(a)   Telecommunications switching equipment belongs to the 'high technology public procurement group' (Group 1). Sectors in this group were characterized by high non-trade barriers, but low price dispersion. Single market measures were expected primarily to increase the scope for exploitation of economies of scale.

(b)   Beer may be classified as a 'traditional public procurement or regulated market sector' (Group 2). Sectors in Group 2 were, pre-single market measures, heavily protected. Intra-Community trade was weak and price dispersion was considerable. Buigues et al. argued that the impact of integration was likely to be greatest for sectors in Group 1 and Group 2.

(c)   Cars and domestic appliances may be classified as sectors with moderate non-trade barriers (Group 4). The key impact of integration on Group 4 sectors was expected to be a reduction in the degree of price variation between Member States.

Air travel is a service sector and therefore is not covered by the Buigues study. But it may be classified as a highly regulated sector with substantial non-trade barriers. Soda ash, on the other hand, was *a priori* not expected to be significantly affected by integration measures.

Table 6.1 below summarizes trends in trade creation for selected market studies.[40]

Table 6.1.   Intra-EU trade creation (intra-EU imports as a percentage of demand)

	1980–84	1985–88	1989–93
Telecom. equipment (Group 1)	16.0	13.4	12.3
Domestic appliances (Group 4)	20.8	25.2	29.4
Group 1 average	24.8	25.8	26.0
Group 2 average	4.9	6.2	7.9
Group 4 average	26.1	29.9	31.0

Table 6.1 illustrates the following trends.

(a)   For telecommunications equipment, where, as with all Group 1 sectors, expectations were quite high, there was a fall in intra-EU trade (as a share of demand). The

---

...tunately, due to data limitations, sectoral-level analysis was only possible for two of our selected market studies.

telecommunications equipment sector was in fact one of only 6 NACE sectors, out of the 46 analysed, where trade has weakened over recent years.

(b) For the domestic appliances sector, there has been a substantial increase in intra-EU trade over the last decade or so, indicating deepening European integration. The growth in intra-EU imports as a share of demand was in fact significantly in excess of the Group 4 average.

Table 6.2 presents trends in trade diversion:

Table 6.2.   Trade diversion (intra-EU imports as a percentage of all imports)

	1980–84	1985–88	1989–93
Telecom. equipment (Group 1)	44.2	45.8	45.6
Domestic appliances (Group 4)	75.8	71.6	73.8
Group 1 average	47.5	49.3	47.9
Group 2 average	79.9	84.6	84.8
Group 4 average	64.0	63.9	62.5

Table 6.2 demonstrates the following trends.

(a) For the telecommunications equipment sector, there has been an increase in trade diversion over the period, despite falls in trade creation. This suggests that integration between the EU and elsewhere has been weakening, and that this trend is more marked than that of weakening integration within the EU.

(b) Trade diversion has fallen in the domestic appliances sector suggesting that world integration has been deepening, and at a faster rate than EU integration. This pattern seems to be typical among the Group 4 sectors.

6.2.2. Trends in price convergence

The DRI study[41] on changes in price convergence provides some detailed information on price trends in our selected market studies. In this section we review their findings for the following industries:

(a) beer;
(b) cars;
(c) telecommunications equipment;
(d) white goods.

---

[41]   DRI, E. de Ghellinck, Horack, Adler & Associates, *Study on the emergence of panEuropean markets*, draft final report, February 1996.

For our other case studies, soda ash and air travel, the DRI study does not provide sufficiently detailed information.

Beer

Beer is classified by DRI as a consumer good with high advertising intensity. Non-tariff barriers are considered high, and both intra- and extra-EU trade is low. The trend in price dispersion for beer is given in Figure 6.1.

Figure 6.1.   Coefficients of variation for beer

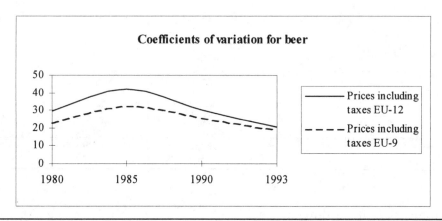

Source: DRI, E. de Ghellinck and Horack, Adler and Associates, *Study on the emergence of panEuropean markets*, draft final report, February 1996.

There is a clear trend towards a reduction of price dispersion from 1985 onwards within both the EUR-9 and the EUR-12, but there are considerable fluctuations around this trend. In particular, there is an unusual increase in price divergence from 1980 to 1985. Not surprisingly, price disparities are lower in the EUR-9 than in the EUR-12.

Cars (motor vehicles)

The DRI study classifies motor vehicles as consumer goods with a high intensity of advertising and R&D. Non-tariff barriers are considered to be medium, and intra-EU-trade is high, but trade with extra-EU countries is low. Trends in price convergence are illustrated in Figure 6.2.

For the EUR-12, there is a clear trend towards price convergence from 1980 onwards. However, when we consider price dispersion for the EUR-9, the coefficients of variation show a trend towards increasing disparities. This disturbing persistence of price differentials makes cars an interesting market study.

Figure 6.2.   Coefficients of variation for motor vehicles

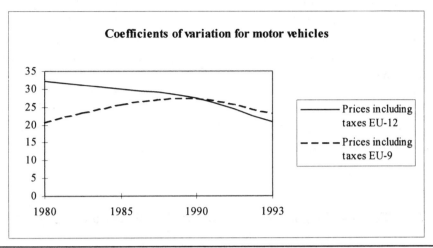

Source: DRI, E. de Ghellinck and Horack, Adler and Associates, *Study on the emergence of panEuropean markets*, draft final report, February 1996.

Telecommunications equipment

Another product category analysed by DRI is telecommunications equipment and meters. Products in this category are characterized by high R&D costs. Non-tariff barriers are high. Intra-EU trade is low, whilst extra-EU trade is high. The coefficients of variation for the EUR-12 are suggestive of a trend towards price convergence, despite some considerable fluctuations, as illustrated below.

Figure 6.3.   Coefficients of variation in the EUR-12 for telecommunications equipment

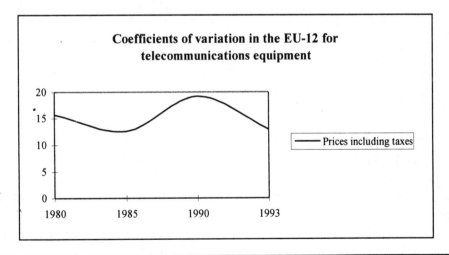

Source: DRI, E. de Ghellinck, Horack, Adler and Associates, 'Analysis of changes in price disparities in the EU following the launch of the single market programme', in *Study on the emergence of panEuropean markets*, draft final report, February 1996, Vol. 1, Table 4.2.1.

Domestic appliances

In Volume II of their report, DRI et al. provide a number of case studies in price convergence, one of which is the white goods sector. Products in this sector had relatively low price disparities at the start of the investigation period. The report comments that this sector is characterized by the dominance of large multinational producers operating multi-location manufacturing and selling under major brand names. Here we summarize the results for washing machines and dryers.

Figure 6.4 illustrates the results for washing machines and tumble-dryers. The coefficients of variation for both the EUR-12 and the EUR-9 point to a significant reduction in price disparities. As is to be expected, price disparities were greater within the EUR-12 than within the EUR-9.

Figure 6.4.   Coefficients of variation for washing machines and tumble-dryers

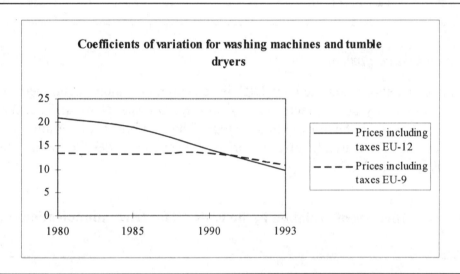

Source: DRI, E. de Ghellinck and Horack, Adler and Associates, *Study on the emergence of panEuropean markets*, draft final report, February 1996.

6.2.3. Summary

Our statistical indicators suggest that:

(a)   for beer, a Group 2 sector exhibiting considerable price dispersion prior to the advent of the single market programme, there has been a marked trend towards price convergence over time;

(b)   for cars, a Group 4 sector, substantial EU price differentials pre-single market measures have persisted;

(c)   for telecommunications equipment, a Group 1 sector characterized by relatively low intra-EU trade flows, there has been a fall in trade creation as single market measures have progressed, but a trend towards price convergence;

(d)   for domestic appliances, a Group 4 sector, there appears to have been a marked trend towards price convergence.

Our statistical indicators suggest that whilst the single market programme has had a significant impact on beer and on white goods, quite the contrary is true for cars, while its effect is ambiguous for telecommunications equipment. In the remainder of this section, we assess whether this is in fact true, and explain the key drivers behind trends in integration and competition in our selected case studies (see London Economics [1996] for fuller details of the development of competition in these markets). We also review our studies on the air travel and soda ash markets.

6.3. Integration and competition in the European soda ash industry

Trade in soda ash, a key raw material for the production of glass, has traditionally been subject to tariff barriers. Within the Common Market these have been abolished, but for extra-EU imports they remain significant. For most of the 1980s, soda ash imports from the US and Eastern Europe were subject to anti-dumping duties, and this affected trade flows considerably.

In terms of the single market programme, most of the technical measures that addressed non-tariff barriers in the chemical sectors concern a series of issues related to dangerous chemical substances. No single market measures, either technical or fiscal, directly concerned the soda ash sector. The only discernible impact of the single market programme, therefore, would stem from the removal of border controls and the reduction in the administrative costs of transporting soda ash across Member States. Full integration is not, however, possible in this industry, given the importance of transport costs.

The direct impact of the single market programme on the soda ash industry has been limited. Competition and trade policy are the two main policies that have affected the soda ash market.

The soda ash market provides an example of how a few dominant firms maintained nationally partitioned markets through cooperative, non-competitive arrangements. This partitioning was challenged by the Commission in 1990 through a series of decisions based on Articles 85 and 86 of the Treaty of Rome. At the same time, the expiry of anti-dumping duties further stimulated competition. As a result, consumers had access to soda ash from a variety of suppliers across the EU, and Solvay, for example, faced competition in Continental Europe.

Stimulated by favourable exchange rate movements, and the liberalization of the EU market, US exporters found European markets profitable again and started to export. However, following a complaint by the European Chemical Industry Council on behalf of soda ash producers, the Commission opened an investigation that led to the imposition of preliminary anti-dumping duties on US imports in April 1995.[42] These duties were confirmed in October 1995, after a protracted debate in the Commission and the Council of Ministers.

Since the 1990 competition decisions, which imposed severe penalties, producers are increasingly marketing their product into each other's national markets. Whilst the tonnage involved in this new trend in the soda ash market is relatively small, it marks a significant change from past behaviour. The break from the cooperation of the past has brought with it the possibility of a structural change in competition. Brunner Mond has emerged as a serious

---

[42] Commission Regulation (EEC) No 823/95, OJ L 83, 13.4.1995, p. 8.

alternative supplier, whose plans now clearly involve competing and acquiring market share in Continental Europe. Moreover, the evidence presented in the detailed market study seems to point to a gradual increase of competition in the soda ash market in the EU since 1990.

Despite the discrepancies in Eurostat trade data, trade flows seem to show that competition in the EU is possibly eroding the position of dominance enjoyed by the local producers in the EU Member States. Intra-EU trade in 1993, the last year for which data is available, shows the highest level since 1981, with intra-EU trade flows representing more than 13% of EU production. This is confirmed by an analysis of the changes in concentration in four large EU national markets for the 1986–94 period. Despite the fact that in 1994 the local producers still enjoyed extremely large market shares in their domestic markets, new competition has been provided by extra-EU imports, and by a modest appearance of EU soda ash producers supplying outside their domestic markets. The Herfindahl-Hirschman Index shows a slight decline from the high levels in all the national markets examined[43] (see London Economics, 1996). While the relative quantities shipped may not be substantial, events following the 1990 decisions reveal a change from the past collusive behaviour of market players. There are indications of a movement from local markets defined along national borders, to geographic markets defined according to the location of firms, their cost structure and transport costs.

Interviews with customers have also confirmed that the nature of competition has significantly changed over the last decade. Where previously customers were faced with national price lists, and had to negotiate on a country by country basis, today large customers can negotiate on an EU-wide basis, subject only to regional price differences.

In sum, all indicators point towards a picture of an EU soda ash market that is slowly moving away from the segmented market, which characterized the previous 100 years, towards a market integrated along regional lines. The main driver of change has not been the single market programme but trade policy and competition policy decisions. However, we need to accept that there are economic limits to the level of integration achievable in the soda ash market, given the importance of production and transportation costs, notwithstanding the policy efforts.

Even in the absence of collusion and anti-dumping duties, it appears extremely difficult to achieve complete market integration in the soda ash market. In other words, an EU-wide market for soda ash is unachievable and not economically efficient. The breakdown of collusion in the EU, and the removal of anti-dumping duties in 1990, increased the level of competition in the EU. EU producers started to compete in markets which were previously the exclusive domain of local producers. Together with the inflow of high quality and very competitive US soda ash, the increased competition put EU producers under pressure. The restructuring process that followed appears likely to have reduced the marginal production costs of the EU soda ash suppliers. Moreover, the implementation of the single market programme could have slightly reduced transportation costs within the EU.

---

[43]   The only exception to this trend is the Spanish market, where large inflows of US-produced soda ash explain the sharp decline of the Herfindahl-Hirschman Index in 1992.

6.4. Trends in integration and competition in European beer markets

6..4.1. The basic economic drivers

The potential size of the market for any individual brewer has grown over the last forty years with the fall in transport costs and increase in shelf-life because of new technologies (e.g. pasteurization). However, competition is mainly in the dimension of quality: price sensitivity is small and brand loyalty is high. Thus entrant brewers can compete only when they have large marketing budgets and where there are low quality incumbent products.

Tying of outlets helps to pre-empt competition, since it allows the brewer to make sure that the quality of his product is maintained outside the brewery (an efficiency effect), and by restricting the potential market for entrants (a market power effect). In the absence of ties, large-scale brewers (with large marketing budgets) will tend to dominate the market. Even where a significant proportion of beer is sold for consumption in the home, tying in the on-licence market may represent an important barrier since a significant proportion of the promotion of new brands takes place in the on-licence market. The barrier to entry effect of tying is dependent on a concentrated market structure that allows tying to lead to foreclosure.

6.4.2. Development of competition

Concentration ratios in all Member States apart from Germany have now reached very high levels. Thus expansion is increasingly likely to occur across national boundaries. Entry into local markets has been achieved in one of four ways. Physical exports from one Member State to another have been an important source of competition where geographical proximity has allowed it. This has been particularly marked in the case of brewers from smaller countries exporting to larger beer consuming countries: Denmark (e.g. Carlsberg) and the Netherlands (e.g. Heineken) to Germany; Belgium (e.g. Stella Artois) to France; and Ireland (Guinness) to the UK. Trade flows across national boundaries within the EU are important and have increased significantly over the last 20 years. For example, while EU production has grown at an average rate of 1.4% per year, imports have grown at 4.3% per year and exports at 5.6% per year; 96% of beer imports in Europe come from other Member States while about one- third of EU exports leave Europe. The second form of entry has been where brewers have acquired production facilities, either through a majority investment (e.g. Guinness owns 88% of Cruzcampo in Spain) or a minority investment (Danone owns a minority share in San Miguel in Spain). The third form, greenfield entry, is rare, although the recent case of Anheuser Busch's acquisition of Mortlake brewery in the UK has a greenfield element, since the production facility will be greatly expanded to brew Budweiser. Finally, licensing agreements represent an important alternative entry strategy for brewers.

6.4.3. The interaction of these drivers with competition policy

Until recently, EU competition policy can be considered almost entirely permissive. Thus there have been no significant contested mergers, the EC block exemptions have placed only limited restrictions on tying agreements, and licensing agreements have not been regulated. Tying agreements have been restricted in terms of duration (five years for all drinks or ten years for beer only), but this is a relatively weak restriction.

This situation may be about to change. Firstly, the EU's intervention in the Carlsberg/Interbrew licensing agreement signals a concern with the implications of exclusive distribution agreements in markets where brewers have significant market shares. Secondly, the 1989 merger regulations offer the possibility of intervention if a trend toward large cross-border mergers were to develop. Finally, the 1990 review of the block exemption signalled increasing concern with the possible anti-competitive effects of the tie, particularly in relation to the UK. The decision as to whether to renew the block exemptions, and if so in what form, will probably be the most important competition policy decision over the foreseeable future. The Commission will have to decide on the likely effect of complete or partial abolition of the tie and the desirability of these effects.[44]

The evidence of the growth of cross-border activities, particularly by brewers from smaller Member States (Guinness from Ireland, Heineken from the Netherlands, Stella Artois from Belgium, and Carlsberg from Denmark), may be taken to suggest that the tie has not restricted entry, and therefore there is no pressing need to amend or abolish it in order to promote cross-border activity. However, if it were believed that tying forced brewers seeking to enter new markets to adopt licensing strategies, when direct entry would be feasible in the absence of ties, then there would be pressure for change.

However, even if the Commission believed that the tie was inhibiting cross-border activity, to the extent that diminishing the tie would lead to concentration in the industry and therefore a narrower range of beers available, then it might still seem on balance desirable to retain the block exemptions. In markets where diversity and tradition are prized, it may be seen as undesirable to promote concentration, even if this reduces costs to the consumer. Yet the relationship between concentration and consumer choice is not a simple one. It may be the case that individual consumers face a wider range of choice today than they did 100 years ago because, although there are many fewer brewers, each bar serves a larger number of beers. Furthermore, effective choice may have increased. Although there were more beers in the past, many were of inferior quality, so that increasing competition has driven low quality beers out of the market. Finally, large brewers may have the financial resources to develop new products which are attractive to consumers (the case of 'lite' beers in the US is an important example), so that concentration may promote improvements in the choices available to consumers.

6.4.4. The interaction of these drivers and the single market programme

In terms of the areas highlighted by the study on the cost of non-Europe, namely the German purity laws, the single market programme does not as yet appear to have had any significant effect. German imports of beer appear to have been more affected by reunification than anything else in recent years. Thus imports grew by 77% in 1990, reflecting the significance of Czech beer in the former East Germany. Since 1991 imports have actually fallen slightly. While consolidation inside Germany has continued, there is no evidence that this trend has accelerated since 1992. Thus there is also no reason to suppose that cost-efficiency has increased dramatically, either through reduction in X-inefficiency or through economies of scale. In Denmark the packaging restrictions remain in force. Beer imports constituted 0.7% of total consumption in 1994, up from 0.3% in 1993, but still too small a figure to represent a significant increase in the degree of competition.

---

[44]   In the US and Australia, abolishing ties contributed to increased concentration in brewing. In the UK the Beer Orders have led to concentration in brewing, closure of on-sales outlets and the creation of new retail chains.

However, the single market programme has made an impact, now that consumers face no customs duties when buying in one Member State for personal use in another. Where significant differences in excise duties exist, arbitrage has flourished. Notably, it is now estimated that 5% of the beer consumed in the UK is brought back by consumers from France and Belgium, where excise duties are significantly lower.

In summary, the European Union is best considered as a set of intersecting beer markets based on local tastes and traditions. These markets mostly lie within national boundaries and are generally not as large as the relevant Member State. Demand is price inelastic, and competition between brands through marketing is more significant than price competition.

Trade flows across national boundaries in the EU have increased significantly over the last 20 years, but even so the share of imports in domestic consumption is relatively low in the principal beer drinking countries of the EU. The degree of competition faced by national beers from imported beers is therefore not generally high. Competition from foreign beers is further reduced in the numerous cases where large brewers in national markets have been granted licences to sell and/or manufacture the beers of leading foreign producers.

Brewers' strategies in these regional or national markets are centred around expansion to exploit economies of scale, maintaining brand image with consumers and influencing the distribution and retail networks. The first strategy has led to increasing concentration in all markets. Whilst the German industry in particular has remained significantly less concentrated than the industry in other Member States, the trend is the same across all Member States. The second strategy has led to an increasing focus on marketing and the development of entry strategies based primarily on brand licensing and, in some instances, on direct entry with a premium brand. The third strategy has led to significant tying of Horeca outlets through direct ownership or exclusive dealing agreements based on loans and other inducements. This has been a particular feature of the UK market and is also to be found across other Member States.

Competition policy within the EU has been permissive until quite recently. Trade between Member States has grown much faster than overall beer consumption in the past twenty years. Trade growth has been particularly strong between adjacent Member States, and brewers in smaller Member States appear to have benefited disproportionately from the openness of EU markets. This rosy picture does not necessarily imply that markets are completely open, and it may be that tying, in particular, has prevented consolidation of specific markets, and that this has adversely affected efficient brewers who would otherwise enter neighbouring markets. Recently the Commission has shown some concern about the anti-competitive effects of exclusive licensing and distribution agreements by brewers.

6.5. Trends in integration and competition in the European car market

Fifteen years ago, the EU car market was characterized by three main features:

(a)   markets segmented along national lines, with local producers accounting for the largest shares of sales in their domestic markets;
(b)   significant price differentials between EU car markets.

Despite this market segmentation, intra-EU trade was already significant. The single market programme was intended to reduce the price differentials across the EU, by facilitating increased trade. The competitive challenge to EU car producers has been severely limited by several external trade policy measures, and the Commission also hoped to reduce these external trade barriers to further stimulate pressures to reduce costs. As far as the single market programme is concerned, the Commission has singled out several technical measures and some fiscal measures as the relevant non-tariff barriers that had to be removed.

Table 6.3 lists the measures introduced by the Commission.

Table 6.3.   Single market programme – technical measures that directly affected the car sector

Types of technical measures	Reference to the main measures
Type approval of motor vehicles	Dir. 87/358/EEC; 92/53/EEC
Measures against air pollution by gases from the engines and on permissible sound level and exhaust system	Dir. 88/76/EEC; 88/77/EEC; 88/436/EEC; 89/458/EEC; 92/97/EEC; 94/12/EEC
Other technical measures concerning:	Directives:
• Mechanical coupling devices	• 94/20/EEC
• Spray suppression systems	• 91/226/EEC
• Lateral protection (side guards)	• 89/297/EEC
• Safety glass and glazing materials	• 92/22/EEC
• Pneumatic tyres	• 92/23/EEC; 89/459/EEC
• Masses and dimensions of type M1 vehicles	• 92/21/EEC
• Installation and uses of speed limitation devices	• 92/6/EEC; 92/24/EEC
• External projections forward of the cab's rear panel	• 92/114/EEC

Note: As of April 1995, see European Commission, 'State of Community Law concerning the Internal Market', Doc. No XV/530/95/EN.

The intricate web of national requirements to ensure the safety of users and third parties, and to protect the environment, has been replaced by harmonized rules for the whole of the EU. EU type approval became optional from the beginning of 1993 for private cars, and compulsory from 1 January 1996.

As far as fiscal measures are concerned, differences in VAT rates are a source of post-tax price differences. Between 1987 and 1994 VAT rates charged on cars in Member States have shown a significant convergence.

However, despite the single market measures designed to promote intra-EU trade, quantitative restrictions on the volume of Japanese car imports applied in several national markets throughout the 1980s. Differences exist between, on the one hand, the larger Member States with indigenous car industries, in which restrictive measures were adopted, and, on the other, Member States with no domestic car producers, such as Belgium, Holland, Ireland and Greece, which were free from quantitative restrictions.

The predicted effects of VERs run counter to the implicit goals of the single market programme, namely:

(a)   an increase in the price of cars subject to the restriction;
(b)   the importers' move upmarket, to maximize the value of their quotas;
(c)   an increase in profits for all firms;

(d)   removal of competitive pressures on domestic producers;

(e)   the possible entry into the protected market of producers subject to trade restrictions but not to restrictions on entry.

National import restrictions were justified under Article 115 of the Treaty of Rome. Nevertheless, as part of the single market programme, the Commission has gradually put pressure on Member States to phase out national quantitative restrictions. At the same time, some informal restrictions were established on the number of Japanese car imports allowed in the EU, and an EU VER was formally agreed in 1991, scheduled to expire in 1999. Under the Uruguay Round of the GATT, tariffs on cars imported into EU countries, which currently exceed 10%, will reduce progressively to that level.

France and Italy have both been largely closed to Japanese imports and have been dominated by domestic producers. Ireland and the Netherlands are open markets, whereas Germany and the UK lie somewhere in between. Imports in these six countries now represent almost 55% of registrations, of which intra-EU imports account for 75%. The figure for Ireland indicates a degree of re-exporting.

Between 1982 and 1993, intra-EU trade in cars expanded, to 59% of registrations: this compares to an average of 37% for 46 manufacturing industries in the period 1989–93. The increase was greatest in France, but negligible in the UK, largely because the Japanese transplants in the UK increased their production in this period. The market share of intra-EU imports of cars did not increase at the expense of extra-EU imports, in the EU as a whole, although this did appear to be the case in Italy, France and the UK.

Borders now matter less, as reflected in producers' diminishing dependence on their domestic markets (see London Economics, 1996). This trend has been more marked for the volume producers (PSA, Ford UK and Renault) than for specialists such as BMW and Mercedes. German unification in 1990 reversed the trend for the German car manufacturers.

6.5.1. Price differentials between EU markets

Perhaps the most sensitive test of progress towards European integration in the car market is whether the prices charged in national markets for similar products have differed significantly, and if so, whether prices are converging. In 1981, according to a study by the Institute for Fiscal Studies of car prices in the UK and Belgium,[45] discounted VAT-exclusive prices in the UK exceeded those in Belgium by an average of 39%. The price differential was higher still when allowance was made, using econometric techniques, for quality differences.

By the 1990s, the situation was not noticeably different. A study by the Bureau Européen des Unions de Consommateurs (BEUC) on behalf of DG XI[46] found price differentials between national markets which ranged from 12% to 50% for UK cars, compared with car prices in Belgium, Denmark, Germany, Greece, Spain, France, Ireland, Luxembourg, and the Netherlands. However, the BEUC study was criticized because (unlike the IFS study) it did

---

[45]   M.H. Ashworth, J.A. Kay and T.A.E. Sharpe, 'Differentials between car prices in the United Kingdom and Belgium' The Institute for Fiscal Studies, *IFS Report Series*, No 2, 1982.

[46]   See BEUC, 'EEC study on car prices and progress towards 1992', BEUC/10/89, 15 October 1989.

not take into account variations in car specifications from country to country, and understated the importance of discounts and other financial benefits to customers.

When investigating the supply of new cars, the UK Monopolies and Mergers Commission (MMC)[47] compared car prices in the UK, Germany, France, the Netherlands and Belgium, for models supplied by nine EU-based producers and one Japanese supplier. The comparison sought to take account of differences in model specification and used car transactions, rather than list prices, in making comparisons. Specification differences were reduced but not completely eliminated, as it was difficult to find identical model variants across the six countries.[48] Moreover, the MMC notes that demand conditions for cars differed in each country over the period of study (in 1990 demand was particularly weak in the UK but was rising in Belgium and the Netherlands). The MMC report concluded the price differences were not in general significant. However, prices for models belonging to the smaller segments showed significant differences.

Another report by LAL in 1991 found large variances in prices for the four models investigated, ranging from 13.8 to 35%.[49] The UK was taken as the basis for comparison, and specifications and equipment items in other markets were adjusted to match the UK. Delivery charges were omitted from the study.[50] Flam and Nordstrom[51] found price differences as high as 50% and average price differences of around 12%.

Table 6.4.   Average price dispersion 1989–92

Average for all models	1989	1990	1991	1992
Price (DM)	20,979	21,459	23,188	24,405
Standard deviation (%)	14	12	14	14
Max. price differential (%)	51	42	49	49

Source: H. Flam and H. Nordstrom, 'Why do pre-tax car prices differ so much across European countries?', *CEPR Discussion Paper Series*, No 1181, May 1995.

Most recently, the European Commission's May 1995 survey of list prices[52] reported that price differentials for more than 50% of all models offered on EU markets (55% of all European manufacturers' models, and 37% of all Japanese) exceeded 20%.

---

[47]   See MMC, 'New motor cars. a report on the supply of new motor cars within the United Kingdom', 1992, Ch. 8.

[48]   The procedure could be criticized because, unlike the IFS study, the additional features incorporated into UK models were valued at manufacturers' prices, rather than hedonically.

[49]   See 'Year 2000 and beyond – the car marketing challenge in Europe', *Euromotor Reports*, 1991, pp. 183–4.

[50]   For an example on how to examine price differences between various car models in term of variation in individual car features within the UK, see J. Murray and N. Sarantis 'Price-quality relations and hedonic price indexes for cars in the UK'.

[51]   H. Flam and H. Nordstrom, 'Why do pre-tax car prices differ so much across European countries?', *CEPR Discussion Paper Series*, No 1181, May 1995.

[52]   See European Commission, 'Car price differentials in the European Union on 1 May 1995', Brussels, 24 July 1995, IP/95/768.

6.5.2. Changes in the structure of supply

The market opportunity offered by the single market might have been expected to have induced an increase in the concentration of ownership. This has not been the case. The market shares of the largest producers remained stable between 1982 and 1994; the effects of acquisitions and market entry on concentration seem to have roughly balanced. Instead, the European producers have looked for alternative structural solutions – notably, joint ventures and expansion globally. Joint ventures preserve independence, but at the cost of instability, as illustrated by Rover's desertion of Honda for BMW. Cooperation between producers was relatively rare before the mid-1970s (although Renault and Peugeot had long-standing arrangements for joint manufacturing of engines and transmissions). The 1980s saw the Fiat/Saab executive car project, and the agreement between Renault and Volkswagen to design and manufacture automatic transmissions. More recently, there has been the VW/Mercedes/BMW venture to produce a fuel-saving diesel engine.[53] Cooperation has been very common over multi-purpose and off-road vehicles.[54]

To summarize, the European market has become more integrated, in the sense that there is greater interpenetration of markets. However, borders, and nationality, still matter. Such integration of the market as has occurred has had few effects on the car industry's ownership and physical structure. The pressure to seek economies of scale and scope has provoked few significant mergers, or exits. Producers have become more adept at generating options from a given number of basic platforms, and have sought to spread their fixed costs over greater volumes, by cooperative agreements and by global expansion. Price differentials as high as 50% were reported in 1995, as was a corresponding loss of domestic shares by dominant local producers. There was no apparent convergence in price levels between the EU markets.[55]

However, the prospects of full liberalization of the EU car market, and the limited market-opening contribution of Regulation (EC) No 1475/95, is likely to accelerate progress towards a truly integrated European car market. The opening of the market to Japanese imports after 1999 should be an important factor in increasing competition, and stimulating change.

6.6. Integration and competition in the European air travel markets

The main characteristic of the airline industry with respect to the single market programme is that it is a sector that is moving from a highly regulated environment to a more competitive one. The process has been lengthy and uneven, partly as a result of resistance by Member States, and appears to require some additional time before being completed on an EU-wide basis.

---

[53] See L. Barile, 'Opel e Ford criticano il progetto del diesel "tedesco" per il 2000', Article on Il Sole-24 Ore, 15 August 1995. The fact that the subsidiaries of the American producers, Opel and Ford, have been excluded from the project, and the involvement of some German states (*Länder*), have caused strong criticism.

[54] Examples are the cooperation between Isuzu and GM to produce the Vauxhall/Opel Frontera (4x4), between Nissan and Ford to manufacture a similar vehicle, and between VW and Ford for a Multi-Purpose-Vehicle. On this see Euromotor Report, p. 268.

[55] Several factors in combination give rise to price differences between national markets: VERs on Japanese imports, national differences in VAT, movements in European exchange rates, customer preferences for domestic producers. The distribution system for cars was not the cause of these price differentials, but it does enable them to be maintained.

The single market programme started rather hesitantly with very moderate liberalization measures in 1987, but has challenged many regulatory barriers to entry since then. The single market measures concerning the airline sector are illustrated in detail in Table 6.5. The three packages introduced by the Commission are more far-reaching than the single market measures in most other sectors, aiming at liberalizing a sector that was previously highly regulated. The third package will, by 1997, establish a regulatory framework where entry to any route in Europe will be in principle open to any EU carrier. To the extent that entry by non-national carriers on intra-EU and domestic routes takes place, integration of the European air travel market will have made some progress.

Member States' domestic markets will only be fully liberalized from April 1997, whereas international routes to non-European countries are still governed by bilateral arrangements whose restrictions vary from country to country.

On the individual international routes, the dominance of the national airlines is therefore still strong. Of the 636 international scheduled city pair routes within the Community and EEA countries, 411 (65%) were monopoly routes, 187 (29%) were operated by two carriers and 38 (6%) were operated by more than two carriers (so called multi-carrier routes, (CAA, 1993, p. 117). As Table 6.6 shows, the proportion of national multi-carrier routes varies between countries, with the greatest range in the six large countries. Italy has a very low proportion of routes with three or more carriers.

Table 6.5. **Single market programme policy measures affecting the air transport sector**

Scope	1st Package: from 1 Jan 1988 Int. sched. passenger transport	2nd Package: from 1 Nov. 1990 Int. sched. passenger transport	3rd Package: from 1 Jan 1993 Int. & dom., sched. & charter, passenger & freight transport
Relevant legislation	1. Regulation (EEC) No 3975/87 on the application of the competition rules to air transport 2. Regulation (EEC) No 3976/87 on the application of the treaty to certain categories of agreements and concerted practices 3. Council Directive 87/601/EEC on air fares 4. Council Decision 87/602/EEC on capacity sharing and market access	1. Council Regulation (EEC) No 2343/90 on market access 2. Council Regulation (EEC) No 2342/90 on air fares 3. Council Regulation (EEC) No 2344/90 on the application of the Treaty to certain categories of agreements and concerted practices	1. Council Regulation (EEC) No 2407/92 on licensing of air carriers 2. Council Regulation (EEC) No 2408/92 on market access 3. Council Regulation (EEC) No 2409/92 on fares and rates
Fares	% of Fares approved Fare type ref. Fare by States Discount 66-90 Automatically Deep discount 45-65 Automatically All other Double approval	% of Fares approved Fare type ref. Fare by States Fully flexible 106+ Unless dbl. disapproval Normal econ. 95-105 Automatically Discount 80-94 Automatically Deep discount 30-79 Automatically All others If dbl. approval	% of Fares approved Fare type ref. Fare by States • However, provisions made for the States and/or the commission to intervene against. Excessive basic fares (in relation to long-term fully allocated costs) Sustained downward development of fares
Designation	• Multiple designation by a State allowed if: 250,000 pass (1st year after integration) 200,000 pass or 1,200 round trip flights (2nd year) 180,000 pass or 1,000 round trip flights (3rd year)	• Multiple designation by a State allowed if: 140,000 pass or 800 round trip flights (from Jan 1991) 100,000 pass or 600 round trip flights (from Jan 1992)	No longer applicable
Capacity	• Capacity shares between States 45/55% (from Jan. 1988) 40/60% (from Oct. 1989)	• Capacity shares of a State of up to 60% • Capacity can be increased by 7.5% points per year	Unrestricted
Route access	• 3rd/4th freedom region to hub routes permitted • 5th freedom traffic allowed up to 30% of capacity • Additional 5th rights for Irish and Portuguese • Combination of points allowed • Some exemptions	• 3rd/4th freedom between all airports • 5th freedom traffic allowed up to 50% of capacity • Public service obligations and certain protection for new regional routes • A 3rd/4th freedom service can be matched by an airline from the other State • Scope for traffic distribution rules and restrictions related to congestion and environmental protection	• Full access to international and domestic routes within the EU including routes between States other than the base of the carrier (exemptions for Greek island and Azores) • Cabotage is allowed for up to 50% of capacity if the domestic sector is combined with a route to the home country (cabotage is unrestricted from April 1997) • More developed public service obligations and certain protection for new thin regional routes • More developed scope for traffic distribution rules and restrictions related to congestion and environmental protection
Competition rules	Ground exemption regarding: • Some capacity coordination • Tariff consultation • Slot allocation • Common computer reservation systems • Ground handling of aircraft, freight, passenger and in-flight catering Some sharing of pool revenues	Ground exemption regarding: • Some capacity coordination • Tariff consultation • Slot allocation • Common computer reservation systems • Ground handling of aircraft, freight, passenger and in-flight catering	Ground exemption regarding: • Some capacity coordination • Tariff consultation • Slot allocation • Common computer reservation systems • Joint operation of new thin routes
Licensing of air carriers	Not provided for in the 1st and 2nd packages		Full freedom to start an airline • Uniform conditions across EU • Concept of Community ownership and control replaces national ownership and control • Requirements for financial fitness specified Small carriers subject to looser regulatory requirements

Source: European Commission, *The Single Market Review*, Volume II:2, Air transport, 1997b.

Table 6.6.   Competition on scheduled routes

	Proportion of round trip flights on routes with two or more competitors (%)			
	Domestic scheduled routes		International scheduled routes	
	Dec. 1992	Dec. 1994	Dec. 1992	Dec. 1994
Austria	0	0	12	12
Denmark	3	4	8	11
Finland	9	9	7	0
France	10	9	26	35
Germany	36	40	10	15
Greece	0	0	0	16
Ireland	0	0	36	46
Italy	28	26	7	15
Netherlands	0	0	20	18
Norway	27	38	0	9
Portugal	47	35	14	37
Spain	0	60	14	20
Sweden	47	47	12	12
UK	43	56	40	45
Total	26	36	19*	25*

Source: CAA, 1995, Table 2.2 and 2.3, pp. 91–92.
* Total includes Belgium and Luxembourg.

6.6.1.   Entry strategies in the new European environment

Entry by new carriers has been much more limited than expected, but considerable changes in industry structure have taken place.[56] Some of the carriers which ran into financial difficulties in the past have reduced their capacity (Air France, Aer Lingus, Iberia and Air Portugal). Some of them, like Iberia, Air France and Alitalia, plan to cut capacity further as part of their restructuring arrangements. Their share will therefore continue to decline.[57] On the other hand, British Airways has increased its output considerably, partly as a result of its takeover of DanAir in November 1992.

Behind these aggregate figures are considerable changes in network structure. In general, the flag carriers have tried to concentrate their operations mainly on their home hub. They have withdrawn some international services from non-hub airports (e.g. Air France at Lyon and Nice, or Alitalia non-stop services from Genoa, Pisa, Venice and Bologna). Even at the end of 1994, the flag carriers, together with their subsidiaries, accounted for over 80% of the total scheduled output on routes between or within the EU.[58]

---

[56]   See Table 1.3 in CAA, 1995, p. 71.

[57]   On the other hand, Sabena and Olympic, which had financial difficulties, grew by roughly the same factor.

[58]   See CAA, 1995, p. 29.

The third EU package gives airlines access on routes between and within other Member States. However, these fifth freedom and cabotage services accounted for only about 1% of the flights offered at the end of 1994. There were increases on some routes, but others were discontinued in 1995, so the total share has probably not increased very much. This would seem to indicate that entry by flag carriers has had a small competitive effect.[59]

However, the assessment differs between routes and regions. Some of the entry has resulted in a third carrier on previously duopolistic routes, and there the impact has been significant. Other entry has taken place domestically, moving from one to two competitor routes. This too has resulted in a significant increase in competition, as shown by lower fares, higher frequency, etc. However, one has to assess these developments in the longer term, to see to what extent extra carriers can be supported on these routes and if they can be made more contestable.[60]

The competitive entry by flag carriers must be seen in relation to the emerging hub and spoke system in Europe. Flag carriers will try to strengthen their position at their home airport, and compete only on routes which benefit their network. This allows them to offer certain short-haul services from these hubs even at a loss, when this can result in feeding more prosperous long-haul services.

The degree to which flag carriers are willing to compete has still not been established. The aggressive participation of BA in the German market remains an exception. In France, BA's behaviour is far more subdued, and the other major carriers have also maintained competition in acceptable bands. An important opportunity is therefore emerging for the smaller non-flag carriers, at least as a competitive check on the entrenched flag carriers. However, for them to be effective, barriers to entry need to be reduced further (in terms of runway slots and related facilities, and access to the computerized reservation system (CRS)). However, even then they will have to overcome other scale disadvantages related to Frequent Flyer Programmes (FFPs), special corporate discount agreements, and so on. In other words, they have to compete from a much lower cost base in order to be competitively viable. But it is not clear if they will be sufficiently profitable to attract the continuing investment needed, to remain as forceful and increasingly important competitors.

6.6.2. Trends in joint ventures and mergers

Following the gradual decline in scheduling conferences and the use of interlining agreements through IATA, airlines have recently developed much more market-specific forms of cooperation.[61] They range from code sharing to marketing agreements and equity participation, all the way to fully-fledged mergers. The picture that emerges is one of increasing cooperation among airlines in Europe. Surveys conducted by Airline Business show that in 1985 European airlines were involved in a limited number of alliances (20), including non-EU airlines. By 1990 the number of alliances rose to 59 and by 1995 it had jumped to 71. The question of the

---

[59] Examples of entry by national flag carriers in another country are BA's entry in 1994 on the Brussels/Rome route and Deutsche BA's (DBA) entry on German domestic routes, as well as TAT's increased competitive activity after its takeover by British Airways.

[60] See Encaoua, 1991, p.123.

[61] GAO, 1995.

nature of these cooperative agreements is addressed in more detail in the case study report by London Economics [1996].

Horizontal cooperative joint ventures with feeder airlines are the most natural form in which joint ventures have developed. Another kind of cooperative joint venture is 'regional' franchising, a practice currently implemented by a number of national carriers.

Cooperation in the form of code sharing arrangements is now becoming more and more frequent among flag carriers, as a typical form of 'horizontal' cooperation. 'Code sharing' allows airlines to connect traffic from other carriers to their own network. These agreements may also be supplemented by a marketing agreement, which involves such features as blocked space arrangements on flights, scheduling coordination and joint marketing and sales.

While regional joint ventures with feeder airlines and neighbouring carriers have been the norm in the past, global alliances have recently increased much more in importance. The GAO study reports that the number of global alliances more than tripled between 1992 and 1995 (from 19 to 61).[62]

Since the end of the 1980s some concentration has taken place among European airlines. Most of them concern the acquisition of smaller regional airlines by the largest flag carriers, either attempting to expand in other Member States' domestic markets or reinforcing their position in their own domestic market. Table 6.7 shows the full-scale mergers that have also taken place in recent years.

Table 6.7.   Important merger cases in European air transport

Companies involved	Year
British Airways/British Caledonian	1988
Air France/AirInter/UTA	1990
KLM/Transavia	1991
Air France/Sabena *	1992
British Airways/DanAir	1993
British Airways/TAT	1993
Sabena/Swissair	1995

* Air France's stake was taken over by Swissair in 1995.

While some elements of competition were evident in the early 1980s, it was not until the Community (and some Member States in their bilateral air transport relations) took more decisive action that significantly increased competition began to occur.

The European air transport market is still dominated by national flag carriers with some restructuring as a result of competition. In some cases, airlines may have delayed restructuring in the expectation that state aid would be made available. In addition, some defensive mergers have helped to strengthen national flag dominance. There has been some reduction in aggregate concentration, but the national flag carriers are still dominant, with the largest

---

[62]   See CAA, 1995, p. 3.

national carriers, British Airways, Lufthansa, and Air France, making up over 50% of this total.

However, these are overall concentration measures, which do not reflect what is happening in individual city pair markets. An assessment of the most important city pair routes in Europe shows that there are very few routes which have more than two competing carriers. The role of potential competition is, therefore, of crucial importance. But on the busiest routes there is congestion at one or both airport ends. This means that entry cannot readily take place, and therefore potential competition is inhibited.

There has been a general improvement in productivity among European carriers. Average fare per passenger mile, an indicator of overall productivity, has decreased much faster in the US than in Europe. While differences are due to external factors such as infrastructure and fuel costs, it is clear that there are still productivity reserves that relate partly to traditional labour management practices, non-optimized route structures, monopoly in ground handling, etc. Government support through state aid has certainly prevented some structural adjustment. Some of the carriers which recently received state aid have high operating costs, while others simply have too large a network.

While the amount of promotional fares currently used by European flag carriers has increased compared to the 1980s, IATA fare levels have increased somewhat. The CAA report [1995] and the study carried out by Cranfield University for the European Commission under the Single Market Review Programme show that fare levels have increased over the last six years. 'As far as the impact of liberalization is concerned, there is little evidence from these trends that EU measures had any significant impact on fully flexible fares' (European Commission, 1997b).

The study of European air travel illustrates the transition from highly regulated national markets to a competitive European market. This transition has been brought about by overall trends of national liberalization, more liberal bilateral policies, but to a large extent by policies under the single market programme. As this initiative is still continuing, the forces of restructuring and liberalization have not yet been fully implemented.

However, there is a considerable amount of evidence to suggest that, as a result of the liberalization measures, the airline markets in Europe have become more integrated. But they are not yet fully integrated, given the transitional difficulties on the one hand, and structural problems such as capacity constraints on routes and airport slots on the other. There is also the international dimension of the market, which is still often determined by restrictive bilateral arrangements.

Within this transition framework we see a restructuring of the industry as would be expected as a consequence of a move towards deregulation. Competition policy is crucial in this connection, by facilitating the lowering of barriers to entry for the necessary restructuring of the industry, but also by carefully scrutinizing structural reconfigurations such as mergers and joint ventures which might be used to extend and enlarge existing market power.

This section concludes with a discussion of the case study of air transport for European competition policy more generally. Air transport is not a homogeneous product, but nevertheless offers some generalizations to other service industries that have similar characteristics (network aspects, non-storability, importance of reputation). The continued market segmentation observed in this industry is a direct result of strategic behaviour by dominant firms, usually the flag carriers of the national countries, who together with their governments have some scope to exclude entrants or to collude with each other or, in the form of joint ventures, to increase their market power.

The nature of production, and the importance of networks and reputation are also typical of some other industries such as banking, insurance, etc. In addition, the intervention of the EU authorities provides an example of the contradictions that may arise from the different policy objectives within the Commission (pursuing liberalization and restructuring towards an efficient industry structure, on the one hand, versus state aid and social service obligations that maintain the status quo on the other).

6.7. Domestic appliances

The development of the domestic appliance industry in Europe shows how a market can become integrated at the level of production, but remain segmented in consumer markets. We discuss these in turn.

The process of integration in production in the domestic appliance sector has been driven by the search for economies of scale. This began with the technical innovations of predominantly Italian firms in the 1950s and 1960s. The 1980s was a period of further concentration in the domestic appliances industry. The top ten firms had a combined market share of around 45% in 1980. However, by the end of the decade this had risen to 75% and by 1993 to nearly 90%.

The process of concentration during the 1980s was driven by poor financial performance by many firms, following over investment in capacity during periods of weak demand in the late 1970s and early 1980s, together with a proliferation of models on the market that eroded some of the economies of scale. The concentration was marked by some particularly large takeovers, including notably those of Zanussi by Electrolux in 1984[63] and Phillips by Whirlpool of the US in 1986.[64]

Between 1976 and 1991, Electrolux made around 200 acquisitions and moved from being global leader in a marginal segment (vacuum cleaner production), and national leader in a peripheral market (Sweden), to world leadership in the entire sector, with a share of nearly 20%. Electrolux's growth strategy was based on, first, market entry through the acquisition of brands and local service and distribution networks and, second, cost competitiveness through the integration of production facilities.

Today, Electrolux operates some 40 household appliance and related component plants in Europe. Each is specialized around limited product categories and ships to multiple national markets. Thus at the Arthur Martin site in Revin, France, in 1991 more than 40 models of top-loading washing machines were produced under 9 different brands for 13 countries.[65]

---

[63]   Zanussi, in addition to problems of excess capacity, had also run into trouble through some poor diversifications.

[64]   In addition, Merloni acquired Indesit (1987), Thompson formed a joint venture with Toshiba (1986) and Hotpoint sold out to General Electric of the US (1989).

[65]   Allen, C., Stephen, A. and Bove, Suzanne, *Electrolux Group*, ECCH, Cranfield Ltd, 1991.

The support of local brands by advertising both feeds consumer preferences and facilitates different pricing strategies, both geographically and in terms of product specification against consumer requirements. Intensive advertising, control of local distribution networks, and the existence of significant economies of scale, act as entry deterrents to potential competitors.

However, the multiplicity of brands designed for national markets means that national markets defined by consumer tastes have remained to some extent segmented. This segmentation is based not just on technical preferences – the English prefer front-loading washing machines while the Italians prefer top-loading – but also on brand preferences. These preferences mean that the same brands are marketed differently in different countries and that different brands are marketed in different countries, irrespective of the underlying technical specification. Thus in the UK Zanussi manages to achieve an upmarket position, while in Sweden it is considered middle-market, and in Italy Electrolux in 1991 decided to market group appliances under the Rex brand name as opposed to Zanussi.

More recently, the introduction of Euro-brands represents an attempt to reap some economies of scale for brands. Thus there is, as far as possible, a common approach to advertising and distribution adopted for the Euro-brands of Electrolux and Whirlpool. These Euro-brands aim at market segmentation based on consumer taste, as opposed to geography. Thus Electrolux's international design centres represent an attempt to coordinate product design around a concept of five global lifestyles, characterized by differences in appliance size, energy consumption and sophistication of electronic functions.[66] However, to date the domestic appliance industry is integrated principally at the level of production as opposed to consumer markets.

6.8. Summary

In this chapter we have reviewed trends in integration and competition in the EU on the basis of individual market studies. These trends differ considerably from one market to another. This is not surprising, given that the market studies have been deliberately selected to cover industries with differing degrees of exposure to single market measures and with different product and cost characteristics. A clear-cut result cannot be expected.

All market studies have shown some important changes in competitive conditions over the past decade. Some industries, like domestic appliances and telecommunications switching equipment, have seen major restructuring with production and marketing becoming organized at a European level. The changes in competition in the former most closely reflect the general aim of the single market programme, namely to create larger, more integrated markets across Member States. The changes in market conditions in the latter are more directly associated with technological changes and the reform and liberalization of a previously heavily regulated public procurement sector. Other markets, like soda ash, have changed little, and if they have, the result was due more to decisions of the Commission on trade and competition policy than to single market measures.

Three sectors, with a moderate to high degree of exposure to the single market programme, have also seen complex interactions between different drivers of competition.

---

[66] Refrigerator designer Roberto Pezzetta has argued 'It isn't important whether the customer lives in Munich or Milan. What's important is their lifestyle, not their geography.' *Wall Street Journal,* 20 August 1990.

European beer markets have proved remarkably resistant to European integration, but have seen, nevertheless, significant changes in industry structure. Regional and national market fragmentation appears to persist, partly due to strong regional preferences for local or national brands and partly due to national differences in consumption patterns and distribution arrangements. The market study throws up some provocative conclusions regarding the interaction of two types of strategic behaviour relatively common throughout the European beer industry: (a) cross-country licensing using JVs; (b) selective distribution agreements at the national level. In a number of countries we observe that major foreign brands get manufactured and distributed by one of the leading national brewers under licence. It is arguable that the pricing and marketing policies for these foreign brands would be quite different if the foreign brewers were themselves to enter into direct competition with national brands. Selective distribution agreements and ties between brewers and tenants of pubs, bars and restaurants are common in most countries, but have been subject to several investigations by competition authorities. If these types of arrangement exist in markets that are relatively highly concentrated, their joint anti-competitive effect needs to be carefully assessed.

European car markets are similarly characterized by a relatively high degree of concentration in national markets that are subject to selective distribution agreements. In contrast to beer, however, joint ventures in the car industry play a significant role in production and R&D on new cars. And unlike beer, the European car industry has had a long tradition of trade protection and other types of government support (state aid). Altogether the European car market has been gradually and only slowly moving towards greater integration. This market study provides a good example of the effects of national distribution arrangements on the potential to maintain price differentials between Member States. The continued debate over the persistence of price discrimination, and the lack of price convergence in European car markets, reflects the importance of this competition issue.

The study of European air travel illustrates the transition from highly regulated national markets to a more competitive European market. This transition has been brought about by overall trends of national liberalization and, to a large extent, by policies under the single market programme. As this initiative is still continuing, the forces of restructuring and liberalization have not yet been fully implemented.

There is a considerable amount of evidence to suggest that, as a result of liberalization measures, the airline markets in Europe are becoming more integrated. But they are not yet fully integrated, given the transitional difficulties on the one hand, and structural problems such as capacity constraints on routes and airport slots on the other. There is also the international dimension of the market, which is still often determined by restrictive bilateral arrangements.

Within this transition framework, we see a restructuring of the industry, and can observe a number of responses that raise competition policy concerns. Competition issues relate to barriers to entry, but also to structural reconfigurations such as mergers and joint ventures, which can be used to extend and enlarge existing market power.

Table 6.8 summarizes the key features of the selected market studies. All the major competition issues that will be systematically dealt with in Part II of the study are represented.

Table 6.8. Summary of market studies

	Soda ash	Beer	Cars	Domestic appliances	Airlines
Initial market structure	Oligopolistic national markets	National markets often oligopolistic	Oligopolistic with national champions	Fragmented	Protected national monopolies/ international cartels
Single market measures	Negligible	Technical and physical	Important technical, continued block exemption for distribution	Reduction in cross-border transaction costs	Major liberalization pressures being implemented by 1997
Competition issues	Major collusion case	Cross-country licensing and vertical restraints	Distribution agreements and strategic alliances	Mergers	Dominance, barriers to entry, joint ventures, mergers
Integration	High, but markets limited by transport costs	Moderate	Relatively high at manufacturing level, low in distribution	High with remaining market segmentation limited by taste	Low

Part II   Competition issues

Our previous discussion, in Chapter 3, leads us to characterize integration as a process of convergence of prices across borders (through arbitrage), increasing access to markets and therefore intensifying competition, increasing exploitation of economies of scale, leading to outcomes of economic decisions that are independent of national borders. This may lead to the exit of less efficient firms and lead to higher levels of concentration. As a consequence, firms can expect that the loss of price discrimination possibilities and the intensification of competition will tend to reduce profits.

While some firms will be able to take advantage of the opportunities provided by the single market, others will want to resist the competitive threats that this development implies. That is, market integration might give firms additional motives to behave in an anti-competitive way, where it has the effect of threatening their profits and entrenched positions in the market.

Over the next six chapters we will examine a number of competition issues that arise from the behaviour of firms when they respond to the integration process and the competitive pressures that the single market programme seeks to promote. The order in which we discuss these issues is significant. We first look at those types of behaviour that are most closely related to integration policy and then proceed with a discussion of the more traditional categories. The six categories of behaviour are:

(a)   parallel import restrictions and price discrimination, whereby firms seek to maintain the segmentation of markets and differentiate the prices of their products across national markets;

(b)   access restrictions and entry barriers, whereby firms resist the impact of the single market programme on entry of new competitors;

(c)   collusion, as a type of anti-competitive behaviour which is only indirectly affected by single market measures;

(d)   other cooperative agreements, where the single market programme can be expected to have a significant effect on the motivation of firms to enter into such agreements;

(e)   mergers, which in larger integrated markets may be the consequence of firms desire to exploit economies of scale but also can be based on a motivation to achieve dominance and market power;

(f)   state aids, which are a response by governments who seek to protect firms from the full cost of adjustment that may arise as a consequence of increased competitive pressures in the single market.

These types of behaviour need to be examined on a theoretical basis in terms of their economic rationale, but more specifically in terms of their interaction with integration in the single market. The rich case history of DG IV provides empirical evidence that is helpful for the illustration of the selected issues. Equally, the case studies summarized in Chapter 6 are useful for the illustration of certain issues.

7. Geographic price discrimination

7.1. Introduction

Much of the typical commentary on market integration has focused on the existence of cross-country price differentials within the EU as an undesirable symptom of market segmentation, and on the persistence of such differentials as an indication that the integration process has not yet run its course. Following this interpretation, increasing similarity of prices across EU economies has been frequently understood as a policy aim in itself.

In an integrated market, cross-border price differentials should be bid away through arbitrage. Thus the ability of firms to sustain different prices for their product in different national markets has been regarded as evidence of the presence of restrictions on consumer arbitrage, and any practice supporting such an outcome (for example contract clauses restricting parallel trade) condemned as illegal. Competition policy has been regularly used to this effect, systematically pursuing the elimination of all practices sustaining geographic discrimination.

The purpose of this chapter is to emphasize that, like all forms of price discrimination, geographic price discrimination need not necessarily be welfare-reducing; therefore firm practices which lead to geographic price discrimination should not be automatically attacked as anti-competitive. We will thus bring into focus a possible tension between integration policies which are concerned with removing discrimination *per se*, and competition policy which should pursue efficient economic outcomes and as such should in some cases allow price discrimination. Prohibiting price discrimination across the board is unlikely to be optimal policy, and rather the economic analysis suggests the appropriateness of a contingent response under which the prohibition of price discrimination is made conditional on various tests, for example on market structure.

We begin in Section 7.2 with a brief discussion of the notion of geographic price discrimination and its relationship with practices that prevent cross-border arbitrage. The main focus is on one type of practice: the use of contractual clauses which restrict parallel trade and so prevent arbitrage. Section 7.3 offers an economic discussion of the welfare effects of price discrimination, emphasizing that these are ambiguous. This weakens the rationale for unconditional opposition to geographic price discrimination, and suggests that the competition treatment of practices facilitating price discrimination – such as restrictions on parallel trade – should be based on a careful economic analysis of the costs and benefits of 'constraining' firms to charge a single price across geographical markets. We then consider in Section 7.4 the current position of competition law *vis-à-vis* practices which support geographic price discrimination. Parallel trade restrictions have been systematically attacked by the European competition authorities under the terms of Article 85 of the Treaty of Rome, which prohibits all agreements between firms which 'may affect trade between Member States and which have as their object or effect the prevention, restriction or distortion of competition within the common market'. In this section we seek to evaluate, on the basis of the scant information available, the evidence on cases where the Commission has intervened to eliminate restrictions in parallel trade. We also discuss the case of cars, where price differentials still persist, and discuss the evidence on the role of distribution arrangements between car manufacturers and dealers in supporting cross-country differentials. Finally, we consider that clauses in distribution agreements restricting parallel trade are not the only way of restricting consumer arbitrage and so facilitating geographic price discrimination across countries. Firms may be able to segment the market geographically through other practices, such as quantity discounting, rebates and tying. These are considered briefly, and will be discussed further in the next chapter insofar as they may act as entry barriers.

We proceed in Section 7.5 with an evaluation of the relation between market integration and price discrimination, and of the current approach of the EU competition authorities to practices which may lead to price discrimination.

7.2. Geographic price discrimination

Price discrimination occurs when consumers are charged dissimilar prices, though the costs of supplying them are similar.[67] There are two important differences in consumer characteristics, which may lead to them being charged different prices on a geographic basis.

(a) Differences in price elasticities of demand. Typically, an unconstrained monopolist will set different prices in different markets if it faces differing demand elasticities; the market with less elastic demand will be charged higher prices. In the European context, differing price elasticities may be either due to differences in underlying preferences across countries, or due to different income levels.

(b) Differences in location, implying a difference in the density of competitors being faced by the consumer (given transport costs). Even when consumers are in other respects identical, they may face different prices as a result of being located in different places. As a result of transportation costs, consumers located in different places may face differing degrees of competition between suppliers. For example, consumers located in an intermediate position between two producers may be able to purchase from either depending on price, whereas consumers located close to just one producer may be facing an effective monopoly as supply from distant producers may be prohibitively expensive.

7.2.1. Restrictions to arbitrage and price discrimination

In all circumstances, geographic price discrimination is constrained by consumers' opportunities to arbitrage across countries. In the extreme case of a perfectly homogeneous good which consumers could import costlessly from any country, price discrimination across countries would not be possible. Arbitrage may be limited (and thus price discrimination sustained) for three main reasons:

(a) due to the inherent nature of the good – for example because transport costs are high relative to its value;

(b) due to cross-border transaction costs (such as have been the target of the single market programme) being high relative to the value of the good;

(c) because of contractual arrangements between suppliers and sellers, for example restricting the extent to which a distributor in any one country can effectively start to supply customers in other countries where prices are higher.

---

[67] In first degree (or perfect) price discrimination, the seller charges a different price for each unit of the good, equal to the maximum willingness to pay for that unit. Second degree price discrimination is non-linear pricing, where prices differ according to the number of units bought. Tying and bundling fall into this category. Under third degree discrimination, different buyers are charged different prices (but the price for each unit bought is constant for each purchaser).

The single market measures should make an impact on price discrimination across countries to the extent that such measures are likely to reduce the effective costs of cross-border trading (in the sense discussed in Chapter 4). In principle they should facilitate arbitrage, and thus make it harder to sustain third-degree price discrimination which is based on differences in preferences and income.

Measures such as territorial exclusivity agreements between manufacturers and distributors prevent consumer arbitrage and so facilitate price discrimination. We will approach the analysis of such contractual limits to arbitrage in the following way. First we will look at those aspects of agreements pertaining to price discrimination. Second, we will consider additional effects of such agreements above and beyond the facilitation of price discrimination.

Vertical agreements may help to sustain geographic price discrimination across markets, even after trade barriers have been fully eliminated, if they are effective in preventing arbitrage on a significant scale. This happens where vertical arrangements such as the adoption of an exclusive distributor in each country may be combined with export ban clauses preventing the distributor from selling for export; or with intellectual property restrictions (e.g. the assignment of the trademark by the supplier to the distributor, in order to prevent imports).

In particular, if arbitrage is subject to economies of scale, the imposition of resale restrictions on intermediaries may be effective in curbing parallel imports. For example, though it is possible for an individual consumer to import a car for personal use and thus benefit from price differences, the bureaucratic costs of doing so might mean that parallel importing will not be undertaken on a large scale. In other words, if producers can prevent intermediaries from undertaking cross-country arbitrage on a large scale, then they may effectively prevent arbitrage altogether, since small-scale arbitrage may be inherently uneconomic. Section 7.4 discusses how EU competition policy currently deals with this tension.

However, in addition it is well known that the imposition of such restraints on distributors can in some cases have efficiency justifications. For certain types of goods (for example, cars or hi-fi equipment), the provision of information and pre/after-sale services by retailers is particularly important, and there is a concern that unrestricted price competition between retailers may lead to suboptimal provision of these services. Thus granting retailers some sort of territorial exclusivity may ensure that they have better incentives to provide such services. One might think of this as a diminution of price competition between retailers, leading to tougher non-price competition. The imposition of vertical restraints, such as contracts granting exclusive dealing territories to retailers, may thus enhance the overall efficiency of the distribution system for some goods.[68]

7.2.2. Other practices supporting geographic price discrimination

Although we will focus primarily on contractual means of limiting consumer arbitrage, a firm with market power may in principle achieve geographic price discrimination through a number of other practices. For example, quantity discounting by firms may increase the costs of consumers meeting their demands from multiple suppliers and so increase the costs of cross-

---

[68]   There is a large literature on the efficiency rationale for vertical restraints. See, among others, Mathewson and Winter [1984, 1987], Waterson [1987], Rey and Stiglitz [1988], and, for a summary, Katz [1989].

border arbitrage (at least at the margin). We consider how firms can erect barriers to foreign suppliers entering their domestic market in much more detail in Chapter 8.

7.3. The welfare effects of price discrimination

In this section we examine in some detail the welfare effects of price discrimination. We aim to form a view on whether prohibiting geographic price discrimination, that is constraining firms to charge the same price in all countries, is generally economically justifiable. The conclusion is ambiguous, in that there are some cases in which prohibiting price discrimination is welfare-improving, but others in which allowing price discrimination is beneficial. Competition policy towards price discrimination may need to become more attuned to these cases insofar as it is possible to discriminate between these cases. Although our conclusion will be complicated by this, it will become clear that a policy of *per se* prohibition of price discrimination (for example, as a direct measure to foster integration) is very unlikely to be desirable.

Relative to the first-best scenario in which a policy maker could control all prices directly (and so mitigate the market power of suppliers), third-degree price discrimination is always (Pareto) inefficient, as consumers with similar costs of supply are facing dissimilar prices. The fact that consumers face different prices for the same good means that there are potential gains to trade between them which are not realized. (In particular, the consumer facing the lower prices could sell a unit of the good to the consumer facing a higher price, and charge some intermediate amount between the two prices. Such a trade benefits both and is thus welfare-improving in the Pareto sense.)

However, the first-best scenario is not the relevant comparison for the purposes of competition policy, given market imperfections and the presence of economies of scale which prevent perfect competition. The relevant comparison is then between the conduct of existing monopolists and oligopolists, where they are allowed to price discriminate, and where uniform prices are required.

We now discuss the impact of price discrimination on total welfare according to this second-best notion of efficiency and also considering distributive justice. We identify a number of effects.

7.3.1. Misallocated consumption

The first effect of price discrimination is that there is an allocative efficiency loss associated with the fact that consumers are charged dissimilar prices, though the costs of supplying them are similar. For a fixed quantity of a good sold to consumers, this loss means that there is always a welfare loss from selling at more than one price (this assuming that there are no transport costs of serving consumers).[69] We will refer to this as the 'misallocated consumption effect' caused by price discrimination. If only this effect were at work, eliminating price discrimination would be desirable.

However, as well as efficiency effects, the elimination of price discrimination always has distributive implications. Consider, for example, two markets with different price elasticities

---

[69]   See Varian [1989].

of demand. In this case, it is profit-maximizing for a price-discriminating monopolist to charge a higher price to the market with lower elasticity. If price discrimination across the two markets were prohibited, then the monopolist would have to charge a price which was intermediate between the previous prices charged to the two markets. Thus, in this second-best world, prohibiting price discrimination benefits some consumers and harms others.[70]

In the context of market integration, if we want to consider the effects of eliminating price discrimination over a wide range of goods, the crucial issue is the distribution of winners and losers. In many ways, this may be a difficult assessment to make, as it is unlikely that the prices of all goods will be systematically lower in particular countries, and this means that a particular country may be a 'winner' with respect to the elimination of price discrimination for some goods, but it might be a 'loser' for others. However, it is also plausible to assume that demand will be more price-elastic in low-income countries, and therefore that there should be a systematic pattern of price dispersion with lower prices on a wide set of goods in low-income countries.

If this is the case, it is possible that eliminating price discrimination may increase average welfare, but at the same time the ensuing losses may be borne disproportionately by low-income countries. In these circumstances, eliminating price discrimination might be inequitable, and might even conflict with the policy objective of promoting greater cohesion across Member States.

We may summarize the argument thus. For a given total quantity of output, selling it by price discriminating lowers average welfare relative to setting uniform prices. However, eliminating price discrimination in favour of uniform pricing always makes some groups of consumers worse off (this is quite apart from any output effect), in that they will be facing higher prices than before. Because of systematic patterns in price dispersion, it is likely that a disproportionate burden of losses would be imposed on low-income economies, and this is obviously not desirable for equity considerations. Thus the absolute change in average welfare might not be an appropriate criterion to assess the impact of eliminating price discrimination. For example, a more appropriate welfare indicator by which to assess European policy intervention might be that of an EU-wide Pareto improvement (i.e. a change where some country is better off, but none is actually worse off).

Thus far we have only considered the case of a fixed stock of output being sold. In general, allowing or prohibiting price discrimination may affect the quantity of output produced. This gives rise to additional effects which should be taken into account in a full cost-benefit analysis of price discrimination. Some are discussed with reference to the case of a price-discriminating monopolist (which is the most studied in the literature, and the one which is best understood). We also consider the effects of price-discriminating oligopolists.

---

[70] Of course, in a first-best world, price discrimination could be removed in a way which is Pareto-improving, since (as we have seen) gains to trade resulting from consumers facing different prices could be realized in a way which makes all better off. In particular, this would require transferring some of the gains from consumers now facing lower prices to those now facing higher prices, but this could be done in such a way that makes everybody better off.

7.3.2. The output-expansion effect

We have seen that price discrimination is a source of allocative inefficiency due to the 'misallocated consumption effect', since consumers with similar (marginal) cost of supply are facing dissimilar prices. Prohibiting price discrimination removes this allocative inefficiency.

However, there is also a basic result that, with fairly general assumptions, price discrimination increases static welfare (the sum of consumers' and producers' surpluses) if total output increases sufficiently to outweigh the 'misallocated consumption effect'. If allowed to price discriminate, a firm's total output may in some circumstances be higher than if not allowed to price discriminate; moreover this increase in output may be sufficiently large to outweigh the misallocated consumption effect and to increase consumer welfare. However, general conclusions on the sign of the welfare change are not possible (see Varian [1985], Schmalensee [1981], and Scherer and Ross [1990]).

Thus a full cost-benefit analysis of the elimination of price discrimination must consider whether there are any output-enhancing effects which can overturn this loss of allocative efficiency.

7.3.3. The market-opening effect

The most dramatic example of the output-expansion effect occurs where allowing price discrimination leads to a firm serving more market. It might be optimal (i.e. profit-maximizing) for a uniform-pricing firm to set a price which excludes a segment of demand. In this case, price discrimination might lead to new market opening, which implies a Pareto welfare improvement (see again Schmalensee [1981]).

In summary, when new markets can be served, the probability of a welfare increase is greater. In addition, most of the literature concerning this issue has considered the case of constant returns to scale. Where marginal costs are falling, this market-opening effect could lead to lower prices for all consumers due to the lower costs resulting from the increase in output if price discrimination is allowed (see Hausman and MacKie-Mason [1988]).

It is interesting to note that a consequence of the market-opening effect is that even if market integration is adopted as a direct objective in itself, regardless of its effects on economic welfare, then it is not clear that price discrimination should be prevented in order to obtain similar outcomes in different countries. Similarity of prices across countries – strictly in the sense of Chapter 3 – is just one aspect of market integration. More fundamentally, we might ask that firms serve all geographical markets. However, firms may choose not to serve particular markets if they cannot price discriminate. Thus it is possible that preventing price discrimination could actually lead to a less integrated outcome, namely that only some geographical markets are served.

7.3.4. The potential pro-competitive effect in oligopolies

Although most of the theory of price discrimination concerns firms with monopoly power, and Article 86 proscribes price discrimination by a dominant firm, it is possible for firms in an oligopoly to price discriminate; all that is required is that firms have some degree of market power. For example, Neven and Phlips [1985] show that price discrimination might also be chosen by competing duopolists, when demand has different price elasticities in the different sub-markets in which they operate. In this case, discrimination is shown to emerge as the non-cooperative Cournot-Nash equilibrium (provided that arbitrage is not operative for some reason).

An interesting argument in favour of price discrimination in an oligopolistic context is that it might have potentially beneficial pro-competitive effects. We must emphasize that while market segmentation and price discrimination have already been identified as possible outcomes of collusion, the occurrence of price discrimination can also be associated with more competitive situations.

This is particularly the case, as we shall see, in the context of spatial price discrimination models. Discrimination based on differing elasticities and income levels tends to reflect market power; with more firms in competition with each other, the price differentials between markets should gradually decline (even without arbitrage) as prices become more reflective of underlying common costs. However, price discrimination can also arise as a result of vigorous competition for particular sub-markets.

The basic intuition for the possible pro-competitive effect of price discrimination is that if firms can set individual prices for each geographical sub-market, then they have a richer set of instruments with which to compete with their rivals than if all firms are constrained to charge a single price in all markets. As a result, competition may be tougher if price discrimination is allowed.

In other words, where firms are competing on price, they might face stronger incentives to undercut their rivals' prices where price discrimination is allowed. To see this, suppose first that price discrimination is prohibited. If a firm lowers its price, then it loses revenue on infra-marginal consumers in all geographical markets. However, if price discrimination is allowed, then a firm which cuts its price in one geographical market will lose revenue just in that market. Roughly speaking, price discrimination leads to more consumers being 'marginal'. An extreme, but very clear example of this phenomenon would be where firms could set individualized prices for every consumer, i.e. where there was maximal price discrimination. In this extreme case, every consumer becomes marginal and is competed for by firms.[71]

The 'pro-competitive' effects of price discrimination are clearly demonstrated in the economic literature on spatial pricing policies. Anderson, de Palma and Thisse [1989] consider the pricing policy adopted by duopolists who are located at different geographic points, and incur transport costs in serving consumers. So-called 'mill pricing' involves the following scheme: each duopolist sets a price; consumers decide which producer to purchase from and pay the quoted 'mill price' plus the transport cost. Anderson et al. show that profits are lower and consumer surplus higher under a spatially discriminatory pricing regime in which rather than quoting a single mill price, the producers specify entire price schedules giving the price paid by a consumer at a particular location. The reason is that under mill pricing, the duopolists are competing only over the marginal consumers who are indifferent as to which firm they

---

[71] As mentioned, we consider this effect in terms of models of spatial pricing policies. These models have a sufficiently rich structure to capture this idea that price discrimination results in 'more consumers being marginal'. It is worth noting that in both the homogeneous good Cournot model and the differentiated good Bertrand model dividing up a market into a number of sub-markets and allowing different prices for each sub-market does not change the outcome (prices and total quantities) of the Nash equilibrium.

purchase from. In contrast, spatially discriminatory pricing allows firms to compete for each individual consumer. Thus this formal result captures our earlier intuition that price discrimination might give rise to tougher competition.

A similar point is made by Thisse and Vives [1988]. They present similar results in which spatial price discrimination leads to firms earning lower profits than under mill pricing. They show that the choice of spatial discriminatory pricing regimes has similarities to a prisoners' dilemma game, in that given the pricing policy of the other firm, each firm prefers to use a spatially discriminatory pricing policy. However, profits would be higher for both firms if they could commit to mill pricing and forego the opportunity to price discriminate spatially. Further theoretical examples of the pro-competitive effects of price discrimination can be found in Anderson and Thisse [1988] and in Matutes and Regibeau [1989].

Phlips [1983] finds some empirical justification for this view that price discrimination could have pro-competitive effects. He cites the example of French cement producers who successfully lobbied for legislation enforcing mill pricing. This accords with Thisse and Vives' view of spatial price discrimination as a coordination problem: firms would like to escape the tougher competition resulting from price discrimination, but have a private incentive to adopt it. The imposition of a legal requirement not to price discriminate spatially removes this private incentive to price discriminate, but leads to higher profits for firms and lower consumer surplus.

Nevertheless, we should not assume that the argument that 'allowing price discrimination yields pro-competitive effects' is a universal one. For example, in the standard Cournot model of oligopoly, there is no such pro-competitive effect and output may not increase.[72] We have already seen from our analysis of the price-discriminating monopoly that price discrimination is only welfare-improving when output is increased sufficiently to outweigh the distributive loss effect identified above.

In summary, in an oligopoly there is a potential additional output-enhancing effect above and beyond the market-opening effect identified in the previous subsection. Although there are some cases in which this pro-competitive effect is absent (e.g. Cournot competition), it is never overturned.

7.3.5. The effect on entry

Allowing price discrimination may have effects on the entry of new firms. First, allowing firms to price discriminate may allow them to take predatory actions against potential entrants who are threatening at least some of the geographical sub-markets in which the incumbent is present. Typically, prices would be lowered on those markets facing potential entry. This argument suggests that allowing price discrimination provides firms with an additional way to deter entry. Indeed, predatory pricing is an extreme form of price discrimination and may be

---

[72] The simplest example is given by taking a Cournot model and dividing the market into two sub-markets, to which firms supply specific quantities and in consequence prices may be different. Division of the market into two sub-markets does not affect the outcome of the Cournot-Nash game. The total quantity supplied to the entire market remains the same. Also, Neven and Phlips [1985] consider the case of price-discriminating Cournot duopoly and show that allowing price discrimination produces a welfare loss. The reason here is that there is no output expansion effect, and price discrimination only leads to an allocative efficiency loss.

used by dominant firms to induce exit of rivals. The classic case is AKZO (1986). However, the analysis of predation and entry deterrence is deferred to the next chapter.

For completeness, it is worth mentioning that price discrimination may also have some positive effects on entry. This is the case if allowing price discrimination means that firms may enter new markets, which they would not enter if they could not price discriminate. We can identify the following effects.

Entry encouraged by increased profitability under price discrimination

Consider an oligopoly in which there is potential entry by new firms. In such a situation, if price discrimination is allowed, firms might make higher profits (taking the number of firms as fixed). Therefore, if price discrimination results in higher profits for a given number of firms, it may encourage entry by new firms; this ultimately gives rise to more competitive outcomes, and it makes it more likely that the total quantity sold will be higher under price discrimination (output-expansion effect).[73]

Effects of price discrimination on entry deterring strategies

Matutes and Regibeau [1989] show how if a firm can commit to charge a single price in all sub-markets, then this can lead to effective entry deterrence from at least some sub-markets. This is because the incumbent's commitment not to price discriminate means that the entrant faces tougher competition the more sub-markets that are entered. By doing this, the incumbent induces the entrant to enter a smaller number of sub-markets than would be the case if the incumbent price discriminated. Thus, in this situation, it is conceivable that a prohibition of price discrimination may discourage entry.

However the empirical significance of these theoretical possibilities is not yet clear.

7.3.6. The effect on the sustainability of collusion

Finally, whether firms set a single EU-wide price, or else set country-specific prices, may affect firms' abilities to sustain collusion. In particular, it would seem likely that setting a single EU-wide price would facilitate collusion by making monitoring of compliance with the collusive agreement easier. If prices are country-specific, as when the price schedule is a complex one, then there are certainly many more prices which need to be observed when determining whether firms have deviated from a collusive outcome. This might make monitoring more difficult, and undermine collusion (see Chapter 9).

7.3.7. Summary

In summary, we have identified in this section a number of effects of geographic price discrimination on economic welfare:

(a)   an allocative efficiency loss due to consumers with similar costs of supply facing dissimilar prices;

---

[73]   See Borenstein [1985].

(b)   an output-expansion effect in which allowing price discrimination can in some cases increase total output and overturn the loss identified in (a);

(c)   a market-opening effect (which can be reinforced by economies of scale) in that more markets are served if price discrimination is allowed that if it is prohibited;

(d)   pro-competitive effect of price discrimination due to competition for marginal consumers;

(e)   effects on entry, which are generally difficult to forecast;

(f)   a reduction in the sustainability of collusion by rendering monitoring more difficult.

Of these, effect (a) is negative (though it might not be very important due to the equity and cohesion considerations discussed in 7.3.1). Effect (e) is difficult to assess, while the other effects are positive. The total welfare effect is thus difficult to sign.

In addition to these issues of economic efficiency, we have also noted that the prohibition of price discrimination has implications for distributive justice since prohibiting price discrimination causes prices to rise in some sub-markets and fall in others. If prohibition of price discrimination leads to price increases across a range of goods being concentrated in particular countries (for example, comparatively low-income ones), then there will be an adverse effect on distributive justice.

However, we may offer the following preliminary considerations.

Price discrimination is likely to be symptomatic of market power. Thus if a firm price discriminates, there may be a prima facie case that the firm has **some** market power. It may be more appropriate for the competition authorities to address the issue of market power directly rather than prohibiting price discrimination which is itself a symptom of market power.

In many cases competition authorities are limited in what they can do about market power due to absolute entry barriers or economies of scale. In such circumstances the question is that of whether prohibiting or allowing price discrimination is more desirable. If the market is relatively competitive and price differentials are relatively small, then we can assume that the welfare loss from the 'misallocated consumption effect' is relatively small (in fact of second order in the size of the price differentials), and in any case may be outweighed by other positive effects. Thus in this case it seems reasonable to allow price discrimination since there is no demonstrable case that price discrimination is leading to significant welfare losses. Hence we conclude that a necessary condition for the prohibition of price discrimination should be significant market power of the price-discriminating firm.

This leaves us with the case of a price-discriminating firm with market power to consider. Should price discrimination be allowed or prohibited in this case? There is no easy general rule due to the existence of the countervailing effects listed above. Again we may argue that if price differentials across countries are small, then welfare losses are likely to be very small and so are unlikely to be sufficiently large to justify the costs of intervention. But what if firms have significant market power and price differentials are large? In such a case it is quite possible that price discrimination is producing significant welfare losses and so prohibition is justified. However, we would ideally like to allow some scope for the price-discriminating firm to argue that setting different prices is justified as it allows new markets to be served. Although we would like to allow a firm with market power to price discriminate under such circumstances, this may be difficult to capture in a policy rule, and we should maybe have a general presumption of prohibition in such cases.

7.4. Competition treatment of restrictions to arbitrage

Given its commitment to integration, which is often taken to mean price convergence across the different parts of the EU, the Commission generally takes a very severe view of geographic price discrimination. This is prohibited both under Art. 85(1), when it derives from agreements between firms (e.g. vertical restraints), and under Art. 86, when it results from a firm's dominant position. Article 86 does not allow exemptions, whereas Art 85(1) does.

In this section we consider first the case of restrictions to parallel trade. The Commission takes a very severe view of firms which try to prevent cross-country arbitrage through clauses restricting arbitrage. Recognizing on the one hand the existence of efficiency justifications for territorial exclusivity in distribution, and seeking on the other hand to promote the elimination of price differentials, the Commission is treading a difficult path:

> 'Community competition policy has always recognized as a vital part of many distribution or licensing systems the allocation of exclusive territories to distributors or licensees, and generally accepts not only exclusivity clauses in such agreements, but also obligations on the distributor or licensee not to advertise or otherwise to actively solicit customers outside its allotted territory. However, the Commission and the European Courts have consistently maintained that agreements restricting parallel trade are illegal and will attract high fines. Such agreements, which have the effect of resealing borders that have been opened by the single market programme, prevent citizens living in countries where prices are high from benefiting from low price imports' (*XXIVth Report on Competition Policy 1994*, p. 11).

Thus the Commission's position is that while it allows restrictions in distribution for efficiency reasons ('it favours the establishment of efficient distribution systems'), this should not translate into geographic price discrimination: 'these systems should be operated in such a way as to ensure that parallel imports remain possible' (*XVIth Report on Competition Policy 1986*, p. 63). And

> '... barriers to exports resulting from agreements or concerted practices between companies have consistently been considered, in the case law of the Commission and the ECJ, a serious infringement of Art. 85(1), as they challenge the free movement of goods and consequently the objective of economic integration pursued by the Treaty' (*XXIInd Report on Competition Policy 1992*, p. 112).

Thus for the efficiency considerations outlined above (to do with issues of efficient distribution), the Commission generally holds a fairly benign view of contracts such as bilateral exclusive distribution agreements conferring some territorial protection. This is demonstrated by the Block Exemption Regulation (EEC) No 1983/83, which establishes a set of general rules under which exclusive distribution agreements for goods do not infringe Art. 85(1); and the concession of individual exemptions from Art. 85(1) for services (or where the agreement is in some respects more restrictive than the Regulation permits). Analogously, in the case of selective distribution agreements EU competition law recognizes the importance of brand image and level of service (i.e. non-price competition) in a manufacturer's choice of downstream outlets. In a number of cases, the efficiency rationale for exclusivity ('provided that resellers are chosen on the basis of objective criteria of a qualitative nature relating to technical qualifications (...) and the suitability of the trading premises...' Metro case) is deemed sufficiently high for the agreements not to infringe Art. 85(1).[74]

At the same time, absolute territorial protection on a distributor (as conferred by export bans on distributors) is not deemed permissible, if it has the effect of isolating national markets from one another: an exclusive distributor can only be required not to solicit orders from outside its territory, but cannot be forbidden to sell outside its territory. In other words, an obligation on a supplier to protect a distributor from indirect competition from parallel imports is not permitted under EU law.[75]

The Commission (and the courts) have dealt harshly with a very large number of cases in this area. Any export ban contained in these agreements (directly or indirectly – such as refusal of customer guarantees if the good was not purchased from the appointed distributor in the Member State, or withdrawal of discounts to dealers exporting to other Member States) is held to infringe Art. 85(1).

Cases include:

(a)   the action against Sperry New Holland (1985) for the 'illegal barriers to intra-Community trade' contained in the distribution system for its combine harvester;

(b)   Tipp-Ex (1987), where the Commission ended the agreements between the German firm Tipp-Ex and its exclusive distributors in four countries because these were 'aimed at preventing parallel imports or exports of correction products', and 'these market partitioning practices were a serious infringement of Art. 85(1)' (*XVIIth Report on Competition Policy 1987*);

(c)   Sandoz Italia (1987), which was fined for displaying the words 'export prohibited' over a number of years on its sales invoices for pharmaceutical products, a clause whose 'purpose is to insulate the national market, thus affecting trade between Member States and preventing the completion of a single market' (*XVIIth Report on Competition Policy 1987*);

(d)   Fisher Price (1987), where parallel imports of Fisher Price toys from the UK into Ireland had been prevented;

(e)   Konica (1987), where parallel imports of film from the UK into the higher-priced German market were prevented;

---

[74]   Industries which have benefited from this position include cameras, electronic equipment, consumer durables, clocks and watches, computers, perfumes and luxury cosmetic products and jewellery.

[75]   Art. 3 of Regulation (EEC) 1983/83 specifically deals with circumstances in which the benefit of the block exemption will be lost. These are:

(a) when there are horizontal reciprocal distribution agreements, which in practice amount to market sharing (e.g. Siemens/Fanuc, 1985); or non-reciprocal unless one of the distribution systems is small enough;

(b) when there is no alternative source of supply from outside the territory (i.e. there must always be the possibility of parallel importing);

(c) when one or both parties make it difficult for intermediaries or users to obtain the goods from other dealers inside (or outside) the common market, in particular through (i) the exercise of intellectual property rights (e.g. the supplier assigns its trademark to the distributor so that it can prevent imports); and (ii) other measures to prevent dealers or users from obtaining the goods from outside the territory, or from selling in it. Again this is concerned with parallel imports.

(f)   AKZO Coatings (1989), where the Commission obtained undertakings from AKZO in relation to the finding that the prices of car refinish products were persistently higher in the UK than in other Member States;

(g)   Toshiba (1991), where Toshiba was fined for having included an export ban in its exclusive distribution agreements for its photocopiers;

(h)   Gosme/Martell (1991), where Martell was fined for having prevented parallel exports of Martell cognac to Italy;

(i)   Newitt/Dunlop Slazenger International (1992), which had used various means to block exports of tennis balls by its British traders to countries where it had sole distributors;

(j)   Parker Pens (1992): Parker Pen and its distributor in Germany were fined for having included an export ban in an agreement concluded between them: 'The Commission took the view that the infringement was such as to obstruct the achievement of a fundamental objective of the Treaty, namely the integration of the common market' (*XXII Report on Competition Policy 1992*);

(k)   Tretorn (1994), where a tennis ball producer prohibited its exclusive distributors from selling for exports.

These are discussed below.

7.4.1. Discussion of available evidence

The Commission's record on price discrimination clearly demonstrates its systematic opposition to practices preventing arbitrage. While it is accepted that a manufacturer can provide dealers with exclusive territories, these cannot be absolute. In practice, this means that distribution contracts can only specify that appointed dealers will not actively seek customers outside their allocated area, but cannot refuse to supply them outside that area when approached. This applies also where territorial agreements are protected by a special block exemption, as in the case of cars (as shown by the two cases involving restrictions placed by car manufacturer Peugeot on dealers' ability to engage in parallel trade – see Peugeot-Talbot (1986), and Eco System/Peugeot (1991)).

The Commission's stance appears quite independent of whether the manufacturer holds a dominant position (reflected in its market share), and the degree of sophistication of the products (in terms of the product characteristics: Peugeot cars, Ford trucks, and cameras received essentially the same treatment as tennis balls, toys or Tipp-Ex correction fluid).

No contingency on market structure

Our earlier analysis suggested that it would be desirable to adopt some dominance criterion in the treatment of price discrimination and to make the holding of a dominant (or jointly dominant) position a necessary condition for prohibition of price discrimination. That holding a dominant position is not a crucial factor in the Commission's assessment is clear for example from the two recent cases concerning tennis balls manufacturers – Dunlop Slazenger International (1992), and Tretorn (1994).

While the British manufacturer Dunlop may have market power with a share of 39% of the EU market, the Swedish firm Tretorn was only the fourth largest firm with 11% of the Community market (1986 estimates). The Dunlop investigation was initiated by a complaint on the part of British sports goods wholesaler/retailer Newitt (and others) that Dunlop had prevented exports of tennis and squash balls in order to protect its exclusive distribution system. Dunlop had a system of exclusive distributors on the Continent, while in the UK it sold directly to retailers and to some wholesalers. It also had two price lists, one for the UK market and a (generally) lower one for the export market. Its exclusive distributors were charged the export price minus a discount which officially was 20%, but generally was much larger and reached 50%. Dunlop was found to have used a variety of practices to erect barriers to trade within the Community (in collaboration with its distributors): these included export bans, specific refusals to fill orders, pricing measures against UK wholesalers to prevent them from exporting at competitive prices, marking products, and buying back parallel imports. Newitt in particular saw its supplies halted, and faced price increases up to 54% for some types of balls. In 1994 a similar investigation was launched against Tretorn, and documentary evidence was uncovered that it had been actively erecting barriers against parallel imports within the Community – through practices very similar to those used by Dunlop (including export ban clauses in contracts and measures to enforce them). Tretorn even stopped supplying the US market because it was unable to prevent tennis balls shipped to the US from reappearing as imports in the Netherlands and Switzerland.

The Commission concluded that the distribution contracts between both tennis ball manufacturers and their dealers were aimed at absolute territorial protection and exclusion of parallel trade. Both Dunlop and Tretorn were fined, though the fine imposed on Dunlop was significantly larger, reflecting its larger sales. Dealers who collaborated in the prevention of trade were also fined.

Limited and contradictory consideration of efficiency in distribution

The distinction between absolute protection and partial protection deserves particular attention. There is an inherent contradiction in the notion of 'partial protection' as pursued by the Commission. The reason why an exclusive distribution system may be 'optimal' is that, because of the characteristics of the product, it is efficient that the retailer has monopoly power over a territory for the specific brand. Allowing arbitrage simply eliminates this monopoly power. It is therefore not a consistent position for the Commission to allow exclusive dealing contracts on the one hand, while at the same time condemning manufacturers' practices to enforce such exclusivity. Hence, at least when block exemptions apply, efficiency considerations should be taken into account openly in considering restrictions to parallel trade. In the case of non-sophisticated products, with little need to support pre- and after-sales services, it is not clear that there is an efficiency rationale for allowing exclusivity, and for the same reasons there is no efficiency rationale for territorial protection. It is thus appropriate that in the case of Tretorn, the Commission makes it explicit that its distribution system would not have qualified for an individual exemption even if Tretorn had applied for one, because the agreements were not indispensable to the efficiency of Tretorn's distribution system. However the case appears to be different for example for car manufacturers.

The 1991 Peugeot-Eco System case was initiated by a complaint lodged by Eco System against Peugeot, after Peugeot sent a circular to all its dealers in Belgium, Luxembourg and France requesting that they suspend supplies to Eco System on the grounds that it was acting as a reseller. Eco System is a specialist intermediary for import purchases of cars by French final consumers, whose services included looking for favourable purchasing terms, and concluding purchases for its customers. Because it was merely collecting orders from final consumers, and never acquired ownership of the imported cars, the Commission decided that

Eco System never acted as a reseller (it did not incur the usual risk that a reseller incurs – storage risk, credit risk, financial risk).

Most importantly, the Commission made explicit that the existence of a block exemption cannot result in a prevention of parallel trade: 'It is apparent that an agreement designed to prevent parallel imports between Member States does not satisfy the criteria for applying article 85(3) of the EEC Treaty' (OJ L 66, 11.3.1992, p. 7). It is also made explicit that block exemptions cannot completely eliminate intra-brand competition. Thus, the Commission accepts that efficiency considerations may recommend a distribution system organized around exclusivity. The distribution system itself is not challenged. However, when it results in price differences such that it encourages arbitrageurs to undertake parallel imports, and manufacturers and appointed dealers to try to prevent these imports, this is taken as evidence that the purpose of exclusivity is to price discriminate, and this is considered unlawful.

Occasionally there is some evidence that consideration is implicitly given to issues of efficiency of the distribution network: for example in the Martell case (1991, where cognac producer Martell withdrew the usual discounts to French wholesaler Gosme because it had resold cognac to Italy, where prices were higher), the Commission stated explicitly that there was no significant issue of efficiency in distribution to justify exclusivity. And in cars, where an exemption exists, the efficiency considerations which justified the exemption appear to be have been taken indirectly into account in deciding the size of fines (for restricting parallel trade). For instance, no fine was imposed on Peugeot in 1991, as the Commission considered this case a clarification of the block exemptions.[76] Yet in other cases, the decisions of the Commission do not appear consistent with considerations of efficient distribution. For instance, a significant fine was imposed on Toshiba (1991) for protecting the exclusive territories of its appointed distributors, even though the product sold (photocopiers, lap-tops, printers, and fax machines) was sophisticated (like cars).

All this strongly suggests that efficiency considerations should be taken into account explicitly and openly, especially when block exemptions apply, to make the process more transparent.

The current approach to the competition treatment of arbitrage restrictions very much confirms that, for all practical purposes, the Commission regards competition policy as another tool to achieve market integration. In this sense, its application is intended to have the same effects as tax harmonization, or agreements on common standards: making it hard for producers to segment the market along national boundaries. This area is a prime example where competition policy has been pushed beyond its usual goals, and has aimed at integration itself (which is understood as a sort of 'law of one price').[77]

---

[76] Similarly in the earlier Peugeot case [1986] the fine was extremely low (ECU 4,000), not intended to punish these actions but the incorrect and/or negligent information deliberately furnished by Peugeot to the Commission. (The case concerned obstacles put by Peugeot to purchases of right-hand-drive vehicles on the Continent, with the aim of protecting is exclusive distributors in the UK.)

[77] The only caveat is that the size of fines has been historically so small that it can hardly be argued that they are a deterrent at all (indeed it is very likely that in many instances the profits from discrimination exceed the foreseeable fine). Furthermore, the length of the litigation process may discourage potential arbitrageurs who incur costs of advertising and promotion, only to find that wholesalers halt their supplies.

General welfare implications (apart from efficient distribution)

We have argued in Section 7.3 that a *per se* prohibition of price discrimination is not economically justified, even when efficiency considerations regarding optimal network distribution are not present. Indeed, we have argued that the welfare implications of price discrimination are ambiguous, because the welfare loss which this creates may be more than outweighed by increases in total supply, possibly enhanced by competitive effects and new entry.

To what extent is it possible to assess whether any of these positive effects of discrimination had been 'at work' in the cases actually investigated by the Commission? Some tentative deductions are as follows.

(a)   Firstly, it appears that in most cases the manufacturers tried to track the origins of grey imports, halted their supplies to arbitrageurs and/or requested all dealers to stop supplying these agents. This suggests that the 'competitive effect' was not present in these cases: discrimination did not force strong competition.

(b)   It would also appear that in preventing parallel trade manufacturers have kept total quantity down – though this statement should be interpreted with great caution. What it says is that at the prices set by the manufacturer in trying to discriminate, arbitrageurs find it profitable to sell more in the high-price countries than they have been allowed to; it does not say that the quantity sold when arbitrage is prevented is lower than the quantity that would have been sold had a single price prevailed. For this an investigation of the evolution of prices and quantities after the cases should be carried out. This certainly goes beyond the scope of this report, but the Commission should consider a study which revisits some of the past decisions and seeks to establish in a more structured way (using company data) the welfare implications of forcing arbitrage.

A final issue is whether there are systematic losers. Price differentials may reflect different demand elasticities for the product across countries. Price elasticities for a product may differ for various reasons. For instance, if French consumers have a preference for French cars, Peugeot will be in a position to set higher prices in France than elsewhere (except in the presence of arbitrageurs). Similarly, Dunlop may be able to sell at higher prices in the UK be because of strong brand loyalty. Generally speaking, to the extent that consumers in one country are loyal to one brand, they can be induced to pay more for it (if arbitrage can be prevented). Another reason why consumers in a country may face higher prices is that competition might have been historically weak in that country for that type of product. This may be the reason why toy manufacturer Fisher Price (1987), with divisions in all Member States, sold toys at prices even 30% higher in Ireland than in the UK, before this practice was found illegal. A final reason why consumers in one country may pay higher prices is if they are (on average) wealthier: in this case firms may not need to compete intensely, and will set higher prices. This could be the explanation behind the Konica case (1987: the Japanese manufacturer of photographic goods sought to prevent parallel trade arising from higher prices being set for film in Germany than in the UK).

It is very difficult, however, to identify from the available case material any systematic pattern of 'winners' and 'losers'. Nevertheless, we should be cautious about blanket prohibitions of price discrimination if only for the reason that some countries may then face systematically higher prices across a range of goods.

7.4.2. The case of cars

The car industry remains a rather unusual case. The car dealership system which is common to the whole of the EU is characterized by exclusive and selective distribution agreements which enjoy a block exemption (Regulation (EC) No 1475/95). This is justified by the Commission on grounds that motor vehicles are a complex product, for which after-sales service is important and there are efficiency gains in combining car distribution with repair and provision of spare parts. Though the Commission has been involved in a few decisions against the most obvious restrictions to parallel trade,[78] parallel imports on a large scale are effectively discouraged by car manufacturers; and this regime has been quite effective in retaining a partitioning of markets along national lines. Parallel imports of cars remain small.

The case of cars is interesting because it is one where – in spite of the Commission's general opposition to geographic price discrimination – markets remain to a significant extent segmented along national borders, with sizeable price differentials being sustained.[79]

While on the one hand the Commission is worried about price differentials (Regulation (EC) No 1475/95 has a general promise that the benefits of the block exemption would be withdrawn where prices in different Member States display 'substantial differences' for a considerable period; and indeed a biannual report on *Car Price Differentials* has been produced since 1992), on the other hand it has designed a block exemption which contributes to supporting the differentials.

The practical implication is that while it is possible for individual citizens to purchase a car in a different Member State, it is likely that the transaction costs of doing so will deter many; it may be that dealers are prevented from selling to intermediaries for fear of the manufacturer's reaction although this is difficult to substantiate. This frustration of large-scale arbitrage, especially given the economies of scale involved in this activity, means it is unlikely that price differentials will be eliminated (up to a limit defined by transport costs).

The interesting question is whether there are positive welfare effects which derive from allowing price discrimination. Davidson et al. [1989], after examining price discrimination in an oligopolistic setting, also seek to draw some conclusions on the car market in the European Community. They consider first the case of symmetric duopolistic competition in two countries, and show that reducing price discrimination through imposing constraints on cross-country price differentials may reduce output for both countries, as well as social welfare.

They further consider the distributive consequences of applying constraints on prices. This is done in a model of symmetric duopolistic competition in three countries, with one country having no home producer and lowest prices. In this case, the imposition of constraints on price

---

[78]   See for example Peugeot-Talbot [1986], and Eco System/Peugeot (1991).

[79]   Empirical studies have shown substantial differences across national markets both for prices of individual models and for average prices (the maximum difference has been found to be as much as nearly 50% of the average pre-tax price - though these measures are generally controversial because it is difficult to account properly for example for model specifications). A comparison of country price indices also seems to suggest that differences tend to be stable over time and size class. See among others BEUC, 'EEC study on car prices and progress towards 1992', 1989; MMC, 'New motor cars. a report on the supply of new motor cars within the United Kingdom', 1992, Ch. 8; 'Year 2000 and beyond – the car marketing challenge in Europe', *Euromotor Reports*, 1991, pp. 183–4; Mertens and Ginsburgh [1985]; Gual [1993]. Flam and Nordstrom [1995], the most recent study, found average price differences of around 12%.

discrimination unambiguously increases prices and reduces welfare in the third country, while the effect on total welfare is indeterminate (though consumers are better off in the other two countries). This is taken as a possible explanation of why Belgium (little domestic production of cars, relatively cheap prices) might not be in favour of any regulation directed at reducing price discrimination across countries.

In terms of the effects we have listed above, it may be argued that the 'market-opening' effect does not appear very important in the case of cars, because demand conditions in most EU markets are rather similar. This is debatable, but we suspect that even if geographic price discrimination were outlawed, then producers would still serve most markets.

Thus in terms of welfare analysis the important question is whether the output-enhancing, pro-competitive effects of price discrimination are present, and are sufficiently large to overturn any distributional losses. For this purpose, we would need to develop an empirically formulated hypothesis concerning the pro-competitive effect of price discrimination, i.e. the idea that where geographic price discrimination is allowed (with significant price differentials) competition is intense. For example, we could test to see whether smaller price differentials (proxying easier consumer arbitrage) are associated with higher industry profit, or with entry due to weaker product-market competition.

However, testing such a hypothesis would require appropriate data, and in particular we would need to see sufficient variations in the ease of consumer arbitrage to be able to test this hypothesis with any power. Unfortunately, it is extremely difficult to find examples of industries in which such variation has occurred in consumer arbitrage possibilities, due to the single market programme or indeed for any other reason.

In other words: according to our discussion it is possible that in the car industry prevention of arbitrage and price discrimination are actually welfare-enhancing. However, proving this would require evidence which is simply not available: because we have never seen any significant variation in arbitrage possibilities, we cannot compare industry profits across regimes of different arbitrage possibilities.

7.4.3. Competition treatment of other practices supporting geographic price discrimination

Price discrimination is also condemned as anti-competitive under European competition law for firms that have been found to occupy a dominant position. Art. 86(c) explicitly mentions price discrimination as an example of an abuse of a dominant position. The main reason is that it has a foreclosing effect on competition.[80] Examples of price discrimination include loyalty rebates (Hoffman-La Roche, 1985), target discounts (Michelin, 1981), predatory price cutting (ECS/AKZO, 1986) top-slice rebates (soda ash cases involving Solvay and ICI, 1991).

In most of these cases, price discrimination was exercised on a territorial basis. In the AKZO case the predatory practices were targeted at a UK based company that wanted to expand into more lucrative Continental markets.[81] In the soda ash cases, Solvay and ICI were accused of maintaining market segmentation along national boundaries.

---

[80]   See Whish [1993] for a discussion of the approach taken by the Commission and the ECJ on a number of cases.

[81]   See Harbord and Hoehn [1994] and Phlips and Moras [1993] for a discussion of this case.

The best-known case of geographic price discrimination by a dominant firm is undoubtedly United Brands (1978), where the major supplier of branded bananas into the EC was held to have abused its dominant position by charging different prices according to the destination of the product. West Germany had the highest prices whereas Ireland had the lowest prices in the Community, but this was not justified by the actual cost differences in supplying these different markets. The case was brought by a Danish distributor who was refused supply of bananas by United Brands because he did not participate in UBC's advertising campaign and had earlier supported a rival brand. The Commission found UBC guilty of four abuses of Article 86: (i) prohibiting its distributors/ripeners from reselling of green (unripened) bananas, (ii) charging discriminatory prices, (iii) charging excessive prices in some EC Member States, and (iv) refusing to supply a Danish distributor.

The ECJ determined that for UBC it was not permissible to charge according to local market conditions whereas this was permissible for local distributors. In other words there was not an obligation to charge similar retail prices, only an obligation for competition/arbitrage to bring about convergence of prices with costs of supply at the wholesale level.

The ECJ also condemned geographic price discrimination in the second Tetra Pak case (1992). The company was accused of engaging in a number of exclusionary practices with the effect that the market became segmented with higher prices being charged in some Member States then others.

We deal with these issues more fully in Chapter 8.

7.5. The interaction between market integration and price discrimination

The existence of significant price differences across markets is often taken as direct evidence of the lack of integration of markets. Thus price discrimination is in a sense the competition issue most directly connected with integration policy. The view has also been advanced in some quarters that price discrimination should be directly prevented as an integration objective *per se*. However, we have seen that this is an overly simplistic view.

If we ask whether market integration is likely to lead to a reduction in price differentials and so to less geographic price discrimination, then the conclusion is fairly clear. Market integration facilitates cross-border arbitrage and so should reduce the scope for geographic price discrimination. Moreover, to the extent that market integration should lead to demand characteristics being more similar across economies (for example as a result of macroeconomic shocks being less idiosyncratic to individual economies), then the underlying incentives for firms to price discriminate should be reduced. Market integration should also lead to tougher product competition, since firms in different countries may be brought into competition with each other. Such a reduction in market power should again lead to reduced price differentials, since prices will more closely reflect common costs.

Where firms manage to maintain market segmentation despite the progress of market integration, for example due to contracts, the erection of entry barriers or by collusion, then price discrimination may persist, but in all cases only as far as cross-border arbitrage possibilities allow. The case law listed above demonstrates a significant number of examples in which such behaviour has occurred. Moreover, these cases show that the pressure of cross-border arbitrage can often be very weak even for consumer goods, and as a result firms can in some cases sustain significant price differences in different geographical markets.

Despite there being a very strong case that market integration should lead to less geographic price discrimination, this does not imply that it is desirable directly to prohibit price discrimination as an object of integration. In some cases price discrimination may be desirable.

An important reason for allowing price discrimination is that (even for a monopolist) constraining firms to charge a single price in all markets may lead them to exit some markets. In the context of integration, the presence of a supplier in all geographical markets may be a more important objective than requiring similar prices in all markets. However, this 'market-opening effect' does require sufficient asymmetries between markets. If geographical markets become more similar, then the force of this argument becomes less, since it becomes less likely that prohibiting price discrimination will induce firms to exit from some markets.

The second important reason for allowing price discrimination is what was called the 'competitive effect'. If firms have the ability to make price cuts targeted towards selected groups of consumers (for example a particular geographical area) then this can lead to more competitive outcomes. Prohibiting price discrimination would prevent such potential price cuts and lead to less competitive outcomes. It is very important to note that even if, in equilibrium, firms in fact set similar prices across geographical markets due to these markets having similar characteristics, then it is having the potential to charge different prices that is pro-competitive even if in equilibrium such prices are not set. In markets in which this pro-competitive effect is important, then it is crucial that integration is achieved by making economic fundamentals more similar across countries and reducing border costs, thus leading to firms choosing similar prices in different geographical markets. Directly constraining prices in different geographical markets to be the same would be counter-productive.

This suggests strongly that we should see reductions in price differentials as a consequence of market integration changing the incentives for firms and reducing the incentive to price discriminate. We should in no way consider price homogenization to be a direct objective of policy.

7.6. Conclusions

Measures taken by firms to support geographic price discrimination usually require arbitrage restrictions that are incorporated in territorial distribution agreements. Distribution agreements which grant territorial protection and are thus effective in segmenting EU markets along national borders are deemed to be in conflict with the integration objective. At the same time, EU competition policy has accepted the view that vertical agreements granting some form of territorial protection might be desirable, for they may be efficient where non-price competition is enhanced. In effect, EU competition policy seeks to strike a balance between efficiency considerations and integration objectives. A similar balance should be struck with respect to price discrimination and measures supporting price discrimination. This is the main conclusion drawn from this chapter which explores some of the positive and negative effects of geographic price discrimination. We have concentrated on the pure welfare effects of price discrimination and tried to isolate these from other efficiency effects of vertical restraints that are typically found in territorial distribution agreements.

First we recognize that where price discrimination is a symptom of collusion and market power, the latter should be addressed directly. In other words, price discrimination is likely to be symptomatic of market power, and in this case intervention is justified – though attacking the discrimination directly may not be the best response.

We have focused particularly on other cases, where price discrimination results for example from differences in location. This area is certainly more controversial, and deserving of a wider debate. We have particularly emphasized that although the theoretical literature is worried about the impact of allowing geographic price discrimination on total welfare, this approach may not be wholly desirable for policy. This is because there may be inequitable consequences from forcing prices to be uniform, if it means that the low-income countries bear a disproportionate share of the losses.

These considerations appear to weigh against any interpretation of the integration objective purely as convergence of prices in absolute terms, and against any absolute presumption against price discrimination. Indeed there are circumstances where price discrimination through vertical arrangements or other means may be welfare-enhancing, i.e. it may be good *per se* (over and above the well-known argument of the efficiency of distribution networks).

In the light of the analysis in this chapter, there should be no presumption that geographic price discrimination is always welfare-reducing, and intervention against it should not be automatic.

There are cases in which we can presume that the welfare losses due to price discrimination are at most small and possibly non-existent. If firms have little market power or if price differentials are small then the 'consumption misallocation loss' is small. In such cases it would be sensible to have a presumption of non-intervention.

Where price discrimination is a symptom of market power and price differentials are large, there is more reason to be concerned and prohibition can be warranted. However, even in this case it is possible that price discrimination is welfare-improving and care must be taken that prohibition does not lead to adverse consequences such as exit from some markets.

In addition, the practical difficulties of identifying price discrimination should not be underestimated. Cross-country price comparisons are difficult for most goods, as graphically demonstrated by various studies on car price differentials. This implies that unless a good is internationally traded, with a clear world price, the evidence for price discrimination may not be satisfactory. Detecting price discrimination may be difficult if not impossible for firms who 'tweak' their products slightly for sale in another country at a different price.

8. Barriers to entry and access restrictions in integrating markets

8.1. Introduction

An evaluation of the ability of firms to cross national borders and enter into hitherto distinct national markets is crucial to assess the competitive impact of market integration. If entry can be prevented by incumbent firms, market integration measures may have very small effects.

The task of dealing with entry barriers erected by firms falls to the Commission's competition authorities, chiefly by force of Articles 85, 86 and 90 of the Treaty of Rome. As stated for example in the 1994 *Report on Competition Policy*:

> 'One of the Commission's main tasks in enforcing competition rules is to ensure that companies do not conclude agreements, or, where they hold a dominant position, engage in unilateral practices, which have the effect of limiting the ability of other firms – usually those from other Member States – taking advantage of the possibilities offered by the Single Market to compete. Under Art. 85, such agreements may typically consist of networks of distribution agreements whereby incumbent producers tie up all available distributors. Under Art. 86, a dominant firm may, for example, attempt to prevent its customers from using different suppliers by means of loyalty rebates, or attempt to remove an existing competitor by predatory pricing.' (p. 12)

The main focus of this chapter is on strategic barriers, i.e. barriers to (cross-border) entry created by incumbent firms to protect their position, in response to the elimination of institutional barriers through the integration process.[82] To the extent that the single market programme has been successful in removing institutional barriers protecting incumbents in certain markets, the incentive for the incumbents is to replace such barriers with strategic behaviour. Similarly, there is an incentive for strategic behaviour where public policy has lifted previous restrictions to entry into legally protected monopolies, and may have forced the incumbent to open access to an asset which is a necessary complement for supplying the final market. In these circumstances, an integrated incumbent may seek to protect its advantage over new entrants by setting terms of access which are disadvantageous to competitors.

We identify two main classes of strategic behaviour by firms which are aimed at excluding actual or potential competitors from the market: creating restrictions of access to a complementary asset, and pursuing exclusion through pricing strategies. These are discussed below in Sections 8.3 and 8.4 respectively. In Section 8.5 we emphasize how, even in cases where entry appears prevented by institutional factors, the exclusionary effect may be actually due to a combination of such institutional factors and the behaviour of the incumbent(s). In such cases, competition intervention may remain the appropriate policy instrument. Empirical material and case law will be used where appropriate. Section 8.6 evaluates the treatment of entry barriers under EU competition policy, and Section 8.7 concludes with a summary of the

---

[82] Our general concept of 'barriers to entry', encompasses the classic definition by Stigler [1968, p. 67] as 'a cost of producing...which must be borne by a firm which seeks to enter an industry but is not borne by firms already in the industry'.

main areas of concern for the competition authorities in addressing strategic behaviour which prevents entry.

8.2.   Barriers to cross-border entry erected by firms

While a variety of strategic entry barriers have been identified in the economic literature,[83] we will here confine ourselves only to those which are most relevant from the perspective of market integration. To the extent that integration measures have lifted previous legal and institutional restrictions to entry into a national market, the incumbent firm(s) in that market will have an incentive to replace them with strategic behaviour. This predatory behaviour (induced by integration) towards potential competitors – both *de novo* entrants and firms already operating in another geographical market – may take essentially two forms.

(a)   Restriction of access to a complementary asset: the incumbent in a market may control an input which is essential for the final supply of the end product to consumers, and most importantly cannot be (realistically) replicated – either because it is in scarce supply, or because there are natural monopoly characteristics on the cost-side. As integration policies remove some of the institutional obstacles to cross-border entry, the incumbent controlling an essential complementary asset in each geographical market will have an incentive to prevent the entry of foreign rivals by strategically setting the terms of access to the asset. This may include the following methods.

   (i)   Refusal to supply, where access to the complementary input is refused by the incumbent which owns or controls it.

   (ii)   Setting access charges in a way which discriminates against new entrants. This is particularly important in the context of the deregulation and liberalization process affecting the network-bound industries, which used to enjoy statutory monopolies at the national level. As trade is opened up with these established monopolies, access terms to inputs with natural monopoly characteristics are crucial.

   (iii)   Use of vertical restraints (e.g. exclusive dealing agreements between manufacturers and distributors) for purposes of foreclosure: this may occur if the incumbent is able to tie up a complementary asset at a different level of the market, to stop entry at its same level of the market.

(b)   Exclusionary pricing: an incumbent firm may preclude the entry of rivals into the market directly through its pricing behaviour, by setting its effective price below the level at which it is worthwhile for an outsider to compete. This includes predatory pricing, where the incumbent adopts an aggressive pricing strategy as a response to entry.[84] Another barrier arising from pricing on markets are non-linear pricing structures such as selective discounts and 'fidelity rebates' (which reward customers in exchange for not purchasing from new entrants).[85]

---

[83]   For a review see, among others, Harbord and Hoehn [1994].

[84]   Limit pricing is a way for the incumbent to signal instead to the potential rival that its post-entry behaviour would be aggressive, and thus prevent entry.

[85]   We will not consider in detail here entry barriers such as sunk costs in R&D, or advertising, which have been identified in the literature as endogenous determinants of market structure (these are costs which are deliberately sunk by incumbent firms in a way that increases their first-mover advantage, and thereby makes rivals' entry unprofitable; see for example Sutton [1991], Lyons and Matraves [1995], and Davies and Lyons [1996]). While this is reasonable as a theory of long-run market structure, it appears less plausible as a response to integration (and to any sudden threat of

8.3. Restrictions of access to a complementary asset

Access to a complementary input which is essential for supplying the final product market may be controlled by the incumbent, because the latter is vertically integrated or holds a special long-term right to the input. There is a barrier to entry when the potential entrant's access to the complementary input is restricted, while at the same time the input cannot be duplicated – for instance because it is physically scarce, or there are elements of natural monopoly in its cost structure. This means that entry will be hampered if the incumbent controls access to a complementary asset, which either cannot be duplicated or is too costly for the entrant to duplicate. Competition policy should ensure that restrictions are not strategically placed by incumbents on access to such complementary inputs.

8.3.1. Refusal to supply

Supplying a final market generally requires the combination of complementary inputs in production and distribution. 'Refusal to supply' is characterized as a situation where access to a complementary input is denied by the (integrated) incumbent which owns or controls it, while it is not feasible for the entrant to replicate the same input. In its effort to favour integration and eliminate barriers to entry (especially cross-border entry), the Commission has developed in recent years the 'essential facilities doctrine' (see below Section 8.6), whereby an incumbent 'refusing to supply' an essential complementary input to a rival (and in particular to new entrants) abuses its dominant position.

A number of points must be made on refusal to supply a complementary asset.

Firstly, it is crucial that the input is non-replicable. If the new entrant could set up an equivalent facility, or could use an alternative complement without incurring a significant disadvantage, then this could not be described as a barrier to entry. The relevant criterion here must be whether the new entrant could enter at minimum efficient scale. All activities have a certain amount of fixed and sunk costs; therefore the relevant criterion is whether the investment which the new entrant must make to replicate the complementary input has relatively low cost in relation to the value of what he wants to sell. Secondly, dominant firms have given various efficiency defences for refusing access to an essential input. We will now look at these two points in more detail.

The first important point to establish is always to what extent the refusal of access is really a matter of exclusion, i.e. it effectively impairs the viability of the entrant. As mentioned, an exclusionary effect can be claimed only where there are no alternative complementary inputs which could be used. This appears to be so, for example, in the case of access by a smaller airline to a flag carrier's computer reservation system (CRS), if this is the only way in which travel agent bookings are effectively made. Initially, each Community flag carrier had its own (unsophisticated) CRS, and to the extent that travel agent reservations are made through this CRS a small carrier which is denied access to it will not be able to enter. The Commission intervened both by introducing 'fair access rules' (similar to the policy of the US DoJ), and also, in one case, by taking direct action against the incumbent. In 1987, the small UK carrier London European Airways had sought access to the CRS managed by the Belgian airline

---

entry: there is a timing problem). In addition, there is not much that competition policy can actually do about these types of sunk costs.

Sabena (Saphir) for the Brussels/Luton route, so that it would be listed on the terminals of Belgian travel agencies. The system was operated, where possible, on the basis of 'reciprocity' (i.e. Sabena would give access to other companies free of charge, provided that they did the same); when this was not possible, a fee was charged by Sabena to the company using the system. In LEA's case, access was refused altogether on grounds that 'it was not in Sabena's commercial and positive interest to collaborate': LEA's low air fares were for Sabena 'a potential threat to traffic from Belgium', its limited timetable 'virtually ruled out any possibility of interlining connections via Brussels', and LEA's refusal to grant Sabena the contract for ground servicing of its aircrafts meant that Sabena could not 'offset' in this way the lost income from 'possible passenger losses'. In cases such as this, particularly as the incumbent had not incurred a substantial investment to develop the facility (Saphir was an adaptation of the Alpha-3 system developed by Air France), the loss of income from the entry of a rival is clearly not an efficiency defence. The Commission correctly decided against Sabena, because it considered that unless LEA had access to the CRS there was no other way for its flights to appear on the terminal of Belgian travel agents, and this would not allow it to operate.[86]

Refusal of access to port facilities has also been a cause of complaints. In 1993, a complaint was lodged by the cargo carrier Sea Containers against the British ferry operator Stena Sealink – which runs ferry services between the UK, Ireland and France and is also the port authority at Holyhead (Wales). The port of Holyhead was the only port on the British side serving on the central corridor route between the UK and Ireland. Sea Containers had been refused access to Holyhead for commencing a high-speed ferry service through the central corridor between the UK and Ireland. The Commission found there was a prima facie case that Sealink was thereby protecting its own ferry service from competition; and, once the complaint had been lodged, Sealink offered suitable berths to Sea Containers (Sea Containers/Stena Sealink, 'Holyhead II', 1993).

As mentioned, the case for defining an asset as an 'essential facility' may not be sustainable when there would have been – at least in principle – alternative complementary inputs which the rival/new entrant could have used. In Morlaix (1995), the Commission dealt with the refusal of the Morlaix Chamber of Commerce, in its capacity of port authority for the Brittany port of Roscoff, to give Irish Ferries access to the port, and ordered Morlaix that access should be granted for the 1995 season. In fact, Morlaix was Irish Ferries' second-best choice, having originally applied to the port of Brest in Brittany. This fell through when the authorization for

---

[86]   Less clear-cut appears 'refusal to interline' (Lufthansa/Air Europe (1990), regarding interline facilities on the London-Munich and London-Düsseldorf routes, and Aer Lingus/British Midlands (1992)). Interlining has been seen by the Commission as a way to facilitate entry on some routes, on the principle that 'sufficient interlining should exist to allow a newcomer to compete on equal terms' (Lufthansa/Air Europe). The Irish carrier Aer Lingus, which is the dominant firm on the London-Dublin route, terminated its interline relationship with British Midland (BM), after the latter announced the start of its own service on that route in 1989. BM's claim was that the withdrawal of interline facilities made its flights less attractive to travellers, especially the business ones, and to travel agents. The Commission decided that the incumbent's behaviour amounted to refusal to supply and Aer Lingus was ordered to resume its interline relationship. However, the Commission also stated that new entrants should not be able to rely indefinitely on frequencies and services provided by their competitors, but must be encouraged to develop their own frequencies and services. Accordingly, the duration of Aer Lingus' duty to interline was limited to two years.

the construction of a new jetty at Brest was turned down by the French authorities, at which point Irish Ferries turned to the port of Roscoff.[87]

Claims by the parties of capacity constraints must also be evaluated carefully. The incumbent may argue that access cannot be granted because the capacity of the asset is already fully used. What must be considered in these cases is the opportunity cost of creating new facilities, including the cost which would have to be incurred to increase capacity (in particular, in the case of a port, whether it would be easier for the incumbent to build new mooring facilities etc.). Where capacity is effectively limited, a regulatory approach may be appropriate.

Refusal to supply and intellectual property rights

In contrast to the cases discussed above, it is not desirable to apply 'refusal to supply' arguments (and the 'essential facilities doctrine') in the case of intellectual property rights. This possibility has received much attention after the Magill case[88] (see also below Section 8.6). In particular, the Magill decision has adopted the position that IPRs – which by definition confer dominance in one market – may be used strategically to foreclose rivals' entry in a different but related market (notion of 'leveraging' power from a market where the firm is dominant to another). [89]

Given the special role which is played by IPRs, this approach does not seem appropriate. The very function of IPRs is to confer exclusivity to the holder, in order to provide sufficient incentives for innovation. IPRs therefore confer by design an absolute advantage to the holder. While IPRs can be used strategically (for example where firms take out sleeping patents), it is

---

[87]   Up to that point, the only operator at Roscoff was Brittany Ferries. After a preliminary agreement with Irish Ferries for the 1995 summer season, Morlaix argued that it would not make the required investment without assurances that Irish Ferries would use Roscoff also in 1996 – rather than move to Brest. It appears that a contract existed between Brittany Ferries and Morlaix, whereby the latter was guaranteed certain revenues for a number of years – thus justifying its development of the Roscoff port – in return for priority in use of the port (it also appears that Morlaix was a shareholder in Brittany Ferries).

[88]   In 1986 the BBC, ITV and the Irish broadcaster RTE held copyrights in their respective TV listings, and provided weekly TV listings magazines each of which featured solely their own programmes (that is, each channel published a guide covering exclusively its own programmes and claimed copyright protection for its weekly programme listings). As no comprehensive weekly guide existed on the Irish market, the small Irish publisher Magill saw an opportunity; however it was unable to meet this demand because the copyright holders refused to grant it licences to use their listings. Magill challenged the right of the copyright holders to behave in this way under Art. 86. The Commission's position, which was later upheld both by the CFI and finally (April 1995) by the Court of Justice, was that the three broadcasters held legal and factual monopolies of the 'basic information' produced as a result of their broadcasting activities, which was required to produce a derivative product (television guides). The court confirmed that the abusive conduct was the reliance on copyright covered by national law to prevent Magill from publishing. The broadcasters had abused their dominant positions in order to give themselves an unfair advantage in the derivative market - thereby preventing the emergence of a new, competing product (the comprehensive guide). The Commission ordered the broadcasters to supply third parties with advance weekly programme listings on a non-discriminatory basis. This decision (subsequently confirmed by the courts) raised concerns that, under certain circumstances, IPR owners may be effectively required to grant compulsory licences.

[89]   The Commission in fact sees a clear difference between the Magill case and the protection which IPRs must confer to their owner on the specific market to which they refer. The use of competition policy to attack dominant positions conferred by IPRs in the market to which they refer is not deemed acceptable, as stated for example in the recent vaccine case Lederle-Praxis Biological (1994): 'at the current stage of EU competition law, it is highly doubtful whether one could impose an obligation upon a dominant firm (...) as a remedy to ensure the maintenance of effective competition (...) to share its IPRs with third parties, to allow them to develop, produce and market the same products which the dominant firm is seeking to develop, produce and market ...' (*XXIVth Report on Competition Policy 1994*, p. 410).

not desirable that their incentive function should be undermined by claims that they confer a dominant position in one market which can be leveraged into separate markets.

A more appropriate approach is the careful definition of the scope of a patent (length, breadth and field of use, see for example Klemperer [1990]). Indeed an issue which is put into sharp relief by the Magill case is that the problem in many cases is the scope of copyright and patent protection. In Magill, the TV networks had been able to copyright their TV schedule: while it is appropriate that the single programmes which are part of the schedule are covered by copyright (to reward the creative effort involved), there is no such rationale for TV schedules (which simply 'fall out' of the decisions on the day's programming) – and essentially for obtaining a copyright twice.

In principle there is of course an interaction between patent law and competition law, as the two are to some extent jointly determined. However, one must be careful that application of competition law in this delicate area does not lead to a reduction of the benefits conferred by patent law. Competition law should respects the limits of a patent, though patent rights should only be conferred where there is a creative or innovative effort to be rewarded and protected.

8.3.2. Access pricing

'Refusal to supply' is a special case of setting access terms. Even if there is a legal requirement that access be granted to competitors, incumbents may reproduce the effect of refusal to supply through very high access prices. Again an important test should be whether the new entrant could enter at minimum efficient scale, i.e. whether the investment which would have to be incurred to replicate a complementary input would exceed the value of the new entrant's sales.

The issue of access pricing and foreclosure has acquired great practical relevance following the gradual deregulation and liberalization of network-bound industries which used to be legal monopolies (gas, telecoms, electricity, water), where there are elements of natural monopoly (e.g. the local loop in telephony) and therefore reproduction of the input by the new entrant may not be feasible or desirable.[90] Access pricing is also the focus of much recent economic literature on regulation, in particular on how access charges should be optimally set while letting the former monopoly compete.[91]

A full review of progress in the liberalization process is outside the scope of this study. The question which we will address is the economic and policy question of whether access pricing issues – which have been traditionally dealt with by regulators – should be tackled in future by the competition authorities, as former statutory monopolies are being gradually opened up and competition develops. It is important to emphasize that competition and regulation have very distinct characteristics: regulation involves the ongoing monitoring of firms' activities, the collection of information about costs, for the purpose of setting prices. Competition policy is

---

[90]   An alternative approach, followed in the US, is to prevent the owner of the network to supply the final market. For example, 'the local network monopolies in the telephone industry have been prevented from entering the value added markets, as well as the long-distance markets, because of the DoJ's belief that [given the asymmetries of information involved] it is impossible to define access to the network which creates fair competition in these markets' (Laffont and Tirole [1994]).

[91]   See, among others, Armstrong and Vickers [1993, 1995], Armstrong and Doyle [1994], Baumol and Sidak [1994, 1995], Laffont and Tirole [1994].

instead a specific, selective intervention often on the basis of a complaint, and it is not aimed at directly setting prices. Because of their monitoring role, regulators have much more information on market and cost conditions than a competition authority (though as competition develops in these industries, specific complaints will tend to be brought by informed players, and the competition authorities may thus be able to rely on more detailed information).

This does not mean that it is not possible – in principle – to design a competition policy approach which includes price controls, effectively based on a regulatory-type intervention. However, any competition policy which relies on setting prices becomes effectively a form of price-cap regulation. The setting of prices presupposes a regulatory context. Thus in spite of the drawbacks of a regulatory approach (permanent monitoring is costly, and the effectiveness of regulation may be undermined by regulatory capture), a switch to a policy instrument which is less finely tuned to specific industry conditions is undesirable. This issue will be discussed further below in Section 8.7, and in our policy conclusions (Chapter 13).

8.3.3. Foreclosure through vertical restraints

The traditional concerns of competition policy in relation to vertical restraints are that in an oligopolistic setting (multiple manufacturers in competition with each other) such restraints may lead to distortions of interbrand competition, facilitating horizontal collusion; and that they may affect the ease of entry in a market (foreclosure effect). The treatment of vertical restraints in antitrust has been widely debated since the 'Chicago school' (especially Bork [1978] and Posner [1981]) took the non-interventionist position that they should be *per se* legal. The view that vertical restraints are harmless, as long as they do not have exclusionary effects, has since made its way also into the policy approach (see Section 8.6 below), and is being advocated today by most practitioners and commentators.

Over the past 15 years, a large body of economic analysis has challenged the traditional view of vertical restraints as restrictions of competition. This body of research has emphasized first of all the efficiency-enhancing role of vertical restraints in correcting externalities and distortions in the retailer's decisions on downstream pricing and provision of effort, as well as contractual opportunism.[92] Though some of this work is based on restrictive assumptions (it often takes the form of a simple principal/agent analysis of the manufacturer/retailer relationship, with a monopolist manufacturer and a competitive retail sector), it has made the important contribution of identifying rather compelling efficiency reasons for vertical restraints.[93] While some models have yielded ambiguous results, there are many cases where the private and social effects of vertical restraints have been found to go in the same direction;

---

[92]   See, among others, Mathewson and Winter [1984, 1985, 1987], Rey and Tirole [1986], and Waterson [1987]. They have shown how the externalities in the manufacturer-retailer relationship can be internalized by various combinations of quantity-dependent pricing (including franchise fees), quantity forcing, retail price maintenance, and territorial exclusivity. These may achieve the same result as full vertical merger.

[93]   Vertical restraints may correct free-rider effects also between manufacturers. The classic example is the case of sophisticated technical training provided by the manufacturer to the retailer (i.e. pre-sales services), which may work to the benefit of other manufacturers if the retailer also carries rival brands. This free-riding effect may lead to suboptimal investment by the manufacturer in dealers (and investments that create customer-drawing power). Exclusive dealing may correct this, as emphasized particularly by Marvel [1982], Steuer [1983] and Ornstein [1989]. However, exclusive dealing also corrects the 'competition externality', i.e. the tendency for firms to set lower prices because they are concerned not to confer a benefit to rival brands. Thus exclusive dealing should also lead to higher prices, and while this is privately optimal for the manufacturer, the welfare implications are ambiguous.

that is, vertical restraints may not only be privately optimal, but also increase total welfare. For example, if there is excess entry at the downstream stage, vertical mergers or restraints which reduce variety (as well as eliminate double marginalization) may be Pareto-improving under rather general assumptions on preferences (see Kühn and Vives [1994]).

Other reasons for a cautious policy approach to vertical restraints include the fact that attempts made to model their exclusionary effects have not produced very robust results. This is because for the exclusionary effect to operate, there are two essential features which a model must incorporate: the incumbent's incentive to deny access, and a complementary input which is non-replicable by the new entrant. Building a model which satisfactorily incorporates these two conditions is not trivial.[94]

Overall, the contribution of the economic literature on vertical restraints has been to establish that there should be no competition policy intervention, except where they are used strategically by the incumbent to foreclose the market to a new entrant, essentially by reducing rival manufacturers' access to downstream distributors.

The foreclosure argument here is analogous to the case of access restrictions examined above (under 'refusal to supply' and 'access pricing'). A long-term exclusivity arrangement which prevents retailers from dealing with another supplier may mean that such a supplier is denied access to the downstream market (if there are constraints on the supply of retail outlets). Indeed, models of exclusive dealing tend to obtain the foreclosure effects only when assuming that the retailing sector is not perfectly competitive, i.e. there are economies of scale in retailing:[95] this implies that there is a constraint on the availability of a complementary input (downstream distribution), and that to replicate such an input (i.e. establish an independent network) may be infeasible. The analogy with the case of access to network or essential facilities is clear.

Alternatively, if the incumbent ties up all high-quality retailers (or retail locations), these arrangements may force rivals to use less efficient marketing channels. Exclusivity agreements may thus affect rivals' entry on two levels: firstly, there may be an outright exclusionary effect if they effectively mean that access to the downstream market is denied; secondly, purchasing exclusive rights to particular retailers is a variation of the 'raising rivals' costs' strategy (Salop and Scheffman [1986]). Also the entry cost of a new rival could be increased if distribution were to involve significant economies of scope (in which case setting up a parallel distribution network may be wasteful).

---

[94]   For example, Comanor and Frech [1985] and Mathewson and Winter [1987] showed that exclusive dealing can indeed have foreclosing effects, provided that the retailing sector is not perfectly competitive, and there is some asymmetry between incumbent and entrant, e.g. in consumer preferences or production costs. That is, in both of these model complete foreclosure is possible as a result of entry barriers in retailing which protect incumbent retailers from competition, and an asymmetry between manufacturers. In the absence of either an asymmetry between manufacturers, or retailing barriers, attempts to foreclose entry completely may not be profitable.

[95]   For example, Comanor and Frech [1985] and Mathewson and Winter [1987]. Dobson and Waterson [1994a, 1994b] and Besanko and Perry [1994] also show that with differentiated retailers and differentiated producers, exclusive dealing allows manufacturers to set higher margins due to the absence of in-store interbrand competition, and the fixed costs of retailing which limit the number of retailers of each brand which can be supported in the market. Social welfare is reduced.

Therefore – as in the case of refusal to supply – the crucial question for the competition authorities in assessing vertical restraints such as exclusive dealing is whether these arrangements effectively prevent entry at minimum efficient scale. If not, they cannot be considered exclusionary. In practice, this means that the potential for exclusive dealing to foreclose a market will depend on the proportion of the retail sector which is thus tied up and inaccessible, and the residual opportunities for competing manufacturers to find an outlet for their goods.

We consider below the issue of vertical restraints and foreclosure in the case of ice cream.

8.3.4. The case of ice cream

The use of exclusivity agreements between dominant local producers and retailers in the market for 'impulse' (single-wrapped) ice cream has been the focus of major competition investigations (at both the Commission and national levels), on grounds that such agreements foreclosed retail outlets to new entrants.

In 1992, the US manufacturer Mars complained to the Commission that it was being excluded from the Irish and German markets as a result of the exclusivity agreements put in place by the local ice cream manufacturers (HB Icecream in Ireland, a Unilever subsidiary; Langnese-Iglo GmbH – also a subsidiary of Unilever – and Schöller Lebensmittel GmbH in Germany). HB has been dominant in the Irish ice cream market since the late 1960s, and in 1989 it estimated its share of the Irish market to be 78% (in volume terms). Langnese-Iglo is the dominant brand of ice cream in Germany, accounting in 1991 for almost 50% of all the ice cream sold in Germany through the grocery trade (where about 35% of all impulse ice cream sales are made); Schöller was the only other producer to occupy a dominant position in the market, with approximately a 20% share of the grocery trade. Mars claimed that the exclusive dealing arrangements resulted in partial or total foreclosure of the Irish and German markets to new competition.

Single-wrapped ice cream is mostly sold through relatively small retail outlets, and some larger food stores. The product market is highly differentiated, with firms competing over price, quality and product range. There are no significant entry barriers in production (local dairies find it fairly easy to enter into production on a small scale). There are significant barriers in marketing and distribution, as brand name and product recognition (and therefore advertising and promotion) are very important in this market. But a company like Mars, with a 'transferable' brand name, was in a more favourable position than any *de novo* entrant.

According to Mars, the most important barrier to entry in this market was the availability of retail space (freezer space) in small outlets. Mars claimed its ability to penetrate the market for impulse ice cream was being harmed by HB's practice (as Schöller and Langnese in Germany) of providing freezers on loan (i.e. 'free') to a large proportion of retailers (71% in Ireland), which were to be used to stock and sell exclusively HB ice cream. Mars identified the entry options facing any new entrant as:

(a)   renting existing freezer space in retail outlets;
(b)   supplying freezers to retailers in addition to the freezers they already had;
(c)   encouraging retailers to swap their HB freezers for the entrant's freezers;
(d)   creating new retail outlets.

Of these options, (a) was not feasible for the large proportion of retailers to whom freezers were supplied by the incumbent with exclusivity restrictions (80% of outlets in Ireland); (b) was limited by retailers' ability and willingness to take an additional ice cream freezer (according to a survey presented by Mars, 65% of retailers with an exclusive freezer agreement said they did not have space available to take another manufacturer's freezer – though this survey-based evidence was contested by HB); (c) was considered by Mars to involve significant transaction costs and costs of financial inducements, especially for new, untested product ranges; and (d) was argued to involve very high sunk costs of entry.

Mars' conclusion was that in a situation where retail space was scarce, exclusivity arrangements amounted to foreclosure of entry. As a result of these arrangements, 61% of retail outlets in Ireland (53% of the market) were entirely foreclosed to new entrants, because an entrant would have to displace the incumbent's freezer to get retail space; and 19% (26% of the market) were 'partially foreclosed' in that, while they had exclusive freezer agreements, they might take an additional freezer. Only 20% of outlets had retailer-owned freezers, or manufacturer-owned freezers which were not exclusive, and therefore available for small-scale ('niche') entry. To gain access to the other 80% of outlets, a new entrant would have to invest in freezers, as well as inducements to retailers, which would necessitate entry on a large scale, and with an entire product range, and mean large fixed (largely sunk) costs. That is, where retailers already had space allocated to ice cream, and total retail space was scarce, they will either be unwilling to take another freezer, or require substantial financial inducements (i.e. very high margins) in order to do so. Mars concluded that either the entrant will need to be much more efficient than the incumbent (i.e. sell more attractive products at very competitive prices), or will need to expend substantial resources to induce retailers to take the product. Thus the dominant firm's strategy of vertical exclusivity arrangements in exchange for the free freezer frustrated entry by new brands, because it increased the cost of entry to the point of excluding it altogether.

In fact, Mars' arguments must also be evaluated carefully. In this case, the duration of the exclusive contracts is an essential factor, and where exclusivity is only established for a limited period, the foreclosure effects will be less severe. In addition, the argument that offering a replacement freezer involves costs of financial inducement, especially for new untested product ranges, is not convincing. It may only hold if the new freezer also comes with an exclusivity clause. Without exclusivity restrictions, there is no need for the supplier to give financial inducements (in a market with competing brands, the retailer will select the 'strongest' products). Most importantly, it should be considered that if it would be worthwhile for Mars to offer an additional exclusive freezer, then it should be even more profitable to provide a non-exclusive replacement freezer (and extract the retailers' profit through a rental fee). Therefore claims by Mars that freezer exclusivity by the incumbent did not leave any viable alternative for entry (i.e. that there was no way of entering at minimum efficient scale) required cautious assessment.

Eventually the Commission accepted the legality of freezer exclusivity, in exchange for some undertakings from HB (essentially selling off some 1,750 'front-of-shop' freezers – 10% of HB's stock – in 1995–96, and introducing an optional 'hire purchase' scheme for freezers being supplied, though exclusivity is retained for at least five years). In the German cases (Langnese-Iglo and Schöller-Lebensmittel), the Commission also ultimately found in favour of

Mars, because the dominant firms were not able to provide convincing efficiency justification for their conduct.[96]

Exclusion effects of tying

Tying is a specific type of vertical restraint between the manufacturer and the final user. It describes the case where the manufacturer makes the sale (or price) of a particular product (the 'tied' product) conditional on the customer also purchasing another – often complementary – product (the 'tying' product). The concern is that this type of practice may be used by the firm to modify the structure of the market for the tied product. In particular, where the firm has power in one product market, tying the sale of this product to another one in which it has no power may produce an exclusionary effect. Rivals may not be viable in that market, which can thus be monopolized, and market power is 'leveraged' across markets.

The feasibility of 'leverage' has been contentious since the Chicago school challenged the traditional opposition of the competition authorities to tying, and argued that such a strategy is not profitable for the firm. As there is only one monopoly profit to be earned in a chain of supply, it cannot be rational nor possible to 'leverage' power from one market into another.[97] More recently, it has been shown that tying can have an exclusionary effect, provided that there are scale economies in the tied good. In this case, tying can reduce the sales of rival producers of the tied good below the point at which it is viable for them to remain in the market. Exit will occur, and the market can be monopolized (Whinston [1990]).[98]

Overall, the implications of a tying strategy for market structure are quite sensitive to the degree of complementarity between the tying and the tied product, and the distribution of consumers' preferences for the tied good (and therefore their valuation). Whinston [1990] showed that the firm has no incentive to exclude rivals through tying in the case of complementary products which are used in 'fixed proportions' (i.e. when the products are essentially 'components parts' of a 'system'). In this case tying is not profitable: the firm actually makes greater profits when there is a rival supplier of one component in the market, because greater sales of the component supplied competitively increase sales of the component which is monopolized.

---

[96] As a result, the benefits of the exclusive purchasing block exemption were withdrawn from certain Langnese agreements, and Schöller was denied individual exemption; in addition, the market leaders were prohibited from entering into exclusive purchasing agreements altogether in Germany for five years after the decision. This last point was overturned in 1995 by the Court of First Instance (CFI), which argued that in prohibiting these companies from concluding exclusive purchasing agreements in future, the Commission exceeded its powers. Such agreements can still be signed, either under the term of the block exemption (provided they do not make access by other suppliers to the various sales outlets difficult to a significant extent), or if they meet the terms for an individual exemption.

[97] Consumers' purchases depend only on the sum of the prices of tying and tied product, and the 'bundle' will be purchased only if its overall price does not exceed the consumer's valuation of the monopolized product, plus the price of the other product. Hence the firm cannot earn more than the monopoly profit it would get if it sold the first product independently.

[98] Whinston also finds the overall effects for consumers and for aggregate efficiency to be ambiguous. There is a loss for consumers if tied market rivals exit, because prices may rise and the level of variety in the market necessarily falls; in some cases there may be a uniform increase in all prices, making consumers uniformly worse off; but more generally – as in models of price discrimination – some consumers may be made better off by the introduction of tying. The effect on aggregate welfare is uncertain because of both this ambiguous 'price discrimination' effect, and the inefficiencies of entry in the presence of scale economies.

The best-known case in Europe in recent years is the Hilti (1987) case, where the firm's tying practices were condemned as exclusionary and anti-competitive. Hilti is the dominant European producer of power-activated nail guns for the construction industry. Hilti tied the supply of nails and cartridge strips for the gun, by only selling its cartridge strips (where it was dominant) together with the corresponding number of nails (which could have been supplied competitively). Two small producers of compatible nails (Eurofix and Bauco) complained that this had exclusionary effects for potential suppliers of nails, and the Commission upheld the small rivals' claim that this practice was abusive – leveraging market power from cartridges to nails.

Given that cartridge strips and nails can only be used together in fixed proportions, it is not clear, however, that the decision was justified. If Hilti had market power in cartridges, it could have set the cartridge price at the monopoly level regardless of the tie; then sales of rivals' nails at the competitive price would have only increased sales of cartridges (at the monopoly price), and Hilti would have thus benefited from the presence of rivals. (The question is rather why rival nail producers were not able to find an alternative supplier of cartridges, which together with their nails could have provided a nail/cartridge 'bundle' in competition with Hilti's own. The evidence suggests that Hilti had been able to prevent this by tying with long-term exclusive contracts the only other three producers of cartridges in Europe.)

Tying and aftermarkets

An interesting variety of the tying problem arises with aftermarkets, i.e. markets for complementary products which are bought subsequently to an original durable good purchase.

Empirical observation shows that suppliers of a durable good often face little competition in the supply of subsequent complementary products. However, the fact that manufacturers of primary products have large market shares in related aftermarkets should not lead to the conclusion that aggressive competition intervention is warranted. The general principle remains that the manufacturer's ability to raise prices in the tied product will be constrained by the consumer's possibility of purchasing an alternative tying product from another manufacturer (i.e. on the effective degree of market power in the tying product). Thus what matters is competition in the primary *ex ante* market for the supply of the durable good, and consumers will choose between competing goods by taking account of the likely costs of the product over its entire operating life.[99]

What makes the analysis of aftermarkets different from that of a firm jointly producing a number of complementary products is the issue of timing and imperfect information: it can be argued that consumers lack the necessary information to perform the lifetime-cost calculation, and thus the producer might be able to raise prices in its aftermarkets (i.e. engage in 'installed-

---

[99]   Consider the example of two photocopier manufacturers who compete with each other in the supply of photocopiers, but who each have a monopoly on the maintenance of installed machines they have manufactured. Here consumers should look at the likely lifetime costs of the two producers' machines, taking account of maintenance costs, and purchase the machine with the smaller lifetime costs. Even if a manufacturer raises the price of maintenance services, it can only do this at the expense of lowering the initial purchase price of the photocopier.

base opportunism' for example by increasing maintenance charges) without necessarily a significant effect on new demand in its primary market.[100]

However, the theoretical possibility of such behaviour must be distinguished from it being plausible in practice. Whether a strategy of installed-base opportunism will be in the private interests of a manufacturer will depend on whether the benefit to be gained from exploiting the current installed base exceeds the resultant loss of future demand for the primary good. Shapiro [1995] has shown that even if consumers are not rational and forward-looking (which makes them potentially liable to installed-base exploitation), it is still possible that they may be protected by primary market competition. If competition in the primary market is vigorous, then any profits that manufacturers expect to make through high prices in their aftermarkets will be competed away in the primary market, with prices in this market being set below costs. Thus, if there is vigorous competition in the primary market, then the potential for installed-base opportunism due to consumers' inability correctly to forecast aftermarket prices should not be of concern to competition authorities.

In addition, even if we take objections to the lifetime cost argument seriously, this does not necessarily lead us to the conclusion that aftermarkets need tough antitrust intervention if consumers are to be protected. Rather, this may be an argument in favour of encouraging firms to offer contracts which bundle the purchase of a durable good with aftermarket services for a single price. Informational problems are thereby avoided, since there is an explicit contract giving the terms on which aftermarket services will be available. Under such conditions, manufacturers of the primary good should engage in competition in the contracts which they offer. Provided the *ex ante* market is competitive, interbrand competition in the primary market should be sufficient to protect consumers and we need not worry about aftermarket power.[101]

To summarize.

(a)   If primary market competition is strong, and firms offer contracts bundling the purchase of a good with aftermarket services for a single price, then the fact that a manufacturer has a high share of its own aftermarket should not worry the competition authorities (provided that contracts for aftermarket services are sufficiently transparent): this much reduces the need to worry about aftermarket power whether or not consumers are rational and forward-looking.

(b)   If there is market power in the primary market it is no longer obvious that profits earned in aftermarkets will be dissipated by primary-market competition. That is, prices in primary markets will not be low enough to compensate consumers fully for higher aftermarket prices. In this case direct competition action against the primary market

---

[100]   This is the reason why this 'lifetime costs' argument was rejected by US Supreme Court in the Kodak (1994) case. The Court argued that consumers were in fact not able to calculate lifetime cost with any accuracy, either because necessary information was not available to them or because of 'bounded rationality'. In particular, forecasting future costs requires consumers to anticipate when, if at all, manufacturers might exploit an installed base by raising maintenance costs.

[101]   What is more, intervention may not even be necessary to encourage firms to offer such contracts. If consumers face large informational problems in calculating lifetime costs, firms will have strong incentives to offer contracts which fix the terms of future aftermarket services in advance, and so remove this informational burden on consumers. For example, laser printers are often advertised stating the low price of the toner cartridges.

power tends to be most desirable, but there may be a limit to how much primary market concentration can be reduced.

The recent Commission decision on the Pelikan-Kyocera case suggests a contrast between the current US position (as established by the Kodak case), which appears to be dismissing the possibility that primary market competition is sufficient to protect consumers from abuse in aftermarkets, and the EU position, which appears rather more economically justified. In 1995, Pelikan, a German manufacturer of toner cartridges for printers and photocopiers, made a complaint against Kyocera, a Japanese manufacturer of computer printers. Pelikan alleged that Kyocera had engaged in various practices intended to drive it out of the toner cartridge market. The Commission found that Kyocera was subject to intense competition in the primary market for laser printers, and that this restrained its behaviour in the secondary market. The costs of switching to a different printer if the cost of consumables rose too much was felt to be low, and consumers were thought to be well informed.

8.4. Foreclosure through exclusionary pricing

In principle, incumbent firms in a (geographical) market may seek to prevent new entry (both *de novo* and cross-border) through conduct which is meant to signal unequivocally that entry would be met with aggressive retaliation, or that its advantage is such (e.g. level of costs) that the rival would not be able to compete effectively, were it to enter. The main focus for these types of signalling strategies is the incumbent's direct pricing behaviour in the market. The important economic issue is when and under what circumstances these strategies may be deemed credible.

From the perspective of the single market programme, to the extent that this removed some artificial barriers to cross-border entry, the incentive for incumbent firms to engage in these types of predatory strategies to protect themselves from foreign entry will have increased. Unlike investment in capacity, R&D or advertising, which may provide the incumbent with a credible advantage but require time, pricing is a strategic weapon which lends itself to use as a rapid response. At the same time, there are reasons why market integration might in fact undermine the efficacy of some of these strategies, for example if the new entrant is an incumbent in another market and would have the resources to sustain retaliation, or if the information asymmetries which support certain types of signalling are reduced.

8.4.1. Predatory pricing

Predatory pricing by the incumbent in a market essentially describes the response of the incumbent to actual entry, in order to induce exit *ex post*. Here the incumbent incurs a short-run cost in order to achieve a longer-term gain – the exit of a rival which allows prices to be raised again.

Various doubts have been expressed as to whether this strategy is a rational and credible course of action, as it is costly to the incumbent as well as to rivals and may not be sustainable for long (even more so if the incumbent is larger than the entrant and cannot cut prices selectively where it is challenged).

Two main categories of arguments have been developed to justify predation as a rational and credible strategy. The first is some variant of the 'long purse' (or 'deep pocket') story, whereby an incumbent with substantial funds can outlast rivals in any price war that induces losses. The other has to do with asymmetric information – the signal jamming and reputation effects, which are in fact closer to limit pricing because they will deter new entry before it occurs.[102]

The 'long purse' story (originally due to Telser [1966], and later formalized particularly by Bolton and Scharfstein [1990]) emphasizes imperfections in capital markets and therefore in firms' financial constraints. This story depends crucially on financial market imperfections. Predation may lead to a tightening of the financial constraint for liquidity-constrained firms, while it is difficult for a bank to assess the prospects of the firm; in this context the long purse story makes sense.

In the context of integration, the 'long purse' story is likely to be empirically more relevant, as it describes how firms with greater financial resources might be successful in expelling from the market rivals with greater financial constraints (indeed there is empirical evidence on the negative relationship between effective cost of capital and the size of a firm). This means that entry may not occur in national markets dominated by a strong established incumbent with substantial resources. In an integrating market, this may also provide an additional incentive to merge, if the parties feel that merging will strengthen their financial resources – thereby allowing them to deter entry successfully.[103]

The main problem with predation from the point of view of the competition authorities is detection. If entrants could be sure that predatory behaviour could be detected and punished, then such strategy would not be used. However, the detection problems are very serious, and there is no single satisfactory test or technique to prove that a firm is predating.

The traditional approaches all consider evidence derived from the pattern of pricing over time. The best-known test is the Areeda-Turner rule, whereby prices which are below marginal costs – as proxied by average costs – are deemed to be predatory. In fact, there are situations in which pricing below marginal cost is legitimate, and therefore this test may not be considered safe. Baumol [1979] suggested considering in addition whether firms return to higher prices after a period of aggressive pricing. The approach which is most likely to be helpful is a composite criterion as suggested by Baumol et al., which includes:

(a)   an analysis of market structure (predation is more likely in a market where firm sizes are very asymmetric, e.g. there is one large firms and a few fringe players), and evaluation of the financial strength of the firm (to see how sustainable predation is);

(b)   considering the pattern of prices over time.

Overall, the record on successfully proving predatory behaviour in the courts has been poor: few cases have been brought, and even less have led to a decision that predation was occurring.

---

[102]   The 'signal jamming' story (Fudenberg and Tirole [1986] and Roberts [1986]) emphasizes inferences from prices. The 'reputation' story (Kreps and Wilson [1982], Milgrom and Roberts, [1982]) postulates that firms may obtain a reputation for predation – though it is not really observed empirically.

[103]   In view of these types of effects, in fact, in German competition law conglomerate mergers may be prevented if firms acquire too much financial power relative to competitors in some markets in which they are active. On the merits and problems of this approach, see Kühn [1994].

A crucial problem is the need to identify an appropriate measure of the firm's costs – to be compared with prices. This is always a contentious issue in predation cases, where there is a sort of 'indistinguishability problem' (the incumbent will always argue that its pricing conduct is in fact compatible with keen competition), and therefore much hinges on the level of costs. These types of difficulties are well exemplified by the case of AKZO (the largest European supplier of bleaching agents), which was investigated following a complaint that its conduct threatened to force out of business a smaller UK competitor, Engineering and Chemical Supplies Ltd (ECS).[104]

In 1982 ECS complained to the Commission that AKZO UK had systematically attempted to drive it from the market by offering 'unreasonably low prices' to its main customers. The Commission considered evidence largely based upon AKZO UK's internal management accounts, which showed that from 1981 to 1983 AKZO UK's flour additives business was being operated at a loss, and argued that some products were being offered 'below cost'. The Commission also rejected AKZO's argument that it needed to 'compete vigorously' in the UK flour additives market in order to recoup profits lost from being undercut by ECS on the chemical additives market. The Commission argued that as AKZO UK was selling flour additives at a loss, it could hardly be recouping lost profits.

The difficult issue of the case was the definition of 'pricing below costs'. AKZO argued that it always included a profit margin in its prices, which the Commission understood to mean a margin over average variable costs (AVC). The dispute centred on what should be included in variable costs. AKZO included only the costs of raw materials, energy, packaging and transport. The Commission noted that items such as labour, maintenance, warehousing and dispatching were being treated as 'fixed' costs, whereas they are usually treated as 'variable' in standard accounting systems. Under AKZO's definition, its prices were probably between AVC and ATC (average total costs). Under the Commission's definition, AKZO's prices on a number of items 'fell well short of covering variable costs'.[105]

---

[104]   Benzoyl peroxide is a bleaching agent used in the plastics industry, and the only one which may be used for flour in the UK and Ireland. AKZO UK (a wholly owned subsidiary of the Dutch group AKZO Chemie BV) was one of only three suppliers of benzoyl peroxide for flour in the UK, the others being ECS and Diaflex. In 1983 AKZO was dominant in the UK with a 52% market share, followed by ECS with 35%, and Diaflex with 13%. The AKZO group accounted for 50-55% of European sales of organic peroxides for the plastics industry.

Before 1977, ECS purchased benzoyl peroxide in bulk from AKZO and blended it for sale. In 1977, after a series of price rises from AKZO, ECS began to manufacture its own benzoyl peroxide, and by 1979 it was supplying one-third of the UK market for flour additives. In 1979, ECS began to produce benzoyl peroxide also in a form suitable for the plastics industry, which is a more lucrative sector. This was initially sold only in the UK, but later in the same year ECS made its first shipment to the continent, supplying BASF (one of AKZO's major customers) at 15-20% below AKZO's then price. ECS then claimed that in response to this, AKZO UK ended their previous 'swapping' arrangements ('assistory' or 'co-producer' deliveries between producers were the norm in this business); moreover it threatened to price flour additives (ECS's main market) below cost in the UK, and to direct its price cuts particularly at ECS customers, if ECS did not exit the plastics market. ECS obtained a court injunction on AKZO not to reduce its normal selling prices for benzoyl peroxide additives 'with the intention of eliminating ECS as competitors'. In fact, after 1980 there were various rounds of price cuts in the UK market for bleaching agents, with all three suppliers cutting their prices significantly. AKZO approached ECS's customers with very low prices, while attempting to keep its prices high for its traditional customers. Later, in response to price cuts from ECS, AKZO also substantially lowered its prices to them. By 1983 AKZO had won from ECS several of its key customers, and between 1980 and 1984, ECS's sales were halved in real terms.

[105]   The ECJ ruled on 3.7.1991 (case C-62/86) that no costs are fixed or variable *per se*. On the basis of AKZO's accounts, the court deemed that labour costs were fixed in this case and that AKZO's prices were therefore between AVC and

Predatory behaviour may also be adopted jointly by the members of a collusive organization, in order to eliminate competition from a new player. This has recently been the case with predatory behaviour by a marine shipping conference. Following complaints from the Danish Government and several shipowners, the Commission initiated proceedings in 1991 against 11 shipowners' committees, and 4 liner conferences (CEWAL, MEWAC, COWAC and UKWAL) for practices adopted in traffic between Europe and West-Central Africa. In particular the members of CEWAL (a grouping of several shipping companies to provide a regular service between North-West Europe and Zaire/Angola) were found to have engaged in a variety of practices to eliminate their chief competitor G&C (a common service between Belgian Cobelfret and Italian Grimaldi). Their predatory practices included in particular the 'fighting ship' method: if a competitor offered a cheaper rate than those set by CEWAL, the conference would hold a meeting to undercut him, and ensure that CEWAL members scheduled their sailings at or around the same time as those of the competitor in order to win over its customers. Charges equivalent to the losses incurred by the competitor would then be shared out among CEWAL members.[106]

8.4.2. Non-linear pricing

The incumbent in a market may seek to deter entry by offering to customers discounts which effectively amount to penalties for purchasing from a competitor. Discounts and rebates are essentially equivalent to making it more expensive for the customer to buy from a variety of sources, and in this sense there is an analogy with exclusivity requirements. In fact, it is important to distinguish between straight quantity discounting for a single purchase, and discounting which is based on aggregate purchases over time.

Quantity discounting for a single purchase is a price discrimination scheme which tends to be pro-competitive, in that it implies more competition for customers 'at the margin'. The case is different for discounts on aggregate purchases over time. These include various fidelity discounts and explicit loyalty rebate schemes to customers, such as the concession of special discounts on condition that the customer does not deal with the rival. An example is the distribution agreements concluded by Coke's Italian subsidiary (Coca-Cola) with a number of Italian firms, under which a fidelity rebate was granted to large distributors who did not sell cola-flavoured drinks other than Coca-Cola (Coca-Cola, 1987). Other schemes directly 'bribe' the customer for not dealing with rivals: for example British Gypsum (the UK subsidiary of British Plasterboard Industries, the dominant plasterboard producer in the EU) responded to import competition from Spain and France into the UK by offering regular lump payments (and priority treatment) to UK builders' merchants who agreed to procure all of their needs from it (British Plasterboard, 1988). In other cases the rebate may take the form of selective price discrimination: for example the system of 'top-slice' rebates put in place by Solvay and ICI (dominant soda ash producers on the Continent and the UK) was a two-tier pricing structure by which the tonnage the customer would have bought 'in any event' was charged at normal prices, while the remaining tonnage which the customer would have bought from the alternative supplier was charged at a substantial (and secret) discount. The special discount

---

ATC. Nevertheless, the prices were predatory because there was no evidence that they were necessary in order to match competitors' offers and there was evidence of an intention to drive ECS out of the market.

[106] A heavy fine was imposed primarily on CEWAL in 1992 for infringing Articles 85 and 86. This was the first decision against a liner conference, which benefits from a block exemption from EU competition rules under certain circumstances (Regulation (EEC) No 4056/86).

depended on customers buying most, if not all, of their requirements from Solvay. The system was implicitly a way of committing to match every discount offered by rivals.

Loyalty effects may be achieved in principle (though there is no case history as yet) through pricing schemes which raise customers' switching costs, i.e. the transaction or learning costs which are incurred in switching between different brands – thereby effectively reducing the elasticity of demand faced by the firm. Klemperer [1987] showed that in markets where consumers have switching costs, new entry may be deterred either by a large customer base or by large switching costs, which deny customers to an entrant.[107]

Discount and rebate schemes which are based on aggregate purchases over time may be effective in foreclosing entry, if they imply an effective 'penalty' for customers in dealing with other suppliers, and this makes alternative sourcing unattractive to them. The effect here is similar to exclusive distribution, as the discounts may effectively 'tie' customers to the incumbent, with the result that the rival may not be able to enter at minimum efficient scale.[108] The relevant question to be asked by the competition authorities in cases of complaints against an incumbent's discounts is therefore the same as in exclusive distribution: namely whether new entry at minimum efficient scale would feasible.

As we shall see in Section 8.6, this approach does not appear to be followed consistently by the Commission. The presumption seems to be that discounts are 'bad' whenever they are offered by dominant firms, but the effective scope for entry at minimum scale is not explored. In the Coca-Cola (1987) case, for example, the view was that as Coca-Cola held a dominant position on the Italian market for cola-flavoured soft drinks, and the effect of the rebates was to get distributors to sell only Coca-Cola, competing producers were prevented from having access to a substantial part of the Italian market for cola-flavoured soft drinks. However it is not clear to what extent rivals' entry at minimum scale was prevented.

In this perspective there appears also to be some asymmetry between the competition policy treatment of exclusive distribution, which benefits from an exemption under Article 85(3), and discounts by dominant firms, which are treated quite severely under Article 86. In fact, discounts may not be as 'bad' as exclusive dealing in foreclosing entry, because while exclusivity tends to be supported by long-term contracts, in the cases of discounts there is nearly always the possibility of 'opting out' (and the possibility that the new entrant could offer to supply the customer at a price which is lower than the incumbent's discounted price).

8.5. Institutional entry barriers and incumbents' behaviour

Cross-border entry into a market may be hampered – or slowed down – by various 'institutional' barriers: rules and regulations introduced by national governments (or local

---

[107] However Caminal and Matutes [1990] have shown that when there are endogenous switching costs, the effect depends crucially on the precise form of the discounting scheme.

[108] Coordination problems between customers may mean that the incumbent can foreclose entry even if the benefit of fidelity for the individual customer is small. Rasmusen et al. [1991] consider the case of a monopolist asking customers to sign agreements not to deal with potential competitors. Although the benefit of buying from one supplier is small, if each customer believes that the others will sign, each also believes that no rival seller will enter; hence an individual customer loses nothing by signing the exclusionary agreement, and will indeed sign. Thus if there are 100 customers and the minimum efficient scale requires serving 15, the monopoly need only lock up 86 customers to forestall entry ('naked exclusion').

authorities) which effectively increase an outsider's cost in supplying that market and put it at a permanent disadvantage relative to the incumbent(s). An example may be differences in technical standards across borders: while these may reflect differences in local preferences, the need to conform to different requirements also increases firms' costs of supplying foreign markets.[109] Lengthy and complex border procedures will add to the cost of shipping goods across national frontiers, and these barriers to trade will also tend to reduce a firm's ability to supply a market from another national market. Insofar as these factors imply that the incumbent enjoys an absolute cost advantage over the potential rival, which persists post-entry, they are absolute barriers to entry.

The single market programme set out to eliminate several categories of these (non-tariff) barriers which were found to restrict artificially cross-border trade and entry – by increasing either the variable cost of supplying a market or the set-up cost of direct entry (see Chapter 2). In parallel, the Commission has been supporting the slow process of liberalization and deregulation which has been initiated by national governments in some network industries (such as, for example, the utilities), in the deliberate effort to promote a competitive and integrated market in such sectors.

It is important to emphasize, however, that in some cases the institutional features of a market can be strategically exploited by the incumbent for the purpose of excluding rivals. In these cases, entry into the market is prevented by a combination of legal rules and restrictions, and the strategic behaviour of the incumbent(s). In these circumstances, the most appropriate policy response is often not a change in the regulation, but again a challenge to the behaviour of the incumbent(s) through competition policy. We consider some examples below.

8.5.1. Dominance through regulation

A possible example of regulations being used in this way is the case of the beer market in the UK. Licensing restrictions on opening a retail outlet (which imply that there is, supposedly, a 'fixed' stock of pubs), combined with exclusive purchasing agreements between brewers and pubs and typically the 'bundling' of finance and beer sales, have been claimed by new brewers to be a significant entry barrier. Indeed, European brewers have claimed that the tying system for British pubs has not allowed them entry into the UK market at minimum efficient scale, and has required them to adopt production licensing arrangements instead.

The strategic exploitation of local regulation for foreclosure purposes is well illustrated, for example, by the case of bottled mineral water in Germany. In 1990, an environmental rule was introduced in Germany promoting the use of recyclable glass bottles for mineral water. Multi-way glass bottles are manufactured by a monopoly, the GDB (Genossenschaft Deutscher Brunnen, German Cooperative for Spring Water). After the rule was introduced most supermarkets and wholesalers refused to accept bottles other than those manufactured by GDB. European mineral water producers complained to the Commission that access to GDB's standardized packaging pool was reserved for German mineral water producers. Supply to producers from the rest of the Community was refused – thereby raising their costs of entry into the German mineral water market. The Commission took the view that the combination of GDB's monopoly and the environmental legislation constituted an effective entry barrier from

---

[109]   Which is the reason why incumbent firms may in some cases play a part in erecting such barriers, e.g. lobbying the authorities for the introduction of national standards.

other Member States. This was deemed to be an abuse of dominant position, and the GDB had to grant all European producers access to its pool.

A very different outcome was obtained on a similar complaint to the Commission in 1987, i.e. before the introduction of the environmental legislation. The Chambre Syndicale des Eaux de Source ou Minérales (Belgium) also complained that the GDB refused to grant foreign mineral water producers access to its pool, compelling them to use only non-standard returnable or disposable bottles and thereby restricting their access to the German market. The Commission rejected the complaint on grounds that no evidence was provided of restricted access to the German market, and at the same time it was established that German distributors generally did not object to mineral water in containers different from those in use in the GDB. That is, up to the point when it was still feasible to sell water in Germany in containers other than the special glass bottles, there was no exclusionary effect, and no reason for the competition authorities to intervene. By restricting the available technology, the new regulation essentially conferred a dominant position on the GDB; and in the new circumstances, the behaviour of the GDB was in fact exclusionary and competition policy intervention appropriate.

8.5.2. Airport slots and traffic distribution rules

The airline industry offers a variety of examples of 'institutional' restrictions of entry. Traditionally, bilateral agreements between government agencies (and/or flag carriers) decided on capacity and number of carriers per route (the two flag carriers in most cases). Slot allocation was a secondary concern. Airport slots were generally allocated by governments (or an employee of the flag carrier) on the basis of 'the principle of self-regulation and consensus'. Another established principle of slot allocation was the concept of 'grandfather rights', whereby an airline which used a slot in one season was entitled to use the same slot in the same season the following year. Once slots had been allocated, trading was not possible.

Since the mid-1980s the industry has been the focus of a wide-ranging liberalization programme, aimed at increasing competition between carriers and at encouraging new entry on most routes. Given the severe physical capacity constraints at several European airports, which are likely to persist for some time, the system through which slots are allocated becomes crucially important.

As part of the liberalization programme, the issue of slots has been addressed by assigning *de facto* property rights over them to airlines. Regulation (EEC) No 95/93 ('on common rules for the allocation of slots at Community airports', July 1993) stipulates that 50% of slots which are unused are to be requisitioned and allocated to new entrants. However there are a number of issues which remain open. First of all, as full tradability of slots has not yet been established, the nature of the property rights recognized to the airlines remains unclear. Secondly, even if such property rights were fully transferable, it is not clear that a pure trading system would necessarily lead to an efficient allocation of slots.[110] Thus, attributing property rights to the current incumbent carriers may not be a solution, and allocating them for example to the airport may be more reasonable.

---

[110]   In the extreme, given that the monopoly profit exceeds the (joint) duopoly profit, a bid for monopoly would always be greater than a bid for duopoly – which suggests that in a fully tradable system, the incentive for the incumbent airline to bid for all the slots would be strong (unless, for example, the airline also operates all the airport catering services, in which cases it will want to maximize the throughput of passengers).

In any case, the bureaucratic procedures for allocation appear to be still strategically exploited by the incumbents to foreclose the entry of new carriers. Regulation (EEC) No 95/93 emphasized the legal obligation of Member States to play an active role in slot allocation, and to create institutional arrangements for such allocation, with legally binding rules. Member States are specifically required to appoint a coordinator whose task is to allocate slots, monitor slot usage and withdraw slots in the event of non-usage. But while the coordinator is required to carry out its duties in a 'neutral, non-discriminatory, and transparent way' (and an obligation is imposed on Member States to ensure that it acts according to these principles), in practice in most cases the coordinator is an employee of the domestic flag carrier.[111] A recent survey of the implementation of the regulation found that 'the rights of incumbent carriers are well established at most airports. [...] In contrast, it appears that the rights of new entrants are rather less well protected. [...] It appears possible for incumbents to pre-empt the access of new entrants to new capacity' (Coopers and Lybrand [1995, p. 63]).[112]

Another way in which flag carriers have sought to reduce their exposure to competition has been to lobby their national governments for the adoption of favourable traffic distribution rules (these are the rules according to which airlines are distributed between different airports located in a same 'catchment' area). Suppose that national flights only leave from one airport, and an airline is restricted to the other. Then the latter would not be able to obtain feeder traffic from the national market, which may make the potential rival unviable.

This has been well exemplified by the traffic distribution rules in the Paris area, where the French Government tried to protect its national carrier from intra-European competition by reserving Orly airport for it (and leaving the rest for Charles de Gaulle)[113]. Frustrated entry attempts by Viva Air, the Iberia subsidiary, by TAT, Lauda Air, KLM and Lufthansa led to a number of complaints. The Commission took formal action in the cases of Viva Air and TAT, as a result of which Orly is more accessible. A similar exclusionary effect of traffic distribution rules was contemplated in Italy in the Milan area, as the Italian administration planned to move other airlines to Malpensa, while leaving the flag carrier Alitalia at Linate. This would have hampered other airlines' ability to interline with Italian domestic traffic.

Finally, member governments have sometimes sought to favour carriers by granting them exclusive route concessions on domestic routes on grounds of public service obligations.[114] That is, a certain route would be reserved for a particular carrier on grounds that traffic on that

---

[111] And even if the coordinator were a civil servant, its independence would be put in doubt by the fact that – with the exception of British Airways, KLM and Luxair – all flag carriers are state-owned.

[112] The case of two small new entrants in Italy is a useful illustration of the incentives that flag carriers still have for exploiting their control of the coordinator to disadvantage the operation of new competitors (or induce their exit). In March 1996, the Italian coordinator – who is an employee of the flag carrier Alitalia – assigned the slots for the summer season of 1996. Two small companies that entered the domestic market in the second half of 1995 (by obtaining 'unused' slots from Alitalia) saw their slots reduced for the following summer season (Noman from 122 in the winter 1995/96 to 52, 12 of which were at 'impossible hours', against the 104 it had demanded; Air One from 168 to 126, against 172 demanded). The reason was the application of the 'grandfather rights' principle, which means that the coordinator took as a basis the summer season of 1995 (when they were not in the market). Alitalia, on the other hand, was assigned 43 slots more than it had the previous summer, plus 42 assigned to its subsidiary Eurofly. After the Italian competition authority threatened to intervene, the parties appear to have come to an agreement. However this episode reflected the residual powers of the flag carriers to influence slot allocation and thereby disadvantage new entrants.

[113] CAA, 1995, pp. 42 ff.

[114] While domestic routes (cabotage) will be liberalized only in 1997, consecutive cabotage rights were already permitted under the First Package (1987).

route was thin and would not support competing airlines, but at the same time there are public service obligations which require that the route is served.

Institutional factors often create the scope for anti-competitive behaviour on the part of the incumbent. This may be the case where institutional restrictions to entry are introduced by governments under pressure from the incumbents in their national markets; where the incumbents exploit rules and regulations to their advantage and to the detriment of competitors; and generally in all cases where exclusionary effects are due not to standards and regulations alone, but to a combination of these and the behaviour of the incumbent.

8.6.   EU competition treatment of barriers to entry

In the previous sections, we have argued that the elimination of artificial barriers to entry and the institutional liberalization of certain sectors will increase the scope for exclusionary behaviour by firms already in the market. We have then identified the forms of exclusionary behaviour which are most relevant in the context of integration. In this section, we consider how these classes of entry barriers are dealt with in European competition policy. We begin with some preliminary consideration on jurisdictional/procedural matters, and on the use of the concept of leverage.

8.6.1.   Jurisdiction and procedure

From a jurisdictional point of view, entry barriers erected by the dominant incumbent in a market are mostly caught under Article 86. As described in the previous chapter, this generally prohibits all abuses of a dominant position, and lists some specific instances of such abuse: setting 'unfair prices', 'limiting production, markets or technical development to the prejudice of consumers', price discriminating between 'equivalent transactions', and imposing unjustified onerous conditions in contracts. The list is clearly not exhaustive, and has been applied to a variety of practices which are not specifically mentioned.

The procedure requires first that the firm is found to be dominant (a process which relies on a preliminary market definition and has led at times to controversial outcomes). Once dominance has been established, abuse must be shown: holding a dominant position is obviously not an offence *per se*. This does not mean, however, that there is a burden on the Commission to prove that a dominant firm did in fact act with exclusionary intent. Rather, the Commission's inquiry is to be limited to the foreclosing effects of the practice in question.[115]

Article 86 should also cover abuses of a dominant position held by more than one firm (joint dominance), and may thus be used to attack entry barriers arising from the strategic conduct of the incumbent firms in the market. However, where barriers to entry result from agreements between firms (e.g. in the case of foreclosure through vertical agreements or joint ventures), then Article 85 applies. As certain practices can only have serious anti-competitive effects in a concentrated market, an important point is that the approach of Article 86 is generally

---

[115]   In the ECJ's decision on Hoffman-La Roche (1976), it is made explicit that an abuse is any practice hindering competition 'in a market where, as a result of the very presence of that undertaking competition is weakened'. There is also a view that firms which are dominant should be charged, by virtue of this fact, with a 'special responsibility' not to engage in practices which would be legitimate for non-dominant companies (for example the ECJ declared in 1983 that a firm in a dominant position has a 'special responsibility not to allow its conduct to impair undistorted competition on the Common market' – ruling on the Michelin case).

preferable: in conditioning competition intervention on dominance, it makes it contingent on market structure (though there are problems with the current definition of relevant market and dominance). Article 85, on the contrary, does not have such contingency provisions. Although the *de minimis* provision requires there to be significant effects for Article 85 to be applicable, in practice this excludes only a very small number of cases of firms with tiny market shares and so cannot be considered to be an effective market structure contingent rule.

8.6.2. The use of the 'leverage'

There is a rather long line of Court jurisprudence and Commission practice on foreclosure which relies on the notion of 'leveraging market power'. Abuses under Article 86 have often been found in markets where the firm is not dominant, but which are in some way related to markets where it is dominant. The condition is that there is some form of 'associative' link between those markets: for example these 'secondary' (or 'derivative') markets can be 'vertically linked' to a 'principal market' through the control of an essential input (e.g. Commercial Solvents, 1984; Telemarketing, 1985; London European/Sabena, 1987). Predatory pricing and loyalty rebates have also been identified as abusive practices by firms holding a dominant position in a related market (e.g. AKZO, 1991 and Tetra Pak II, 1994). In all these cases where the firm is accused of 'extending dominance into neighbouring markets', or 'abuse in associated markets', it is important to be clear what the 'association' is based on.

For example, in Tetra Pak II (1994 – Case C-333/94), the CFI upheld the Commission's earlier finding that Tetra Pak had abused its dominance in the market for aseptic packaging machines and cartons by operating a predatory pricing policy and other practices in another market (described as 'adjacent and indeed associated') in which it was not dominant – namely the market for non-aseptic packaging machines and cartons. In the view of the Court, 'the fact that Tetra Pak had nearly 90% of the markets in the aseptic sector meant that […] it was not only an inevitable supplier of aseptic systems but also a favoured supplier of non-aseptic systems'. As aseptic and non-aseptic packaging are not complements, and the customers are not the same, it is difficult to see a reason for this. The Court went on to say that '(m)oreover, by virtue of its technological lead and its quasi-monopoly in the aseptic sector, Tetra Pak was able to focus its competitive effort on the neighbouring non-aseptic markets, without fear of retaliation in the aseptic sector […]', and on this basis 'Tetra Pak's practices in the non-aseptic market [where Tetra Pak was not dominant] are liable to be caught by Art. 86 without being necessary to establish the existence of a dominant position in those markets taken in isolation, since (Tetra Pak's) leading position on the non-aseptic markets, combined with the close associative links between those markets and the aseptic markets, gave it freedom of conduct compared with other economic operators on the non-aseptic markets, such as to impose on it a special responsibility under Art. 86 to maintain a genuine undistorted competition in these markets' (para. 122).

This judgement appears hard to justify. More generally, this framework (and in particular the distinction between 'principal' market and 'secondary' market) does not appear to be particularly helpful. More helpful would be to use the notion of 'complementarity' of assets and inputs.

8.6.3. Access to complementary assets

Refusal to supply and the 'essential facilities doctrine'

Refusal to supply is dealt with under Article 86, as an instance of abusive behaviour on the part of a dominant firm. As explicitly stated in Polaroid/SSI (1983), 'as a general principle an objectively unjustifiable refusal to supply by an undertaking holding a dominant position on a market constitutes an infringement of Article 86'.

Since the late 1980s, the focus on the integration objective has meant the Commission has tackled an increasing number of cases in which 'refusal to supply' concerned access to an infrastructural input (such as a port, or an airline facility), which was claimed to be 'essential' for operating a particular service, and without access to which potential rivals were prevented from supplying the final market. Thus Article 86 has been used in a number of recent decisions to require the owner/operator of an infrastructural facility to grant access to competitors. These have been described as 'essential facility cases' to indicate that, without access to the facility, competitors could not provide services to customers.[116]

The nature of the abuse in these cases tends to be viewed by the Commission again in terms of 'leverage', i.e. as the use of monopoly in one market (the 'essential' complementary asset) to exclude competitors in a related market (the final market which can only be supplied if access is obtained to the complementary asset). For example, in London European/Sabena (1988), the Commission held that by refusing LE Airlines access to its CRS, Sabena had abused its dominant position 'in the market for computerized flight reservation systems' in Belgium. Sabena's CRS was deemed an essential facility in the Belgian market for any company to compete actively on this route.

The first important issue for the competition authorities is to establish the extent to which a particular access can be actually considered an 'essential facility'. Thus, in all cases, it is essential to evaluate carefully whether alternative entry can be achieved at minimum efficient scale (e.g. in the case of a port, whether there are alternative ports which could be used to run a ferry service);[117] and the cost (including the opportunity cost) of creating a new facility.

Having established that a facility is truly essential in the sense just described, it is appropriate that access should be ordered. However the doctrine is not very helpful when it comes to the conditions at which access should be granted. In 'Holyhead I' (1991), the Commission enunciated the principle that a company which both owns and uses an essential facility 'should not grant its competitors access on terms less favourable than those which it gives its own

---

[116] This has most often concerned airline and port facilities, though in 1995 the Commission also adopted a notice applying the essential facility principle to cross-border credit transfer systems (where a cross-border credit transfer system constitutes an 'essential facility', it must be open for further membership, provided that the candidates meet appropriate, objectively justified criteria).

[117] There are cases in which this is not very clear. For example, as seen in Section 7.3, in Morlaix (1995) the Commission applied the 'essential facility doctrine' to force access by Irish Ferries to the port of Roscoff for ferry services between Ireland and Brittany – though in fact there was a variety of other ports in Brittany to which Irish Ferries could have potentially turned (indeed Roscoff was a second choice for Irish ferries, after an application had been turned down by the port of Brest). The Commission found that Morlaix was dominant because it was 'the only port providing port facilities under acceptable conditions between Ireland and Brittany' (though the qualification 'under acceptable conditions' is unclear). The refusal of the port authority (Morlaix) to allow access to Irish Ferries, thereby preventing competition with the incumbent Brittany Ferries, was deemed an abuse of that dominant position. Morlaix was ordered to allow Irish Ferries 'reasonable, non-discriminatory access' to Roscoff for the 1995 season (pending final resolution).

services'. In 'Holyhead II', the principle was formally declared to apply also to new entrants.[118] It is important to emphasize that non-discriminatory access is not the issue here: an integrated company can charge a high access price both to its downstream subsidiary using the facility and to rivals, and then recoup its own losses through the access charges paid by the rivals. Thus when it comes to issues of access conditions (i.e. price), an obligation of 'fairness' to rivals will not be sufficient to exclude strategic behaviour by the incumbent.

In truth, setting the conditions of access is a regulatory rather than a competition issue, because (as seen in Section 8.3) it requires adequate cost data. Indeed the 'essential facilities doctrine' has been used to date only to require access, but not to deal with refusals of access based on excessive or discriminatory pricing. While it is possible that this may change as competition increases, and more comparative data gradually becomes available, it also highlights the difficulties of using competition law to define specific access conditions. As discussed below, this is particularly relevant in the case of network industries.

Access pricing

The process of deregulation and liberalization of the former statutory monopolies has raised the question of whether access pricing problems should be addressed in future by the EU competition authorities under Article 86, rather than by regulators. In this approach, the 'essential facilities doctrine' is viewed as a point of departure for the application of competition policy to industries where there is still dominance at least in an important segment of the market (due for example to bottlenecks on particular portions of the network infrastructure – e.g. the local loop in telephony).

The application of Article 86 in particular to network industries has been advocated on occasion, on the grounds that there is already a general obligation under this Article on dominant firms to deal 'fairly' with customers and competitors. In Holyhead I (1992) the Commission made this explicit by arguing firstly that 'a port, an airport or any other facility, even if it is not in itself a substantial part of the common market, may be considered as such insofar as reasonable access to the facility is indispensable for the exploitation of a transport route which is substantial'; then recognizing that this argument can be extended to any infrastructure, and not merely to transport routes; and finally acknowledging that 'this consequence of Article 86 is of essential importance in the context of deregulation' (*XXIInd Report on Competition Policy*).

In practice, in the sector where the liberalization process is most advanced – telecommunications – the Commission has so far pursued the introduction of competitive market conditions through a combination of Article 85 and regulatory measures, rather than by bringing a series of Article 86 cases.[119] In its 1987 Green Paper on telecoms, the Commission

---

[118]   Already there was a body of Article 86 cases where a general duty is imposed on the incumbent of 'acting fairly towards competitors' who are dependent on supplies of a particular material (Commercial Solvents, 1985), or on access to essential services (Telemarketing, 1984).

[119]   A variety of Article 85 cases in the telecoms sector (joint ventures and cooperative agreements) have also dealt with entry issues. In this area, the attitude of the Commission has been to grant negative clearance or individual exemption subject to the provision of undertakings to grant access to third parties to the facilities in question, and that the price of access be 'fair and reasonable' (e.g. BT/MCI (1993), BS/BT (1994), Nordic (1995), and, early on, Eirpage (1991), a joint venture between the Irish TO and Motorola to establish and operate a paging system. The operating agreement reached between the two partners regulated access to infrastructural facilities which would have effectively excluded third parties from competition. The Commission therefore obtained undertakings from the Irish TO that it would make

explicitly took the view that a strategy based on bringing cases against Member States and TOs would be too cumbersome and slow. The regulatory route was chosen instead, in particular the development of a series of 'Article 90 Directives' aimed at removing the exclusive rights of TOs to provide equipment and services.

However there is some evidence that competition rules may be used more in the future. For example, in the Green Paper on the Liberalization of Telecom Infrastructure (January 1995), while still choosing a regulatory approach in preference to case-by-case application of the competition rules, the Commission recommended the use of Art. 86 to deal with interconnection disputes – in particular with regard to access to the local loop. Thus as competition develops in these industries, it is conceivable that more use will be made of Article 86 to deal with cases of abuse by the incumbent.

Foreclosure through vertical restraints

European competition policy has largely adopted the notion that vertical restraints between manufacturers and distributors, or manufacturers and licensees, can be welfare-enhancing. At present vertical restraints benefit from a system of block exemptions which exempt certain categories of vertical agreements from the prohibition of interfirm agreements contained in Art. 85(1). There is in particular a block exemption on exclusive distribution (Regulation (EEC) No 1983/83), and one on exclusive purchasing (Regulation (EEC) No 1984/83, with special rules for beer and petrol). Both of these are due to expire at end-1997. Individual exemptions may be given for selective distribution, and there is a specific block exemption on car distribution and servicing agreements (Regulation (EEC) No 123/85, replaced by Regulation (EC) No 1475/95 in 1995). Special rules also exist on franchising.

As well as traditional considerations of efficiency in distribution, the favourable treatment of vertical arrangements in EU competition law has also been supported by the view that appointing a local distributor may facilitate the penetration of foreign markets, and stimulate cross-frontier trade, thereby favouring integration. At the same time, as seen in the previous chapter, there is a rather uneasy balance between the position that agreements conferring territorial exclusivity have efficiency justifications, and should be allowed, and at the same time that this should not translate into market segmentation.

However, there are also concerns about the possible market monopolization and foreclosure effects of certain agreements. For example, the Commission's position that exclusive purchasing agreements should not hamper entry is apparent in the refusal to exempt such agreements in the case of German ice cream manufacturers Langnese and Schöller. It was stated that 'In general, the Commission considers these agreements to be beneficial to competition in normal market conditions because they strengthen the position of the undertaking which has concluded the exclusivity agreement. If, however, access by other suppliers to the relevant market is impeded as a result of the market structure and other significant barriers to entry to this market, any further strengthening of that position by exclusivity agreements cannot be accepted. Such a situation arises in the present case, where Langnese and Schöller operate a duopoly and where access to the market is made particularly difficult as a result of freezer exclusivity arrangements'.

the infrastructural facilities available to third parties on the same conditions as applied to Eirpage. The Commission also insisted on the possibility of 'fair access for third parties' even if the facilities were not strictly 'essential').

More generally, the block exemptions contain a number of conditions and criteria which make the agreement eligible for exemption. The length of the agreements is an important consideration (exemption is granted only for limited periods), and indeed long-term exclusive arrangements between a dominant firm and its customers may be considered an abuse in the sense of Article 86, because they preclude customers from switching to alternative suppliers, and they may foreclose competing suppliers.

While at this stage the Commission's future orientation on vertical agreements is not known (a Green Paper is expected), it would be appropriate if this incorporated a market structure test, with intervention being conditional on such a test. In this approach, the competition authority would only intervene if, having regard to the structure of the market, it appears that competition is being effectively impaired. Under this 'structural approach' only restraints by firms with market power would fall within Art. 85(1).

This is also an opportunity for the Commission to address the criticism that its current system of block exemptions puts too much emphasis on the legal form of arrangements.

In the meantime, the block exemption for motor vehicle distribution has been renewed, though only for another seven years (Regulation (EC) No 1475/95), and there are views that it will not be renewed again. A new position has emerged on multi-make dealers: individual exemptions may be granted to a dealer which represents two makes, as long the showrooms are in separate premises.[120] The Commission appears to be gradually warming to the position that sales and servicing need not be carried out in the same premises or by the same dealer; and the established efficiency defence for exclusivity/selectivity mostly applies to service. Hence the traditional approach – where clearance of exclusive rights is linked for new car sales, and exclusive servicing rights – may be outdated, especially if market practices develop which show that such a link may not be indispensable. The current evidence appears in favour of this approach, as it increasingly shows manufacturers owning or appointing dealers with large showrooms for sales, and separately franchising service centres in different locations (this is for example the entry strategy followed by the Korean company Daewoo).

8.6.4. Exclusionary pricing on markets

Predation

Predatory pricing falls under the category of abusive conducts which are caught in EU competition law under Article 86.

As we have seen, the classic predation case is AKZO (1986): it abused its dominant position in the EU organic peroxides market by implementing a strategy of selective below-cost pricing in the flour segment of that market, when its threat to a small rival to deter it from entering the market was ignored. Apart from this, there are very few examples of cases being brought specifically on predation charges. More often, predation is accessory to a wider set of complaints made against a dominant firm, mostly to do with issues of refusal to supply (e.g. in Tetra Pak II (1991), the main issue was the 'tying' of a durable good with the supply of complementary inputs by the dominant firm, however predatory pricing was also identified by

---

[120]   Though it was later stated that those premises can be in the same building.

the Commission in the fact that one type of carton (the non-aseptic type) had been 'sold at a loss' in seven states).

Non-linear pricing

It has been a long-standing policy of the Commission to prohibit under Art. 86 the practice by dominant firms of offering, as a means of supporting their dominant position, loyalty/fidelity rebates (Hoffman-La Roche, British Gypsum); rebates related to sales targets (Michelin, Coca-Cola) or 'top-slice' rebates (Solvay and ICI).

In all these cases, the Commission view (upheld by the CFI in 1993) was that although 'promotional payments are standard practice in a normal competitive environment', this is indeed an abusive conduct when pursued by a dominant firm. According to Court jurisprudence and Commission practices, rebates offered by dominant firms are excusable only if 'they are based on objective cost-based criteria, and therefore produce actual cost savings'; their terms are transparent; and they are non-discriminatory. Conversely, rebates are abusive if they are discriminatory, i.e. 'based on estimates of customers' capacity to absorb additional expenditure' (e.g. Hoffman-La Roche); if they are aimed at attaining the entire requirements of a customer (HLR); if they are based on the decision of a customer whether or not to buy a competitor's product (Hilti); if they are totally discretionary; if they are accompanied by 'pressure' on customers to sell the supplier's products.

Recent Commission administrative practices indicate, however, that the Commission may be willing to enter into a settlement with a dominant firm if it can be assured that a sufficient degree of competition is not foreclosed through that firm's rebate and pricing policies. Indeed, more recently the Commission has gone further, allowing dominant companies the possibility to benefit from an Art. 85(3) exemption for their various distribution practices. Also, the Commission appears willing to treat some rebate schemes favourably if they satisfy certain conditions, even if the firm is dominant (e.g. application by BPB for four rebate schemes). In a series of Notices published in 1992, the Commission stated that rebates which are transparent, non-discriminatory, based on objective cost-based criteria, linked to actual savings or 'intended to facilitate market entry' will be judged favourably (even when the firm has a significant market share) because they are 'capable of promoting competition'.

Overall, the competition policy rules in this area are not really coherent and consistent. For example, while loyalty bonuses are regarded as infringements of Art. 86, frequent flier programmes are not objected to. However, this also reflects the fact that in this area there are as yet no clear guiding economic principles as to what should be objected to.

8.7. Conclusions

To the extent that the single market programme has been effective in removing institutional factors preventing entry into markets, we would expect that firms' incentives to replace these barriers with strategic behaviour have increased.

In this chapter, we have discussed a variety of ways in which this may have occurred.

(a)   First, we have emphasized how even where barriers to entry are of an institutional nature, the exclusionary effect can be determined by a combination of these factors and the behaviour of the incumbents, which makes competition policy intervention the appropriate instrument.

(b) We have identified two main categories of exclusionary behaviour which is likely to prevent entry (both *de novo* and cross-border), and thereby hamper integration, retaining artificial market segmentation along national borders. The first is restricting access to a complementary asset, the second is pricing on markets.

(c) On access issues:

(i) We have identified the basic conditions under which access restrictions placed by the incumbent can be considered exclusionary (that the asset is essential and non-replicable by the entrant, so that entry at minimum efficient scale is not possible). We have reviewed the 'essential facilities doctrine' in this light.

(ii) We have discussed access pricing as a special case of refusal to supply, and argued that wide application of Art. 86 to these cases may not be desirable, given the intrinsically different nature of competition policy and regulation, which makes the latter more suitable for the task.

(iii) We have considered the conditions under which vertical restraints may have exclusionary effects and conclude that they should be treated conceptually the same as other access restrictions.

(d) On pricing on markets:

(i) Predatory strategies based on the 'long-purse' story are the most relevant in the context of integration, though detection remains a difficult issue. In these cases, a composite tests which considers market structure and the firm's financial strength, as well as the pattern of prices over time, appears the most appropriate.

(ii) In considering 'non-linear pricing' we have emphasized the analogy between various instances of discounts and rebates for aggregate purchases over time, and exclusivity in distribution. We have also noted the asymmetry in EU competition law between the harsh treatment of discounts, and the benevolent treatment of exclusive dealing.

9. Market integration and collusion

9.1. Introduction

Firms would typically prefer to achieve and support some form of 'joint action' in place of direct rivalry. Collusion is a general term which includes 'all types of conduct or forms of behaviour whereby decision-takers agree to coordinate their actions' (Rees [1993a, p. 27]). Collusive agreements include direct price-fixing, whereby firms agree on a mechanism to determine and adjust prices; arrangements on quantities supplied to the market; or mutual 'stand-off' agreements, whereby firms commit themselves not to enter each other's markets. In addition to prices and production levels – which are the focus of standard analysis of collusion – firms choose other strategic variables, such as investments in physical capital and R&D, and may also collude in these.[121] Collusion also includes cases where outcomes are effectively coordinated, but in fact there is no explicit agreement between firms to achieve that outcome – 'tacit' collusion.

Collusion in setting prices or quantities leads to adverse allocative efficiency effects, as it enables prices to be sustained significantly above costs. It may also imply productive efficiency losses, if it blunts firms' incentives to remove slack. For these reasons, it is a major focus of competition policy under all jurisdictions.

In EU competition law, the prohibition of collusion has a further dimension. Art. 85(1) of the Treaty of Rome, under which collusion is captured, explicitly prohibits agreements, decisions and concerted practices between firms 'which may affect trade between Member States and which have as their object or effect the prevention, restriction or distortion of competition within the common market'. As a result, the practice of the European courts on collusion has been characterized by the pursuit of a dual objective: collusive agreements should be eliminated because they increase market power and reduce economic efficiency, but also because they undermine the process of integration as such. Evidence for this dual objective may be found for example in the Cement case (1994), where the Commission explicitly stated that 'the practice of cement producers not to sell in one another's home markets [...] has the sole objective of limiting competition between companies from the different Member States, and frustrates the fundamental EU aim of the creation of the single market' (*XXIVth Report on Competition Policy 1994*).

Given the emphasis on collusive agreements affecting trade, the Commission has typically focused on two types of collusive agreements: cross-border agreements through which firms effectively share markets on a geographic basis (i.e. mutual 'stand-offs'), and agreements between domestic firms which might prevent the entry of a rival into a national market.

This chapter addresses the nature of the relationship between the process of integration and the incentive for firms to collude and sustain cooperation. In particular, we consider how the achievement of integration might be hindered by existing or new collusive agreements between

---

[121] Indeed the overall evaluation of collusion on prices and quantities should take into account its effects on the competitive interaction in these other dimensions. The economic literature has shown for example that collusion on prices and quantities may yield lower overall profits (compared with not colluding at all) if it intensifies competition in an earlier stage of the game in variables such as capacity investment or R&D.

firms. We also consider whether measures to remove artificial barriers to trade may be expected to undermine existing collusive practices; or whether they might provide instead an incentive for firms to seek renewed or new forms of cooperation.

We would expect the single market to affect collusion firstly through its direct impact on some devices which made collusion sustainable. For example, the promotion of market integration measures might undermine some of the intangibles which helped firms sustain collusion in the past. The achievement of a collusive outcome is generally facilitated if firms share a common history, or know each other well from their past experience of interacting in the market place. In such a case, the entry of new rivals spurred by market integration measures might undermine collusion, as achieving coordination is more difficult without mutual knowledge between firms.

Further, where single market measures achieve the harmonization of rules and standards across Member States, they reduce the importance of national regulations and thereby should reduce the importance of regulatory capture for sustaining collusion at the national level. That is, firms within each country might be able to 'capture' their regulators, and obtain the imposition of standards or rules which effectively discriminate against foreign firms (by making their entry too costly). Where these rules were superseded by common rules (or at least by the recognition of each other's standards), then within-country collusion through this device might be undermined. This may be particularly important in the case of services, such as in banking (see Vives [1991]).

More generally, two essential concepts must be identified at the start which determine whether collusion might be achieved and sustained, and which must be adopted as an organizing principle in the analysis of collusion. These are the incentive to collude and the incentive to cheat. The 'incentive to collude' is measured by a firm's longer-term gain from complying with the agreement, which means getting a share in the (joint) monopoly profit instead of the profit of short-run competition. The 'incentive to cheat' is the firm's short-term private gain from not abiding with the agreement, which means reducing prices to gain market share from rivals in the short term, but which might also mean foregoing the collusive profit in the long term.

In this chapter we will seek to assess the effects of measures to promote the single market on these two incentives. For example, the removal of artificial barriers to trade should imply an opportunity for more firms to enter a market. This might make collusion harder because each firm's share in the collusive profit is smaller, and therefore the incentive to collude may be smaller. In addition, the incentive to deviate from the agreement might be greater because 'cheating' may become less expensive, and therefore existing cooperative agreements might not be sustainable.

The Cecchini report [1988] emphasized the expected benefits of '...increased trade and sharper competition triggered by market integration', which (will) 'lower profit margins to the extent that they have been artificially sustained above competitive levels' (p. 78). It predicted a 'narrowing of the gap between prices and costs in the wake of the curtailment of monopoly power' (p. 83).

However the Cecchini report also makes a brief reference to the possibility that increased market openness might give firms renewed incentives to collude: 'in this new and blustery climate, there is a good chance that some of the economy's players will seek various forms of shelter from competitive reinvigoration. This happened following the removal of tariff barriers, and it is to be expected that the Community's authorities will face multiple stratagems developed by private and public actors to cushion the competitive impact on them' (p. 90).

Overall we find that as far as market entry is facilitated by the process of market integration, and some 'focal points' for collusion are removed, we should see less collusion occurring. At the same time, it is possible that the single market measures will not diminish the incentive for cross-border collusive practices centred on national boundaries.

We begin in Section 9.2 with a brief summary of selected collusion cases dealt with by the Commission over the past decade. This provides an empirical context for the discussion in the rest of this chapter. We begin the analysis in Section 9.3, by defining the notion of collusion, and discussing how the incentive for firms to collude and to cheat might vary across product markets. In Section 9.4 we consider what effects might be expected from the single market programme. Section 9.5 considers a few examples which reinforce the general arguments of the preceding sections.

In Section 9.6 we address competition policies against collusion. We discuss in particular the detection problem, and then evaluate the possible merits of a more 'structural' approach to the fight against collusion: i.e. to attack directly secondary agreements which are likely to have been entered into for the purpose of sustaining collusion. We discuss in particular the weight to be given to information exchanges (the most frequent form of communication between rivals).

9.2. Selection of some relevant collusion cases since 1985

A variety of markets and industries have attracted the attention of the EU competition authorities under Art. 85(1) ('horizontal agreements'). These include agreements to fix prices, quantities or divide markets in various ways.

Agreements to fix prices and/or other variables, either directly between firms or indirectly through a trade association which sets 'list prices' include the following.

(a) Polypropylene (1986): 15 major petrochemical producers were found to have operated a market-sharing and price-fixing cartel between 1977 and 1983. Documentary evidence was found of regular meetings held to set target prices, decide how to concert efforts to raise prices, and implement and monitor a system of quotas. Users within the Community were argued to be adversely affected by the manipulation of the selling price.

(b) Meldoc (1986): five Dutch diaries were found to have operated a cartel involving market sharing through quotas, and the protection of the home market against imports (in particular by dropping the price of UHT milk after imports were started from Germany, or dumping milk on the Belgian market). Trade was argued to be affected between Member States, as penetration of the Dutch market was made more difficult.

(c) Belasco (1986): seven Belgian producers of roofing felt were found to have operated a cartel between 1978 and 1984. Through general meetings of their trade association (Belasco), they sought to organize the Belgian market and protect it from external competition. A common price list was adopted with minimum prices, the allocation of quotas, and joint action to deal with any disturbance to the collective interest arising out of new entrants into the market, increased competition or the development of substitute products.

(d)   Italian flat glass (1988): a number of flat glass producers in Italy were found to have adopted agreements and concerted practices which isolated the Italian flat glass market (including price-fixing, quotas, market sharing).

(e)   PVC and LPDE (1988): two decisions were taken by the Commission concerning cartels involving the majority of EU thermoplastics producers. Collusive practices (which included fixing target prices, planning concerted initiatives, sharing the market and 'exchanging detailed operational information in order to obtain better coordination') were agreed to by producers at regular secret meetings.

(f)   Welded steel mesh (1989): 14 undertakings were fined for having engaged in 1981–85 in a series of agreements or concerted practices designed to fix prices, quotas, and share markets.

(g)   Soda ash (1990): Solvay and ICI were found to be involved in long-term concerted practices to share the EU market between them (supported by 'swaps' of products).

(h)   VOTOB (association of undertakings offering tank storage facilities in the Netherlands, 1992): six undertakings decided to increase prices as of April 1990 by a uniform, fixed amount by means of an 'environmental charge'. This was considered incompatible with Art. 85 by the Commission.

(i)   SPO (federation of construction industry associations, Netherlands, 1992, first case in the construction sector): 28 construction associations in the Netherlands were found to have operated a cartel in the Dutch building and construction industry through their joint federation SPO: this consisted of a set of complex and detailed regulations adopted to coordinate the competitive conduct of building firms when engaged in competitive tenders. The Commission found that these rules severely restricted competition between participants, by prohibiting each bidder from freely setting the price and other conditions of his offer. These rules were deemed to affect intra-Community trade appreciably.

(j)   CNSD (customs agents association, Italy, 1993): Italian customs agents were found to have fixed prices in the form of joint tariffs set by their association CNSD. This was the first time that this principle was applied to a service.

(k)   NVL (lift industry association, Netherlands, 1993): members of the association were operating through it a system allowing price-fixing and market sharing.

(l)   Steel beams (1994): a cartel was found to operate since 1984 between 17 companies, implemented via Eurofer (the European steel industry association). These companies had agreed to fix prices and quotas, 'and regularly exchanged a wide variety of what would be normally considered highly confidential information in order to ensure that the cartel was operated effectively'.

(m)   Cement (1994): 23 cement producers were found to operate a 'home market' cartel, i.e. agreed – via their national cement associations – not to sell in each other's home market. A widespread exchange of information 'that would normally be considered confidential' also took place.

(n)   Cartonboard (1994): a cartel was found to be operating involving 19 companies. It consisted of periodic 'price initiatives', and an agreement on market shares.

In a few cases the fact that information was exchanged, again directly between firms or through a trade association, has been interpreted as evidence in favour of collusion.

(a)   Fatty acids (1986) was the first case in which fines were imposed with respect to an information exchange agreement. Three major EU producers of fatty acids were found to have operated such an agreement to exchange confidential information about their sales, after having established their respective market shares in the previous three years. The

Commission's decision was justified on grounds that the agreement set up means of monitoring the firms' future performance, and thus had 'an inherent restrictive effect upon competition'. The agreement 'made for artificially increased transparency between the parties, ... enabling them to react more rapidly and efficiently to one another's actions'. Trade between Member States was thus affected.

(b)   UK agricultural tractor registration exchange (1992): prohibition of a system (set up in 1975) for exchanging information on retail sales and market shares for agricultural tractors sold in the UK. The Commission's view was that 'exchanges of information identifying the sales of each competitor in a highly concentrated market with no significant competition from outside the EU restricted competition'. The agreement poses the risk of 'eliminating any hidden competition through the creation of an artificial and undesirable degree of transparency in a highly concentrated market'. It was also considered a barrier to entry.

9.3.   Factors affecting the likelihood of collusion

An interesting stylized fact which emerges from the list in the previous section is that a high proportion of collusion cases tried by the Commission have concerned markets for homogeneous products (often intermediate inputs), with high capital costs and significant excess capacity: from Woodpulp (1984) to Polypropylene (1986), Fatty acids (1986), PVC and LPDE (thermoplastics) (1988), Welded steel mesh (1989), Soda ash (1991), Steel beams (1994), Cartonboard (1994), and Cement (1994). This list of cases appears to suggest that there may be some common features to industries where collusion is more likely, in which case-specific identification of these features may assist the targeting of competition interventions against collusion.

In order to explain these empirical regularities it is appropriate to consider in some more detail the notion of collusion, and the lessons to be drawn from economic theory on how collusion might be sustained.

9.3.1. Sustainability of collusion

Collusion may consist of some form of explicit agreement between the parties. It may also be tacit, which describes the idea that firms recognize their mutual interdependence, and therefore 'could agree to coordinate their actions without explicit communication and discussion' (Rees [1993a, p. 28]). Technically, in this case the collusive outcome is obtained as the equilibrium solution of repeated interactions over time in a non-cooperative dynamic game (as opposed to a static setting).[122]

Tacit collusion has been the subject of a large economic literature which explores how firms can resist their incentive to gain privately at their rivals' expense, and thus achieve an outcome which is better for all competitors. The argument is that even if firms do not communicate with each other, they may realize that their actions are interdependent, and it could be privately optimal for them to make choices leading to the 'cooperative' outcome (i.e. closer to the joint monopoly profit) even if there is no explicit agreement between them.

---

[122]   In 'repeated' games, firms repeatedly set prices or outputs, and can respond to rivals' choices. The idea behind repetition is thus to formalize in some way the notion of action-reaction, and play over time, which makes it possible for firms to sustain tacit collusion by anticipating rivals' reactions to their actions.

To be effective, any agreement must be sustainable. As anticipated, this will depend on the balance between the 'incentive to collude' and the 'incentive to cheat': a firm will have a short-run incentive to 'cheat' (i.e. pursue its own immediate interest through secret price cuts, or other forms of 'business stealing'), and will comply with a collusive agreement only if its long-term gain from doing so is greater than the short-term profit from cheating.

A further essential factor for the stability of collusion is the possibility of imposing sufficiently severe punishments on the deviators. If a firm deviates it must expect a response from its rivals, in the form of lower prices or increased output: this is generally interpreted as a 'punishment' inflicted on the cheater. Moreover, punishments must be credible, so that a deviating firm will believe that its rivals will go through with the punishment.

In the light of this, we would expect the likelihood of collusion to be affected by factors such as the number of firms in the market, and the frequency of interaction. A larger number of firms in the market should make it more difficult for them to collude effectively (see among others Selten [1973]). This is because even though the intensity of punishment might be the same, there is more redistribution from cheating, and therefore a greater incentive for firms to deviate. Collusion should also be easier to sustain when firms interact more frequently, because this affects their ability to grant secret price cuts. Although it is possible to identify the circumstances likely to lead to collusion being less sustainable, we should not expect to be able to quantify these effects, e.g. to know how many firms are required for collusion to break down.

Further, collusion should be easier to sustain when monitoring is more accurate. After Stigler [1964], the ability to monitor rivals' actions has become central to the analysis of collusion, given the prevalence of information imperfections: anything that makes it easier for firms to know what others are doing facilitates monitoring, and makes collusion more sustainable. The availability of more disaggregated information on the market, for example, should help to sustain collusion.

With information imperfections and demand/cost uncertainties, it is obviously not easy to tell whether a certain observed outcome (e.g. lower prices) depends for example on a demand shock or on deviation(s) from the agreement. The economic literature has suggested that the only way to support coordination in these circumstances might be to adopt a 'punishment' (e.g. to revert to competitive pricing) in all cases where the observed outcome is consistent with the possibility of one member having deviated. This might imply of course that the punishment is inflicted on all firms even when none of them has deviated. It is precisely the credibility of the threat of future punishments which provides the discipline that supports non-cooperative 'collusive' outcomes. Price wars may thus be a necessary part of optimal collusive arrangements.[123]

---

[123] This result is obtained among others by Green and Porter [1984]. In their repeated market game, it is optimal for firms to produce at the collusive output level, and therefore any observed price war occurs after an unexpected drop in demand, rather than after actual cheating. Price wars are thus the occasional equilibrium outcome of the repeated non-cooperative market game, as a fall in price below a certain threshold 'triggers' the punishment (reversion to Cournot behaviour). A degree of collusion is sustained via 'trigger' strategies that involve switches between periods of collusion and price wars.

Interpretation of stylized facts

Economic theory thus offers some helpful insights into the effects of basic industry and market characteristics on collusion. On this basis, we might be able to propose some explanations for the stylized facts observed above (see also Scherer and Ross [1990]).

A rough measure of firms' incentives to collude is the difference between total profits without coordination, and joint monopoly profits. The more competitive the market is in the absence of collusion, the more there is to be gained by firms from coordinating. This might explain why we could expect to see more collusion in industries where there is excess capacity.

In particular: the incentive to deviate is based on the profitability of deviation, the likelihood of being caught, and the cost of being caught. Features which increase the profitability of deviation may often make it less costly to punish deviations. For example, if firms have significant capacity constraints then this both reduces the incentive to deviate (since firms who undercut the collusive price may not be able to meet extra demand), but also implies a loss of punishment possibilities (since firms are more limited in their ability to increase output and lower price to punish a deviating firm). In such situations, the overall effect on the sustainability of collusion may be ambiguous, but the latter effect may prevail in some circumstances. Both Rey et al. [1995] and Padilla [forthcoming, 1996] have shown in different contexts that the loss of punishment possibilities might ultimately prevail, and hence collusion is more difficult to sustain with capacity constraints; this confirms the converse notion of excess capacity generally favouring collusion.

A similar analysis applies to product homogeneity: on the one hand, in the absence of collusion, competition in prices is tougher in homogeneous goods markets, and this should increase the incentive to collude. Detection should also be easier, and the punishment more severe (though of course homogeneity increases the gain to cheating, making collusion less difficult to sustain). For the idea that product differentiation may better support collusion, see Ross [1992], and Hackner [1994].

Ease of monitoring will also be affected by industry conditions. Firstly, collusion is generally thought to be easier in more concentrated industries, since fewer firms are involved, and therefore monitoring should be easier. Moreover, with homogeneous products it might be easier to observe prices, and therefore to detect deviations. Another important factor is the prevalence of posted prices, as opposed to individually negotiated prices. With individually negotiated pricing, there is greater scope for secret price cuts and monitoring might be more difficult (as well as the incentive to cheat being greater).

Thus although theoretical results about conditions favouring collusion are often ambiguous, it is possible to make sense of the empirical observation that many of the Commission's collusion cases involve industries with common characteristics. Collusion might be observed more often in industries with:

(a)   excess capacity, because while the incentive to deviate is greater, the ability to punish is also credible;

(b)   high fixed and sunk costs, because these lead to higher concentration, which in turn reduces the incentive to cheat, and allows easier monitoring of the agreement; sunk costs also prevent hit-and-run entry if incumbent firms raise prices by colluding;

(c)   product homogeneity, because monitoring is easier, and it is harder for a firm to retain its market share if there is severe punishment (threats against new entrants are also more credible);

(d)   open price lists, as opposed to individually negotiated prices, because they make secret price cutting more difficult;

(e)   repeated attempts by firms to communicate with each other in some way (indeed in virtually all the collusion cases mentioned above, the Commission found evidence of information exchanges in some form, for example through a trade association).

These features should be kept in mind by the competition authorities as generally increasing the likelihood of collusion. For policy purposes, the most important point is the last one on information exchanges, because it is one where specific policy recommendations on how to tackle collusion can be made. These will be discussed in Section 9.6.2 below.

Market entry

One factor which we have not yet considered, but is essential given our focus on market integration, is the effect of entry on collusion. A necessary condition for the stability of a collusive outcome is that it is not undermined by the entry of new firms which undercut the colluding incumbent firms. Entry barriers therefore assist incumbent firms in sustaining collusion, and so industries with significant sunk costs may be particularly susceptible to collusive behaviour.[124] Strategies employed by firms in collusion might in fact have as a secondary effect the discouragement of entry: for example, with imperfect information, entry of a new firm may be misinterpreted as cheating by existing firms, and lead to a punishing price war with the consequent effect of reducing the profitability of entry (Friedman and Thisse [1994].

These issues are explored in greater detail in Section 9.4 below, where we consider directly the relationship between collusion and the single market.

9.4. The impact of the single market on collusion

As was argued in Chapters 3 and 4, the mechanism through which single market measures may affect collusion is through their impact on cross-border selling and market entry costs. In this section we consider how firms' incentives to collude and their ability to sustain collusion may be affected by the integration process, and in particular by the single market programme. We must distinguish two different cases.

Firstly, there is the case where the overall impact of single market measures on firms may not be very significant: for example, if transport costs are high in relation to the value of the product, the effect of reducing artificial barriers to trade might be comparatively small. In this case, the single market programme may not significantly affect firms' incentives to enter new markets (a case in point is soda ash, which will be discussed in the next section). As a result, we should not expect existing (collusive) market-sharing arrangements to be affected by the single market programme; indeed firms will seek to maintain an allocation of markets according to national boundaries even if borders have been formally eliminated.

---

[124]   However, we may distinguish here between the threat of entry, and effective entry which is a direct result of market integration (i.e. removal of barriers). This will be explored in greater detail in Section 9.4.1 below.

The second case is where single market measures might significantly ease entry or market access. This is the case where the single market has in principle a pro-competitive effect: as the size of the market is increased, more firms should be sustainable in equilibrium (even with barriers to entry). In this case we need to investigate how this will affect collusion.

The issue is whether product-market integration – and integration measures – may have affected the way in which rival firms compete, and in particular their willingness to coordinate their actions and their ability to sustain cooperation.

As noted already (Section 9.1), measures to promote the single market might act directly upon firms' ability to sustain existing collusive practices, by affecting intangibles upon which coordination might be based. For example, integration might remove some 'focal points' which served as collusive devices in the past; or – where it encourages new entry of firms – it might lead to the breakdown of coordination based on mutual knowledge, and shared experience of a market. Where they lead to a reduction in the importance of national rules and regulations, in favour of supranational standards, integration measures might also undermine collusion which is sustained by means of regulatory capture by firms in their home markets.

When considering the incentives to collude and to cheat in more detail, a useful distinction to make is between collusive agreements within a country, and cross-border collusive agreements. We would expect single market measures to undermine – at least to some degree – within-country collusion, since domestic markets would be opened to entry by foreign firms. However, there is perhaps less reason to believe that single market measures will necessarily reduce cross-border collusion.

We consider each of these two types of collusion in greater detail.

9.4.1. Pro-competitive effects: within-country collusion

The issue here is how easy is it to sustain collusion in the face of market entry. It is useful at the start to distinguish between two concepts of entry which might impact on the sustainability of a collusive agreement. One is potential entry, or threat of new entry. The other is entry because of market integration. This is the notion that the single market programme, by widening the boundaries of the market and reducing effective transport costs, implies that more firms (which were previously segregated within their national frontiers) are now in competition with each other.

There is a (limited) economic literature on the sustainability of collusion in the face of free market entry. The general intuition is that collusion might indeed be sustained in the absence of entry barriers if the expected 'harshness of punishment' in the post-entry market is sufficient to deter potential entrants. For example, Harrington [1989] investigates the degree of cooperation that firms can support with free entry, and finds that if the discount factor is sufficiently high (i.e. firms are not too 'short-termist') there exists a free entry equilibrium in which they sustain some cooperation. This is because the incumbent firms credibly threaten to respond to entry with a period of very aggressive competition. Stanbacke [1994] treats collusion in a market with free entry as analogous to collusion with asymmetric market shares, and shows that when the expected competitive response is very harsh (i.e. with very severe punishments) collusion is actually sustainable in equilibrium provided that firms again have a sufficiently high discount factor. In all these cases, entry threats depend on how strong the punishment is; and they might actually be very small given the harshness of the competitive response to entry. Empirically, there is some support for the notion that the threat of entry may have very small effects (despite contestability theory): see for example, Borenstein's [1989] study on US airlines.

There is however another aspect to consider: to the extent that the single market programme extends the boundaries of the market, or reduces effective transport costs, more firms can be sustained in equilibrium for any degree of competition. Thus, even if firms expect some punishment, then some degree of entry at the margin will actually occur, because firms expect to be able to survive in the larger market.

The extent to which actual entry as a response to market integration will limit competition will also depend on the characteristics of the market. For example, entry might be greater with product differentiation, because in a differentiated good market an entrant can sometimes survive by serving only a market niche. Thus entry will not be effectively deterred, that is, the incumbents cannot easily induce exit of an entrant in the case of differentiated products. The case is different with homogeneous good markets, where if incumbent firms respond very aggressively, the entrant may not be able to cover its entry costs.

In the context of the EU, where countries have rather similar characteristics and therefore we would expect more intra-industry trade, it is possible that entry might occur in markets for differentiated products (i.e. firms decide to enter a market with a product which is 'niche', or rather specialized). This suggests that entry might take place to a significant degree, and thus the 'limiting' effect of entry on collusion might be large. In homogeneous good markets – such as those where most EU cases on collusion have been identified – we might not on the other hand expect as much cross-border entry.

In summary: economic analysis suggests that within-country collusion might be effective in discouraging potential entry (and thus sustain itself). However, if market integration widens the market and reduces transport and market access costs, then foreign firms on the margin of entering should enter and might be able to survive.

It is less clear what the consequences of entry by foreign firms might be for domestic collusion. Potentially, foreign entrants might simply join a new larger collusive agreement; however, monitoring is likely to be more difficult with more firms who do not know each other from past experience of interacting in the market, and thus we would have a presumption that market integration is overall likely to undermine domestic collusion.

9.4.2. New incentives to collude: cross-border collusion

The effect of market integration on EU-wide collusion is not clear-cut. Market integration affects the sustainability of cross-border collusion in subtle ways, and there is no necessary reason why such collusion should be undermined by integration. Rather, there are at least some arguments that market integration might provide new opportunities for firms to sustain a 'stand-off' with their potential foreign rivals, e.g. implicitly agreeing to segment the market geographically; or – where they are already present in each other's markets – not to undercut prices.

First of all, even if national borders were effectively eliminated by integration, a market-sharing agreement according to national boundaries might still be feasible, because the parties can probably still monitor compliance quite easily. This is because:

(a)   national boundaries may act as 'focal points' for the agreement;

(b)   market sharing according to national boundaries gives rise to better monitoring.

Let us now consider the sustainability of collusion. We have argued that the potential for any agreement (old or new) to be sustained is a function of the participants' pay-offs (short-term returns from cheating vs. longer-terms returns from compliance). Market integration may be expected to have a number of effects on implicit agreements – some of which potentially conflict with each other.

Firstly, there is a direct effect: 'cheating' on an existing agreement (e.g. selling outside one's 'allocated' geographical market) may become cheaper with market integration (lower transport costs etc.). At the same time, reduced transport costs should make punishment cheaper and easier, and could thereby support collusion; overall, the result is ambiguous.[125]

In addition there might be a market size effect: if integration means that the geographical market which a firm could economically supply becomes larger (because transport and transaction costs in general decline), then the gains from cheating become larger, and therefore the agreement becomes more difficult to sustain; i.e. there is a 'market size' effect which may increase the short-term gain from cheating.[126] [127]

Sustaining collusive outcomes also requires firms to monitor the compliance of rivals with the implicit or explicit agreement. A number of effects are possible here.

(a)   The most obvious point is that monitoring problems are presumably more complex where there are more firms. Thus if integration leads to an increase in the number of firms, monitoring might be less effective.

(b)   On the other hand, if integration effectively implies greater convergence of economic conditions (see Chapter 3), then demand in different geographical markets may become more closely correlated. This may make monitoring easier (and therefore collusion more likely to be sustained) with imperfect information, because a deviation could be more easily distinguished from a downturn in demand (effectively there is less noise).

---

[125]   This is the same point illustrated in Rotemberg and Saloner [1986], who show in a dynamic model that the imposition of an import quota by one country can lead to increased international competition, reducing the price in the country that imposes the quota, the foreign country, or both. The reason is that a quota reduces the ability of foreign firms to punish a deviating domestic firm, and therefore the amount of collusion that can be sustained is correspondingly lessened (this is especially true with prices as the strategic variables). These results would seem to suggest that trade liberalization - by increasing firms' ability to punish deviations - may support a degree of collusion.

[126]   This conclusion is obvious in the case of a market in which the non-cooperative behaviour is Bertrand competition without capacity constraints. In this case, market integration should lead to greater incentives to deviate from the collusive agreement. However, punishment possibilities are not toughened by market integration since the potential to drive profits to zero always exists, whatever the size of the market. Therefore in this special case we would unambiguously expect market integration to lead to less collusion.

[127]   One of the few studies of the effect of the single market on the sustainability of collusion is van Wegberg et al. [1994], which suggests an application of the theory of multimarket contact (Bernheim and Whinston [1990]) to European integration. Firms which meet in multiple product markets may thus have an additional incentive to comply with the agreement if they fear that deviation may be punished in more than one market. In fact, this effect is debatable. Multimarket contact theories assume that markets are not linked on the demand-side, therefore multimarket contact increases the opportunity to punish deviations without creating more incentives to deviate. However, this model seems relevant only where transport costs remain high, but market access is easier. If integration coincides with a fall in transport costs, then we are in a potentially ambiguous scenario: lower transport costs imply that punishment is easier, but at the same time the incentive to deviate is also stronger.

(c)   Another way in which collusion may be made easier by integration is through the effects of consumer arbitrage: if greater arbitrage reduces price dispersion – and in the extreme, if it leads to a single price – defection may be easier to monitor.

While general conclusions are difficult to draw, we argue that on balance, we cannot expect integration measures always to undermine collusive behaviour. It is therefore appropriate for the EU competition authorities to retain vigilance.

9.5.   The case of soda ash: an illustrative example of cross-border collusion[128]

In its decision of 19 December 1990,[129] the Commission found that Solvay and ICI, 'the two major producers of soda ash in the Community, participated in a concerted practice contrary to Article 85 of the EEC Treaty by knowingly continuing in concert and complicity to observe and apply the essential terms of … a restrictive market sharing agreement dating from 1945 or earlier and which they had purported to terminate in 1972, by coordinating their respective commercial activities, by avoiding all competition with each other and by confining their soda ash activities in the Community to their traditional home markets namely continental Western Europe for Solvay and the United Kingdom for ICI'. (OJ L 152, 15.6.1991).

The collusion case against Solvay and ICI, the claim that markets were separated was based on the following evidence:

(a)   up to about 1980, ICI's list prices in the UK were lower than list prices in neighbouring markets;

(b)   since then, prices in the UK have risen relative to those charged in adjacent markets, price premiums in the UK being sometimes as high as 20%;

(c)   despite these price differences, there has been no significant trade in the product in either direction,[130] although final prices (accounting for transport costs) to UK customers for imports from Continental Europe would for some time have been lower than the prices charged by ICI;

(d)   ICI supplied soda ash only to the Scandinavian market where no domestic producer existed and where price levels, despite the transport costs that have to be incurred for imports, were lower than in countries with an indigenous producer;

(e)   ICI bought soda ash from Solvay as 'purchase for resale' in order to meet its medium- and long-term commitments in its traditional markets, where customers were not aware of the origin of the material.[131]

Some of this evidence, however, does not give a conclusive proof of collusive behaviour. In particular, price differentials and the absence of actual trade does not *per se* give evidence of collusion. Competition may involve Nash equilibrium prices which are limit prices deterring imports, and which may differ according to asymmetries in production costs, transport costs

---

[128]   See Case Study 1 in London Economics (1996) for a fuller description of the soda ash industry.

[129]   The Commission dealt with the soda ash market in a number of cases. Here we focus on the collusion case which was complemented by separate action brought against ICI and Solvay under Art. 86 on abuse of their dominant position.

[130]   The only movement of soda ash were 'co-producer' shipments from Solvay to ICI.

[131]   Following the closure of one ICI plant in 1984, production capacity was not sufficient to meet the whole domestic demand. Furthermore, all of ICI's sales to South Africa were made with material purchased from Solvay.

and different volumes of demand by those customers located closest to each competitor (see Phlips [1995, p. 136 ff.]).

Spatial price discrimination may alleviate this problem of indistinguishability between collusive and competitive outcomes. However, in the presence of a transport cost supplement for serving foreign markets (a discontinuity in the transport cost function) which would result from cross-border trading costs (before market integration), the absence of actual trade flows does not imply collusive market-sharing agreements. Although such costs should have been reduced by market integration, in the case of the UK and Continental Europe, the discontinuity in transport cost will remain due to cross-Channel transport.

Therefore, it may be difficult to detect and identify collusion without more specific information about demand and cost conditions. In the ICI-Solvay case, however, the additional evidence (in particular the purchase-for-resale arrangement) leaves little doubt on the assertion that the observed market segmentation was indeed the result of collusive behaviour.

It is difficult to gauge the impact of the collusion case brought against ICI and Solvay on the competitive outcomes in the European market because, at the same time, the anti-dumping duties which had protected the soda ash market from external competition since 1983 were also eliminated after a request for review from the US producers and the glass industry.[132] It is arguable (from evidence of prices and statements by major purchasers) that competitive conditions changed significantly once a more liberal external trade policy was pursued. Up to the 1980s purchasers bought soda ash from national suppliers facing different price lists from country to country. Today major purchasers can negotiate on a European-wide basis and agree single purchasing deals across markets that are determined by economic boundaries rather than by national borders.

As a result of these actions and the effects of the recession in the early 1990s, prices decreased and small changes appear to have emerged in trade patterns. This is illustrated in Table 9.1 which shows the evolution of market shares in four major national markets.

---

[132]   It is well known that anti-dumping measures may have anti-competitive effects as they reinforce collusion between domestic producers.

Table 9.1.   Soda ash – evolution of market shares in selected European markets (%)

	1986	1989	1992	1994
France		0		
Solvay	55.1	57.3	47.8	47.5
ICI/Brunner Mond	0	0	0.2	1.6
Rhone Poulenc	42.9	40.2	40.7	34.2
AKZO	0.2	0.2	0.7	4.0
Lars Christensen	0	0	0	1.5
E. European Producers	1.8	1.2	2.3	6.4
Turkey	0	0.8	0	0
USA	0	0.4	8.4	4.9
Total ('000 MT)	1,165	1,295	1,315	1,316
Italy				
Solvay	97.3	95.5	86.2	84.1
ICI/Brunner Mond	0	1.2	1.2	1.7
AKZO	0.3	0	1.2	0
Lars Christensen	0	0	1.2	2.3
E. European Producers	2.5	2.4	2.0	3.4
Turkey	0	0.9	2.9	0.7
USA	0	0	5.3	7.7
Total ('000 MT)	773	849	850	870
Spain				
Solvay	100	99.8	69.4	98.1
E. European Producers	0	0	0.3	0
Turkey	0	0.2	0.6	0
USA	0	0	29.7	1.9
Total ('000 MT)	555	602	680	690
UK				
Solvay	0.8	0.2	0.5	4.7
ICI/Brunner Mond	94.4	94.8	92.6	89.1
Rhone Poulenc	0.6	0	0	0.2
AKZO	0	0.5	0.5	3.1
Lars Christensen	0	0	0.2	0.2
E. European Producers	0.2	1.1	2.3	2.5
USA	4	3.3	3.8	0.2
Total ('000 MT)	850	910	940	965

Source: Harriman Chemsult.

There are thus a number of implications to be drawn from the soda ash case.

(a)   The single market programme, by means of reducing the cost of cross-border trade, may not be expected to achieve more competition in markets where the collusion is likely to be sustainable and where the incentives to collude are strong.

(b)   The only effective way to break up existing market-sharing agreements appears to be policy intervention: the Art. 85 (and 86) cases brought by the Commission against soda ash producers in 1990 seem to have stimulated some internal trade and led to major changes in purchasing behaviour for major customers who now can satisfy their requirements within single European-wide purchasing agreements.

(c)   Trade policy with the outside world is also essential: competition from extra-EU countries started to emerge when anti-dumping duties were eliminated in 1990, and their provisional reintroduction in 1995 (after lobbying from soda ash producers) certainly runs counter – and may even undermine – the impact of the competition investigations. The relationship – and the tensions – between competition policy and trade policy will be addressed in the final chapter on policy conclusions.

9.6. Competition policy against collusion

An important aim of competition policy is to punish collusive behaviour, though this is hard to detect and to prove in practice: documentary evidence of cartelization is not often easy to find.[133]

A more conceptual problem in dealing with collusion from an antitrust perspective is the notion that collusion may be tacit: a large body of theory, as we have seen, is dedicated to show that collusive outcomes may be sustained as equilibria of repeated interactions in a non-cooperative dynamic game. The equilibrium collusive outcome does not in this case result from an explicit agreement, but from the 'rational pursuit of individual self-interest in a situation of perceived mutual interdependence' (Rees [1993a, p. 38]).

The application of this notion poses obvious problems to antitrust systems, such as the EU's, which are based on a prohibition of collusion (and therefore on a behavioural notion). It is true, however, that recent developments in the interpretation of Art. 85 suggest that the European courts have become more sensitive to the notion that collusive behaviour would be likely to occur when there is significant scope for it; in which case 'restrictions of competition' come to encompass any activity which significantly increases the scope for collusive behaviour. This is graphically illustrated by the ECJ's interpretation of Art. 85(1) as given in the UK Tractor Exchange (1992) case: '... Art. 85(1) of the Treaty prohibits both actual anti-competitive effects and purely potential effects, provided that they are sufficiently appreciable ...'.

Our discussion of appropriate competition policy actions against collusion starts from the premise that there are two possible approaches (obviously not mutually exclusive) to combat collusion: one consisting of directly attacking collusive agreements (i.e. agreements through

---

[133]   However this difficulty should not be overstated: there are cases where substantial evidence has been found, as in the case of Polypropylene (1986). Fifteen major petrochemical producers (thirteen within the EU) were found to have operated a market-sharing and price-fixing cartel between 1977 and 1983, and direct documentary evidence was found of regular meetings held to set target prices, decide how to coordinate efforts to raise prices, and implement and monitor a system of quotas. Another case is Steel beams (1994).

which firms fix prices or quantities). The other is to attack those agreements which indirectly facilitate collusion ('secondary' agreements), i.e. to eliminate the conditions that make it easier for firms to sustain it.

In the rest of this section we consider the problems raised by these approaches. First, the necessary condition for being able to attack collusive agreements directly is for the competition authorities to detect collusion, and this may present formidable difficulties. Secondly, the secondary agreements which may be singled out for their role in sustaining collusion must be carefully identified.

In particular, Section 9.6.1 considers the extent to which it might be possible to make inferences on collusion from observed outcomes (price and quantity data). This is a particularly difficult topic. The notion that bouts of price wars indicate cartel disciplining, and therefore reveal coordination, appears quite robust. What can we infer, however, in the absence of a price war? Without detailed information on demand and costs, how can a competition authority tell whether the observed price path describes a cooperative or a non-cooperative equilibrium?

This question has been put into sharp relief by the Woodpulp case: the 1989 Commission decision that firms were colluding was rejected in 1993 by the ECJ, essentially on grounds that the same price path could have been explained by an alternative non-collusive model, i.e. it could equally have been the equilibrium of a non-cooperative game. This may have set a precedent to the effect that if any alternative explanation for price data other than collusion can be found, then the competition action might fail. While it may be in principle correct to try and 'discriminate' between a collusive and a non-collusive outcome by direct testing of a calibrated game-theoretic model, this requires extreme care because of the 'indistinguishability theorem'.

Section 9.6.2 focuses on information sharing as the main category of secondary agreements which might be used by firms to sustain collusion, because it makes monitoring easy. We consider in detail which types of information sharing between rivals may actually sustain collusion, and should thus be directly eliminated.

9.6.1. The problem of detection

When collusion cannot be proven through documentary evidence, the antitrust authorities are left with the option of seeking to infer collusion from price and quantity data. Indeed the approach adopted by the EU competition authorities has been to '... spend a lot of time trying to collect evidence of direct communication between competitors, threats of punishment or actual punishments of deviators', Phlips [1995, p.8].

This is in general a quite formidable task. More conclusive results could be derived where there was sufficiently firm evidence of a price war, or (even better) alternate periods of price stability and conflict (this could be supported for example by tests showing a 'structural break' in the price path between the two periods). Of course interpretation would have to be careful, and would have to consider such factors as the possible impact of the business cycle etc. In practice, however, few cases appear to have actually used this type of argument.

However, the most serious problems from a methodological point of view arise when no punishment phase can be observed, in which case there is a clear difficulty in distinguishing tacit collusion from parallel price movements resulting from non-cooperative strategic interaction between firms. The question is: in the absence of any evidence of price wars or other punishments, and without knowing costs, how is it possible to tell at all whether the observed prices are in fact the product of tacit collusion? Given that apparently collusive outcomes might be achieved without there being anti-competitive conduct, how can we tell whether behaviour is collusive or non-collusive?[134]

This is the recognized 'indistinguishability problem' between two different equilibria, which captures the difficulty presented by MacLeod [1985] in his work on 'conscious parallelism': as long as the profit functions are not known, there are no systematic differences between the size of price responses to exogenous shocks at the collusive and non-collusive equilibria. Hence looking, for example, at evidence of price parallelism between firms in a market may not tell us anything on whether they are engaged in collusion.

For the practice of competition policy, this raises a host of problems. Ultimately, the firms under investigation will always try to argue that observed sales, prices and profits are typical for a non-collusive equilibrium sustained in a repeated non-cooperative game; while the antitrust authority will seek to show that the same indicators are typical of a collusive equilibrium. Information asymmetries between the parties in the judgement would be decisive here.[135]

The empirical literature has also recently produced a stark example of the kind of problems which are encountered in making inferences on collusion from market data. Ellison [1994] re-examined the experience of the Joint Executive Committee (the 1880s US railroad cartel), to assess the applicability of the Green and Porter [1984] and Rotemberg and Saloner [1986] models of price wars. The main point is that while Green and Porter had found evidence of little collusion (the outcome was close to Cournot), Ellison obtains virtually perfect collusion by introducing in his model the assumption that demand is serially correlated. Thus model specification greatly affects the collusions that are drawn.

Thus two good econometric analyses, based on a very good data set, generate rather different results.[136] This suggests the following points:

(a) it is difficult to make reliable inferences even with a rich data set on prices, quantities, costs, etc.;

(b) in order to identify trigger strategies correctly, one would need several years of detailed data, which present a formidable information requirement (quite simply these are often not available);

(c) there is also a need for strong assumptions on functional forms.

---

[134] The 'Folk Theorem' shows that several more or less collusive equilibria can result from repeated non-cooperative play when deviations can be punished in a credible way.

[135] As anticipated, the potential for conflicting interpretation has been put in sharp relief by the Woodpulp case (1984). Fines were imposed on several extra-EU producers for having imported woodpulp into Europe in a regime of announced and enforced parallel price changes. The absence of deviations from the parallel time path (together with information exchanges, see above) was used as evidence of collusion. However the decision was annulled by the ECJ in 1993. Though it was not used in the final reasoning of the Court, the concept of a Cournot-Nash equilibrium was mentioned by the Advocate General – i.e. the notion that the observed result could be compatible with a non-collusive equilibrium in quantities.

[136] Another example is Rees [1993a], who used data presented to the UK Monopolies and Mergers Commission Report on White Salt – a homogeneous market, with a price-setting duopoly where firms are subject to capacity constraints. He finds that the possible explanations of the collusive equilibrium in terms of joint profit maximization are not supported by the data; the equilibrium outcome can be rather explained by threat strategies of the type of Abreu's 'simple penal codes'. However the explanation of the equilibrium remains an open question.

If these conditions are satisfied, then in principle it would be possible to estimate demand, cost and reaction functions and compare collusive and non-collusive outcomes of the game with the actual observed outcome (as in Slade [1987]). One should not underestimate, however, the exceptional informational requirements of these techniques. Most importantly, in most circumstances it does not seem sensible to make inferences only from observed outcomes, because of the indistinguishability problem – i.e. the lack of an agreed-upon benchmark that can be used by the Courts to identify collusion from price and quantity data.

9.6.2. Agreements facilitating collusion[137]

Given the above discussion on the difficulties of detecting collusion, and making inferences from market data, it might be advisable to adopt an approach based on the notion that firms will tend to collude whenever there is scope for them to do so.

Thus competition policy could put more emphasis on 'structural' measures, in particular focusing directly on secondary agreements which increase the scope for collusion. In this sense the current legal setting, which relies on showing that there has been some contact/negotiation between firms, corresponds quite well to the lessons from the theoretical economic analysis of collusion.

The most important form of secondary agreement which firms might enter into, and which might facilitate collusion through greater ease of monitoring, is information exchanges.

The European courts have devoted much attention to information exchanges between firms, as this is often the only form of communication between rival firms which can be substantiated in any way (i.e. of which there is any evidence). Indeed virtually all the cartel cases which have survived the proceedings of the EU courts have been based on some evidence like protocols of meetings within trade associations, which were taken to document the existence of a price agreement.

The Commission's understanding of information exchanges in relation to collusion is summarized effectively in the Suiker Unie & Ors (1975) decision, where such exchanges are seen as conflicting with a notion of 'competition' interpreted as 'independent decision making' by firms, or 'absence of market coordination'.[138] In a few cases, this has been taken by the courts to mean that an information agreement by itself can be an infringement of Art. 85(1).

While it is self-evident that information sharing can help sustain collusion through improving monitoring possibilities, it is manifestly true that not all forms of information sharing can do so in the same way, and to the same degree. In this section, we will briefly review which types of information sharing should be considered more effective in increasing the scope for tacit

---

[137]   This section draws heavily on Kühn and Vives [1995].

[138]   'The criteria of coordination and cooperation ... must be understood in the light of the concept inherent in the provisions of the Treaty relating to competition that each economic operator must determine independently the policy which he intends to adopt on the Common Market... Although it is correct to say that this requirement of independence does not deprive economic operators of the right to adapt themselves intelligently to the existing and anticipated conduct of their competitors, it does, however, strictly preclude any direct or indirect contact between such operators, the object or effect whereof is either to influence the conduct on the market of an actual competitor, or to disclose to such a competitor the course of conduct which they themselves have decided to adopt or contemplate adopting on the market', ECR 1663).

collusion; we will then argue as a desirable policy development that these types of information sharing should be treated as infringements *per se* of Art. 85(1).

The most important point is to what extent does an information-sharing agreement facilitate monitoring. When monitoring is not effective, then we should expect collusion to break down frequently, while if monitoring is good, then firms can sustain near-perfect collusion (or at any rate longer collusive periods).

Secondly, the degree of aggregation of the data also matters (both at the industry vs. firm level, and in geographical terms). The Commission already distinguishes sharply between exchange of aggregate industry data and individual firm data, with only the latter presenting a real problem. Though it may not be appropriate to draw such a sharp distinction in terms of their effects, this is broadly justified as individualized data clearly facilitates punishment strategies that single out a deviating firm.

Other important features include the frequency of information exchange, as exchange of yearly data hardly seems to increase the scope of collusion.

Also who is made party to the information matters, i.e. whether it is shared only among producers, or whether consumers are also included. In Woodpulp, the Commission argued that the increased market transparency provided by information exchanges is detrimental to competition, because it discourages 'secret price cuts' which are the essence of competition. There are two effects here: on the one hand, consumers benefit from increased transparency, because it reduces their search costs; on the other hand it may be true that in a dynamic context, increased 'transparency' may support collusion by making secret price cuts more readily detectable (it improves monitoring of collusive arrangements). The result is therefore ambiguous, which suggests as a possible rule that information exchange may be objectionable if it is limited to producers at the same level in the production chain (e.g. internal trade association statistics); however it may not be unambiguously negative when it extends to downstream consumers (e.g. announcements in the trade press). That is, overall we should be suspicious of information-sharing agreements where there is no market transparency benefit for consumers.

In conclusion: if competition authorities could directly attack collusion on prices, there is no reason why information exchanges should be a worry for competition policy. However, it is difficult in most cases to prove effectively infringements of Art. 85(1) in the form of price-fixing agreements; at the same time, it is the case that these agreements can only be sustained if firms have access to sufficient information about the actions of their competitors. Thus the competition authorities should consider acting directly on those contacts which might be motivated by an attempt to facilitate collusion. This might mean regarding certain types of information exchanges (mainly direct exchanges of price and quantity information) as a restriction of competition in themselves, as direct infringements of Art. 85(1).

Another reason why this course of action would be desirable is that acting on information exchanges is also powerful in cases where no agreements to collude exist in the real sense, but firms are able to obtain collusive outcomes through their understanding of interaction in the market: i.e. tacit collusion.

9.7. Conclusion

Most collusion cases which fall under the jurisdiction of the European courts fall into two categories: 'stand-off' agreements, and within-country collusion to keep potential entrants out. We expect the process of integration to affect these in a different way.

In particular, we expect some entry to occur into the various national markets as a result of market integration – especially where products are differentiated – and this could undermine the internal collusive agreement between incumbent firms to some degree.

Conversely, we do not expect geographical market-sharing agreements to be much affected by the single market, as the incentive to use national boundaries as focal points for these agreements is not reduced. On the contrary, if the cost of trade is reduced, then it might be even easier to ship goods to a market – and thus punish deviators.

Our main conclusion is thus that market integration measures may not reduce the incidence of collusion. Although within-country collusion is likely to be discouraged to some degree, the effect is more ambiguous for cross-border collusion.

There is therefore no reason for the competition authorities to relax vigilance on collusion, though pursuing actions against colluding firms remains difficult (though there are some principles which might be followed, e.g. looking more carefully at certain types of markets where collusion is more likely; looking for evidence of price wars).

In particular, the 'indistinguishability problem' poses serious problems to anyone seeking to infer collusion from market data. Soda ash (1991) is another good example. Several cartel agreements spanning various decades had shared the market between the two main producers, with UK/Ireland assigned to ICI, and Continental Europe to Solvay. When these were terminated in 1972, both firms continued to serve their former markets. In the 1980s, when UK prices increased by 15–20% above those of the Continent, there was no attempt by Solvay to enter into the UK. The Commission interpreted the fact that neither ICI nor Solvay entered each other's market as evidence of tacit collusion. However Phlips [1995a, p. 13] argues that 'the absence of market penetration can be rationalized as a feature of the non-collusive Nash equilibrium in a repeated game' (see also Boehnlein [1994]).

As no robust inferences can be made at all in some cases, our view is that competition policy should adopt some more 'structural' measures, i.e. measures which reduce the likelihood that collusion might be achieved. Thus we believe that more attention should be paid to secondary agreements with a potential for favouring collusion. One important instance is the elimination of various types of contracts that make it easier to sustain collusion, possibly by making them independent infringements of Art. 85; another possibility is further trade liberalization.

The latter comes from the observation that the main worry remains cross-border collusive agreements to share markets by national boundaries. These kinds of collusive agreements are potentially difficult to attack, since it is obviously not possible to 'force' a producer in one country to enter another country's market. However, since we have concluded that market integration may reduce the opportunity for within-country collusion, by the same argument opening the external borders of the EU is a possible policy response to reduce cross-border collusion within the EU. Thus one additional option might be to further liberalize trade policy with the rest of the world.

10. Efficiency defences for cooperative agreements

10.1. Introduction

In the previous chapter we discussed the treatment of collusion on prices and production in European competition policy, exploring in particular the effects of market integration on firms' incentives to enter into new agreements, and their ability to sustain collusion in a more integrated market.

It is possible however that 'collusive agreements' on dimensions other than prices and quantities may also have efficiency-enhancing effects. Various efficiency defences are routinely used by firms to argue that an agreement produces benefits far outweighing the potential harm to competition. Emphasizing the expected efficiency gains, such agreements are generally described as 'cooperative', and are treated with indulgence in EU competition policy. In particular, the general prohibition of interfirm agreements contained in Art. 85(1) is weakened in this area by a variety of exceptions under Art. 85(3), in the form of block exemptions and individual exemptions.[139]

In this chapter we examine the credibility of these efficiency defences, and the adequacy of the current EU competition rules in finding an appropriate trade-off between the potential social benefits of cooperation, and its social harms. We also critically evaluate the economic rationale for the widely held belief that in an integrated market collaborative agreements should be entered into more frequently between EU firms. The launch of the single market programme was accompanied by hopes for more intense competition between firms across Europe, and at the same time by great enthusiasm on the part of the Commission for an expected increase in cross-border collaboration between enterprises. More intense cooperation was expected to accelerate integration, and thus unlock substantial unexploited efficiency gains.[140] Indeed, the White Paper *Completing the Internal Market* [1985] identified intra-EU industrial cooperation as a major policy aim for the Commission:

> 'Community action must [...] create an environment or conditions likely to favour the development of cooperation between undertakings' (p. 34),

and promised to deploy 'all means available to the Commission' for the purpose of facilitating cross-border cooperation, including competition policy:

> 'The Commission will also continue to deploy competition rules by authorizing cooperation between undertakings which can promote technical or economic progress within the framework of a unified market' (ibid.). [141]

---

[139] EU competition policy draws a distinction between 'cooperative' and 'concentrative' joint ventures, the former being dealt with (as any interfirm agreement) under Art. 85, the latter under the Merger Regulation. The rationale for this distinction is discussed further below. This chapter is however concerned mainly with agreements falling under Art. 85.

[140] Though some have argued vigorously against this hypothesis: see for example Kay [1991].

[141] Other instruments were to be technology policy (subsidies to joint R&D programme), and regional policies ('The Commission will also seek to ensure that Community budgetary and financial facilities make their full contribution to the development of greater cooperation between firms in different Member States. [...] The Regional Fund must also be enabled to contribute to greater cooperation between firms' (White Paper, pp. 34-5)).

After examining how firms' incentives to cooperate relate to market integration, we emphasize that in fact market integration should remove some of the incentives for these agreements (such as overcoming artificial barriers to entry in a discrete geographical market). In an integrated market, many cross-border agreements – particularly those joining together firms with substitute assets – simply have anti-competitive aims.

We start in Section 10.2 with some empirical evidence on recent trends in cross-border cooperation, which may shed some light on the motivation for firms' actions in this area. In Section 10.3 we consider the economic foundations of the 'efficiency defence' for cooperative agreements. While there may be efficiency motives for cooperation, which imply they may be socially beneficial (for example through increased variety for the consumer), firms seeking to enter into an agreement will always overemphasize its prospective benefits to the competition authorities, and their claims should be evaluated with great care. We are generally sceptical of the true size of the gains being claimed. Our assessment is different for R&D, where we believe that the potential efficiency gains are of a different order of magnitude and there is therefore a more clear-cut case for preferential competition treatment. In Section 10.4 we consider some examples of agreements which have received approval from the Commission over the past decade, and seek to evaluate the significance of the efficiency defences in each case. The impact of integration is considered in Section 10.5, where we evaluate the expectation that a more integrated market should be characterized by greater incidence of cooperation. Finally, in Section 10.6 we discuss the current EU competition policy approach towards cooperation. We conclude in Section 10.7.

10.2. Empirical evidence on trends in cooperation

Under the broad heading of 'cooperation', we consider in this chapter a variety of agreements between firms (involving both equity participation in a new entity, or long-term contracts) whereby the parties commit assets and skills (inputs) to a certain task. This includes the case of agreements whereby a firm grants another firm exclusive use of an input, which may consist of a physical input or derive from an intellectual property right.

The range of possible collaborative arrangements includes joint ventures (which encompass a variety of ownership arrangements, from equity participation in a separate undertaking, to other financial arrangements[142]); various agreements between partners, for example research partnerships and co-production agreements; and some forms of licensing (of a know-how, a distinctive product, or a trademark) between (potential) rivals.

Empirical research on cooperation between firms tends to be limited to a number of firm-level case studies in the business literature. Systematic information on cooperative agreements is not collected in official statistics, and most of the available data is put together by tracking announcements in the financial press.[143] For this reason, different sources tend not to be

---

[142]   Traditional joint ventures are created when two or more partners join forces to create a newly incorporated company in which each has an equity position, thereby each expecting a proportional share of dividends. They thus involve two or more legally distinct organizations, each of which invests in the venture and actively participates in the decision-making activities of the jointly owned entity. Other financial arrangements are possible however (see Bresnahan and Salop [1986] for a discussion of their incentive properties).

[143]   This has implications: in particular, in many cases the source of the information is likely to be press releases by the firms involved, which may be biased accounts of their purpose: e.g. participating firms may seek to mislead competitors

consistent or easily comparable, and firm conclusions are not easy to draw. However, while the absolute number of agreements which is reported may not be accurate, it is still possible to piece together a picture by considering the proportion of agreements in different categories, and how these relative numbers evolve over time.

Some insight into the evolution of interfirm cooperation can be gleaned from a database of collaborative agreements collated at INSEAD (from announcements in the specialist press) since 1975. We compare below the picture for the decade 1975–85 (as given in Hergert and Morris [1988]), and for the period 1986–93.[144] A few stylized facts are worth noticing:

(a) Firstly, there has been a decline in the proportion of intra-EU agreements since 1986. below, on origins of the partners, shows a percentage decline in within-Europe agreements after 1986, from around 30% over the period 1975–85 to 24% in 1986 and to only 17% in 1993. Conversely, EU firms appear to have entered into more agreements with the 'rest of the world' (especially Eastern Europe) over the same period, as did US firms – which suggests that these ventures are frequently used to circumvent obstacles to direct entry.

(b) Secondly, the incidence of cooperation with rivals in the same product market remains very high, relative to cooperation with 'complementary' firms. Both in the 1975–85 and the 1986–93 periods, according to the INSEAD database, collaboration with 'rivals' accounted for around 70% of all agreements. This may support the notion of cooperation being sought for its effects on competition.

(c) Thirdly, there has been a shift from agreements on R&D to agreements having as their purpose joint production and joint marketing: i.e. cooperation has become 'closer' to the product market.
Table 10.2 below considers the purposes of the collaboration, for the three main trading blocs, and compares patterns across time. Over the period 1975–85, the majority of all cooperative ventures in the INSEAD database were formed to engage in joint product development (39%), followed by production (22%) and – at some distance – by marketing (8%). The breakdown by origin of the partners shows that in the early period, collaborative ventures within the EU were even more likely to concern R&D than the total (this is also true for the US, suggesting that agreements between different blocs are often formed for the purposes of reaching a market). Over the next period, the proportion of all agreements concerning R&D declines to a third, while marketing increases to 21%. In Europe, the proportion of R&D agreements declines from 42% to 31%, while agreements on marketing increase to 23%.

---

over their motive and activities by misrepresenting themselves. In some cases, joint ventures may go unreported because the parents maintain strict confidentiality.

[144] The interpretation must be cautious, however, because of the variety of other factors which might have affected the prevalence of cooperation, in addition to EU market integration. For example, the rate of technological change and the emergence of world-scale competition in some sectors are both powerful incentives for entering into joint ventures, and their relationship with internal EU integration may not be easily disentangled.

Table 10.1.   Origin of the partners (%)

	Intra-EU	EU-US	EU-Jap	EU-Row	US-US	US-Jap	US-Row	Row	All blocs (absolute numbers)
1975–85	30.8	25.8	10.1	7.0	8.4	8.4	4.2	5.4	
1986	24.1	24.1	10.5	7.0	11.8	9.2	3.5	9.7	228
1987	27.0	12.6	11.7	12.6	10.0	7.4	7.0	7.4	230
1988	32.6	17.8	12.9	10.2	11.0	6.4	3.8	5.3	264
1989	29.4	16.5	6.6	11.8	8.8	10.3	6.6	9.9	272
1990	21.0	19.8	13.9	14.7	8.8	5.0	8.8	8.0	238
1991	18.7	12.9	7.1	18.7	8.7	11.6	12.0	11.6	241
1992	13.8	14.4	2.5	22.0	8.6	12.2	11.9	14.7	327
1993	17.4	14.5	4.2	22.2	7.1	6.4	14.2	14.5	311

Source: INSEAD database.

Table 10.2.   Purposes of collaboration by economic bloc (%)

	Dev.	Prod.	Mktg	Dev.& Prod.	Dev.& Mktg	Prod.& Mktg	Dev.& Prod. &Mktg	Total* (absolute numbers)
Intra-EU								
1975–85	42.1	18.0	5.1	24.1	1.5	2.6	6.7	195
1986–93	31.2	21.6	23.4	10.9	1.8	5.3	5.8	394
EU-US								
1975–85	40.0	21.3	8.3	14.8	3.0	5.3	7.7	169
1986–93	31.9	14.3	24.8	9.8	2.6	9.5	7.2	307
EU-Jap								
1975–85	29.0	31.9	11.6	11.6	4.4	7.3	4.4	69
1986–93	17.5	38.3	20.8	12.3	2.6	5.8	2.6	154
Intra-US								
1975–85	57.1	21.4	3.6	3.6	5.4	3.6	5.4	56
1986–93	54.4	15.4	14.2	4.7	5.3	2.4	3.6	169
US-Jap								
1975–85	11.6	21.7	14.5	16.0	20.3	13.0	2.9	68
1986–93	32.5	23.4	14.3	12.3	1.0	8.4	8.4	154
Total								
1975–85	39	22	8	17	3	5	6	562
1986–93	33	21	21	10	2	7	6	1,211

* does not include rest of the world (ROW)
Source: INSEAD database.

Table 10.3 below describes in more detail the decline in R&D and the increase in joint production agreements within the EU over the period 1986–93, particularly towards the end of the period.

Table 10.3.   Purposes of collaboration within Europe, by year

	Dev.	Prod.	Mktg	Dev.& Prod.	Dev.& Mktg	Prod.& Mktg	Dev.&Prod. &Mktg	Total*
1986	18	7	8	9	0	0	0	55
87	24	8	10	5	0	4	6	62
88	24	9	22	7	3	0	4	86
89	20	7	19	4	2	4	7	80
90	12	13	3	9	0	1	4	50
91	13	14	1	5	0	1	0	45
92	8	12	4	3	1	7	1	45
93	4	15	25	1	1	4	0	53

* includes 'other'
Source: INSEAD database.

Supplementary information may be obtained from a few empirical studies of the UK.

Glaister and Buckley [1994] examine joint ventures entered into by UK companies over the period 1980–89 (the database of over 500 ventures was collated from announcements in the press[145]). Joint ventures between UK firms and other European partners were found to be less likely to be marketing-related than joint ventures with US or Japanese partners (45% of agreements with US and Japanese partners involved marketing[146]). This is taken to indicate that market entry is a powerful motivation for joint ventures ('... joint ventures with more geographically remote partners such as the US and Japan may be used as market entry mechanisms and thus have to involve marketing activities. This is not the case as often in Europe to the extent that UK firms are already in the market'). However it must be noted that this evidence would also be compatible with an anti-competitive motive, if more intense competition was coming (in the relevant sectors) from the US and Japan. It is difficult to draw firm conclusions without more information on what proportion of joint ventures involved a combination of assets and skills which are genuinely complementary (e.g. manufacturing and distribution), rather than an alliance between firms with similar capabilities, which is aimed at neutralizing rivalry between them in the product market.

The study of Millington and Bayliss [1995], on transnational joint ventures between UK and EU-based partners, is based on a survey of 812 UK manufacturing (quoted) PLCs, 100 of which (around 17%) were found to have one or more cross-frontier joint ventures with a

---

[145]   The industries with the greatest incidence of joint ventures were found to be telecoms, aerospace, financial services, and to a lesser extent automobiles – though the pattern differs somewhat depending on the origin of the partner. Joint ventures with other European partners more often concern aerospace and financial services; with US partners telecoms and financial services; with Japan financial services, electrical and automobiles.

[146]   There are, of course, important sectoral differences: pure R&D is found to be the purpose most often for aerospace, telecommunications, and other electrical; production for chemicals, and automobiles; development and production for aerospace, automobiles and telecoms; and marketing for food and drink, telecoms, distribution, and other services.

European partner. Almost 80% of these joint ventures involved companies operating in two very different types of industries: either mature industries, fairly open to import penetration, using established technologies with limited or exploited economies of scale; or growth industries, with high incidence of R&D, also open to international trade, with strong competition from other trading blocs.

A significant difference is found between large and smaller firms both in terms of propensity to cooperate, and in motives for cooperation. Firms with a turnover in excess of UKL 100 million are over 3.5 times more likely to enter into a joint venture with a European partner than firms with a turnover of below UKL 20 million. Firms in the lower size class also tend to form joint ventures mainly in order to 'penetrate markets in which they do not yet operate', while large firms identify as the main cause for cooperation the 'increase in competitive pressures stemming both from an increasingly unified EU market, and increasing global competition (especially in mature and high-technology sectors)'. Again an important criterion for assessing the claim that an agreement is necessary to 'achieve market entry' is the extent to which the joint venture effectively combines complementary capabilities, rather than pools similar assets and skills. Of 46 joint ventures studied in depth, 32 (70%) gave as their reason 'circumventing national barriers and achieving market penetration'. However, of these only less than half (14) had a vertical element, involving for example a producer and a distributor. The rest were between firms producing similar goods.

Overall, the available empirical evidence indicates that firms setting up a joint venture or another form of partnership tend to mention three main motives: to combine their resources or assets in a way that is somehow more efficient, to enter a market where they are not present, and to carry out joint R&D. In the next section, we discuss the economic rationale for these efficiency defences of cooperation.

10.3. An economic analysis of efficiency defences

Our main tool of analysis in the evaluation of efficiency defences is the distinction between complementary and substitute assets and skills.

'Complementarity' refers to the fact that the production of a good (or service) requires the combination of different inputs and assets. All factors of production which are needed to manufacture a good, or supply it to the market, are therefore in this specific sense complementary (for that particular purpose). Conversely, 'substitutability' refers to assets and inputs which have effectively the same function in the production or supply of a particular good. In this framework, an agreement between firms may be described as bringing together complementary assets where the partners contribute distinct skills and inputs which can be combined either for producing an entirely new good (for example a telecom operator and a publisher offering an on-line news service), or for supplying a product to the market (for example an agreement between a manufacturer and a distributor for the sale of the good in a different geographical market, where there is an element of selective vertical integration). The agreement brings together substitute assets where it joins together firms which have at least the capability of manufacturing similar products.

The more recent economic theory of the firm provides some insights into the efficiency effects of (selective) asset integration, which may be helpful when assessing efficiency defences for cooperation. The traditional view of the firm is that of a combination of assets, in a way that makes it possible to produce (and sell) more efficiently than its constituent parts separately. That is, assets are integrated in a single entity because this is the efficient (cost-minimizing) organization. Some more useful insights are offered by the 'incomplete-contracting' theory of the firm.[147] This develops the earlier 'transaction cost' approach, which argued that vertical integration of assets may be preferable to market transaction when there are dangers of inefficient investments. The 'incomplete-contracting' theory addresses the concern that agents may underinvest (relative to what would be socially optimal) because some of the benefits of their investment are dissipated in future bargaining over the stream of profit from an asset. Hence efficient investments by agents depends on the control structure over the assets; and assets are efficiently assigned when they mitigate this underinvestment.

The concept that a control structure is optimal when it provides the agents with (second-) best incentives to invest is used to understand the boundaries of the firm. In particular, it is shown that common ownership of assets is likely to increase overall efficiency when the assets are complementary. That is, integration of complementary assets has particularly strong efficiency reasons.

There are of course also 'non-efficiency' reasons why assets may be integrated into a firm, rather than acquired through market transactions, in particular the exercise of monopoly power on the product market. However, the dangers of market monopolization may be more significant where the firm brings under its control substitute assets.

In the context of interfirm cooperation, an agreement which brings together firms with substitute assets has thus greater potential for collusion – provided of course that the structure of the market is sufficiently concentrated (where concentration is low, the anti-competitive effect will be negligible and there is no real reason for concern). In a concentrated market, a cooperative agreement between firms with substitute assets provides an explicit framework for coordinating behaviour (e.g. through the discussion of pricing policies, and the sharing of cost information). There are also clear commitment and credibility effects (the parties commit resources explicitly, or make an investment in a joint asset), and the ability to monitor a rival is increased, all of which makes collusion sustainable. A common subsidiary may also be the vehicle for the side payments which may be necessary to redistribute the rents from collusion.[148]

Conversely, an agreement joining together firms with complementary skills and assets may be expected *ex ante* to have greater potential for net efficiency gains. This may also allow deployment of inputs and assets in new ways which may not have been achievable by one firm alone.[149]

---

[147] See in particular Grossman and Hart [1986], Hart and Moore [1990] and Moore [1992].

[148] Bresnahan and Salop [1986], among others, showed how collaborative links between firms affect the parties' incentives to compete. As the nature of joint ventures implies financial interests among competitors, the parties will not compete vigorously with the venture – or indeed with each other. In particular, the sharing of the joint venture profits between the parents/stockholders reduces their incentive to expand output and thereby lower prices. A related feature is that the parents have a private incentive to structure the agreement in a way that removes the discretion of the venture's management over prices and output, and replaces it either with direct control by the parents or with a formula.

[149] However, even in this case there may be anti-competitive horizontal effects, for example if the agreement effectively forecloses access to a particular input, which is scarce or not replicable.

We apply this general framework to discuss the main efficiency defences invoked by firms when entering into cooperative agreements, which fall under the following categories:

(a)   cooperative agreements may generate cost reductions and rationalization of capacity through the sharing of existing assets;
(b)   cooperation may generate efficiency gains by bringing under joint control assets with strong complementarities (vertical integration effects);
(c)   they may allow access to a new geographical market when entry without a partner would be difficult or may not occur at all;
(d)   they may lead to the development of a new product or process (R&D) which the partners could not have achieved individually.

10.3.1. Efficiency gains from sharing or coordinating existing assets

Firms often claim that they entered into a cooperative agreement with each other because of cost savings to joint operation, for example in production. The argument that efficiency gains may be realized through sharing an asset or input, and achieving more efficient organization of production, is often used by firms with substitute assets. It is, however, doubtful that cooperative agreements may be indispensable to generate the claimed efficiency gains, and that alternative arrangements would not produce comparable results. The case is different where the efficiency gains to the agreement are expected to come from coordination of complementary assets, in which case the agreement has characteristics of selective vertical integration. We review these efficiency defences briefly below.

(a)   Capacity sharing: in the presence of demand uncertainty, firms may need to keep a certain amount of spare capacity to cope with positive shocks. An agreement which enables firms to share capacity also allows them to rationalize the amount of excess capacity in the market, because they can essentially 'swap' their constraints. However, in order for this argument to be valid, a convincing case would have to be made demonstrating why effective capacity sharing could not be achieved through the market.
(b)   Economies of specialization: firms may mutually agree to focus on a smaller range of products (i.e. effectively to share the manufacture of a product line between them), and then distribute each other's goods in their respective markets. One argument which is sometimes made is that 'a firm is at a disadvantage if it does not offer a full range of products'; this may however overstate the significance of consumer search costs. A very common argument is that this type of agreement is beneficial because it allows firms to realize economies of scale, as well as learning economies. As these economies of specialization could be achieved by firms on their own, it is not clear why a cooperative agreement is necessary. Where returns to scale are significant, firms should have an independent incentive to specialize, and inefficient under-specialization in production could be eliminated without the need for an agreement. On the other hand, if the argument is that by agreeing to specialize production and to distribute the full range, each firm gains access to a new geographical market, a case would have to be made that there are very strong asymmetries in accessing each other's market (agreements which have as their object entry into a new geographical market are considered in more detail in Section 10.4.2).
(c)   Economies of scale are also often claimed as a justification for cooperation. In fact, economies of scale in production are difficult to achieve if there is no integration of production facilities and production continues to be managed at the plant level. Cost

efficiencies may be obtained, however, through multiplant organization, firstly through managerial economies, but also though a selection effect, i.e. if production is reorganized to reflect the relative technical efficiency of different plants, or if capacity is better utilized. Whether these effects may outweigh the anti-competitive effects of a reduction in competition is ultimately an empirical issue. Overall, the evidence of actual cost savings achieved through joint operations in mergers is mixed (see Chapter 11 below). It is difficult to imagine that a cooperative agreement – where management remains in principle separate – may achieve significantly better results than a complete integration of assets.

(d) Vertical integration: efficiency gains from coordination of assets should be expected to be substantial where the agreement joins together complementary assets – as where it has characteristics of selective vertical integration. An aspect which must be considered in this case, however, is the effect of the agreement on assets which are substitute to the complements. Where the agreement ties assets together to the exclusion of rivals, there may be a horizontal foreclosure effect which needs to be explored.

10.3.2. Expansion into new geographical markets

An oft-quoted reason for cross-border cooperation between enterprises is that it makes possible the penetration of new geographical markets by firms lacking local knowledge or expertise. The essence of the agreement in this case is the transfer of an existing product or technology to the partner, in exchange for local information and marketing skills. This is clearly a vertical issue: a firm manufacturing a product in one market requires complementary skills for selling into another market, and may achieve informational benefits from cooperating with a local firm with superior knowledge of local market conditions. Forming an alliance with a local partner also enables firms to circumvent certain absolute or artificial barriers to entry – including artificial restrictions to trade (high tariffs and quotas) and discriminatory public procurement barriers.

This type of cooperation should be seen as efficiency-enhancing, if it involves the combination of manufacturing skills in one market with distribution expertise in another geographical market: that is, if the agreement joins together firms with truly complementary assets.

The assessment must be much more cautious when the agreement for entering into a new market joins together firms with substitute assets. In several cases a firm has licensed the manufacture of its product, or its trademark, to a firm which produces similar goods in other geographical markets. This has been justified on grounds that new market entry typically requires costs to be sunk, while the profitability of entry is *ex ante* very uncertain; a licensing arrangement thus provides a way of 'experimenting' with a new market, without necessarily incurring the large sunk costs of full-scale entry, and reducing the exposure to risk.

While this is true, the key issue remains the extent to which entry through this means is in fact a way of removing the competitive effect of entry, or foreclosing the market to rivals. Market entry through licensing (of know-how or trademarks) essentially removes competition between partners with substitute assets. Indeed this form of entry is effectively a commitment not to enter the market directly. In these cases, while there is a positive welfare effect in the form of increased variety for the consumer, it is also important to evaluate whether there was any other possibility of achieving direct entry at minimum efficient scale. If there was, there are strong reasons to be suspicious of the licensing agreement.

10.3.3. Joint development of a product or process

Firms may enter into cooperative agreements (of various forms) for jointly developing a new product or process – rather than undertaking the necessary research and development in-house, or purchasing the relevant inputs and assets on the market. In particular, the reasons most often given for cooperation in R&D include:

(a)   synergies in collaborators' existing assets or skills;

(b)   cost savings made possible by sharing fixed assets and sunk costs, and thus generating economies of scale;

(c)   prevention of waste, if cooperation pre-empts rival firms from simultaneously carrying out research which is duplicative;

(d)   capital market imperfections leading to limited financial resources, and consequent inability of firms to acquire relevant assets independently;

(e)   sharing of risk across the collaborating partners, which makes it possible to undertake more risky projects, as well as expand the number of projects being carried out (this may be especially the case when associated with investments that serve uncertain demand or involve uncertain technology).[150]

Cooperation in R&D has some characteristics of joint production, and may join together firms with both substitute and complementary assets. For example, firms manufacturing and supplying a similar good (substitute assets) may combine their R&D effort to develop a new technique, or a new version of the product; while firms with complementary assets may combine their skills to develop an entirely new product (the scope for complementarities is large in new product development).

As in the previous efficiency defences, there may be reason to be more suspicious of cooperation when it brings together firms which own or control substitute assets, because in these circumstances any agreement is more likely to affect the intensity of product-market rivalry. However this may have different relevance for the cases of product innovation and process innovation. In product innovation the potentially anti-competitive effects of joint R&D for rivalry in the product market are more significant than in process innovation, because in the former the partners will either jointly or separately produce the same good; in the latter it may be easier to enforce some separation of R&D from the production of goods incorporating the new technique.

Innovation has, however, very distinct characteristics, which increase the size of the efficiency gains to be expected from joint R&D – relative to cooperation in production.

Firstly, the protection conferred on research findings through intellectual property rights is not perfect, and as a result there may be technological spillovers: successful research results by one firm also benefit its competitors. The existence of spillovers is an externality which dampens a firm's incentives to carry out R&D, if it fears that rivals will at least partially free-

---

[150]   This may be confirmed by the empirical evidence on the type of industries which are most often interested in R&D joint ventures: in the US, the traditional focus is on computers, electronic components, medical equipment and financial services: all high-tech industries requiring large high-risk investments. It is also confirmed by the high incidence of collaborative links in the European aerospace and defence industry, and heavy engineering industries in general, such as rail transport. Common characteristics are heavy investments in technology, and long lead times, plus shrinking market and global competition.

ride on its effort. The incentives for R&D may thus be suboptimal and there may be undersupply of R&D. Joint research can internalize the problem by allowing the potential users to take account of these spillover effects. Cooperation should thus correct the externality and reinstate the incentives for R&D. The increase in R&D following the elimination of the externality should be particularly significant at least in sectors where these spillovers are large.[151]

In addition, economic analysis has also identified another reason why joint R&D may be efficiency-enhancing. While the incentive for each firm to undertake research may be suboptimal in the presence of spillovers, the overall volume of R&D carried out may be excessive from a social welfare point of view, if firms duplicate each other's effort. A joint R&D programme should enhance efficiency by preventing needless duplication of R&D expenditures.

Overall, there appears to be more convincing efficiency justifications for cooperation in R&D than for other forms of interfirm cooperation, and this has informed public policy towards design R&D. Joint R&D activities have been a natural candidate for preferential treatment in competition policy, and a more lenient treatment is reserved to them both in US competition law (National Cooperative Research Act 1984, which put joint R&D under a 'rule of reason'), and in Europe (Block Exemption 1985).[152]

However it is important to consider the impact of joint R&D not only on product market competition, but also on competition in R&D itself. The concern is that cooperative R&D ventures may end up doing less research, if cooperation eliminates the incentive of independent firms to innovate before their rivals, i.e. to beat their rivals in the 'race' to produce an innovation and appropriate the benefits. This results from the fact that the market rewards only those who are first in the innovation race (rather than rewarding them on the basis of their R&D inputs).[153] Especially in concentrated industries, joint research may effectively be a way for rivals to avoid R&D competition, and may slow down the pace of research (relative to what would be socially desirable).

This is an important aspect which is often underestimated, as discussions of the efficiency of joint R&D tend to give more weight to the benefits of eliminating needless duplication, and 'excessive' R&D. In fact, the notion that R&D may be socially wasteful because there is 'too much' of it may be of relevance only to the (not very plausible) case in which independent firms would undertake exactly the same R&D programme. In practice, R&D programmes are

---

[151]   There is a significant empirical literature seeking to assess the existence of technological spillovers, which suggests that these are important particularly in sectors such as computers, communication equipment, electronic components and aircraft, where the productivity of R&D is high. However their importance should not be overestimated. In particular Geroski [1993] emphasizes that the transmission of information is not costless, and indeed imitation costs and time tend to vary with the amount of basic research done by the imitator. Spillover effects may also be different for basic research and for development activities embodying innovation into a product (the latter is often too specific to spill over; more costly; has more competitive feedbacks from output markets), and may change systematically over the life of a collaborative programme. Technological spillovers are likely to be larger in the case of basic research than for development activities: hence cooperative research is likely to increase innovation more than cooperative development.

[152]   Evidence suggests that the NCRA in the US encouraged joint research: as reported by Shapiro and Willig [1990], reports of joint venture formation rose markedly at the time the NCRA was being considered by the US Congress.

[153]   Both Ordover and Willig [1985] and Grossman and Shapiro [1986] argue that by replacing competitive decision-making with joint decision-making, joint research may prevent a patent race and thus decrease the pace of R&D.

easy to differentiate, and the parallel development of similar strands of research may be socially beneficial.

In summary, joint R&D may create concerns for competition in two dimensions: in the product market, and in the R&D market. At the product-market level, joint R&D may affect the ease of collusion (especially where firms with substitute assets are involved). Anti-competitive outcomes are particularly likely where cooperation is allowed to extend to further stages (such as production, or even marketing).[154] However there are special efficiency reasons – to do with the special characteristics of innovation – for allowing interfirm cooperation in R&D programmes. In the market for R&D, however, it is possible that competition in R&D may be stifled by cooperation. This aspect is often underestimated, and should be evaluated carefully when assessing the efficiency defence for cooperation in R&D.

10.3.4. Summary

Economic analysis suggests that there may be social benefits from joint operation between firms. However, agreements can only be justified when the efficiency defences for such behaviour are significant. Claims of efficiency gains from collaboration should thus be considered very carefully. An essential distinction must be drawn between agreements which join firms with *substitute* or *complementary* assets. We must also distinguish collaborative agreements in terms of whether their effect is merely that of *horizontal concentration*, or includes elements of *vertical integration*.

A more robust case can be produced in favour of joint R&D, though the distinction between substitute and complementary assets for inventing new products/services remains important – both for competition in the product market and competition in R&D (the dynamic process of innovation). In this sense it is important to consider the extent to which cooperation removes from the market assets which could give rise to competition in R&D (as well as in the product market).

10.4. Case evidence for the efficiency defences

In this section, we discuss some of the available evidence on efficiency defences for cooperation, as may be derived from a selection of cases approved by the Commission. It is worth noting at the outset that, as the evaluation of the efficiency gains is inevitably difficult, much effort appears to be spent by the Commission and the courts in deciding whether the parties to an agreement are at all competitors in the relevant product and geographical market. Where it is concluded that they are not, obviously the restrictive effect on competition is negligible. The analysis of the efficiency effects does not appear very systematic.

10.4.1. Sharing and coordinating existing assets

In a number of cases, agreements have received individual exemption by the Commission from Art. 85(1) on grounds that the expected productive efficiency gains from sharing an asset, or joining together complementary assets, outweighed the restrictive effects on

---

[154]   EU competition policy often has a difficult job in trading off incentives for innovation against reduced product-market competition. As discussed below in Section 8.6, the EU approach of allowing collaboration further down the chain of production is potentially likely to lead to less product-market competition than the US regime of allowing collaboration only at the R&D stage, though it may have positive effects on incentives to innovate.

competition. A review of these cases suggests, however, that the empirical evidence in support of this efficiency defence is not always very convincing, particularly where the declared aim of the agreement is to rationalize the deployment of assets owned/controlled by firms which are product-market rivals (substitute assets). The first-order effect on the intensity of direct rivalry appears difficult to overturn.

Joint production/distribution by competitors

For example, in 1986 Ford UK and the Italian company Iveco set up a joint venture (Iveco-Ford Truck Ltd) for the joint production and distribution of heavy vehicles in the UK. Both companies were already producing and selling heavy vehicles in the UK and the rest of the EU, Ford UK above 6 tonnes gross weight (the 'Cargo' line), and Iveco above 3.5 tonnes. Ford was thus offering a more limited range, and as a result of this – it argued – its sales had declined. The joint venture had a dual purpose: to take over the production and sale of the 'Cargo' line of heavy vehicles previously manufactured and marketed by Ford UK (for this purpose Ford UK sold and transferred to the joint venture the necessary equipment and personnel); and to market in the UK the heavy vehicles produced by Iveco which complemented the Cargo line (i.e. heavy vehicles above 4 tonnes). In the UK, the joint venture was to combine the two specialized Ford and Iveco dealer networks, and distribute the Iveco products under the combined Iveco/Ford trademark.

As a consequence of the agreement, Ford UK agreed not to manufacture heavy vehicles in Europe (so did Ford USA); while Iveco agreed not to compete directly with the joint venture in the UK with its heavy vehicles above 6 tonnes, and to market its 'complementary' products between 4 and 6 tonnes in the UK only through the joint venture (neither party included in the joint venture lighter transport vehicles, below 4 tonnes).

This was clearly an agreement between two major producers, direct competitors in a market which is fairly concentrated both at the European and at the UK level. In the market for heavy vehicles above 4 tonnes, Ford was the leader in the UK with a 19% market share (1985), and the 4-firm concentration ratio (C4) was 58% (including Ford, Leyland, Daimler Benz and GM); Iveco was in eighth place with 4%. In Europe, however, Iveco was the second largest producer after Daimler Benz. It is difficult to imagine that a company like Ford would not have the ability and resources independently to develop and supply a complementary range (between 4 and 6 tonnes) to the UK market, where it was the leader with a wide and efficient distribution and assistance network; indeed it did produce other heavy vehicles outside Europe. The main aim of the agreement appears to be the coordination of operation between two rivals, one of which is leader in the UK market, and the other a major player in Europe and potentially in the UK.

In Ford/Iveco (1988), the Commission acknowledged that '(t)he joint venture is a business formation between competitors. It cannot be considered to be an independent new competitor in the heavy vehicles sector (because) the transfer of its previous heavy vehicles production by Ford UK to the joint venture does not preclude Ford from producing heavy vehicles elsewhere overseas. Ford remains an important supplier there, and one which could export to Europe'. Iveco also remains a competitor, because 'it continues to produce heavy vehicles which in principle compete with the joint venture's (though not in the UK)'.

The Commission then noted that '(a)s a result of the agreement, Iveco is required to sell its heavy vehicles in the UK only through the joint venture, and in conjunction with the Cargo line. Iveco is also required not to supply certain heavy vehicles to the UK insofar as they are in direct competition with Ford's Cargo. Competition between the two parties' various heavy vehicles ranges is thus restricted and consumer choice in the UK reduced' (para. 25). Similarly: 'The production and supply ban imposed on Ford UK from producing heavy vehicles above 4 tonnes in Europe or from supplying them to Europe reduces the number of suppliers in this sector' (ibid.).

Nonetheless, the Commission granted an individual exemption under Art. 85(3) on grounds that the agreement 'improves the distribution of goods, while allowing consumers a fair share of the resulting benefit, without (a) imposing on the undertakings restrictions which are not indispensable, and (b) eliminating competition' (para. 30). The Commission goes on to say that 'the joint venture makes it possible to achieve rationalization effects' (para. 31): complementing the Cargo line is 'good' for consumers with large heavy vehicles fleets, as they can take advantage of uniform maintenance and spare parts systems ('the addition of the complementary Iveco models will improve Ford dealers' competitiveness'). It also 'allows Iveco to penetrate the UK market (of which it had only a small share) by filling the existing gaps in Ford UK's range'. Moreover, the joint venture and the attached restrictions were regarded as 'indispensable' because they allowed 'the rationalized and smooth transition from the old range of models to a new generation of vehicles. This could not be achieved with the same prospects of success in any other way' (para. 34).

Most importantly, 'the agreement does not result in competition being eliminated ... It is to be assumed that effective competition exists in the common market in the heavy vehicles sector' (para. 37). The only support for this argument is a notion of 'relevant market' which is taken to include all heavy vehicles (not only those covered by the joint venture). Thus while Ford had in 1985 a 37% market share of sales of 6-16 tonnes vehicles in the UK, when all heavy vehicles are considered the combined total of Ford and Iveco was only 24%. The Commission concludes: 'Given this market structure, it may be assumed that effective competition exists...'. Similarly, 'competition is not affected in other areas of the common market' (Ford and Iveco together accounted for only 20% of total sales of all heavy vehicles in the EU in 1985 – and the actual range of the joint venture accounted for a mere 5%).

Overall, 'the advantages to be expected from the agreement on the whole outweigh the disadvantages associated with the restriction of competition' (para. 42): consumers are to enjoy a 'fair share of the resulting benefit' because they now can purchase complementary vehicles to the Cargo, and 'can now look forward to a new and complete range of vehicles produced by the joint venture'. Joint production also means a reduction of costs through economies of scale, and 'given the intense competitive pressures from other manufacturers, the cost reductions will be passed on to the consumers' (para. 43).

In fact, it would appear that the achievement of efficiency gains in production and distribution from this agreement may be of a second order of magnitude, relative to the inhibiting effects on competition between the partners in the UK market for heavy vehicles.[155]

---

[155]   Another case of a joint venture to 'pool' the operations of two competitors in a market is Apollinaris/Schweppes (1991): Cadbury Schweppes (UK) and Brau und Brunner (Germany) pooled their Austrian and German operations into

Coordinating the selection of plants

In a few cases, agreements have been deliberately approved as ways of cooperatively achieving selection of plants. This has happened most often in 'ailing' sectors, in preference to more drastic solutions: in particular, various agreements received individual exemption from the Commission in the 1980s concerning the European chemical industry, which was plagued by structural overcapacity and was making large losses. These included ENI/Montedison (1986), ICI/Enichem (1987), PRB/Shell (1987), EMC/DSM (1988), and Bayer/BP Chemicals (1988).

However there have been other cases where rationalization of production has been sought through agreement. For example, in Philips/Osram (1994), competing firms have recently entered into an agreement for the joint production of an input.

Agreements incorporating licences to use/manufacture an input

Productive efficiency gains are also claimed by firms in agreements where one partner obtains from the other access to a product/technology which is an input in the manufacture of a final good. Again substitutability or complementarity of assets between licensor and licensee plays a crucial part for the competition assessment. Where the parties originally supply a (similar) final product to different geographical markets (i.e. have substitutable assets), the agreement may be a way of effectively sharing the market along national boundaries. That is, where one firm obtains from another the exclusive use of a certain know-how on a certain territory, but their assets are in fact fully substitutable, the anti-competitive effects of eliminating rivalry in each other's territory may be strong.

An example is the case of Mitchell Cotts and Sofiltra. A joint venture was set up in 1984 in the UK between Mitchell Cotts Engineering, a UK producer of (among other things) air filters, and Sofiltra, a French manufacturer of various glass-based products (including filters). The aim of the joint venture (Mitchell Cotts Air Filtration Ltd) was to manufacture and market high-efficiency air filters using a type of small pleated paper made of superfine glass fibres, produced by Sofiltra. This paper is the major cost component and the key technological element in the finished product. Mitchell Cotts did not possess either the relevant technology or the R&D to manufacture this independently, and since 1975 it had purchased it from Sofiltra.

The joint venture essentially took over Mitchell Cotts' manufacture and sale of air filtration equipment, while Sofiltra conferred its technical know-how ('secret data and other information relating to the design and manufacture of high-efficiency filters using small pleated paper'), in exchange for a royalty. As a result, there was no need for Mitchell Cotts to import the pleated glass fibre paper. The licence was exclusive: Sofiltra was not to grant further licences in the UK and could not sell directly in the UK, while the joint venture could not manufacture and sell competing products, and was prohibited from establishing any commercial sales branch/agency outside its allocated territory (UK, Ireland, and a few non-EU countries – though passive sales were permitted). Before the agreement, sales of Mitchell Cotts filters

a partnership for the manufacture, distribution and sale of water and soft drinks in Austria, Germany and export markets. While acknowledging that the joint venture was likely 'to give rise to a division of markets between the parents and the joint venture', the Commission found that it also 'enabled the parties to improve the distribution of their products outside their home market, and to intensify competition with producers of soft drinks'.

accounted for approximately 10% of the UK market (the share was negligible in Europe), while Sofiltra had around 15% of the whole European market and was dominant in various national markets (e.g. 54% in France).

In Mitchell Cotts/Sofiltra (1987), the Commission argued (correctly) that the relevant product market was that for the finished product; however Mitchell Cotts and Sofiltra 'could not be considered competitors at the manufacturing level' because 'Mitchell Cotts was marketing a finished product incorporating an input purchased from Sofiltra, whereas Sofiltra produced the finished product without recourse to outside assistance'.[156] Further below, it is however acknowledged that Mitchell Cotts and Sofiltra are in fact competitors in the 'sales and distribution of the final product'.

The Commission then puts forward that the joint venture 'enables both parties to become more competitive within the UK': MC could develop its manufacturing activities, while 'Sofiltra expands its activities to other parts of the Common Market' (though the terms of the exclusive licence actually restricted Sofiltra from selling in the UK), where 'Sofiltra would not have set up its own manufacturing facility in the UK without substantial uneconomic expenditure'. Therefore 'this obligation cannot be considered to constitute an appreciable restriction of competition within the meaning of Art 85(1) ...' (para. 22).

In the end, the Commission recognizes that the 'mutual ban on active sales' (i.e. the fact that the joint venture is prohibited to sell 'actively' in territories reserved for Sofiltra, and Sofiltra is prohibited to sell 'actively' in the UK does fall within Art. 85(1), 'since such restrictions result in the sharing of markets between Sofiltra and the joint venture which have become competitors and are offering competing products' (para. 24).

However, an exemption was granted, because 'to enable the joint venture to establish itself and develop, it should not be subject to competition from other production units established by Sofiltra or other licensees'. Furthermore, 'it is in the interest of the joint venture not to be distracted from developing the market in its exclusive territory by attempting to sell outside it. Such a restriction should enable the joint venture to concentrate its efforts on its exclusive territory, building on the experience of MC's sales network. The territory can therefore be easily supervised with the result that there is better market knowledge based on closer contact with consumers. Accordingly, the agreements contribute to an improvement in production and distribution' (para. 25). Furthermore: 'As a result of the agreements, the products are manufactured by an integrated production process and technological improvements are made more widely and rapidly available to consumers and users' (para. 26).

In the light of the restrictions included in the agreement, these claimed efficiency gains appear unconvincing.

---

[156] 'As regards manufacture, MC was not an actual or potential competitor of Sofiltra since (it) lacked the requisite know-how and R&D facilities for the production of pleated fibreglass paper, the crucial component in the finished product and the subject of the technology transfer in this case. The mere availability of purchases or licences from other sources does not alter this analysis: MC had evident economic and commercial interests in developing its own technology in this field and has not been able to do so, resorting first to purchases from Sofiltra and later to a joint-venture coupled with a know-how licence. Therefore, MC and Sofiltra were neither actual nor potential competitors for the manufacture of the complete finished product incorporating the essential technical component which is also the major cost component' (para. 19).

10.4.2. Entry into a new market

There is a rather rich body of case material on cooperative agreements which are entered into for the declared purpose of achieving entry into a new geographical market. The issue is in what circumstances may this type of entry be considered beneficial, and when is it aimed instead at eliminating the competitive effects of entry (outweighing the benefits of increased variety for the consumers).

A useful example to illustrate possibly different (expected) effects of cooperative agreements on entry is the recent history of the European telecommunications sector. This has been significantly transformed over the past decade by two main events: first, the Commission's 1987 Green Paper which encouraged deregulation and liberalization (still largely ongoing); secondly, the technology-driven phenomenon of 'convergence' of telecoms and information technologies. As a result, national telecom operators (TOs), which had hitherto operated as monopolists within their national boundaries, were faced for the first time with the prospect of having to accommodate competing suppliers of telephony services. In addition, new local TOs emerged and gained market share, while established operators from other national markets (within and outside Europe) now had the opportunity to enter any EU national telecoms market. A wave of agreements and strategic alliances followed. In particular, a number of alliances have been formed between foreign TOs and local companies not yet active in telecoms, for the purpose of providing telecoms services in competition with the incumbent.[157] In these cases there are clear elements of complementarity and selective integration.

Other agreements have been formed between foreign operators and minority groups in individual countries (usually companies owning an alternative network), aimed at establishing a presence in these markets for their future opening to competition. In a network industry like telecoms, where direct entry is not possible without access to the network, teaming up with a local operator controlling an alternative network may be the effective way of achieving entry and bringing competition to the incumbent. However, as the parties have (in principle) substitute skills and assets, the question must be carefully considered of whether direct entry was not possible by the foreign TO, and/or effective competition could not have been waged on the incumbent by the local TO alone.

The concern of horizontal concentration is very much present in all cases where the joint venture includes already dominant TOs: for example, a case like BT-MCI (1994) raises in principle more concerns than IPSP (1994).

Entry into a new geographical market can also be achieved through licensing of know-how and trademarks. There are indeed several examples of firms granting licences to a firm in another geographical market for the manufacture of their product, or the use of their trademark. The agreement often includes exclusive production and distribution rights for the licensee at least in one part of the common market. Again in this case, where the licensee has substitute assets and is already supplying similar products, the licence may be an effective device for sharing markets between the parties, and avoiding the competitive effects of entry.

---

[157] Examples include: in Germany BT-VIAG; Tyssen-Bell South; Vabecom (an alliance of Cable & Wireless and Veba); and RWE plus six small electric utilities. Similar coalitions are being formed in France, Italy (Albacom: BT-Banca Nazionale del Lavoro), Sweden (Telenordic: BT, Teledenmark and Telenor in Sweden) and Spain (Megared: BT and Banco de Santander).

In the European beer industry, for example, brewers have in some cases adopted the practice of licensing a rival brewer in the destination market for the production, distribution and marketing of a brand (as well as its on-premises retailing, in some cases). Thus, for example, Heineken licensed their name to Whitbread in the UK (even though Whitbread have altered Heineken's recipe); Löwenbrau was originally licensed to UK brewer Allied Lyons, while Courage brews Foster's lager. The practice has also developed in other EU Member States: for example Interbrew brews Carlsberg in Belgium and Holsten brews Foster's in Germany.

The brewers have inevitably claimed significant efficiency gains from this entry strategy, emphasizing that licensing an incumbent brewer makes it possible for them to achieve niche entry at low risk and relatively small cost (especially where the existence of ties makes direct entry difficult); and this can be a springboard for full-scale entry once the brand name is established. However, these are ultimately 'horizontal' arrangements which must be viewed with serious concern. Licensing to an upstream rival in the destination market essentially implies the delegation of all relevant decisions on a brand (price, advertising, market positioning, distribution, etc.) to the upstream competitor, in exchange for a licence fee. This will not lead to fierce interbrand competition, but the licensee will price and position the 'entrant's' beer in a way which does not compete with its own brands. Also, licensing arrangements tend to be of relatively long duration, which casts doubts on brewers' claims that this may be only a prelude to full-scale entry.

For example, UK brewer Whitbread was granted the exclusive right to brew and market Canadian Moosehead beer in the UK. The Commission approved of the agreement (Moosehead/Whitbread, 1990) on grounds that given that most of the on-licensed premises in the UK are owned by brewers and tied to them, 'it is essential for a foreign firm to gain assistance of a British brewer in order to enter the UK market'. According to the Commission the agreement was likely to contribute to the improvement of production and distribution of Moosehead in the UK and to 'promote economic progress', while consumers would benefit from a wider choice.

A less favourable stance was taken when the Danish beer producer Carlsberg and Courage (second largest brewer in the UK) entered into an agreement whereby Courage acquired the right to brew some Carlsberg beer under licence in the UK for 10 years, and also received exclusive distribution rights for Carlsberg beer to the off-premises trade (5 years) and non-exclusive rights to the on-premises trade (10 years). In Carlsberg-Courage (1992), the Commission argued that it could not accept the exclusive distribution rights for Courage, since there was no justification for granting such rights to a competitor. The parties then had to limit their arrangements for the on-trade to the supply of Carlsberg beers to the pubs that were tied to Courage.

Thus the Moosehead example was one in which a JV was thought to aid the entry of a new product. The rationale for the Carlsberg/Courage JV was presumably that this JV was not necessary to facilitate entry, but was rather about coordinating the pricing and marketing of competing products; Carlsberg had another means of maintaining its presence in the UK through a deal with Allied Lyons.

10.4.3. Research and development of new products/processes

In EU competition law, pure R&D agreements benefit from a specific block exemption (see below Section 10.6). Other types of cooperative agreements which have as their object the development of a new product or technology may receive individual exemption under Art. 85(3).

The phenomenon of 'convergence' in the telecoms/media/IT sectors provides some good recent examples of agreements joining together firms with complementary assets and skills for the purposes of developing a new product. In particular the emergence of cable operators, often with their independent infrastructure for the delivery of TV programmes to the home, has created the opportunity for new complementarities and synergies, for example with input providers (e.g. of programmes and movies). As new possibilities have arisen for combining complementary assets and developing new products, there has been an increase in joint ventures and strategic alliances for the provision of the new services created by convergence. Examples of complementary skills being joined together include alliances between TOs and publishers (e.g. Europe Online, a joint venture of AT&T and a number of European publishers); other TOs have sought to extend into cable-TV networks (e.g. Telefonica-Prisa, Telecom Eireann-Cablelink, Telecom Italia).

Alliances between partners with complementary skills are more likely to be socially beneficial, as they may speed up the development of a new product or service – thus delivering technological progress and lower prices to consumers. Another case is BP/MW Kellogg (1985).

The issue is – as usual – more problematic in the case of R&D which is carried out jointly by firms with substitute assets. In this case, an important question is whether cooperation is in fact essential for carrying out a particular research or development programme, or whether firms could have proceeded alone. There is also the question of whether cooperation does not in fact dampen the incentives for competition in R&D, effectively slowing down the pace of research.

In many cases, especially where large multinational firms are involved, it is very difficult to believe that they are doing research together because they did not have sufficient resources individually. Indeed, in the majority of cases, the Commission reaches the conclusion that the parties to the agreement would have the means of carrying out the research or development individually, but then it also argues that a result would be achieved 'more rapidly' by pooling resources.

Examples of research joint ventures set up between large multinationals (which are also competitors in the product market) include the cases of Continental-Michelin (1988) and more recently Asahi-Saint Gobain (1994).

The world tyre market is rather concentrated (84% of all sales accounted for by 10 groups). The French manufacturer Michelin is the second largest in the world (after Goodyear) with an 18% market share (1987), while the German Continental Gummiwerke AG is the fourth largest, with a 4% market share. In the EU, Michelin is the largest and Continental the second largest supplier. In 1986, Michelin and Continental applied to the Commission for individual exemption of a cooperation agreement commenced in 1983 for the development of a new run-flat tyre/wheel system for passenger car tyres (the block exemption does not apply because the tyres manufactured by the parties amount to more than 20% of all tyres manufactured in the EU).

Continental had been working on the development of a new tyre/wheel system (known as the 'reverse hooking tyre' system or RHT) since 1979. The objective was to develop a tyre/wheel system such that, in case of a puncture, the car can be driven for several hundred miles at reduced speed with a flat tyre (this potentially makes it possible to dispense with the spare wheel, which in turn has various advantages). The purpose of the agreement was first to assess the RHT system developed by Continental, and then to develop RHT tyres further.

Continental and Michelin argued that the agreement was justified by (a) the need for further development of Continental's prototype to the manufacturing stage (there were various technical problems) and (b) the fact that an individual tyre manufacturer cannot on its own introduce a new system like RHT into the market, since 'the motor industry strictly avoids becoming dependent on a single tyre manufacturer' (para. 9). They also emphasized that their cooperation is 'restricted to areas which are directly connected with the development of the new tyre/wheel system' but they will otherwise remain competitors (i.e. they will differ in terms of compounds, profile and non-system related structures).[158]

From the notified agreement, the Commission inferred that although Michelin had for years been working independently on the development of a flat tyre system, but no results from this effort were included in the agreement, its attempts had not been successful. The parties therefore agreed to concentrate on a joint development. This restricted competition 'insofar as the agreement will not lead to the development of competing systems' (i.e. cooperation may eliminate the benefits of competition in R&D).

The Commission also commented on some restrictions on the parties' freedom to market the product in the initial stage, but eventually it granted the exemption on grounds that the agreement generally led to 'improved production of goods and promotion of technical progress', and the 'consumers' share of the advantages resulting from the agreement' was significant. In principle, the JV was to grant non-exclusive production licences, including to third parties, thus ensuring competition in production and the passing of benefits to consumers. Continental was unable on its own to resolve the numerous technical problems involved, and there were safety advantages from a dual set of safety tests. In addition, the Commission agreed with the 'need to avoid supply bottlenecks in the motor vehicle industry' (dubious argument).

Technology transfer and other agendas

In several cases, agreements on joint product development have received exemption from the Commission on grounds that they make possible a degree of technology transfer from an extra-EU firm to a European partner. The agenda here is clearly one of industrial policy, as it is hoped that access to outside technology will enable EU firms to compete effectively with large multinationals. On a few occasions, the competition authorities have stated that they will not allow any restriction of competition within the EU 'for the sake of helping EU undertakings in the world market: competition "at home" can be beneficial in making

---

[158]   It should also be noted that the joint venture set up by Continental and Michelin was to grant non-exclusive licences, i.e., third parties could, in principle, have access to the new technology.

companies more effective on a global scale' (*XXIst Report on Competition Policy*, point 45). However this commitment is not firmly upheld in practice.

The case of Olivetti and Canon is quite typical. In 1987, Olivetti and Canon formed a joint venture (Olivetti-Canon Industriale) for the purpose of 'developing, designing and manufacturing copying machines, laser printers and facsimiles'. In fact, in the first phase the joint venture was to take over (on licences from Olivetti and Canon) only the manufacture of certain models of Olivetti and Canon copying machines in the speed range of 10-20 copies per minute (cpm). The joint venture had exclusive manufacturing rights for Europe. In a second phase – to start in 1989 – 'the parties may decide to produce other office automation products such as laser printers and fax machines. They may also consider the production of higher-speed copiers.'

In 1987, the low-end range of the plain-paper copier market in Europe (which includes the 10-20 cpm range) was dominated by Canon, with a 24% market share and a strong innovation record. Of the nine largest brands in Europe at the time, seven were Japanese: this reflected the difficulty of European copier manufacturers since the 1970s to keep pace with the technological developments of Japanese manufacturers.[159] Japanese companies also progressively set up a manufacturing base in Europe, while an anti-dumping duty was imposed in 1986 on their sales of imports from outside the EU (a 20% duty was imposed on Canon). 60% of Olivetti's sales of copiers in 1986 were Japanese machines sold under its brand name (OEM arrangement); the rest were manufactured by Olivetti, in the low range only. Canon was also a major name in fax machines, with a full product range (at 20% it had the second largest market share in Europe in 1986 after Panasonic), while Olivetti's sales, limited to Italy and Spain, were all on an OEM basis from Sharp and accounted for 2.5% of the EU market. In laser printers, Canon was one of the two most significant manufacturers in the world, and in 1985 accounted for 18% of sales in Western Europe (as well as supplying the engines for the market leader Hewlett Packard). Olivetti only sold a few units in 1984/85, procured from Hitachi.

Olivetti was to transfer to the joint venture its copier research and production activities, while Canon was to make a substantial investment in 1987–88 and to transfer technology to the joint company. In addition, Canon was under obligation to 'expose its product plans to the joint venture from time to time' (Commission Decision OJ L 052 26.2.1988, para. 24). Also, each party was under the obligation of 'promptly disclosing to the other any improvement made by it to the licensed products'.

The Commission judged that 'the joint venture had been formed between actual competitors for copying machines of low-speed range, and for fax machines (of which Olivetti was an important OEM seller in Italy); and between potential competitors in copying machines of the medium range.[160] The parties were non-competitors in the markets for high-range copiers

---

[159] The main remaining EU producers are Rank Xerox (UK, full range) and Océ (Netherlands, upper range), but most of the smaller companies converted (totally or partially) to 'Original Equipment Manufacturers' (OEM) distribution of Japanese machines, i.e. distribution under their own brand name of Japanese products.

[160] 'Olivetti's skills and technology for copying machines could be extended to higher-range models: the input products are largely the same, demand is sufficient to support such business and these machines sell at larger margin, Olivetti is a profitable and healthy group. It could therefore bear alone the technical and financial risks associated with production of mid-range machines' (para. 39).

(Canon's share negligible, Olivetti none) and laser printers (Canon major competitor, Olivetti not active). As a result, the Commission found that the joint venture restricted competition between the parents in the low-range copiers market, and in future possibly also for mid-range copiers and fax machines. The argument rested on the (dubious) notion that joint production 'will result in identical production costs for both, with an inevitable influence at the sales stage. The products will be substantially the same (and) each party will have less autonomy in determining its sales prices than it would have if its production costs were different. The scope for competition at the sales stage is thus limited'. Moreover, 'the joint venture restricts competition in terms of development and designing of the relevant products' (para. 42).

These arguments were ultimately offset by the consideration that the agreements 'offer benefits for the Community which outweigh the restrictive effects on competition' (para. 53). In particular, the joint venture was seen as 'improving technical and economic progress' in a field where the technology is fast moving. An attempt was made to emphasize the productive efficiency gains from the joint R&D, as 'the expansion of production in the EEC which results from the joint venture enables the parties to spread the cost of these investments over a larger number of products; otherwise the cost of those products would be too high for producers to be able to sell them at a competitive price. The joint venture is therefore apt to avoid duplication in costs of development' (para. 54). However, in the same breath the Commission recognized that 'research does not fall directly within the scope of the joint venture' (ibid.).

The decisive factor was the acknowledgement that the joint venture 'enables a transfer of the benefits of advanced technology to Olivetti (...) from Canon which is a leader of innovation and whose policy is R&D oriented' (ibid.) – while 'the granting of a licence would not have allowed the transfer of a technology to the same extent as allowed in a joint venture: the major involvements of the partners in a manufacturing joint venture permits a permanent and intense flow of technology' (para. 56).

As in this case, also in other cases agreements which are branded 'joint product development' concern in fact joint manufacturing of a product by firms which are effectively competitors on the product market (substitute assets). Even in these cases, the Commission has tended to grant exemptions when the agreement was perceived as 'desirable' from an industrial policy perspective. A rather obvious example is that of the joint venture formed in 1992 between Ford (US) and Volkswagen for the joint development and production of multi-purpose vehicles (MPVs) in Portugal. It is easy to see how the Commission did not turn down an agreement which was large, relatively high-tech, and included production from a greenfield site in a less developed region of Europe. The agreement was exempted under Art. 85(3), though it was made subject to some conditions 'given the high degree of cooperation in the car industry'.

10.5. Cooperation and market integration

In this section, we address the expectation that European market integration should be associated with an increase in the number of cross-border alliances between enterprises. In particular, we discuss how market integration relates to firms' overall incentives to enter into cooperative agreements, as well as on the form of such cooperation.

The main expected contribution of the 1992 programme to cooperation was the removal of barriers such as disparities in company law, tax law, and rules on capital movements, which were perceived as a major obstacle to the formation and survival of cooperative agreements in the past:

'... Cooperation between undertakings of different Member States is still hampered by excessive legal, fiscal and administrative problems, to which are added occasional obstacles which are more a reflection of different mental attitudes and habits. The absence of a Community legal framework for cross-border activities by enterprises and for cooperation between enterprises of different Member States has led [...] to numerous potential joint projects failing to get off the ground. As and when the internal market is developed further, enterprises [...] will become more and more involved in all manners of intra-Community operations, resulting in an ever-increasing number of links with associated enterprises, creditors and other parties outside the country' (White Paper, *Completing the Internal Market*, pp. 34-6).

Emerson et al. [1988] also identified a number of obstacles to cooperation in Europe, and speculated that the 1992 programme would eliminate 'the paradox (...) that cooperation with Community partners has so far been less frequent than cooperation with partners in non-Member countries' (p. 175).

Undoubtedly much of the enthusiasm for cooperation and alliances was associated with the view that these would strengthen European capabilities especially in high-technology sectors, and thus support European 'competitiveness' on the world scene. This position was echoed by the Cecchini report ('Market integration brings with it a number of factors giving European firms the chance to regain technological leadership [through] the rapid development of cross-frontier business cooperation for R&D', p. 75). To substantiate its commitment to encouraging collaborative links between enterprises, the Commission also set up a variety of specific programmes to stimulate and even fund cross-frontier R&D cooperation, and much effort has been spent on developing a European dimension to industrial research work.[161] These programmes were explicitly conceived also as one way of furthering European integration. As argued by the Cecchini report, 'EC-sponsored R&D programmes like ESPRIT, way beyond their monetary significance, are a crucial focus for fusing cross-frontier innovation and business' (p. 89).

The questions to be addressed are whether these expectations are justified from an economic point of view, and what interpretation should be given to changes in cross-border cooperation as a response to market integration.

As was argued above, when markets are geographically segmented (e.g. along national boundaries) by differences in regulation and standards, or in the legal framework, firms may seek to overcome these artificial restrictions and gain entry through cooperative agreements

---

[161] This followed the example of large-scale interventionist programmes in the US or Japan. The majority of the programmes set up by the Commission involve the provision of funds, while others (such as BC-NET) aim at helping firms find possible partners in the EU. For example, the ESPRIT programme was aimed at promoting pre-competitive collaborative research (i.e. applied research between basic research and the product development stage) by linking together the largest electronics firms. Several other programmes were implemented by the Commission under the umbrella of the Framework Programme: ESPRIT and RACE (now ACTS) were specifically tailored to information technology; MAST, BIOTECH and AIR to the biotechnology and agriculture sectors. Various other programmes cut across sectors to promote new manufacturing technologies (BRITE), technology transfers (SPRINT), regional technological initiatives (STRIDE), or to avoid duplication of basic R&D programmes in the EU (EUREKA).

with a local partner. Firms' propensity to enter into such agreements should be increased by uncertainty on the characteristics of the local market and issues of idiosyncratic risk.

In addition, differences in the institutional environment may be expected to affect also the choice of the particular form of collaboration, and in particular the choice of contracts versus equity. Where the ability to form contractual relations is limited, for example due to issues of contractual incompleteness and hold-up problems, firms might favour equity participation. If writing contingent contracts is not feasible, ownership may have preferable incentive properties: giving an independent firm adequate financial incentives for the optimal allocation of its time and effort among relevant activities may be costly, especially where it is difficult to measure performance. Equity participation may thus reduce the need for strong performance incentives. Also, where investments are specific and have sunk cost character, equity participation may create a more irreversible commitment to a market, and thus reduce the mutual hold-up problem. This may find some support in the fact that joint ventures are more frequently adopted between firms in dissimilar economic blocs. If we view joint ventures as a response to contractual incompleteness, this is easily explained: for example, transactions which might be market-mediated or contractual between two EU firms may not be feasible between an EU firm and an Eastern European firm, as a result of the greater difficulty of writing contingent contracts in the second case. This is also the situation in which there is more likely to be tariffs and quotas, and joint ventures may well be a response to these restrictions.

If artificial barriers to trade and direct entry are removed, three possible effects could be expected.

(a)   *Increased opportunities for direct entry*

We have argued that in some cases the cooperation of a local firm is sought for gaining access to a market which is protected by artificial or absolute barriers to direct entry. To the extent that market integration reduces artificial obstacles to direct entry into a market, this incentive for entering into cooperative agreements might be weakened. Some support for this hypothesis may be inferred from the case of the US, which is an example of an integrated market: there are fewer joint ventures between domestic firms, relative to those involving US firms and an outside partner (see Tables 10.2 and 10.3, Section 10.2).

(b)   *Anti-competitive responses to integration*

In an integrated market, firms may enter into cooperative agreements in order to reduce the intensity of competition from firms which are now able to supply their market: for example, in order to avoid the competitive effects of entry. As was discussed in the case of beer, licensing arrangements when the licensee has fully substitute assets might be an anti-competitive alternative to direct market entry, in order to eliminate competition between the licensor's product and the incumbent/licensee's product. The pecuniary externality (business-stealing effect) that the entering product would have on the incumbent product is internalized.

More generally, cooperation may provide a framework for coordination with rivals, which might be felt as necessary by firms in an integrating market.

(c)   *Reduction in information asymmetries (monitoring and enforcement costs)*

To the extent that the single market programme may reduce information asymmetries in identifying a suitable partner in another country, and eliminates certain obstacles to the establishment of an agreement, it is possible that cooperation may be facilitated. For example, where market integration implies less idiosyncratic shocks across countries, it is possible that monitoring of a partner's actions improves and cooperation becomes more feasible. Also, to the extent that a more uniform legal and institutional framework develops across the Community (e.g. company law, auditing standards, rules on taxation, issues which were given significant weight by the Commission in all its pronouncements on the subject), there should be less uncertainty on the true position of the prospective partner (for example on its financial position, or the resources which it can credibly dedicate to the venture), and this could stimulate agreements. This expectation was echoed by various commentators, who saw significant potential for some measures to encourage cross-border cooperation.[162] This may be particularly true for contractual agreements, as differences in legal frameworks were never a very significant obstacle for firms to enter into joint ventures. To the extent that market integration improves monitoring and enforcement possibilities, and reduces idiosyncratic differences between countries, firms might find it easier to enter into contracts, rather than equity participation. Integration may thus enhance contracting possibilities relative to ownership.

To summarize: to the extent that cooperation is motivated by firms' efforts to overcome regulatory and other barriers to market access, it is conceivable that integration would reduce the incentive to cooperate; however the strategic motive for cooperation may become stronger for the same reasons (as competitive pressures increase both inside the EU and from rivals in other trading blocs). Paradoxically, integration may make these agreements easier, if it eliminates information asymmetries and artificial barriers (differences in institutional and legal framework) and reduces these disparities.

10.6. Interfirm cooperation in EU competition law

The task of competition policy in this area should be to differentiate effectively between cooperation which has socially beneficial aspects, and should therefore be allowed, and agreements which effectively support anti-competitive outcomes, and should be rejected. In practice, in order to avoid altogether the problem of having to quantify the significance of the efficiency defences, much effort is spent by the Commission and the courts to show that the undertakings which are part of the agreement do not in effect compete in the product market, and therefore there is no appreciable restriction on competition. As indicated in Section 10.4, this has led in some cases to rather paradoxical descriptions of competition in a market.

---

162   See for example Buigues and Jacquemin [1989]: '...there are several obstacles to the conclusion of a cooperation agreement. In addition to the difficulties of finding a partner able to make a balanced contribution, setting up a management structure to minimize the running costs of cooperation, and ensuring a full and fair use of the proceeds, there is also a set of regulatory and political obstacles to cooperation in Europe. Differences in company law and tax systems, for example, are often considerable. This raises the problem of Community-level consolidation for tax purposes and financial transfers between companies within the group. Barriers to the mobility of human resources arising out of social legislation [...] are also important. Completion of the single market will remove a number of obstacles to cooperation, whether discrimination in the shape of national industrial policy measures or disparities in the standards, rules and regulations governing products.' (pp. 63–4).

Apart from the way it is applied, Community competition law accords a privileged status to many cooperative agreements, and appears to have been effectively informed by the persuasion that the potential social benefits from interfirm cooperation are likely to be large.

On the one hand, it is acknowledged that cooperative agreements may in practice have effects which are very similar to mergers: joint ventures which respond to certain criteria are deemed 'concentrative' and must be notified to the Merger Task Force, to be dealt with under the Merger Regulation. However, the criteria for distinguishing between 'concentrative' and 'cooperative' joint ventures[163] remain dubious and most unsatisfactory. All 'cooperative' joint ventures are dealt with under Art. 85, together with all other forms of cooperation between enterprises. This implies significant procedural differences, and also leaves room for manipulation of the system through strategic choice of jurisdiction (see for example Neven, Nuttall and Seabright [1993]).[164]

The law's favourable attitude towards cooperation finds expression in a substantial body of special rules, which define a set of exceptions – or exemptions – to the prohibition of Art. 85(1). The exemption is the main legal instrument for allowing interfirm linkages when efficiency gains are believed to ensue. In addition to the possibility for individual exemptions, the Commission has issued a variety of block exemptions, to avoid having to deal with a flood of applications for individual exemption even for relatively straightforward cases. These grant immunity from prosecution, for a certain length of time, to agreements conforming to a given set of criteria.[165]

For cooperative joint ventures there are specific guidelines detailing the circumstances under which an agreement may be individually exempted, or it may be given negative clearance (i.e. is deemed to fall outside of Art. 85(1) altogether). From a procedural point of view, the position is that there is no necessary notification requirement for these joint ventures; the parties may decide to notify them only if they fear that the Commission might question their validity at a later stage, because of effects on competition or EU internal trade. Most notifications are dealt with through informal non-binding 'comfort letters' (the Commission has committed itself to come to a decision within two months), and do not give rise to any final decision (they are not binding for national courts).

There is a consensus that the Commission's attitude towards (cooperative) joint ventures has softened over time. After an 'interventionist' earlier phase with wide application of Art. 85(1), the Commission became more lenient after 1983 (*XIIIth Report on Competition Policy*); in 1993, a special *Notice on Cooperative Joint Ventures* was issued, identifying some agreements as falling outside of Art. 85(1) altogether, and allowing a variety of ancillary restrictions (e.g. restrictions specifying the product range of the joint venture, restrictions on field of use, and restrictions on the parents in competing initially with the joint venture). The *Notice* also

---

[163] Formally, a joint venture is deemed 'concentrative' if two conditions are fulfilled: that the joint venture is an 'autonomous' entity, and that 'it has not for its purpose the coordination of the activities of the parent companies'.

[164] For example, it is well known that firms generally tend to structure a joint venture as concentrative whenever they can, because of the advantages of doing so in terms of procedures (the MTF must respond within one month) and the greater certainty associated with an MTF pronouncement (see below). See for example Bensaid et al. [1994].

[165] While this approach has obvious advantages in terms of transparency and is economical from an administrative point of view, it is also criticized for its rigidity, and exposure to manipulation on the part of firms – which can ensure exemption by carefully tailoring the terms of their agreement.

defines the 'checklist' of criteria to be applied for granting an individual exemption, including whether the agreement restricts competition between the parents; between the parents and the joint venture ('this typically manifests itself in the division of geographical markets, product markets or customers'); whether it establishes a network of joint ventures that could restrict competition; and whether it affects third parties 'excluding them from economic opportunities' especially in oligopolistic markets, or erecting a barrier to entry by pooling the parents' market power. The effect on competition must also be appreciable. As we have seen, the case history on cooperative joint ventures suggests, however, a rather lenient application of these criteria (see Section 10.4).

Special block exemptions exist for other categories of collaborative agreements, including R&D agreements (block exemption Regulation (EEC) No 418/85, amended by Regulation (EEC) No 151/93); specialization agreements (block exemption originally issued in 1972, subsequently replaced by Regulation (EEC) No 3604/82, then Regulation (EEC) No 417/85, and amended by Regulation (EEC) No 151/93); and various forms of intellectual property licences (block exemption on patent licences Regulation (EEC) No 2349/1984, and on know-how licensing Regulation (EEC) No 556/1989; these are being replaced by a single block exemption, to provide a unified approach in this area).[166]

The Commission's favourable stance on R&D agreements also reflects in part – as we have seen – considerations of industrial policy, sectoral policy, and integration aims. Initially, the agreements originally eligible for block exemption were 'pure' R&D agreements, those extending to joint exploitation (including manufacturing and licensing), and joint exploitation flowing from an earlier R&D agreement. The only condition was that joint exploitation was limited to goods and services resulting from the research; and if the parties were competing manufacturers, their combined market share should not exceed 20% of the EU market for the products in which they compete.

An important restriction was the prohibition of joint selling, which meant that R&D agreements which extended to the marketing stage were not to benefit from the block exemption. However this condition was deleted in 1993, as Regulation (EEC) No 151/93 extended the scope of the exemption to the joint distribution of products resulting from joint R&D – on condition that the parties' joint market share does not exceed 10% of the relevant market.[167]

Another *ad hoc* block exemption exists for specialization agreements, whereby firms agree to specialize only in manufacturing certain goods, and to distribute each other's products. The Commission tends to look favourably on these agreements, '... since in (this case) each firm

---

[166] Of course for all agreements which do not qualify for block exemption remains the option of the individual exemption, which will be granted on the basis of the usual requirements of Art. 85(3): (a) that the agreement implies an improvement in economic and technical progress; (b) that consumers receive a fair share of the benefit; (c) that the restrictions included in the agreement are indispensable for its operation; and (d) that there should not be a substantial elimination of competition.

[167] This development undoubtedly raises a number of concerns on the effects of joint R&D on competition in the product market. Indeed this formal development had been anticipated by some Commission decisions, which gave signs of increased flexibility: e.g. in Alcatel Espace/ANT Nachrichtentechnik (1990), a 10-year exemption was granted (under Art. 85(3)) to a cooperation agreement on R&D, production and marketing of certain electric components for satellites between Alcatel and ANT. The justification was that 'in this field the nature of demand means that the benefits of joint research and development and manufacturing can be obtained only if they are combined with some degree of joint marketing' (*XXth Report on Competition Policy 1990*).

continues as an independent producer' (Whish [1993]). Only in a few cases has the Commission worried that these agreements may be used in practice by firms to fix quotas and divide the market.

Finally, a number of exemptions have been issued in relation to licensing of intellectual property rights. The Commission tends to be more guarded towards cross-licensing (agreements whereby competing firms license each other to use a technology), being concerned that firms will 'use them to effectively pool their patents and agree not to license to third parties, while at the same time fixing quotas and prices' (Whish [1993]). However, the attitude is more lenient towards 'vertical' licensing, for example where the producer of patented goods (or goods embodying valuable know-how) grants manufacturing licences to third parties.

The Commission tends to view these types of agreements (including the case where the licence contains restrictions on the quantity of goods produced by the licensee or their price) essentially as restrictions on intra-brand competition, on grounds that 'these restrictions relate to the patentee's own product'. There may be, however, serious effects on interbrand competition – especially when the licensee is also a potential competitor in the product market. Non-competition clauses are also mostly allowed, forbidding the licensee from handling goods which compete with the licensor's, or 'field of use restrictions', whereby the licensor limits the licensee's authority to produce goods for a particular purpose. The rationale here is that the law should not be too rigid on these restrictions, to the extent that they encourage the patentee to license a new technology and the licensee to invest, which means the technology is disseminated; and again the restrictions mostly affect intra-brand competition, while interbrand competition may be increased by introducing a new licensee onto the market. The main anti-competitive concern is that 'licences of intellectual property (...) may be used in a way that compartmentalizes the market' (Whish [1993, p. 625]). Though territorial restraints are allowed, the Commission employs its usual compromise criterion that 'passive sales should not be restricted'.

10.7. Conclusions

In this chapter we have considered the economic rationale for a variety of efficiency defences applied to cooperative agreements between enterprises. The critical issue for the competition authorities is to evaluate when the restrictive effects of an agreement on competition (coordination in the product market, elimination of the competitive effects of entry, and so on) may be overturned by certain efficiency gains from joint operation.

There were two main reasons for discussing these agreements separately.

First, in spite of its occasional claims to the contrary (see *XXIst Report on Competition Policy*), EU competition policy is informed in various places by an overall agenda in which industrial and integration policies occupy a prominent place. Though cooperation is often suspicious on competition grounds, the policy approach has been to look at it rather favourably when it allows EU firms to remain 'competitive' with the rest of the world, or when it furthers the 'integration' objective. As a result, EU competition law contains a plethora of *ad hoc* exceptions to the general prohibition of Art. 85(1), generally issued on grounds that interfirm cooperation may deliver important 'efficiency gains'. (In addition, the Commission and the courts often go to great lengths to argue that an agreement should be exempted because the two partners are not in any significant way 'competitors' in the product market, and therefore competition is not affected.) Secondly, the launch of the single market programme was accompanied by expectations that EU firms would enter into cooperative agreements much more freely and frequently in an integrating market, and that this would in turn contribute to the completion of integration.

In this chapter we have argued two main points:

(a) In order to establish which agreements are most likely to generate efficiency gains of significant magnitude, it is important to consider the degree of asset substitutability or complementarity of the firms which are joined together in the agreement. We would expect *ex ante* the size of the efficiency gains to be larger where the agreement combines firms with complementary assets (e.g. where there is an element of selective vertical integration); while where the partners have substitute assets, there is greater potential for horizontal concentration – subject to the condition that the market is sufficiently concentrated.

(b) A more robust case exists for cooperation in R&D, where we expect the size of the efficiency gains to be more substantial.

It is not clear that the current approach of EU competition policy effectively differentiates between agreements which are socially harmful and those which are welfare-enhancing. Claims by the partners of large efficiency gains to be generated by the cooperation are inevitable, and should not be overestimated.

As for the impact of market integration on cooperation, we have emphasized that cooperation with local partners is often used by firms as a way to access a market and circumvent absolute and regulatory barriers. To the extent that markets become more integrated, the incentive to enter into such arrangements may become weaker. In such a case, the main reason for an increase in the prevalence of cooperative activities would be the anti-competitive motive, whereby firms seek mutual agreements to defuse the impact of increased competition or entry into their national market.

11. Mergers

11.1. Introduction

In the previous chapter we have described cooperative agreements between firms as a selective combination of the parties' assets and skills (for a given purpose). Mergers are instead a complete combination of the assets and control of the firms involved – which may have competed beforehand in the same market (horizontal mergers), or may own or produce complementary assets and inputs. Joint ventures which are legally defined as concentrative may in practice have effects close to that of a merger; although a JV may be a selective combination of the parties' assets, it may be a complete combination of those assets relevant to serving a particular market. Such concentrative JVs we include in our understanding of the term 'merger'. This notion of a complete combination of assets is equivalent to stating that the JV has functional autonomy from its parents and represents a long-lasting commitment which is one of the conditions that the Commission uses when deciding on the applicability of the Merger Regulation (EEC) No 4064/89.[168]

The distinction in the previous chapter between complementary and substitute assets in the evaluation of efficiency defences thus remains highly relevant also to the analysis of mergers.[169] And as in the case of cooperative agreements, the competition assessment of mergers raises greater concerns when the merging parties' assets are substitutes. With complementary assets the presumption of benefits (efficiency gains) from common ownership can be stronger (see the 'incomplete contract' literature in Chapter 10). Conversely, the danger of market monopolization is greater where the merging firms own substitute assets (provided that the structure of the market is sufficiently concentrated).

There is, however, an important difference between mergers and cooperative agreements: this is in the respective degree of commitment which is taken on by the parties. Cooperative agreements tend to be limited to a given time horizon, while mergers entail a much more permanent change in the firms' ownership. Even if in principle demergers are always possible, they are much more costly than for example interrupting a cooperation agreement; hence changes to market structure which result from a merger are significantly more permanent and costly to reverse. It is therefore worthwhile for any competition authority to devote significant effort and resources to the evaluation of a merger.

The main focus of this chapter is on horizontal mergers, which raise the greatest concerns as they describe the combination of assets and activities between former competitors in the product market. We begin in Section 11.2 by mentioning various factors which may affect merger activity, and the occurrence of merger waves. This suggests that it is generally difficult to isolate the possible effects of integration on mergers activity in Europe from all other factors which might have had an impact on firms' behaviour over the same period. The

---

[168]   The Commission published a *Notice on Cooperative and Concentrative Joint Ventures* (OJ[1990] (C-203/6)) which seeks to clarify under what circumstances the Merger Regulation applies and when a JV is to be treated as cooperative under Art. 85. See also Whish [1993, p. 711].

[169]   A merger brings together complementary assets if the merging parties contribute clearly distinct assets which can be combined to produce a new product, or supply it to the market. It brings together substitute assets where the parties would have the capability of manufacturing similar products individually.

available data indicates that merger activity has followed rather closely the economic cycle. In Section 11.3 we discuss firms' private incentives to merge, in particular market power and the realization of efficiency gains, and in Section 11.4 we evaluate how the market integration process should be expected to have affected these incentives. In Section 11.5 we discuss the Commission's current approach to merger analysis, and consider how this could be affected by market integration. Finally, in Section 11.6 we emphasize the impact of integration on the incentives to modify the institutions of merger analysis. We conclude in 11.7.

11.2. Patterns of merger activity

A variety of reasons have been identified in the literature for firms merging: from enhancing market power, to achieving cost reductions and other efficiency gains in combining the parties' assets,[170] to managerial and financial motives (the last two focus on managerial labour and financial market aspects, rather than the product market).

The characteristic feature of mergers is that they have historically occurred in waves. Such waves are very clearly defined in the US and the UK: for example, the US has experienced four distinct merger waves over the past century, in 1887-1904 ('great merger wave'), 1916–29 ('merger movement'), late 1960s ('conglomerate merger wave'), and in the 1980s;[171] these have been echoed in the UK by virtually synchronous waves in the 1920s (mass production and economies of scale), the 1960s (as a response to internationalization), and the 1980s (in parallel to the evolution of the market for corporate control).[172] In countries other than the US and the UK, a history of merger waves is less clearly discernible, partly also because the existence of a market for corporate control is a largely Anglo-Saxon phenomenon.

Various reasons have been put forward for the existence of merger waves. For example, Stigler [1950] argued that 'merger waves are the result of exogenous changes in the environment leading to an increase in the potential benefit of certain types of acquisitions. Thus each merger wave should be associated with a specific change in the regulatory, financial or other relevant environments'. Thus the reasons may be:

(a)   institutional (e.g. changes in rules on tradability of shares);
(b)   financial (for example merger activity in the UK and the US tends to coincide with peaks in the stock market cycle – except for the 1980s wave which coincided with a stock market slump; see Bishop and Kay [1993]). It has also been shown that merger and takeover activity tends to follows an improvement in financial balances, with a lag of about two years (Comment and Schwert [1995]);
(c)   economic (as noted by Scherer and Ross [1990], the beginning of US merger waves in 1925, 1932 and 1967 coincided with booming economies);
(d)   a 'bandwagon effect', as mergers may become a fashionable activity (Hay and Morris, 1991). This may help to explain economy-wide merger waves when business cycles only

---

[170]   This includes, for example, the pursuit of economies of scale and scope by exploiting one of the parties' brand name and know-how in several product markets, which is a powerful driver of 'diversifying' mergers.

[171]   See Scherer and Ross [1990].

[172]   Town [1992] went further by seeking to establish statistically whether mergers are a 'structural event'. He found that 'the underlying pattern in the M&A data can be characterized by dichotomous shifts between high and low levels of activity'. Considering in particular data for the US between 1895 and 1989, Town identifies **nine** merger waves – of which three major ones: 1889–1902 ; 1925–32 ; and 1967–69.

affect industries with cyclical demand: there may be a multi-market bandwagon effect from the cyclical industries to the others.

Others (e.g. Town [1992]; van Wegberg [1994]) have proposed instead a more 'structural' approach, whereby merger waves are a structural phenomenon which depends on such factors as cyclical changes of capacity constraints, and growth in firms' intangible assets.

Against this background, 'stripping out' the effect of market integration on merger activity over the past few years is not an easy task. While we can observe actual trends in merger activity, causality remains difficult to establish.

Merger activity at the European level has been traditionally dominated by mergers and acquisitions in the UK. The pattern of merger activity in the Community since 1986 is illustrated in Table 11.1. In the number of deals, UK firms have, since 1990, been more active as purchasers than other EU firms in respect of non-cross-border deals and acquisitions of non-EU companies (see Table 11.2). However, Germany has become the leading target country for cross-border acquisitions in general, while French companies have taken the lead as acquirers of other Community enterprises.

Table 11.1. Merger activity in the EU (number of transactions)

	National*	Community**	International with EU bidder***	International with EU target***	Total
	1308	162	316	96	1882
1987	1928	262	401	116	2707
1988	2604	548	675	181	4008
1989	4344	1330	698	523	6895
1990	4225	1479	691	552	6947
1991	4292	1160	501	498	6451
1992	3792	968	476	573	5809
1993	3543	875	538	608	5564
1994	3764	913	588	729	5994
1995	3492	989	706	693	5880

Source: AMDATA.
* Deals between EU firms of the same nationality.
** Cross-border deals between EU firms.
***Deals between EU and non-EU firms.

Table 11.2.   Breakdown by Member State of EU merger activity, 1990–95

Country	National	Community		International	
		Bidder	Target	Bidder	Target
B	417	221	418	55	69
DK	920	302	271	151	114
D	5316	821	1395	548	1116
GR	19	5	29	2	13
E	607	86	599	57	195
F	3415	1270	900	493	453
IRL	162	215	61	62	23
I	1444	276	482	136	194
L	2	87	52	12	7
NL	1185	624	523	239	210
A	47	138	99	25	28
P	24	13	101	0	13
FIN	1405	257	183	122	124
S	1027	532	285	248	155
UK	7118	1243	835	1280	888
Multiple		294	151	70	51
Total	23108	6384	6384	3500	3653

Source: AMDATA.

Aggregate figures (source AMDATA) for the EU as a whole show an increase in cross-border merger activity in 1994 compared to 1993 (from a value of ECU 43.2 bn to ECU 66.5 bn, an increase of 54%). In 1994/95 the number of European cross-border deals rose 7%, from 2,230 to 2,388, but the increase in value terms was 37%, to a peak of ECU 91.3 bn (concentrated especially in particular sectors: media, banking, telecoms and pharmaceuticals accounted for 30% of all M&A deals in 1994). This recovery follows the drop in 1991–93, and overall the economic cycle appears to play an important part in the intensity of merger activity.

11.3. Private incentives for merger

In this section we focus on the product market incentives for firms to merge (as opposed to managerial labour market and financial market incentives). We consider in particular two kinds of motivations for horizontal merger: increasing market power, and achieving cost reductions and more generally efficiency gains. We also discuss the empirical evidence on the significance of these motivations for merger.

11.3.1. Market power incentives

Market power is the ability to raise price profitably and sustainably above marginal cost. The extent to which a firm can exercise market power depends on the demand responses of consumers, and on the supply responses of actual and potential competitors. Merger can enhance market power in the following ways.

Firstly, merger may enhance market power directly by 'internalizing' the price externalities between firms competing in the same market. Firms tend to be constrained in their incentive to raise prices by the fact that some of the benefits will accrue to competitors (who will increase sales as a result). Merger may reduce this problem, and thus on the whole improve the incentive to raise prices. As a result, a market with fewer firms and significant barriers to entry is more likely to see higher prices, post-merger.

Secondly, it is possible that merger may enhance market power by facilitating collusion between rivals in the product market. With a reduction in the number of independent firms, bargaining costs are lower. Merger can also affect the balance of benefits and costs to a firm of deviating from the collusive strategy, and therefore the ease with which tacit collusion can be sustained. With fewer firms, the profits per firm in the collusive equilibrium are higher and thus the incentive to deviate should be reduced. In addition, when there is a smaller number of firms it will be generally easier to observe individual deviations from the collusive strategy, and thus to punish the deviating firm. Thus merger may facilitate tacit collusion. In addition, if there is a free-rider problem in the provision of entry deterrence through pricing, that is if the incumbent firms in a market cannot successfully coordinate their actions to exclude a new entrant, a merger may reduce this externality.[173]

It is also possible that horizontal merger could facilitate exclusionary behaviour (and thus enhance market power) if there are scale benefits to such behaviour: for example, under the assumption of imperfect capital markets, a large firm may have access to financial resources that enable it to sustain temporary losses in order to drive out rivals (the 'deep pocket' story).[174] Large firms can also coordinate and deploy lobbying activities more effectively.

11.3.2. Efficiency gains from mergers

A frequent justification for mergers is that these achieve cost reductions, for example rationalization of capacity through the sharing of assets between the parties, or the achievement of more efficient organization of production. In particular, mergers may induce efficiency gains and reduce industry average costs through rationalization, selection effects and/or synergies.

Rationalization occurs when the total output of the merging firms is allocated more efficiently across existing plants, due, for example, to economies of scale. If a firm's average cost is decreasing in output over some range, the acquisition of a new plant could reduce average production costs. In addition to rationalization between plants, industry average costs can also be reduced through rationalization between firms: these are the selection effects whereby industry output is shifted from high-cost firms to low-cost firms.[175] Finally, synergies occur through the combination of complementary assets, and operate by shifting downward the marginal cost curve. Examples of synergies may include managerial restructuring, marketing gains and complementary patents.

In this area, many of the arguments seen in the previous chapter on efficiency defences for cooperation apply. For assets which are complementary (i.e. for which the marginal returns from deploying them together are higher than deploying them separately), there are significant

---

[173]   See Gilbert and Vives [1986] for an analysis of the conditions under which there is a free-rider problem in entry deterrence.

[174]   In view of these types of effects, in German competition law conglomerate mergers may be prevented if firms acquire too much financial power relative to competitors in some markets in which they are active.

[175]   The selection benefits of mergers are emphasized in the Cournot analysis of Farrell and Shapiro [1990].

advantages of common ownership.[176] However, for substitute assets the benefits are less clear-cut. In particular, economies of scale in production may be limited given the existing plants and production facilities. More significant efficiency gains may be induced through multiplant organization, in the form of managerial economies and selection effects between plants (i.e. if production is reorganized to reflect the relative technical efficiency of different plants, or if capacity is better utilized).

More generally, a claim that a merger allows the realization of significant economies of scale must be set against the alternatives of similar economies being achieved by firms through internal organization. Where returns to scale are significant, firms should have an independent incentive to exploit them, and inefficient production should be eliminated. The extent to which the 'buy' decision can be a substitute for the 'build' decision will depend for example on delays in plant construction and/or artificial entry barriers in a market – when these are important then build is a poor substitute for buy.[177]

11.3.3. Empirical evidence

A number of studies have sought to evaluate the empirical evidence on the significance of market power and cost reduction incentives for mergers. Some caution should be used, however, in interpreting these results. First, the construction of a sample of mergers always implies period selection, and this gives each research a historical context with a unique political, regulatory and (global and financial) economic environment. Further, the availability of appropriate data often forces a bias upon empirical research in favour of large US firms which are quoted on the stock market, and this gives the results a distinctly American flavour.

Inferences on the market power motive have been attempted from both price studies and event studies. The evidence from price studies is not very systematic, but they tend to find that prices tend to increase following a merger.[178]

The event studies approach explores the effect of a merger announcement on the stock market price of the merging firms and their competitors, and seeks to make inferences on the welfare effects of the merger. The rationale is that considering the stock price of the merging firms alone does not identify the source of possible expected higher profits, which could be either cost savings or market power (or both). Looking at the stock market response of the merging firms' rivals may help to sign the welfare effects. For example, if a merger is expected to lead to price increases, then its announcement should be followed by positive abnormal returns to the stock prices of the rivals (as well as the merging parties), because the rivals should benefit from the price 'umbrella' created by the merging firms. Conversely, if the merger is expected

---

[176]   In contrast, with independent assets marginal returns are no higher when these are deployed together or separately. See Hart [1995, Ch. 2] for an exposition of the relationship between optimal ownership structure and the nature of assets.

[177]   See Gilbert and Newbery [1992] for an analysis of the 'build or buy' decision.

[178]   For example, Kim and Singal [1993] examined price changes following a number of US airline mergers in 1985–88 (when mergers usually went unchallenged because of the Reagan administration's relaxation on antitrust policy). They found that prices increased on routes served by the merging firms, relative to a control group of routes unaffected by the merger; and conclude that the impact of efficiency gains on air fares was more than offset by exercise of increased market power. Werden, Joskow, and Johnson [1991] also examined the price effects of mergers in the US airline industry. Two mergers (TWA/Ozark and Northwest/Republic) were found to have been followed by increases in fares and reduction in service on city pairs operated by the merging companies.

to lead to cost savings, the rivals' stock prices will fall as the merging party should be in a better position to compete strongly in the product markets.

In practice, this methodology has not produced very clear results: either there are no wealth effects on rivals at the merger announcement; or where there are positive effects, they either disappear for firms challenged by the antitrust authorities, or they are uncorrelated with pre- and post-merger concentration.[179] In the light of *ex post* results, event studies have been shown to be unreliable for detecting anti-competitive mergers: for example McAfee and Williams [1988] conducted an event study on a challenged horizontal merger which was known *ex post* to be anti-competitive, and found no *ex ante* indication of this.

There are various reasons why the use of the event study methodology for inferring the welfare effects of mergers is a highly imperfect instrument. For example, if rival firms are large multiproduct firms which derive only a small fraction of their revenues from the affected market, their stock prices may not respond strongly to a challenge announcement affecting only one sub-market. Prager [1992] also argues that there may be deterrent effects of antitrust policy: failure of these studies to find evidence of anti-competitive effects may reflect the fact that mergers most likely to have such effects may not have been attempted because of anticipated antitrust prosecution.

In summary, the stock price responses of rivals simply do not convey much information about market power, and the event study methodology does not seem well suited to analyse the market power effects of mergers. The price studies are more informative, but unfortunately too small in number. Given their focus on specific industries operating under different demand, cost, competitive and regulatory conditions, they provide little evidence from which to generalize. Nevertheless, what evidence is available from the price studies appears to support the notion that market power must be taken seriously as an incentive for merger.

The evidence on the cost-saving effects of merger comes from specific studies of gains in scale economies and of productivity changes following changes in ownership. The first type of studies provide some evidence that mergers can allow exploitation of plant-related scale economies, though they also suggest that such mergers may be less necessary when there is strong product-market competition which forces companies to seek out scale economies any way.[180] As argued by Scherer and Ross [1990, p. 165], 'Plant-specific and product-specific

---

[179]   In a study of 11 horizontal mergers Stillman [1983] found no evidence of wealth increases for the rival firms. Conversely, Eckbo [1983] found evidence of positive abnormal returns for rivals at the announcement of several horizontal mergers in 1963–81. However he also found that there were no statistically significant abnormal returns at a subsequent antitrust challenge, and interpreted his results as indication that mergers which had been challenged had, on average, 'increased competition'. Similarly, Eckbo [1984] examined 196 horizontal mergers, 80 of which were challenged, and again found that the merger announcement was usually associated with positive abnormal returns to the rivals of the target firm. However, there was no correlation between the industry wealth effect and the change in concentration implied by the horizontal merger, nor the pre-merger Herfindahl index. If mergers are more likely to be anti-competitive when there is high pre-merger market concentration, or a large concentration increase, Eckbo concludes that the positive industry wealth effect is explained not by anti-competitive effects, but by the identification of cost savings in the merger process that were potentially applicable throughout the industry. A newer strand of research has emphasized the problems of aggregate analyses of mergers, and subdivided merger samples into subsamples (for example distinguishing conglomerate from horizontal mergers). Seth [1990] found that for 'related mergers', the returns to the merger are significantly higher the larger the relative size of the target firm to the bidder; while a higher debt level rises returns for 'unrelated' mergers.

[180]   In a study of 12 industries across 6 nations, Scherer et al. [1975] find some evidence of post-merger product-specific scale economy gains. Such gains were greater in Europe than in the US, which is argued to depend on two factors. First,

scale economies can and do result from mergers. But for a significant fraction of the cases in which they do, it is because competition has failed to stimulate efficient plant investment, specialization, or closure choices. Mergers are a second-best solution, given the failure of competition. It follows conversely that the more effectively competition is working, the less essential mergers are as a source of production scale economies'.

Studies of the productivity performance of plants following an ownership change have found sizeable improvements following an ownership change.[181] This evidence suggests that mergers play an important role in matching assets to their most effective owner. This in turn suggests that merger policy must take seriously the possibility that merger can lead to combination of complementary assets.

In the next section, we consider how the pursuit of market integration and the adoption of policies facilitating integration may affect these incentives for merger.

11.4. The effects of integration on the incentives for merger

Given the incentives for merger described in the previous section, how should we expect firms to react to greater market integration?

As argued at several points in this study, the expected effect of the integration programme was a reduction in two types of cost of doing business across space: the fixed costs of entry into foreign markets, and the marginal cost of providing goods to foreign consumers (equivalent to a fall in transport costs). The outcome of such cost reductions is effectively an increase in market size, and each firm may find itself facing a larger number of competitors than in its pre-integration markets. In equilibrium, this should lead to smaller per-firm price-cost margins, though the effect on the total number of firms in the market is indeterminate – it may be lower than the sum of the pre-integration markets.

As a result, the effect of market integration on the market power incentive for merger is hard to assess. This is because the overall impact of integration on such an incentive is in fact the net result of two distinct effects. On the one hand, a larger market implies that more firms should be sustained in equilibrium than in each of the separate (pre-integration) markets, and price-cost margins should be lower than they would have been in the individual markets. This suggests that in an integrated market the effect of a merger on the price-cost margin should be proportionately smaller than in each of the separate markets. On the other hand there is a quantity effect which is potentially ambiguous, as each firm's sales in the integrated market can be larger than pre-integration. The crucial issue is what happens to the number of firms in the market, and this will depend on the specific market structure and conditions.

---

the much greater size of the US market made it easier to attain most product-specific economies (optimal plant size) without merger, by *de novo* expansion. Second, price competition was fiercer in the US, generating greater pressure on US producers to specialize in products in which they could capture maximum scale economies. In Europe, where product-market competition had failed to enforce specialization, merger was a route to product-specific scale.

[181]   McGuckin and Nguyen [1995] find that transferred plants in the US food manufacturing industry over 1977–87 experienced significant improvements in productivity performance following ownership changes, and conclude that synergy gains were the most important motive for these merger. These results are consistent with those of Lichtenberg [1992] who finds that manufacturing plants involved in ownership change in 1972–78 showed productivity increases relative to a control group; and airline mergers in 1970–84 were associated with reductions in unit cost (both in absolute terms and relative to non-merging carriers), most of which were passed on to consumers in the form of lower prices.

Consider for example two separate geographical markets with two firms each. Suppose that after integration only three firms will be sustainable in the single market: that is, in equilibrium there are more firms in the joint market than in each of the two markets separately, but less than in the sum of these pre-integration markets. The price-cost margin will be lower, and compared with the pre-integration situation a merger will have a smaller effect on such a margin. However, this will apply to a larger amount of output. Hence the market power incentives are going to be ambiguous.[182]

How would we expect integration to affect the cost-reducing incentive to merge?

Enlargement of market size makes it possible to exploit economies of scale which were previously unrealized (for example if minimum efficient plant scale was greater than what was afforded by a domestic market). The question is then whether mergers may be effectively needed to exploit such economies. In fact, market enlargement (i.e. reduction of entry barriers into other geographical markets) should make possible the internal realization of economies of scale by firms, stimulating direct investment strategies to exploit such economies, and thus reducing the attraction of mergers for these purposes.

Some indirect support for this hypothesis may be obtained from the study of Scherer et al. [1975] on post-merger product-specific scale economy gains. This found that such gains were greater in Europe than in the US, which suggests that the much greater size of the US market made it easier to attain most product-specific economies without merger. The inference is that as European integration proceeds, there may be less need for merger to exploit scale economies: the enlargement of market size should enable firms to attain optimal plant size by *de novo* expansion rather than by acquisition.

In addition, price competition was fiercer in the US, which was interpreted as generating greater pressure on US producers to specialize in products in which they could capture maximum scale economies. In Europe, where product-market competition failed to enforce specialization, merger was a route to achieve product-specific scale economies. If integration leads to more intense competition, firms may be induced to exploit scale economies through direct investment, and therefore merger should be less necessary to capture scale benefits. Thus as European integration develops, and product markets become more competitive as a result, companies will be induced to increase productive efficiency internally, and the scale-economy incentive for merger should become weaker.

On the other hand, some integration measures should also be expected to facilitate the movement of assets across borders, and thus to generate new incentives for recombining assets. As discussed in Chapter 10, the task for policy in this case is to distinguish between asset combinations which are complementary, and thus efficient, and those which are substitutes, and thus more likely to be anti-competitive. In particular, it is important from a

---

[182]   As for the 'collusive' incentive for merger (which in any case is a second-order effect), the impact of integration is also going to be ambiguous. Integration enlarges the size of the market, and more firms should be supported than in each separate geographical market (though less than in each market individually). In a larger market with more firms collusion may be more difficult, and the incentives to collude may be lower (each firm's share of the collusive profit is lower). This should reduce the attraction of mergers/takeovers of rivals to facilitate collusion. On the other hand, the incentive to cheat will also be lower, so collusion may be more easily sustainable. More generally, pricing behaviour across markets should become more interrelated, and make it easier to detect deviations from the collusive agreement.

policy perspective that the synergy claim is not allowed to become a *carte blanche* for approving mergers that lead to combinations of substitute assets.

11.5. Mergers and joint ventures in the airline industry

We briefly consider here the airline industry which has recently been the subject of an intense deregulation/integration programme, to assess whether any evidence can be gleaned from case law on the integration effects on merger behaviour.

As the air transport liberalization programme has progressed,[183] there has been a significant increase in the number of cooperative alliances (and other similar arrangements) involving airline companies operating in Europe. Cases which have qualified for notification under the European Commission Merger Regulation were Air France/Sabena (1992), BA/TAT (1992), BA/Dan Air (1993) and Swissair/Sabena (1995).

Some insight into the possible effects of aviation deregulation and liberalization can be provided by the experience of the US, whose airline network moved to a hub-and-spoke system as a result of deregulation in the early 1980s. Hub networks make it easier for a given airline to serve a greater number of city-city combinations, and thus allow airlines to take greater advantage of economies of scope and traffic density. Extensive empirical research has shown in particular that in the US, (a) hub networks have led to fiercer competition at the city pair market level, but an increase in airport and industry-wide concentration; (b) hub networks allow for significant economies of scope and of traffic density; (c) the ease with which an airline can exercise market power depends much more on its dominance at a hub, than on an individual route; and (d) an airline with extensive inter-route contacts is more likely to have market power (through multimarket collusion).[184]

In Europe, research has shown that wherever entry has occurred after the adoption of bilateral liberalization measures in Europe, lower fares followed (Abbott and Thompson [1991]). By allowing provision of flights between any two Member States, it is possible that the European liberalization programme could also encourage carriers to establish hub-and-spoke networks in place of direct city-city flights.[185] However there are also other reasons − such as the characteristics of European geography (shorter distances, etc. − see our case study on airlines) − which suggest that a full move towards a hub-and-spoke system is not very likely in Europe.

In the case of Air France/Sabena (1992), Air France bid to take joint control with the Belgian Government over the Belgian airline. For the affected markets (the routes Brussels-Lyon, Brussels-Nice and Brussels-Paris), the merger would have resulted in a transformation from duopolies to monopolies. The merged parties intended to establish a new hub-and-spoke network centred on the Brussels Zaventem airport, and would have taken all the resulting slots. The merger was cleared by the Commission, subject to a number of undertakings: that one of the companies would effectively withdraw from the Brussels-Lyon and Brussels-Nice

---

[183]   As of 1 January 1993, airlines have been free to fly between any two EU countries, and from April 1997 they will be free to run domestic services in other Member States (cabotage).

[184]   See Brueckner and Spiller [1991], Keeler and Formby [1994], Evans and Kessides [1993], and Borenstein [1991].

[185]   This prediction is also made by Huston and Butler [1993], who anticipated a move towards the hub network in the EU − though less fully than in the US because of political and structural constraints limiting the strength of the competitive environment.

routes; that other EU airlines would be granted access on the Brussels-Paris route (with interline agreements being provided in all cases); and that the merged firm was restricted to 65% of the slots at Zaventem for 10 years.

This case illustrates the importance of examining potential dominance in the airlines sector both on city pair routes and on individual airports. The main implication for competition policy of any move towards a hub-and-spoke system is that it is crucial to ensure that airlines have easy access to airport facilities. Merger authorities should expect some consolidation in EU airlines as output transfers to the more efficient carriers, but mergers which allow airlines to dominate slot access at any given airport should be treated with circumspection.

Eight weeks after the Air France/Sabena decision, the Commission cleared BA's plan to buy nearly 50% of the French regional airline TAT, after undertakings by BA (BA/TAT (1992)). The terms of the initial proposal led the Commission to have competition concerns about the effects on the Gatwick-Paris and Gatwick-Lyon routes, because of the lack of actual competition and the absence of new slots. However, BA promised to give up slots on both routes if rivals want to start or step up their services. This commitment satisfied the Commission that the problems of market entry would be 'eliminated'.[186]

In 1993 the Commission cleared the merger between BA and DanAir, on the grounds that the merger did not create a dominant position on the London-Brussels route.[187] Before the merger BA operated on the Brussels-Heathrow route and DanAir on Brussels-Gatwick. Thus if the two routes were taken as distinct markets the merger had no effects on competition. Taking the London-Brussels route as a whole, BA had 40% of the market and DanAir 9% of the market beforehand. Two competitors, British Midland and Sabena, have greater flight frequency on the Heathrow-Brussels route than BA,[188] and thus were adjudged to provide sufficient competition to restrain BA-DanAir's pricing. Especially important in the Commission's decision-making was the recent entry of British Midland, which entered Heathrow-Brussels in summer 1992 and had within a year greater flight frequency on this route than BA. British Midland had obtained slots at Heathrow by transferring slots from other routes.

Early in 1995, Air France sold its stake in Sabena, and later in the same year a 49.5% stake in Sabena was acquired by Swissair. There were several problems with this acquisition. Again, on the relevant city pair routes (between Brussels and Switzerland's three major airports – Basle, Geneva and Zürich) the merger would transform a duopoly into a monopoly; in addition there was a lack of available slots during peak periods; and furthermore a 1960 bilateral agreement between Belgium and Switzerland provides for state mono-designation of air carriers, so that no airline other than Swissair and Sabena may fly on this route. Negotiations were underway (but not completed) between the EU and Switzerland to extend the EU's air transport market policy to Switzerland. The Commission was also concerned with network effects, as Swissair is part of a cooperative alliance with SAS and Austrian Airlines, which coordinates route scheduling and allows specialization of hubs. Taking into account an

---

[186]   See Neven et al. [1993, pp. 124-125].

[187]   The concentration did not have a Community dimension, but the Belgian Government requested under Article 22 that the Commission examine the effects of the merger on the Belgian market.

[188]   83% of passengers travelling the London-Brussels route use Heathrow.

alliance between SAS and Lufthansa, this agreement accounts for 35% of passenger traffic within Europe, and carries twice as many passengers as the next largest carrier.

The Commission approved of the purchase subject to undertakings: first, that the Belgian and Swiss Governments were committed to change the existing regulatory situation so that the present system of mono-designation will become one of multiple designation. Secondly, the companies entered into a number of commitments relating to slot availability, interlining and Frequent Flyer Programmes (FFPs).[189] The Commission determined that these would allow for effective new entry at the level of both individual routes and the air transport network, and thus cleared the merger.

Two points relating to integration are worth noting here. First, it was clear that one of Swissair's major motives in acquiring Sabena was to establish a secure market position in the EU's deregulated single aviation market. Remaining outside this market, Swissair had felt it was to receive unfavourable treatment at key European hubs. Thus integration within the EU appears to have encouraged entry from outside the EU. Second, the mono-designation regulation was an important entry barrier, and suggests the value of extending deregulation measures to as many markets related to the EU as possible.

This brief survey of cases in the EU airlines industry suggests firstly that integration may be encouraging companies to seek out the most cost-efficient industry structure. In the airlines case this may also mean a partial move towards a network structure more based on hubs-and-spokes. Secondly, integration and increased competition are likely to have selection effects and to lead to some industry consolidation. In all cases, the main point for policy remains to ensure that airlines are not able to acquire control of access to airports, or more generally to any essential facility, and thus to discourage mergers which facilitate dominance over access to such facilities.

11.6. The EU approach to mergers and market integration

In this section we consider the current EU competition policy approach to mergers, and make use of the analysis so far to evaluate how this may need to be revised in the light of integration. As the market power incentive for merger is unlikely to be reduced in a wider (integrated) market, we emphasize the importance of a rigorous analysis of dominance. We then discuss the weight to be given in an integrated market to the efficiency defences for merger, and argue that these should not become more prominent. Finally we emphasize the importance of sound market definition, which in an integrated market become more crucial for taking the correct decision.

The current basis for the analysis of merger in EU competition policy is Council Regulation (EEC) No 4064/89, which came into force on 21 September 1990 (and created the Merger Task Force). This applies to 'Concentrations with a Community dimension' (CCDs), which are assessed on the basis of 'compatibility with the Common Market'.[190]

---

[189]   Swissair also undertook to terminate cooperation with SAS.

[190]   The notion of 'concentration' includes both the case where two or more previously independent undertakings merge, and the case where one or more undertakings acquire direct or indirect control of the whole or part of one or more other undertakings (concentrative joint ventures). The questions of the definition and control of concentrative JVs as opposed to cooperative JVs (which are assessed under Article 85) have been contentious ones. See Chapter 10.

In order for a concentration to possess a 'Community dimension' it must be large and pan-national, which in practice means that it must exceed certain size thresholds, and at least one party should not operate predominantly in one single country. The specific requirements are that (a) the aggregate world-wide turnover of all parties concerned must exceed ECU 5 billion, (b) the aggregate Community-wide turnover of each of at least two parties must exceed ECU 250 million, and (iii) unless each of the undertakings concerned achieves more than two-thirds of its aggregate Community-wide turnover within one and the same Member State. The tests are based on geographic turnover and not upon the location of the parties: the Merger Regulation can therefore apply to transactions involving no EU company, or companies with little connection with the EU.

It is worth noting that the Commission's initial intention was that the thresholds should be eventually reduced to ECU 2 billion and ECU 100 million. Compared with the current average of about 60, it is estimated that such a reduction would increase the annual caseload to about 130 concentrations. This proposal was put on hold in the face of opposition from the UK, France and Germany, but it has been reintroduced by the Commission in the January 1996 Green Paper.[191]

Since the creation of the Merger Task Force and up to November 1995 some 374 cases (including concentrative JVs) had been notified, of which 31 fell outside the scope of the Regulation and 4 have been blocked.[192]

Table 11.3.   European mergers 1991–95

	1991	1992	1993	1994	1995
Notifications to the Commission under the Merger Regulation	63	60	58	95	112
Concentrations cleared during the first month	50	47	49	80	n.a.
In-depth investigation opened	6	4	4	6	7[1]

Source: European Community Competition Policy 1994, *EC Competition Policy Newsletters 1995.*
[1]   Nordic satellite, Crown Cork, Kimberley Clark, Gencor, Orkla, ABB, RTL/Veronica/Endemol.

The guiding principle in the Commission's analysis of merger is that a concentration which 'creates or strengthens a dominant position, as a result of which effective competition would be significantly impeded in the Common Market or in a substantial part of it, shall be declared incompatible with the Common Market' (Article 2). The key role of merger policy is thus in

---

[191]   The Paper also sought to address the problem of multiple jurisdiction for medium-sized mergers in different EU countries that fall below the thresholds, but which may require notification in several countries. Under the proposals, the Commission would take control of those mergers which fall between the old and new thresholds and which have to be notified to more than one national competition authority.

[192]   The 4 blocked cases to date were: Aerospatiale-Alenia/de Havilland (1991), where the proposed takeover of de Havilland was blocked because of its effect on the market for propeller aircraft with between 20 and 70 seats used for regional flights; the MSG Media Service (1994) joint venture formed between Bertelsmann, Kirch and Deutsche Bundespost Telekom, to supply administrative and technical services to digital pay-TV operators; Nordic Satellite Distribution (1995), creating a joint venture that would broadcast programmes by satellite to the Nordic countries; and RTL/Veronica/Endemol (1995), where the three firms proposed creation of a joint venture – Holland Media Group – that would become the largest TV broadcaster in Holland with about 40% of the TV audience.

the first instance to identify and control market power, which is costly (it inflicts direct harm upon consumers, and prevents the realization of the benefits of dynamic efficiency). Conversely, mergers which do not adversely affect competition should be approved without delay or concern as to whether or not they will eventually be privately profitable.

It is, of course, also possible that mergers allow efficiency gains in the form of cost reductions for the merging parties. These may go some way to offsetting the static efficiency losses from the increase in market power; and indeed it is conceivable that the overall welfare effect of a merger may be positive even if the merger leads to an increase in concentration, if there are as a result significant reductions in marginal costs which are 'passed on' to the consumer in the form of lower prices (see for example Hausman, Leonard and Zona [1994]). There is however a major obstacle to the evaluation of cost reductions (and more generally of post-merger induced efficiencies) on the part of the competition authority. Merger authorities do not in practice have complete information about costs and demand, and it is hard for them to measure directly the firm-specific own-price elasticity of demand. The information asymmetries between the merging parties and the competition authority mean that where firms are allowed to use efficiency defences, they have an incentive to behave strategically: i.e. overstate possible cost savings, in order to increase the likelihood of having their proposal approved.[193]

In view of these difficulties, it is appropriate in our opinion that some competition authorities do not give a significant welfare weighting to cost savings claimed to result from a merger. Unlike the US Department of Justice (which places an explicit value on cost savings on the grounds that these enhance the dynamic competitive strength of the market, and shareholder welfare should be valued positively), in Europe the German Bundeskartellamt places no value on cost reductions *per se,* and deems cost savings to be beneficial only to the extent that they reduce prices. Similarly the EU approach is heavily focused on changes in market structure and does not easily accept efficiency defences. The Commission's services procedure for assessing mergers places far more emphasis on market power, and its centrepiece is therefore the analysis of dominance (given a certain market definition).

We consider below, in turn, if and how the process of market integration should be expected to affect the procedure followed by the EU authorities for the analysis of dominance, the assessment of cost savings, and market definition.

11.6.1. Analysis of dominance

The purpose of the analysis of dominance is to evaluate to what extent the merger would weaken competition in the market. There are in principle two parts to this analysis: the evaluation of concentration measures, and entry analysis.

Concentration indices (which should be estimated post-merger) are mainly useful as a safe harbour for excluding harmless mergers (at least 90% of mergers in practice): it will rarely be possible to exercise market power on a highly dispersed market. Much more important for the evaluation of market power is a careful analysis of entry, as the exercise of market power by

---

[193]   Notice that the firm's incomplete information about the regulator (i.e. the uncertainty on how the regulator will assess each case) also implies costs both *ex ante* (some welfare-enhancing mergers will simply never be proposed because the firms place a positive probability on the case being blocked) and *ex post* (the resource costs of mergers that are proposed and eventually blocked).

incumbent firms will be difficult if entry is feasible. This aspect is taken very seriously by the US Department of Justice, which assesses whether entry would be timely, likely and sufficient (to keep prices down).[194] Unfortunately, so far the European Commission's analysis of entry has not always been systematic.

Our discussion of the impact of integration on merger incentives in Section 11.4 suggested an ambiguous effect on the market power incentives to merge. Accordingly, once the relevant market has been appropriately defined, taking into account the effects of integration (see Section 11.6.3 below), there should be no presumption that the analysis of dominance should be any less strict. It is possible that a merger which was previously anti-competitive in a locally-defined market may no longer raise concern if some artificial barriers are eliminated, and the market is wider as a result. However given market definition, there is no justification for relaxing market share criteria, and entry analysis. (Indeed, as we will see below, there might be a presumption that the analysis of dominance should be stricter, since following integration firms may no longer need merger in order to circumvent artificial barriers and exploit scale economies: they can simply expand capacity directly. That is, given that market expansion without merger is facilitated by integration, there is if anything a case for making dominance analysis stricter.)

Undoubtedly the most important effect of integration on the analysis of dominance is that it raises the returns from a systematic analysis of entry. In a few cases, it would appear that the Commission's services have sought to take explicitly into account the effect of integration on entry barriers. In Mannesmann/Hoesch (1992), for example, the geographical market was defined to be national, but the analysis of dominance was carried out taking into account that the German market was in the process of opening up to foreign competitors, in particular because of the harmonization of technical standards for steel tubes and the impact of the European Commission Public Procurement Directive. Similar factors were assessed in Siemens/Italtel and Mercedes-Benz/Kässbohrer (1994) (line buses). However, there may be a case for enforcing a more thorough entry analysis by the Commission's services, perhaps along the lines of the US Department of Justice's guidelines on likelihood, timeliness and sufficiency of entry.

A final point is that, as we have mentioned, there may be circumstances in which collusion may be facilitated by integration, for example adherence to cross-border collusive agreements can be better monitored if integration enhances the observability of pricing behaviour. From this perspective, integration may increase the importance of a well-formulated policy towards the joint dominance effects of merger. The text of the Merger Regulation does not discuss the possibility of joint dominance. However, the Commission's services have shown themselves to be sensitive towards mergers which result in concentrated oligopoly as and when such cases have arisen. For example, in Rhône-Poulenc/SNIA (1993) the Commission concluded that although the concentration lead to a combined market share of 65%, parallel behaviour would not be significantly facilitated because of the structural characteristics of the market, such as a general lack of transparency in prices and competitive pressures from outside the EU. In Nestlé/Perrier, a precedent was established for taking account of joint dominance. Nevertheless, in an integrated market the increased importance of the joint dominance issue

---

[194] The importance of the entry lags depends on the industry in question. For example, entry times are shorter in the electronics industry than in the airline manufacturing industry.

would suggest that it would be valuable to have an explicit policy framework defining joint dominance and clarifying how oligopolistic interdependence should be taken into account in merger cases.

11.6.2. Assessment of cost savings

There was a considerable debate before the Merger Regulation was passed as to whether an efficiencies defence was desirable. Jacquemin [1990] observed that many believed that some horizontal consolidations might help merger firms pursue R&D in high-tech fields more effectively.[195] He further considered it unlikely that the role of potential dynamic efficiency gains in cases would be ignored. Indeed a careful reading of Article 2 of the Regulation, which deals with how concentrations are to be appraised, suggests that paragraph 1(b) does seem to open up scope for such a defence by referring to 'the development of technical and economic progress provided that it is to consumers' advantage and does not form an obstacle to competition'. In practice, thus far, the Commission does not seem to have allowed such a defence.

Neven et al. [1993] note that the current EU approach on cost savings of mergers is not entirely clear. In AT&T/NCR (1991), the Commission took the parties' claims of cost savings from complementarities between technical know-how and marketing of workstations as a negative factor in assessing the merger, since it feared it would allow the merging parties to drive out their rivals. Without a clear statement of the conditions under which cost savings will be considered predatory or beneficial, this may have created a deterrent effect for subsequent firms contemplating cost-reducing mergers. For example in Aerospatiale-Alenia/de Havilland (1991), the parties put forward an estimate of cost savings amounting to 0.5% of combined turnover, to be realized through 'synergies in marketing and product support', and through 'rationalizing parts procurement'. The Commission regarded these cost savings as 'negligible' (it is possible that the AT&T/NCR decision might have caused firms to understate estimated savings).

In another case dealing with the MSG joint venture between two German media companies and Deutsche Telekom, which proposed to offer infrastructure facilities and services for digital pay-TV, the Commission explicitly rejected this type of defence:

> 'The reference to this criterion [contribution to technical and economic progress] in Article 2(1)(b) of the Merger Regulation is subject to the reservation that no obstacle is formed to competition. As outlined above, however, the foreseeable effects of the proposed concentration suggest that it will lead to a sealing-off of and early creation of a dominant position on the future markets for technical and administrative services and to a substantial hindering of effective competition on the future market for pay TV.'[196]

In their review of this case, CJ Cook and CS Kerse [1996] observed that the Commission went on to question whether it was even likely that, given the dominant position acquired by the joint venture, technical and economic progress would in fact be achieved. The Commission identified almost a logical inconsistency between dominant positions and technical and

---

[195] A. Jacquemin, 'Horizontal concentration and European merger policy', *European Economic Review*, Vol. 34, May 1990, pp. 539–50.

[196] Commission Decision, OJ L364/1, 31 December 1994.

economic progress, notwithstanding the reference in Article 2(1). Moreover, the technical and economic progress achieved by the merged enterprises was considered to enable them to out-distance their competitors, and may be a factor which in itself contributes to the creation or enhancement of a dominant position.[197]

The approach appears to be different in US antitrust law, where the trade-off between potential market power costs and benefits of cost reductions from mergers is assessed explicitly: if a merger is expected to enhance market power, then the regulator evaluates whether cost savings from the merger are likely to outweigh the adverse market power effects. This entails a reversal of the onus of proof. At the 'analysis of dominance' stage the onus of proof is on the competition authority, which must demonstrate that a merger has anti-competitive effects. This is appropriate as the majority of mergers have negligible anti-competitive effects. However, at the 'efficiency defence' stage the onus of proof is reversed so that it is incumbent upon the firms to demonstrate to the regulator that the cost savings are large. The reason is clearly that this onus of proof gives the firm better incentives to reveal its private information concerning prospective cost savings.

Considering the effects of market integration on firms' efficiency justifications for merger, we have emphasized the difficulties of the regulator in assessing the cost savings which may result from a merger – given that the merging parties will have both the ability (due to their superior information) and the incentive to overstate these cost savings. Given these problems of incomplete information which inevitably beset competition authorities, a systematic policy of putting more weight on post-merger induced efficiencies is problematic. Market integration does not change this assessment in any way. Indeed, market integration increases the scope for firms to achieve certain efficiency gains (e.g. economies of scale) through organic internal growth rather than via merger. In this sense, the analysis of efficiency defences for cooperation in the previous chapter applies in full.

11.6.3. Market definition

The Commission uses a standard definition of the relevant product market as comprising those products 'which are regarded as interchangeable or substitutable by the consumer, by reason of the products' characteristics, their prices and their intended use.' One weakness of the Commission's approach is that while in recent years there has been a move towards the use of econometric evidence when assessing substitutability, there is still great reliance on technical characteristics of the product, its function and on consumer surveys. Another weakness is that the Commission's definition of the relevant product market tends to focus mainly on demand-side substitution.

Most important from the point of view of integration is the effect on the relevant geographical market. This is defined by the Commission as comprising 'the area in which the undertakings concerned are involved in the supply of products or services, in which the conditions of competition are sufficiently homogenous and which can be distinguished from the neighbouring areas because, in particular, conditions of competition are appreciably different in those areas'. Factors relevant to the assessment of the relevant geographical market include 'the nature and characteristics of the products or services concerned, the existence of entry

---

[197]   CJ Cook and CS Kerse, *EC Merger Control*, Sweet and Maxwell (second edition), 1996, p. 166.

barriers or consumer preferences, and appreciable differences of the undertakings' market shares between neighbouring areas or substantial price differences'.

The effect of integration will be to expand the relevant geographical market, other factors held constant. Thus integration makes it particularly important for the merger authority carefully to assess supply-side substitutability from a geographic point of view.[198] Again, market integration may require a more careful analysis of the possibility of entry by firms for whom entry strategies may have been previously hindered by barriers.

11.7. Institutional implications of market integration for merger control

A very important implication of market integration, which must be emphasized, is that it provides strong incentives to modify the institutions of merger control.

As markets become more integrated, and national market boundaries therefore become less relevant, there are implications for the distinction between mergers falling under the competence of national antitrust authorities, and those falling under the competence of the Commission. Integration should mean that relevant markets are increasingly 'stretched' across national boundaries, and not confined within national borders. In this context, maintaining the current approach to merger decisions would create two types of potential 'costs'.

(a)   To the extent that market definition by national authorities continues to be based on national boundaries, the outcome would be systematically wrong decisions. For example, to the extent that integration enlarges the size of the relevant market, a high level of market share at the national level should raise less concern. In other words, greater intra-EU competition should make it possible to tolerate higher levels of domestic concentration. Thus mergers which would have raised domestic competition policy concerns before integration should be let through after integration – if the firms' post-integration market shares are lower as a result of wider market definition. However, if the national competition authorities still define markets on the basis of their national boundaries, decisions will be systematically distorted.

(b)   Where, instead, national authorities were to adopt the 'right' market definition, and therefore consider relevant markets which extend beyond their national boundaries, the result would be overlapping competencies. This has an obvious duplication cost attached. Furthermore, it means that if the various national authorities have different degrees of stringency, the one with the harshest approach is implicitly that which is adopted.

In this sense, integration raises the important institutional issue of coordination between competition authorities at the national and EU levels, including how to deal with overlapping competencies.

An important consequence appears to be that the analysis of mergers should be reallocated or at least coordinated at the European level. This may imply a reduction in the number of cases

---

[198]   In recent years the Commission appears to have paid more attention to intra-Community barriers to trade. For example, in Direct Line/Bankinter (1994) the Commission noted that in spite of the opening up of the non-life insurance market to intra-Community competition, the markets remain national due to national differences in consumer preferences, regulatory regimes and distribution systems.

which are brought in front of the national competition authorities, and a transfer of competencies to the EU authorities. Alternatively, the implementation of the rules could be delegated to the national authorities. This would appear a good solution to take into account on the one hand the benefits of a unified treatment of mergers across the EU (significant differences in the attitude of national authorities may distort the choice of merger partner), and on the other, the informational benefits of delegating implementation of merger rules to national authorities, wherever possible. In late 1996, the Commission published its *Green Paper on the Review of the Merger Regulation* which includes a proposal to lower the thresholds of the Merger Regulation.[199]

11.8. Summary and conclusion

In this chapter, we assessed the scope for anti-competitive behaviour in the single market through mergers and acquisitions. We discovered the relative importance of incentives to enhance market power and incentives to achieve cost reductions. Unlike other types of behaviour reviewed in earlier chapters, we found no systematic evidence that integration has a major effect on the market power incentives to merge or vice versa.

The ambiguous impact of market integration on the market power incentive to merge suggested that there should be no general presumption that merger policy should become less stringent (provided that markets are defined taking properly into account the effects of integration).

As for the cost-reduction incentive, whilst integration offers companies the opportunity to exploit scale economies, it also makes merger less necessary to attain such economies: that is, mergers are less likely to be needed to circumvent artificial entry barriers, and competition forces firms to behave in a more internally efficient manner without ownership changes. In addition, mergers that might have been pursued in order to overcome certain cross-border barriers are no longer necessary. Generally, no greater emphasis should be placed on efficiency defences, and there is a possible case for making competition analysis stricter. An important caveat should be emphasized, however, for the case of complementary assets: merger may perform an important function in bringing such assets under common ownership, which has beneficial effects, and this should be allowed.

In the light of integration, which should make entry easier, it is crucial that likely entry effects are carefully and systematically assessed. Current EU treatment of entry effects is too often arbitrary. At the stage of market definition this means taking into account geographic supply-side substitutability. At the analysis of dominance stage this requires a more systematic entry analysis, assessing the likelihood, timeliness and effectiveness of entry.

---

[199]   COM(96) 19 final.

12. State aid

12.1. Introduction

Although the framework for control of state aids at a European level has been in place since the foundation of the EU, its importance has increased considerably with the implementation of the single market. In particular, market integration is likely to increase the incentives for firms to lobby for state aid due to increased pan-European competition. On the other hand, market integration may change those circumstances in which the granting of state aid is economically justifiable. We will need to consider these two effects of market integration in detail.

Of key importance to state aid policy is the need to distinguish those circumstances in which state aid is economically justifiable as a response to a market imperfection or failure from those in which it is not. In the latter case, state aid is likely to have effects which are detrimental to economic welfare as a result of distorting the decisions of economic agents. In particular, state aid is likely to bias the exit and entry decisions of firms and thus lead to a distortion of market structure. These distortions of market structure are likely to be of greater concern in an integrated market for two reasons. First, a greater number of consumers will be affected. Second, there may well be greater incentives for national governments to foster 'national champions' following market integration; state aid may have a proportionately greater effect in enhancing the competitive position of the recipient.

These reasons suggest that there is a prima facie case that market integration may lead to increased lobbying for and, possibly, granting of state aid. This may hinder the achievement of the benefits of integration. If firms lobby for state aids, then this may in itself be a wasteful activity, whether or not the state aid is ultimately granted. Thus there is a case that market integration should be accompanied by some toughening of policy on state aids, both to reduce the granting of state aids and to reduce firms' incentives to lobby for aid.

Market integration may also lead to circumstances in which the granting of state aid is beneficial. For example, increased product market competition following integration may lead to the exit of some firms. Where this creates structural adjustment problems, there may be a good case for the use of state aid to smooth the transition process. Thus, like competition policy, state aid policy will always need to be conditional, identifying those cases in which state aid is welfare-enhancing and those in which it is welfare-reducing.

We will first sketch some of the trends in state aid, and then consider some of the effects of granting aid. We then consider how market integration is likely to have affected the incentives for firms to lobby for state aid, the incentives for governments to grant aid, and the effects of state aid on economic welfare. We critically review current EU policy on state aids and develop some conclusions on whether policy needs to be changed as a result of market integration.

12.2. Trends in state aid

Most of the issues raised in this chapter indicate the theoretical possibility that, without a toughening of restrictions, the incentives to lobby for aid and to grant state aid might increase as a response to market integration. However, the only information available on the actual amount of state aid granted in the EU are four surveys conducted by the Commission. Table 12.1, 12.2 and 12.3 show a general decrease in the amount of aid.

Table 12.1.   State aid to the manufacturing sector in the EU

.EUR-12	1988	1989	1990	1991	1992
In % of value added	4.1	3.2	4.2	3.5	3.4
In ECU per person employed *	1,497	1,133	1,475	1,215	1,210
In % of intra-Community export **	22.8	15.9	20.9	17.3	16.9

Source: Fourth Survey on State Aid, European Commission, 1995, p. 8.
* at constant 1991 prices
** intra-Community exports of industrial products

Of course, the level of state aid is affected by several factors. The macroeconomic cycle will influence the number of business failures and hence have an important influence on state aid; during recessions the amount of state aid will tend to grow. The German unification of 1990 had the effect of increasing the amount of state aid granted by the German state. Between 1990 and 1992, 40.5% of all German aid to manufacturing was granted to the new *Länder*; this accounts for the somewhat anomalous figures for 1990 in Table 12.1.

A dampening effect on state aid might among other things also be due to the following factors.

(a)   Greater Community control on the granting of state aid by national governments. For example, the total number of decisions on state aid made by the Commission increased from 294 in 1987 to 527 in 1994. Greater transparency in the application of Community rules may also reduce the amount of state aid granted.

(b)   The criteria of economic convergence set by the Maastricht Treaty in 1990 for participation in the Monetary Union (aiming at a 3% budget deficit and 60% of debt-GDP ratio) may have constrained the ability of states to grant new state aid without raising taxes.

(c)   Table 12.2 shows that the decline in the amount of financial subsidies granted by the Member States has been compensated by an increase in aid at the Community level.

As a political consequence of the Single European Act and the Maastricht Treaty, the Commission has become a more active player in granting aid through its regional and social funds and other schemes. The actual amount of Community aid has increased in recent years.

Although Community aid has rather different objectives to national state aids, it may in part reduce the need for national state aids. For example: EU regional funds may reduce the need for national governments to grant regional development aids; EU aids to promote R&D may substitute for national aid.

Table 12.2.   A comparison of the state aid granted by national states and Community expenditure

(million ECU)	1988	1989	1990	1991	1992
State aid *	37,691	30,254	42,059	35,734	35,673
Community expenditure	30,989	32,618	34,043	40,516	42,880
Total	68,680	62,872	76,102	76,250	78,553
State aid as % of total	54.88	48.12	55.27	46.86	45.41

Source: Fourth Survey on State Aid, European Commission, 1995, p. 85.
*State aid to the manufacturing sector in current prices. It includes EAGGF Guarantee, EAGGF Guidance (payments), Social Fund (commitments), Regional Fund (commitments, part corresponding to the concept of aid within the meaning of Art. 92 of the Rome Treaty), R&D (both DG XII, part intended for large firms and SMEs, and DG XIII) and ECSC grants (resettlements, steel social, coal social, research and interest relief).

Table 12.3 shows that the level of state aid has declined in all the EU Member States, though at a different pace, from 1981 to 1992. Thus, the factors leading to reduced state aid appear to have affected different countries similarly.

Table 12.3.   Overall state aid in the EU Member States, in percentage of GDP

Country	1981–86	1986–88	1988–90	1990–92
Belgium	4.1	3.2	2.8	2.3
Denmark	1.3	1.0	1.1	1.0
Germany	2.5	2.5	2.5	2.4
Greece	2.5	4.5	3.1	2.2
Spain	-	2.7	1.8	1.3
France	2.7	2.0	2.1	1.8
Ireland	4.0	2.7	1.9	1.5
Italy	4.0	3.1	2.8	2.8
Luxembourg	6.0	4.0	3.9	3.9
Netherlands	1.5	1.3	1.1	0.9
Portugal	-	1.5	2.0	1.4
UK	1.8	1.1	1.2	0.6
EUR-12	**2.8**	**2.2**	**2.1**	**1.9**

Source: First, Second, Third and *Fourth Survey on State Aid*, European Commission.

12.3. The economics of state aid

12.3.1. The reasons for granting state aid

State aid provides a subsidy to private producers and/or consumers. While such subsidies can contribute to the achievement of allocational efficiency if they address market failure (resulting from externalities, public goods or market imperfections, e.g. due to asymmetric information), state aid may be used to further national objectives at the expense of other EU countries. In addition, it is also possible that the government can be captured by domestic interest groups engaged in rent-seeking. In this case, subsidies may simply constitute a redistribution of income (rents) to well-organized and politically powerful interest groups rather than being a corrective measure to market failures. Lobbying for such redistributive aid may itself be wasteful. In addition, state aid may also distort competition and increase the tax burden, thus leading to inefficiencies and overall welfare losses. Finally, state aid may be used to pursue political objectives like, for example, an equal distribution of income over different regions.

Basically, we can distinguish three kinds of state aid, based on different reasons for granting subsidies.

(a)   Aid that is intended to correct market failures resulting from externalities or public goods. Typical examples for externalities comprise (positive or negative) spillovers between industries, in particular spillover effects from R&D investment. Of particular interest in the context of integration are capital market imperfections and debt overhang problems.

(b)   A particularly prevalent special case of aid to correct market failures is that intended to smooth structural adjustment. Rapid changes in industrial structure, following market integration, may entail frictions (for example, due to labour immobility) that could be avoided by affecting the way in which, and the speed with which, these changes take place.

(c)   Aid that is intended to promote domestic firms or industries at the expense of foreign suppliers, or that is granted in response to subsidies given by foreign governments to foreign firms.

(d)   Aid granted as a redistribution in favour of particular interest groups by governments.

We will consider the reasons for granting aid that are relevant from the perspective of the interrelation between state aid and market integration in more detail.

Capital market failures and R&D investment

We first consider the main reasons for granting state aid to improve economic welfare. A common feature of all these reasons is that the granting of state aid is only optimal when there is a market failure of the economy elsewhere and state aid is being used in a corrective manner.

Capital markets are particularly susceptible to problems resulting from asymmetric information. Creditors may find assessing the specific merits of an investment project difficult and may face an adverse selection problem. Higher interest rates may attract relatively more investors with high-risk projects. An increase in interest rates may, therefore, increase the average riskiness of the portfolio of projects for which credit is being given and decrease the lender's expected returns. As a result it may be profit-maximizing for banks to improve the quality of their portfolio by reducing interest rates below the market clearing level and rely on non-market means of credit allocation.[200] This credit rationing may make it difficult for firms to get sufficient access to finance and may warrant subsidies to correct this market imperfection.

Because these problems are caused by asymmetric information, one would expect credit rationing to be most severe for types of investment where information asymmetries are large. R&D investments in particular may give rise to the greatest concerns about rationing problems resulting from asymmetric information. However, there are additional potential externalities

---

[200]   See, for example, Jaffee and Russell [1976] or Stiglitz and Weiss [1981].

involved in the process of R&D which may justify the granting of subsidies. For example, there may be positive spillover benefits for other producers resulting from innovation by one firm. To the extent that innovators fail to take account of the benefits they generate for others, there may be a case for subsidy. Also, innovation by one firm may help other firms by allowing them to forecast non-accurately the likely pay-off from innovation themselves. In such circumstances, firms will tend to delay innovation for strategic reasons.[201] Such strategic delay is socially wasteful and provides a justification for so-called 'pump-priming' partial funding of R&D by governments.[202]

However, one has to be cautious in applying these arguments in order to justify state aid given to particular firms. Governments are unlikely to be better informed about the characteristics of investment projects than private borrowers and are therefore unlikely to pick those investment projects that suffer most from credit rationing. A system which decentralizes investment decisions may be preferable to direct government funding of specific investment projects. For example, if credit rationing is felt to be a particular problem for innovative industries, then appropriate corrective fiscal policy for this sector may be desirable, such as an investment tax credit.

Debt overhang problem

Legal provisions for bankruptcy remove control over the firm from equity holders and give it to debt holders in situations of debt default. This may create a situation where efficient decisions to refinance the defaulted firm may not be taken because the marginal benefits to debt holders differ systematically from the social marginal benefits. Government subsidies may help to keep firms in business where it is socially optimal to refinance the bankrupt firm but where the debtors have insufficient incentive to do so.

The following example may help to illustrate the problem.

Debt overhang: an example

Assume that the firm has debt equal to D. Let V be the liquidation value of the company, i.e. the realizable value of its assets. Upon liquidation of the firm debtors obtain pay-off equal to $\min[D,V]$. Equity holders receive the remainder of the value of the firm, equal to $\max[0,V-D]$. If $V < D$, the firm is illiquid and faces bankruptcy. Suppose that refinancing the firm would lead to a value of $V^* > D$ with some probability p, but be completely ineffective with probability $(1-p)$. Finally, assume that the refinancing cost R is covered exclusively by additional debt (i.e. the refinancing is being carried out in a situation of default on existing debt), and that successful refinancing at least covers its cost (i.e. $V^* > D + R$).

Refinancing the firm is socially optimal if, and only if, $pV^* + (1-p)V - R > V$, i.e. if the expected value of the firm with refinancing net of the refinancing cost is greater than the current default value. However, because some of the potential gain from refinancing would accrue to equity holders, debtholders face a different incentive. They will decide to refinance if, and only if, $p(R+D) + (1-p)V - R > V$. Because $V^* > R+D$, there may be cases where debtors have no incentive to provide additional funds to refinance the firm although it would be socially optimal to do so.

---

[201]   See Chamley and Gale [1994].

[202]   We must make the proviso that there are circumstances in which there is too much expenditure on R&D from a social point of view. Recent literature on patent pacts has made the point that R&D competition can lead to wasteful duplication of R&D effort. Thus, it is not always true that the level of R&D investment is suboptimal and that corrective subsidies are needed.

Thus, in the presence of capital market imperfections, there may be economically justifiable reasons for using state aids to rescue ailing enterprises which are viable in the long run, but facing short-run difficulties due to lack of available finance.

Smoothing structural adjustment

Even if firms should go out of business in the long run because they are not competitive, there may be a reason for slowing down the adjustment process because of imperfections in other markets, primarily the labour market. This may be particularly important, for example, if the work-force is relatively immobile (geographically or sectorally) and if the social costs of unemployment are high. This problem may be reinforced by market imperfections such as wage rigidity. By smoothing the transition process, the cost of transition can be reduced.

In this case, the justification for granting state aid is due to an imperfection elsewhere, for example, in the labour market. If the social costs of the transition process have to be borne by the community rather than by the individual firms, then firms will have incentives to diverge from socially optimal behaviour. In this case, corrective measures are necessary to achieve an optimal balance between efficiency gains from restructuring and the social cost of the transition process.

Nevertheless, it is important to note that aid to smooth adjustment may be justifiable even in the case that the enterprise is not viable in the long run, if the social benefits of smoothing transition are sufficiently great. What is at issue is a dynamic trade-off: a (static) misallocation of resources may be tolerated for some time in order to reduce the overall (dynamic) adjustment costs of changing that allocation. It must be stressed, however, that this form of government intervention may carry the risk of perpetuating an inefficient situation unless the government can credibly commit to limit the amount of aid and the time over which it is given to industries that are not competitive.

Strategic promotion of national industries

Subsidies granted to domestic firms or industries may modify the incentives of firms in a way that improves their competitive position relative to firms receiving no aid. For example, recent strategic trade theory has shown that in an oligopolistic market, export subsidies may shift the reaction functions of domestic suppliers and lead to a non-cooperative equilibrium outcome that is distorted in favour of the subsidized suppliers.[203] Under specific assumptions about the nature of competition and the behaviour of foreign governments, export subsidies can be welfare-improving for an individual country even if the subsidies are financed by a lump sum tax levied on the subsidized firms or industries.[204] More generally, in the presence of imperfect competition and increasing returns to scale, state aid will affect the incentives of subsidized companies and can, therefore, be used to promote domestic suppliers. Export promotion may be achieved also by subsidizing domestic producers who compete with imports.[205]

---

[203]   Notice that in this example state aid is granted related to export volumes, rather than just as a lump sum.

[204]   See Brander and Spencer [1981, 1983].

[205]   See Chapters 12 to 14 in Krugman [1994] and, for an overview, Helpman and Krugman [1989].

For example, there is a historical tendency of governments of the Member States to subsidize national champions in the car industry, which has often been regarded as a strategic sector. Over the last decade almost all car manufacturers have received some kind of financial support from state bodies.[206] Despite the fact that often the Commission authorized aid schemes on the basis of supposed beneficial effects on depressed regions or because of the R&D contents, the number of state aid cases involving the car industry indicates the importance that governments attribute to the sector. In 1988, the Commission issued a framework on state aid specifically tailored to the motor vehicle industry,[207] which has had the effect of tightening implementation of the state aid rules by the Commission.

The promotion of national firms may be a response by national governments to market integration. If the number of firms in an integrated market is lower than before integration, then transient subsidies may be an effective instrument by which governments attempt to determine which firms will survive rather than letting the market pick the survivors. The shipbuilding industry is an example of this case: shipbuilding in the UK declined because UK suppliers were not competitive relative to the subsidized industries in other countries. Thus, if a country decides to refrain from granting state aid, those countries that subsidize domestic industries will win out.

These domestic strategic reasons for granting state aid clearly increase national welfare. However, they do so at the expense of international competitors.[208] Thus such policies will give rise to gainers and losers within the EU. In terms of average EU welfare, they may be expected to give rise to an overall loss due to the resulting distortion of competition (however, in oligopolistic settings this will not be universally true for the usual second-best reasons). We consider these welfare losses in more detail in the following section.

---

[206] Most of the cases of state aid can be divided into two categories: aid to support domestic producers and aid to attract foreign direct investment. The following cases belong to the former category: the French government provided new equity capital to Renault (1987); the Italian government gave aid to Alfa Romeo in the form of new equity capital (1985); the UK government aided the Rover Group with restructuring prior to privatization (1986); the French government gave financial aid to Peugeot (1988); the UK government donated further aid to Rover (1990); aid was granted by the German government to Volkswagen and Opel for investments in the new *Länder* (1991); the Italian government gave aid to Fiat to support its Mezzogiorno investment plan (1991); the Italian government aided the SEVEL joint venture between Fiat and PSA (1994). Examples of aid granted in order to attract foreign direct investment or to preserve the company's involvement in the country are the following: the Brussels regional authorities' proposal to grant aid to Volkswagen (1990); aid by Luxembourg to General Motors for setting up a new R&D centre (1990); Portuguese aid to an automotive component manufacturer subsidiary of GM (1990); Derbyshire County Council (UK) grant of indirect aid to Toyota (1990); aid from the Portuguese government to Ford and Volkswagen to set up a new plant for the production of multi-purpose vehicles (1991); aid from the regional government in Belgium to Volvo for innovation and environmental protection (1992); Dutch state aid to Volvo and Mitsubishi (1992); Spanish aid to Renault (1994); regional aid to Jaguar in the UK (1994). This information is drawn from the Annual Reports on Competition Policy. See also Hancher, Ottervanger and Slot [1994], *EC State Aids*, Chancery Law Publishing, 1994, pp. 111–122.

[207] OJ C 123, 18.5.1989. The framework has been renewed every two years since. In 1992, no expiry date was fixed and the Commission interpreted the latter as of unlimited duration. However, this interpretation has been recently overruled by the Court (Case C-135/93 *Spain v. Commission*).

[208] If other countries take retaliatory measures, total welfare will decline, but it will still be in the interest of each individual country to promote its national industries.

12.3.2. Adverse effects of state aids

Competition-distorting effects

State aids will generally distort competition and market structure. Consider the simplest example of a state aid, namely a lump sum subsidy for a firm. This may induce the firm to remain in the market where it would otherwise exit. If this has the consequence that the number of firms in the market is increased, then such a state aid might have a pro-competitive effect. However, the more plausible case is that such aid will (providing the firms included have fairly similar costs) cause the exit of another firm. Thus the state aid has changed the identity of the firms in the market, without increasing the number of firms. This could have an adverse effect on allocative efficiency since the granting of state aid to one firm leads to the displacement of a lower cost producer by a higher cost one.

State aid races

Governments may face coordination problems in the granting of state aid. In particular, it may be individually optimal for each government to grant a state aid, even though it is not in their collective interests. Consider, for example, the location decision of a new plant. Such decisions are often accompanied by subsidy races. Each potential recipient of the new plant has an incentive to grant aid to influence the location decision at the margin. However, in the end, if all governments grant equal state aid, then all that has happened is that there is a net transfer to the builder of the new plant, which must be raised from general taxation with its accompanying dead-weight losses.[209]

Ex ante distorting effects

We have seen that there may be socially beneficial reasons for governments granting state aid. However, even if a government pursues a policy of granting state aid only when (*ex post*) socially optimal, then even this will still distort firms' *ex ante* incentives. In particular, a firm might induce a government to grant it a subsidy if it can move first and commit itself to produce by making an irreversible (sunk) investment. In this case, a government will find it optimal *ex post* to subsidize such a firm even if it would not have given the subsidy without the firm's commitment. However, the firm will clearly anticipate the granting of a subsidy and so its *ex ante* behaviour will be distorted.

Rent-seeking behaviour

Individual companies or industries may have a strong incentive to lobby for government subsidy. As noted above, well-organized groups may be able to receive favourable treatment and subsidies at the expense of less well-organized groups. Rent-seeking behaviour usually not only has redistributive effects, but also leads to inefficiencies because it may lead to inefficient allocations if successful. Moreover, resources will be wasted in the rent-seeking process itself. This effect may far outweigh the 'pure' efficiency loss that results from an inefficient allocation.

---

[209]   For these extensions of the basic Brander/Spencer model, see Dixit and Kyle [1985].

One particular problem for assessing state aid measures is that most of the arguments that can be made for welfare-improving subsidies may be used in the process of rent-seeking. Firms may refer to capital market imperfections or competitive pressure that would force them to shed jobs in order to convince governments that some financial backing is needed. Trying to distinguish bona fide arguments from rent-seeking ones may be extremely difficult.

A study by Neven [1994] has shown that political factors are the main determinants in the variation in the level of state aid granted to the manufacturing sector, though not necessarily of the level itself. This study did not analyse, however, the extent to which state aid may be used as an instrument to promote national interests at the expense of the development of an integrated market.

Distorting effects of state aid on production and pricing decisions

State aid such as lump sum subsidies or inducements to locate plants clearly affect if and where production occurs. However, state aid may also affect competition and welfare if it affects firms' output, capacity decisions or pricing. A specific state aid measure will have such effects depending on the way it changes firms' costs. If the aid affects variable costs (e.g. subsidized input price for a variable input), profit-maximizing production and pricing decisions will normally be affected. By lowering firms' marginal costs, a subsidy allows the receiving firm to charge a lower price (not necessarily by the same amount). Production and pricing decisions will also be influenced by aid that affects fixed but avoidable costs (e.g. subsidized rental of non-specific capital equipment). Following this argument, aid that affects sunk costs (for example, the transfer of a sunk asset from the state to a firm) should not influence a firm's profit-maximizing decision. One has to be very careful, however, in identifying aid that affects sunk costs: for example, a payment to a firm to assist in the acquisition of assets, even of specific assets, does not fall under this heading. At the time of acquisition the relevant capital costs are obviously variable costs, so that the aid would rather affect variable costs.

A more sophisticated analysis would suggest that even state aids affecting sunk costs (the transfer of ownership of sunk assets) might affect pricing and output decisions. The modern theory of corporate finance emphasizes that real decisions may be affected by the financial structure of the firm, and so even state aids affecting sunk costs may have real effects.

12.4. State aid and market integration

There are three broad classes of reasons why firms may seek and why governments may grant state aid:

(a)   efficiency-enhancing reasons, where state aids are welfare-improving due to market failures elsewhere in the economy;

(b)   national self-interest reasons, typically advancing the interests of national producers at the expense of firms in other countries;

(c)   political reasons, when state aid is useful as a means of transferring resources to particular interest groups.

We now ask how market integration is likely to affect these different motivations for state aid. Also, we ask how the granting of state aid is likely to affect the process of market integration.

12.4.1. Effects of integration

We first consider the effects of integration on the three classes of reasons for granting state aids identified above.

Efficiency-enhancing reasons

As noted above, welfare-enhancing reasons for granting state aid have to be based on market failure, the most relevant being capital market imperfections and externalities like those in the debt overhang problem or in connection with rapid changes of the industrial structure.

Market integration is likely to lead to changes in industrial structure (in at least some sectors). In particular, greater cross-border competition is likely to induce the exit of some firms. Thus, in the short term, market integration may require some transitional arrangements to smooth the effects of the exit of firms. We would emphasize that the circumstances in which such state aids would be warranted are quite limited: first, the industry must be one in which integration is likely to have a significant effect on the equilibrium number of firms; second, the effects of firms' exit following integration must be concentrated into particular geographic areas or a particular sector of the economy for which mobility of labour in other areas or sectors is limited.

Where integration leads to exit, we are also likely to see the possible bankruptcy of some firms. Thus state aids may be justified in some circumstances to correct possible debt overhang problems resulting in firms being liquidated too readily from a social point of view.

With regard to capital market imperfections, we would expect that the problem of information asymmetry might decrease a little within an integrated market. The difficulties of assessing the riskiness of an investment project are likely to be lower for foreign lenders than for domestic ones. In cases where domestic lenders have an informational advantage over foreign lenders, there is likely to be a continuation of fragmented capital markets rather than the development of an integrated capital market. Advantages from using an integrated capital market, therefore, are likely to result from the development of more specialized providers of financial services whose expertise will enable them to assess the specific characteristics of an investment project better than their less specialized competitors. Furthermore, advantages could be expected from escaping tightly regulated and restricted national capital markets in which imperfections may have been reinforced by excessive regulation. Unless regulations which are put into effect for the integrated market are tighter than national regulations, we may expect the number of economically justified cases in which state aid is needed to correct capital market failures to decline as a result of integration though this effect cannot be expected to be large.

Thus, in consequence, we might expect that following market integration there will be increased economic justification for the granting of state aids resulting from exit of firms as a result of increased competition. However, this effect is only transient. Economically justified state aids would be a transitory response to smooth the effects of integration. In the long run, we would not expect market integration to expand the set of circumstances in which the granting of state aids is justifiable. Rather, if market integration reduces the impact of market failures (e.g. by integration of capital markets), then, in the long run, market integration should reduce the set of circumstances in which aid is welfare improving.

National self-interest reasons

The gradual removal of non-trade barriers will lower transport costs and reduce firms' entry costs within the EU. As a consequence, firms that have previously been protected from foreign competition will become subject to increasing competition from companies located in other European and extra-European countries. This increasing competitive pressure may induce domestic firms to adopt anti-competitive strategies. In addition to strategic reactions which have been described in the previous chapters, firms may also react to increasing competition by lobbying their own national government to grant them some sort of protection. The incentives to obtain financial support from the state, together with some other type of protection (e.g. technical standards), are, in theory, increased by market integration. Lobbying for state aids may become easier for firms since it might be reinforced by credible threats of laying off parts of the work-force as domestic firms face increasing competition.

Moreover, rather than shielding their national firms from the more intense competition in an integrated market, governments may actively want to create competitive advantages for national firms since these may now be exploited in a larger market. Governments are generally inclined towards supporting sectors that are deemed to be 'strategic' (e.g. steel in the past, semiconductors or computers today) or prestigious (e.g. cars, aeronautics). These industries tend to be highly concentrated and should be able, therefore, to organize their interests very well. If national governments grant aid in order to favour domestic firms, then market integration may not necessarily reduce the incentives for such behaviour. In particular, since integration expands the size of the market, a given expenditure of state aid may increase domestic output more in an integrated market than if markets are separated.

These incentives for governments to grant state aid may differ from country to country, in particular if the process of market integration produces losers as well as winners. The governments of those countries where industries suffered losses may be more inclined towards supporting and protecting their domestic industries. Similarly, firms' incentives to demand financial support from the state could be strengthened in those countries that enjoyed the higher levels of protection and are now facing competition from foreign firms.

Granting subsidies to national companies in an integrated market inevitably gives rise to requests for a 'level playing field': if a firm in country A is subsidized, firms in countries B and C may have a greater incentive to demand a similar treatment from their respective governments to avoid a disadvantage. This reasoning is at the basis of international attempts to regulate subsidies in order to avoid 'subsidies races'.

Political reasons

State aid may be granted to favour particular interest groups. It is hard to provide an economic analysis of such aid and we have not undertaken any analysis of this third type of effect. It is not obvious, however, why we should expect integration to have any systematic effect on such motives for granting aid.

12.4.2. Effects of state aid on market integration

Assuming that the single market programme has had the effect of increasing market integration among the EU Member States, this will influence the impact state aid might have. If state aid is granted to domestic firms that enjoy protection from import competition (e.g. due to the non-tariff barriers whose removal has been object of the single market programme), the possible distorting effects of the state aid are limited, to a great extent, to the domestic market of the receiving firm. If market integration means that the size of the market is expanded, then the effect of one national authority granting financial support to domestic firms is clearly felt in a larger market, affecting a wider number of firms, although, depending on the nature of competition, the effect on each individual competitor is likely to be smaller.

As argued above, the reduction of the costs of cross-border trade, which market integration is likely to have brought about, has the effect of increasing the level of competition in the EU markets. Increasing competition has positive effects on different aspects of economic efficiency. State aids may frustrate this process and prevent the full benefits of integration being reaped.

As competition tends to reduce price costs margins, it will force the least efficient firms out of the market. State aid, affecting variable or fixed, but avoidable costs, introduces a distortion in this process, reducing allocative efficiency first by displacing low cost producers by higher cost, but subsidized, producers, and second by increasing the tax burden with its associated dead-weight losses. Aid may also negatively affect productive efficiency through removing the competitive pressures thought to favour internal efficiency in organizations.

A wider market increases the ability of firms to reap the benefits of economies of scale. Allowing firms that would otherwise exit the market, or would be taken over by the most efficient competitors, to remain in the market might prevent the latter from enjoying the benefits of economies of scale through external growth.

Of particular concern in an integrated market is the use of state aids to influence the location of productive capacity. In an integrated market there is presumably enhanced flexibility in the location of production facilities. Under such circumstances there may be greater incentives for state aids to be used as a means of influencing location decisions. Such behaviour has been seen to a large extent in the car industry, and more generally when multinationals consider a range of EU countries for the location of *ab novo* production facilities.

Of course, all these effects of granting state aid were also present before markets became more closely integrated. Where national markets are only partially integrated, however, subsidizing only some selected firms is likely to have only a modest impact on other national markets, but the situation changes as market integration proceeds. In general, as the degree of tradability of the product increases with market integration, it is more likely that the aid would affect other firms in other countries. Because these firms might seek state aid with reference to the 'level playing field' argument, the risk of an escalation of the 'subsidies race' is, therefore, increased.

In conclusion, we would expect that market integration may in the short run give rise to increased incentives for firms to lobby for all governments to grant state aid. In the absence of appropriate EU-level controls on the granting of aid, this could potentially hinder the achievement of the full benefits of market integration.

12.5. State aid policy

12.5.1. EC Treaty

The Commission takes decisions based on Articles 92 and 93 of the EC Treaty and Articles 4 and 95 of the ECSC Treaty in respect of aid paid by Member States' national or local governmental bodies to public and private enterprises. Article 92 lays down the general principle that aid which may distort competition between firms in different Member States is forbidden, but may be permitted in certain specified circumstances. Article 93 sets out procedures which the Commission must follow in exercising its powers and imposes obligations upon Member States to cooperate with the Commission.[210]

In general terms Article 92(1) declares incompatible with the Common Market 'any aid granted by a Member State or through state resources in any form whatsoever which distorts or threatens to distort competition by favouring certain undertakings or the production of certain goods.' Several tests must be satisfied for a particular measure to be deemed 'aid'. According to Article 92(1) a particular measure must meet the following criteria:

(a) it must be granted from state resources, either directly or indirectly;
(b) it must favour certain undertakings or the production of certain goods;
(c) the aid must affect (or distort) trade between Member States.

Measures that could qualify as state aid include, amongst others, direct financial subsidies, tax exemptions, preferential interest rates, guarantees of loans on especially favourable terms, dividend guarantees, foregoing of profits, indirect state participation in share capital, the acquisition of land or buildings either gratuitously or on favourable terms, provision of goods and services on preferential terms, preferential settlement of public accounts, and the deferred collection of fiscal and social contributions. This list is by no means exhaustive.

Article 92(1) requires the Commission to give reasons why, in each specific case, the aid could be expected to distort competition.[211] Currently, if aid is identified in a financial flow between the state and an enterprise, the conclusion that aid distorts competition is almost automatic.[212] Numerous cases decided by the Commission have been challenged on the basis that insufficient evidence was given that the aid in question distorts trade or competition; however such challenges rarely succeed.

Article 92(2) defines state aids that are compatible with the common market, particularly those which promote the economic development of regions with an abnormally low standard of living and facilitate the development of certain economic activities without adversely affecting trade.

---

[210] See Lehner and Meiklejohn [1991], Chapter 5 for a detailed description of Community state aid law; also Hancher [1994].

[211] Opinion of the Advocate General in Case 173/73 *Italy v. Commission* [1974] 2 CMLE, 593 at 603-604. See generally Hancher, Ottovanger and Slot [1994, Ch. 2]. Also Case 248/84 *Germany v. Commission* [1987] ECR 4013; Case 102/87 *France v. Commission* [1988] ECR 4067; and for a recent review of case law, Cases C-324/90 and C-342/90 *Germany and Pleuger v. Commission* [1993].

[212] Lehner and Meiklejohn [1991, p. 50], and Evans and Martin [1991, pp. 83-89]. However, the Court has ruled that the Commission must at least give reasons why aid will distort trade and competition, and Commission decisions now routinely contain market and trade statistics in an effort to support the conclusion that trade will be affected.

Article 93 is concerned with the application of the European state aid policy, regulating notification of state aid and the possible decisions by the Commission. Most interesting with regard to the integration process, Article 93(1) requires the Commission, in cooperation with Member States, to review the state aid policies of the Member States continuously as well as to propose appropriate measures to the Member States as required by the progressive development of the common market.[213]

12.5.2. The market economy investor principle

The identification of the presence of state aid is the first step in any investigation conducted by the Commission. It is important to recognize that not each and every financial flow between the state and firms may constitute a form of aid. The so-called 'market economy investor principle' (MEIP) is intended to distinguish that part of a financial flow which constitutes state aid.

According to the MEIP, aid should be assessed as the difference between the terms on which the funds were made available by the state to the firm or enterprise, and the terms which a private investor would find acceptable in providing funds to a comparable firm or enterprise when the private investor is operating under 'normal market economy conditions'. Only if public funds are provided at more favourable terms than could have been obtained from a private investor, government funding will be deemed to be 'state aid'. The MEIP, therefore, is supposed not only to help to determine the presence of state aid, but also to help to quantify the amount of aid that is granted. We may interpret the MEIP as a definition of 'state aid': a state aid (according to the MEIP) is that part of a financial flow between a state and a private enterprise in excess of that which would be provided by a private investor. Thus the MEIP provides a benchmark against which financial flows can be measured. If a financial flow from a state to an enterprise would have been forthcoming from a private investor on the same terms, then this transaction does not fall under the remit of Article 92. On the other hand, if the MEIP identifies a state aid, then further analysis is required to determine whether the aid is acceptable. Thus the MEIP is a way of determining whether a transaction falls under Article 92.[214] However, it would be quite incorrect to identify transfers which constitute 'state aid' under the MEIP with transfers that are *per se* incompatible with the competition articles because they reduce welfare, since these transfers may have efficiency defences.

Nevertheless, a fundamental question is: if financial flows from the government to a company are on the same terms as a hypothetical investment by a private investor, then why should the government make this investment rather than leaving it to the market. If a financial flow does not constitute state aid under the MEIP, then government funds have replaced potential private investment. Because the funds have to be raised from either taxation or public borrowing, there can be no presumption that governments have a comparative advantage as lenders relative to the private sector.

---

[213] With regard to coal and steel, the ECSC Treaty contains special provisions relevant for state aid. Specific measures are declared to be incompatible with the common market for coal and steel in Article 4 of this treaty.

[214] The MEIP has been accepted by the European Court of Justice to be an appropriate way to deal with public ownership of an enterprise without violating Article 222 of the Treaty, under which the Treaty provisions may in no way prejudice the rules in Member States governing the system of property ownership (Case C-305/89 or C-303/88).

A recent example for this source of concern has been given by the case of a capital injection of PTA 87 billion to the Spanish flag carrier Iberia in 1996 despite the 'one time/last time' bailout rule invoked in the granting of state aid of PTA 120 billion in 1992. The second capital injection was deemed not to be a case of state aid because the state holding company controlling Iberia was found to have acted in the same way as a private investor would have acted. This begs the question of why such funding was not forthcoming from the private sector.

Although the current system of regulating state aids allows the government to act as a rational private investor and to make investments at market return where it wishes, it is not clear that governments require such freedoms if private investors would provide funds in any case. An alternative regulatory system might consider all investments by a government in an enterprise as potential state aids in need of investigation, not just those investments passing the MEIP hurdle. Such a system would be much simpler and more transparent, although governments would no longer be able to act as private investors. Under such a system, investments by the state would be allowed only if there were demonstrable welfare gains and such investment corrected some market failure. Such a system avoids the problem that the MEIP is likely to be a very difficult rule to apply in practice since it compares an actual financial flow with a putative financial flow (i.e. that forthcoming from a private investor).

A possible, but problematic, counterargument to this alternative system is that governments need to act as investors since capital market imperfections (such as credit rationing) lead to a suboptimal provision of private capital. However, under such circumstances the suboptimal actions of private investors are no longer an appropriate benchmark against which to consider financial flows; strict adherence to the MEIP would then classify as state aid investments which simply corrected capital market failures. Thus the MEIP is of limited usefulness in this case.

Thus we may conclude the following:

(a)   A financial flow which constitutes a 'state aid' under the MEIP may nevertheless be economically justified since funds forthcoming from private investors may be suboptimal due to capital market imperfections. It is, of course, entirely a matter of definition as to whether one should call such a financial flow a 'state aid' or not.

(b)   There may be other reasons (e.g. debt overhang, structural adjustment, etc.) why a 'state aid' as defined by the MEIP is economically justifiable. Thus we cannot equate the existence of state aid with the undesirability of state aid.

(c)   It is not clear that the use of the MEIP as an initial hurdle in identifying state aid is the most transparent method of controlling state aids. Deciding what investment flow would be forthcoming from a private investor in an equivalent situation is difficult since 'equivalent' must be defined.

(d)   Whilst recognizing the implications of Art. 222 of the Treaty which requires private and public ownership structures to be treated equally, as economists we may reasonably ask whether governments need to invest in enterprises at all, except insofar as this corrects market failures.

12.6. The application of state aid policy

The general purpose of state aid regulation is to prevent the distortion of competition through government subsidy or aid. However, as we have discussed above, it can reasonably be argued that in some cases the granting of state aid is justified under an economic point of view. For example, 'market failures' distort competition, and aid which alleviates the effects of market failures may, therefore, be justified.

In its practice, the Commission has taken account of the fact that market failures might exist in certain circumstances. Exceptions granted under certain circumstances for aid to R&D, small and medium-sized enterprises, and for environmental reasons, are all examples of what the Commission considers to be acceptable uses of state aid. However, derogations in favour of certain aids to particular sectors and regions seem to adhere more closely to other objectives of the Commission rather than to the objective of preserving competition.

Table 12.4 gives the breakdown of the decisions taken by the Commission on state aid. Although the number of decisions shows a tendency to increase over time, at the same time both the share and the number of negative and conditional decisions has drastically decreased. In 1994 negative and conditional decisions combined represented only 1% of the total.[215] This data leads us to examine the system of exemptions for state aid. In the following sections we will turn our attention to the policies of the Commission in this field, the economic rationale behind them and the possible changes introduced by the single market programme.

Table 12.4.   Percentage breakdown of the decisions taken by the Commission on state aid

Types of decision	1987	1988	1989	1990	1991	1992	1993	1994
No objection	63.9	73.9	75.5	84.3	82.6	85.7	85.4	83.5
Initiation *	9.5	8.8	10.5	6.9	9.0	5.4	6.9	7.6
Termination	10.2	4.9	6.1	4.1	4.7	4.6	4.1	2.8
Negative **	2.4	3.4	4.7	2.8	1.2	1.4	1.3	0.6
Conditional	2.0	2.2	0.0	0.0	0.3	1.3	0.2	0.4
Other decisions ***	11.9	6.8	3.2	1.8	2.2	1.6	2.1	5.1
Total (in numbers)	294	410	343	492	597	552	467	527

Source: XXIVth Report on Competition Policy, 1994, Brussels 1995, Annex IV, p. 629.
*Including extensions of procedures already initiated.
**Including partly negative decisions.
***Namely, appropriate measures under Article 93(1) of the EC Treaty and decisions made with the assent of the Council under Article 95 of the ECSC Treaty.

Table 12.5 below shows a breakdown of the aid to the manufacturing sector granted by national states for the EU as a whole according to the classification adopted by the Commission.

The objectives listed in Table 12.5 can be interpreted in terms of the economic analysis of state aid presented above. Aid given to promote SMEs or R&D could be attributed to the economic reason of correcting market failure from capital market imperfections. Sectoral aid can be seen as oriented towards smoothing transition processes or correcting externality problems that would lead to inefficient liquidation decisions. Regional objectives may address

---

[215]   However, some cases might receive clearance after changes that followed a negotiation with the Commission.

distributional problems, and trade/export objectives, finally, may reflect the strategic trade policy aspect.

One has to be careful, however, since almost every objective for giving state aid could be an instance of rent-seeking behaviour. Funding of R&D may act as a trade distorting measure favouring domestic firms, as well as a corrective measure for market failures. We want to give a short analysis of the effectiveness of state aid policy in dealing with these issues.

Table 12.5.   State aid to the manufacturing sector; percentage breakdown according to sector and function

Sectors/function	1981–1986 *	1986–1988	1988–1990	1990–1992
Horizontal objectives	**47**	**41**	**42**	**38**
Innovation; R&D	9	11	10	10
Environment	0	1	1	1
SME	6	9	10	9
Trade/export	16	11	11	9
Economization of energy	1	1	1	2
General investment	5	5	3	2
Other objectives	9	3	5	4
Particular sectors	**16**	**20**	**20**	**12**
Shipbuilding	n.a.	n.a.	5	2
Other sectors	n.a.	n.a.	15	9
Regional objectives	**37**	**39**	**38**	**50**
Regions under 92(3)c	18	17	8	6
Regions under 92(3)a	10	9	30	43
Berlin and 92(2)c	9	13	0	0
Total	**100**	**100**	**100**	**100**

Source: First, Second, Third and *Fourth Survey on State Aid in the European Community.*
*It includes 10 Member States, excluding Spain and Portugal.

12.6.1. Capital market imperfections

The main task for state aid policy is to separate those instances of state aid that lead to distortions of competition, inefficiency and an obstacle to market integration from those instances where the measures taken are justified.

The issue of capital market imperfection is dealt with by the Commission only indirectly. The Commission attitude towards SMEs has, generally, been favourable. In particular, the Commission often mentions, among other things, that capital market problems are more acute for SMEs [*VIth Report on Competition Policy*, p. 132 (in Italian)] and consequently it is less restrictive in the application of state aid rules to SMEs. However, as we mentioned before the single market programme may have made a wider range of financial options available to all the firms. If the problem is, as it seems, that SMEs lack internal expertise on how to take advantage of this possibility, state aid does not seem the best measure.

State aid to R&D in public research institutes do not raise any objections from the Commission. State aid to basic R&D conducted by firms is allowed up to a maximum of 50% of the total investment. This threshold is reduced the closer R&D is to the final product market

(25% for applied R&D). Higher thresholds are applicable to small and medium-sized enterprises (SMEs).

In the Commission Decision Regeling Bijzondere Financiering,[216] the Dutch government stated more explicitly that the goal of the proposed aid scheme was to overcome the imperfection of the capital markets in the Netherlands. It was also stressed that 'Dutch banks have a tradition of prudence, due among other things to Dutch bankruptcy laws, and that they are more familiar with short-term than with long-term financing of companies.' However, the Commission rejected arguments that state guarantees may serve to deal with imperfections in national capital markets.

In taking the above position, the Commission might be right. In general, capital is becoming increasingly mobile, and the barriers that impeded domestic firms from seeking financing strictly in their domestic market are no longer in place to a great extent. Moreover, in these circumstances state aid is likely not to be the best measure to deal with national capital markets imperfection.

12.6.2. Restructuring

Special rules apply to sectors such as steel and coal (ECSC Treaty), agriculture, fisheries and transport. We will concentrate on sectors for which the Commission designed special policies to build on the state aid rules. The sectors involved are shipbuilding, motor vehicles, synthetic fibres, textiles and clothing. The main concern that guided the Commission's policy in these sectors is the necessity to restructure and reduce capacity at the same time.

Broadly speaking, it seems that two very different motivations are at the root of these special sector policies. On one side, there are sectors such as steel, and at least in part, motor vehicles, where the main problem is overcapacity. States tend to over-subsidize their domestic firms, inducing them to expand capacity, thus causing cyclical crises. Political reasons, namely the reluctance of each government to stop supporting its domestic firms, are at the basis of the Community policy in these sectors. Although the industrial policies of the Commission for these sectors are likely to cause significant adjustment costs, they might be the only politically feasible way to keep down the level of state aid.

On the other hand, sectors such as textiles and clothing, synthetic fibres and shipbuilding have suffered from very strong import competition from extra-EU firms. In some of these sectors, for example shipbuilding, competitors in the world market are subsidized[217] so that granting aid may seem only a way to level the playing field. The Community has granted aid to the shipbuilding sector for this reason, though not to the textiles or fibres sectors. However, the main aim of state aid in this case is to make restructuring and conversion more gradual. We should see such policies as very much a second-best solution. Clearly it would be desirable to deal with the underlying friction in the labour market that necessitates aid. However, often this may prove difficult and indirect methods of transitional relief may be required instead.

---

[216]   See Regeling Bijzondere Financiering in OJ C 22/6 1992.

[217]   Ehlermann [1994, p. 415].

As far as the effects of the single market programme for sectors such as shipbuilding are concerned, some increase in competition might arise from the liberalization of public procurement. For sectors such as textiles and clothing, the main effect on competition will come through the lowering of tariffs on extra-EU products in the context of the GATT Rounds.

12.6.3. Promotion of domestic industries

A relatively large proportion of state aid measures appear to be devoted to trade and export-enhancing objectives. However, this category is wide-ranging and includes relatively minor measures (such as, for example, grants to SMEs to attend trade fairs). General measures applying to all firms in a Member State do not constitute state aid under EU rules,[218] but export aids are specifically prohibited for intra-EU exports; such export aids would not constitute 'general measures' since they are specific to exporting companies. Nevertheless, the prime mover in restricting such subsidies has been GATT, rather than the EU.

Given that companies from outside the EU receive government subsidies, there may be justifiable reasons for granting export-promoting state aids. However, in such cases it is essential that subsidies should be administered at the EU level in order to remove the incentives of Member States to distort intra-EU trade to their advantage.

12.7. A case study: state aid to airlines

Air transport between different countries has traditionally been heavily regulated, based on the principle of sovereignty of air space established by the Paris Convention of 1919 and the Chicago Conference of 1944. Up to 1993 when the measures of the third Intra-EC Air Transport Policy Package took effect, even between countries within the EU all scheduled air services were governed by air service agreements or bilateral agreements. This package was the last in a series of measures taken in order to liberalize and deregulate air transport within the European Union, following the first package (taking effect from 1 January 1988) and the second package (taking effect from 1 November 1990).

These first two packages gradually removed restrictions on fares, designation, capacity and route access that could be agreed upon in air service agreements or bilateral agreements, and established the applicability of competition rules to air transport. The third package brought about free pricing, unrestricted capacity for intra-EU transport, an abolishment of designation agreements and the full freedom to start an airline. From April 1997, full cabotage will be allowed for any European carrier in any European country. Airlines responded by forming strategic alliances and cross-border mergers, code-sharing and franchising and, in many cases, a revision of their pricing, route developing and planning and scheduling strategies.

Looking at all EU interstate services, the percentage of routes that are served by only one carrier has decreased between 1988 and 1995 (over 60% of all EU interstate services are served by only one carrier). This decrease has been accompanied by an increase in the percentage of routes served by two carriers (below 30%), while the percentage of routes served by three or four or more carriers has remained roughly constant at a low level (around 5%

---

[218]   Ehlermann [1994, p. 413].

each).[219] However, the number of non-stop cross-border routes between European cities has increased sharply (in 1995 alone the number of routes increased by 12% over the previous year).[220] Thus, competition (at least actual) on some routes has increased, and competition between an increasing number of (non-stop) routes may have increased as well, offering better connections and somewhat more choice to passengers.

The economic impacts of these changes, in particular changes in performance and profits resulting from potentially more intense competition, are still more difficult to isolate, because developments in transport volume and yields are affected by general economic developments. The growth of GDP was found to be the major determinant of the development in transport volume with transport volume growing stronger than GDP. While real yield has fallen between 1987 and 1994 to slightly over 80% of the 1987 level, it is difficult to establish an influence of the liberalization packages based on econometric estimates.[221]

Looking at changes in fares, we find that from 1986 to 1995, the level of air fares on average has risen at an annual rate of up to 4%, but that deep discount fares have decreased in some countries.[222] However, given that airlines use complex yield management techniques to maximize their revenue (on the basis of scheduled output), changes in average fares do not give a clear-cut indication of changes in revenue. Furthermore, changes in cost structure and productivity will change the profitability of carriers on specific routes. However, we may assume that different airlines have had different success in adapting to a more competitive environment, leading to some of the carriers losing money in the more competitive, single market. For example, Olympic Airways had a load factor of only 60% in 1992, compared to 68.9% in 1989. With 21% of total available seat capacity for traffic to or from Greece, it carried only 15.5% of the traffic in 1992, dropping further to a mere 13% in 1993, but much of it as a result of increased competition from the already liberalized charter market. Olympic Airways' market share on the main European routes terminating in Athens (which is the starting or end point for 90% of European passengers going to or coming from Greece) fell from 27.6% in 1988 to 22.7% in 1992.[223]

Since the first liberalization package in 1987, the demands of a non-competitive environment have significantly impacted on state-owned airlines and have been associated with the granting of large state aids to flag carriers. For example, in the decision on aid granted to Olympic Airways (OJ L 273, 25.10.1994), it referred to the various obligations and duties that were imposed on the flag carrier after having been made over to the Greek state in 1975.

---

[219] See European Commission [1997b], *The Single Market Review*, Volume II:2, Air Transport.

[220] Ibid.

[221] 'Almost all passenger variations were explained by variations in real GDP and real yield. Frequency competition is likely to have had little effect on the overall market size, but would have been used to increase market shares of individual carriers. Attempts were also made to insert a competition or liberalization dummy variable into the equation from 1989 onwards, with poor results. This was hardly surprising given the gradual introduction of liberalization within Europe, starting as early as 1985 for some country pairs.' (Ibid).

[222] Ibid.

[223] See the information provided in the Commission Decision, OJ L 273, 25.10.1994.

Table 12.6. shows the amount of state aid granted to European airlines since 1991.

Table 12.6.   State aid to European airlines

Year	Airline (financial stake of national government in %)	Amount (million ECU)
1991	Sabena (61.8)	1550
1991–92	Air France (99.3)	843
1992	Iberia (99.8)	929
1993	Aer Lingus (100)	224
1993	Air France (99.3)	228
1994	TAP Air Portugal (100)	914
1994	Olympic Airways (100)	1900
1994	Air France (99.3)	3000

Source: British Airways and News Publications.
The 1995 grant of ECU 562 million to Iberia was not classified as state aid with reference to the MEIP (see *Financial Times*, 1 February 1996).
The aid to TAP included a loan guarantee of up to ECU 858 million.

This massive amount of government aid has invariably been justified in terms of the need to restructure a carrier that was faced with major adjustment problems.[224] Most state aid cases in the airline sector have been very controversial and were dealt with by the Commission in a highly political environment.

12.7.1. Economic reasons for state aid

Going back to the economic reasons for government subsidies, we may want to ask which of them could possibly justify state aid to national air carriers.

Market failures

Although capital market imperfections can be regarded as a potential justification for government subsidies, it is debatable that airlines are faced with this problem. In particular, with government ownership and continued protection on extra-EU routes airlines should be able to borrow any funds needed for restructuring through national or international capital markets. Other market failures that affect airlines are difficult to establish. There may be some problems of stability of competition on low density routes which lead to either monopoly situations or competitive outcomes where no carrier is likely to earn sufficient returns. However, this does not provide a rationale for the granting of state aids in general. Subsidies to keep very low density routes may be justifiable in terms of meeting a public service obligation; they are not justifiable as a means of influencing which of a number of carriers becomes the ultimate sole carrier on a low density route.

---

[224]   See for example OJ L 300, 31.10.1991 (Sabena), OJ L 54, 25.2.1994 (Aer Lingus), OJ L 254, 30. 9.1994 (Air France), OJ L 273, 25.10.1994 (Olympic Airways).

Smoothing the adjustment process

The massive lay-offs that have threatened airlines may well give rise to the need to find appropriate adjustment mechanisms where labour markets are not sufficiently flexible to cope with the huge reduction of demand from a leading employer in an area. Airports regions have become very important job centres. The problem here is that a reduction in demand by one carrier may well be compensated by increases in demand for labour by competitors. More importantly though, the resistance to the adjustment process is due to the desire to protect high wages. In the case of Air France and Iberia, the Commission only allowed aid to be granted on the basis of restructuring plans which foresaw substantial reductions in wages.[225]

Export promotion

State aid to airlines may well be seen as a form of export promotion. However, the incentives to promote domestic firms rest upon the prospect of shifting profits from foreign competitors to the domestic players. When such a transfer of profits occurs within the EU, then there is an overall loss on an average EU-basis due to the distortion of competition. Most state aid measures, however, appear to have been given in order to cover losses rather than for the purpose of increasing profits in this way.

Rent-seeking

It is very difficult for any outside observer not to suspect that seeking state aid is nothing else but the replacement of a previously protected status with another form of protection. While operating in a highly regulated environment inefficiencies and excessive costs were easily compensated by high regulated fares. In a more competitive environment, low-cost carriers exert pressure on fares and subsequently on costs as we have seen above. By seeking state aid airlines can avoid facing the full pressures of competition and continue to earn rents (above returns) even if they get appropriated by staff rather than shareholders.

12.7.2. State aid policy in the airline sector

The Commission has developed a framework for dealing with state aid and public subsidies in the airline sector on the basis of the Competition and Transport chapters of the Treaty of Rome.[226] The rules of state aid that apply to the airline sector are largely similar to the general policy on state aid based on the application of the 'market economy investor principle' (MEIP). The basic elements of the Memorandum can be summarized as follows.

---

[225]   Furthermore, the competitive pressures on flag carriers created by liberalization may be lower than expected, because entry from independent airlines does not seem to occur on a major scale. Based on an empirical analysis of entry and exit decisions post-liberalization, Marin [1995] concludes that 'the liberalization of the market has not provoked a drastic alteration in the identity of the companies operating in the market, but rather a reorganization of the European flag carriers network structure. Moreover, this means that even if the belief that flag carriers are less efficient than independent airlines is true, differences in efficiency are not large enough to offset the positive effect of other advantages enjoyed by the flag carriers. We can conclude that it is difficult to justify the protection and subsidies that many European flag carriers request from their governments.'

[226]   The first guidelines for dealing with state aids in the airline sector were set out by the Commission in its Memorandum No 2 of March 1984 on progress towards the development of a Community air transport policy. In March 1992 these guidelines were reinforced. In December 1994, a further revised memorandum was issued which further tightened the rules for granting aid and sought to increase the transparency of state aid policy in this area.

(a) All state aid which potentially distorts competition is in principle incompatible with the common market.

(b) Only a strongly proven common interest may allow for the acceptance of competitive distortions.

(c) State aid for offsetting the operational losses of an airline is incompatible with the common market. The 1994 Memorandum makes it clear that such a subsidy may only be granted in exceptional circumstances in the context of a restructuring plan with the objective of returning the airline to viability within a reasonable period. A strong case would be required to justify such aid, which would be granted for a clearly specified period only.

(d) The granting of restructuring aid should, in principle, be one-off and the government granting the subsidies must normally commit itself to not grant any further aid in any form.

(e) Compensation for operating a route under a public service obligation is considered not to be state aid if the relevant conditions of Regulation (EEC) No 2408/92 are respected.

(f) The granting of other subsidies to support the operation of domestic routes is not normally permitted, except for regional policy reasons in the Greek islands and the Azores, which are for the time being outside the scope of Regulation (EEC) No 2408/92.

The Commission has to be notified in advance of all proposed state aid or changes to the extent of existing aid.

12.7.3. Effectiveness of state aid policy in the airline sector

Given this explicit policy of the Commission, the practical results captured in Table 12.6 must seem rather disappointing. If restructuring (and, subsequently, privatization) restores the profitability of the carrier, then private investors should be willing to finance the measures for which aid was being granted. If, as noted in the Sabena decision, 'in view of the accumulated debts and the costs of the restructuring programme, no investor apart from the state would at present be prepared to take part in the restructuring programme',[227] then the granting of state aid can be justified only with social inefficiencies which would result from competition driving inefficient carriers out of the market. Thus, unjustified distortions of competition must follow by definition unless failure of other markets (such as the labour market for airline staff, or a second-hand market for equipment) can be proven.

Furthermore, the 'one time/last time bail out' rule, which seems only reasonable if aid is given for commercially successful restructuring plans, has been broken more than once. On the contrary, in its report to the Commission the 'Comité de Sages' for Air Transport (Expanding Horizons, 1994) recognized that state aid to airlines contributes to the problem of overcapacity and uneconomic pricing. While the assessment of uneconomic pricing is more difficult to determine, we can certainly observe a policy of aggressive expansion which was, for example, pursued by Air France and Iberia. The latter would certainly not have been approved as part of a state-aided restructuring plan. This becomes obvious in the recent decision of the Commission on the second large financial transfer to Iberia as state aid, where Iberia will have to divest itself of its 83% stake in Airolinas Argentinas and its 38% stake in Ladeco of Chile

---

[227] OJ L 300, 31.10.1991.

(which is transferred to another joint venture, in which Iberia's parent holding company Teno will have a 40% stake alongside US investment banks Merrill Lynch and Bankers Trust).[228]

The recent Iberia case (also the Air France case) casts doubt on the usefulness of the MEIP to determine the presence of, and to quantify, state aid. The classification of the financial transfer to Iberia as not being state aid, based on an application of the MEIP, is considered debatable by many industry analysts. The use of the MEIP leads to a certain lack of transparency, creating an opportunity for lobbying thus weakening the effectiveness of the EU's state aid control. If cases like Iberia and Air France set precedents for further capital injections into national carriers which do not qualify under state aid, European control over state aid policy is likely to become a blunt instrument and an almost empty threat that can be bypassed by invoking the MEIP.

The danger is that competition-distorting state aids will be granted at the expense of taxpayers and to the detriment of consumers. The airline sector gives particular cause for concern in that substantial state aids continue to be granted against a background of overall total EU levels of state aid falling. Thereby, the desired effects of the major liberalization programme of the Commission is put in doubt. As the Commission itself acknowledged in an evaluation of state aid:

'In a more competitive environment state aids might be of substantial increased importance for the government looking for measures to protect the economic interest of their own airlines. The common interest and the basic objectives of the liberalization process would, however, be at stake if such a subsidy race took place' (SAC (92)431).

12.8. Conclusions

As summarized by Faull [1994], 'competition may be distorted by advantages given by public authorities to certain companies or categories of companies which compete with other, less fortunate companies in the EC'. On the other hand, 'state aid may also have more honourable objectives ... The purpose of the EC's state aid policy is to provide for central control and checking, sorting out the good from the bad, allowing some and prohibiting others.'

State aid measures generally discriminate in favour of a particular firm or group of firms. Since when granting aid a government is unlikely to take account of the EU-wide impact of the aid, it is likely that the aid will distort trade and competition thus lowering EU welfare overall, even if national welfare has been increased. Hence there is a clear rationale for the control of state aids at the EU level. Market integration is likely to increase the size of the negative impact on other states of a state aid increase and so reinforce the need for EU-level controls.

There are economically justifiable reasons for granting state aid in order to correct market failures. Thus, the recognition that 'the prohibition of state aid that distorts competition is neither absolute nor unconditional' (Ehlermann [1994, p. 412]) reflects the fact that some government subsidies may be justified. The legal framework of state aid policy mostly allows the problems that may be regarded as appropriate reasons for state aid to be addressed.

---

[228]   *Financial Times*, 20 December 1995.

Despite acknowledging that the overall objectives of state aid policy accord with economic objectives, we are concerned about the practical usefulness of the MEIP in implementing state aid policy. Due to the difficulties of determining an 'equivalent' private sector transaction, the MEIP is not very transparent and is likely to be subjective in its implementation. It is reasonable to ask why, if a given level of financial support does not constitute state aid since a private investor would be willing to provide it as well, such an investor is not forthcoming. This alternative perspective would suggest that all of a financial flow from a government to an enterprise should be treated as a potential state aid in need of further investigation, not just, as the MEIP would require, that part of the flow additional to the investment that would be forthcoming from a hypothetical private investor. Such a perspective would be extreme and would probably be difficult or even impossible to square with case law on the compatibility of state aid under Articles 92 and 93 with Article 222 of the Treaty which requires equal treatment of diverse ownership/property rights systems.

Regarding the impact of integration on state aid it can be noted that the increased granting of aid at the EU level rather than through Member States is a welcome trend, providing that the EU aid-granting process can be insulated from national lobbying. It should be expected that EU-level aid would be granted with a view to raising EU welfare and so avoid the problem of national governments granting aid to pursue national interests. The example of the airline sector discussed in this chapter offers only little comfort in this respect, a fact that even the Commission acknowledges.

Part III   Conclusions and policy recommendations

We now present our conclusions. Due to the wide-ranging nature of the study, these conclusions are divided into two sections.

First we consider how integration has affected the conduct of firms. Integration has been generally expected to have pro-competitive effects (for example, as predicted by the Cecchini report). We review the evidence for such effects that has been presented in Part II of this report. However, we must also consider potential anti-competitive responses by firms to integration. Although integration can be shown to have led to more competitive outcomes, the full potential benefits of integration may not yet have been reaped as a result of anti-competitive responses by firms. We believe that this is the key question which must be asked. It is insufficient simply to point only to evidence of integration leading to more competitive outcomes. Integration may have pro-competitive effects simultaneous with firms engaging in anti-competitive responses. Thus the relevant comparison is of actual firm behaviour with what might be called 'potential full integration behaviour', that is, how firms would be likely to act if policy could prevent anti-competitive responses to integration. Although this question is a very difficult one to answer, it is clearly the relevant one to ask if we are interested in looking forward to how policy should be framed in an increasingly integrated European economy. To address this question we will need to use three strands of our analysis: quantitative empirical evidence; case studies and case law; and finally our detailed analysis of potential anti-competitive behaviour given in the chapters on competition issues.

Second, we offer some conclusions on policy. Competition policy may require revision in some areas as a result of the changing nature of the European economy due to market integration. However, competition policy may also have a role in preventing potential anti-competitive responses by firms to integration and in doing so helping to realize the full potential benefits of the single market programme. In some areas competition policy has limited effectiveness in preventing such anti-competitive responses, and other policy instruments, such as external trade policy, may be more potent.

13. Conclusions on the evolution of competition in the single market

13.1. Introduction

The Cecchini report, published in 1988, concluded that a substantial part of the benefits of completing the single market would derive from the effects of intensified competition. Reductions in the costs of doing trade across national borders, including reductions in restrictions of competition, due to national systems of regulation and public procurement, were expected to lead to entry of new competitors into national markets. Markets that were previously mainly delineated by national borders would become larger. Economic boundaries would be determined by the economic fundamentals of transport costs, tastes and technology rather than by national borders. Market power and hence margins would be reduced. Within these larger markets tougher cross-border competition would ensure that inefficient firms would either exit the market or improve their performance. These competitive pressures would affect not only product markets but also input markets for labour and capital. Furthermore, larger markets, and reductions in barriers to entry, were expected to be a spur to designing new products and undertaking R&D.

These high expectations of the effect of intensified competition in the single market have some justification in economic theory. Generally speaking our study shares the assumption that competition can be expected to have a beneficial impact on efficiency. The question that this study raises is not, however, whether increased competition in the single market is a good or bad thing. This study seeks to establish the nature of the interaction between integration and competition, and then to assess the role of competition policy in securing the potential benefits of the single market. In particular, we address the question of how integration affects firms' behaviour.

Market integration should reduce the additional variable costs of producers in one EU country serving consumers in another country. It should also reduce the fixed costs of entering a foreign market. Thus market integration should bring producers in different countries into competition with others where previously border costs constrained competition. Other expected benefits were the lowering of production costs through greater flexibility in the location of production facilities and the associated exploitation of economies of scale unreaped by serving just domestic markets. Tougher product market competition may provide stronger incentives for the reduction of internal inefficiencies in firms.

There is a wide variety of behaviours which could lead to these potential benefits of integration not being fully achieved. Barriers to entry may exist which hinder cross-border entry even after market integration. For example, access to essential facilities may not be forthcoming at a reasonable price. Firms may collude and share markets along national borders. Pro-competitive direct entry into foreign markets may be avoided by joint ventures or licensing agreements. Mergers may lead to market power even in a broader post-integration market. Finally, firms may call on governments to protect them from the necessary adjustments to a more competitive environment.

It is important to emphasize that even if we observe apparently pro-competitive effects of market integration, this does not imply that firms are failing to make such anti-competitive responses. It is perfectly possible that although some of the benefits of integration are being achieved, we have yet to achieve the full potential benefits of integration. This could happen even within an individual product market. For example, firms' pricing could be somewhat constrained by the threat of entry into their domestic markets by foreign producers, whilst the threat of entry is itself moderated by an 'anti-competitive response'. In general we may see the balance of pro- and anti-competitive effects being very different in different markets. Such a shortfall in achieving the potential gains of integration is clearly extremely difficult to identify in general.

In an attempt to overcome these difficulties we have used a broad approach and have considered the issue of how market integration affects firm behaviour from a number of perspectives:

(a)   aggregate statistics on trade flows, firm performance and concentration;
(b)   sector-level data on prices, margins and trade flows;
(c)   theoretical analysis of potential anti-competitive responses;
(d)   case study analysis;
(e)   review of case law.

13.1.1. Aggregate statistics on trade flows, firm performance and concentration

We have reviewed the literature and looked at primary data sources on how aggregate statistical measures have moved. These statistics have moved in directions which are broadly consistent with market integration having pro-competitive effects. However, it would be quite incorrect to infer more from aggregate statistics than broad consistency with the hypothesis that integration leads to more competitive outcomes. In particular, there are many possible drivers for these aggregate statistics and we cannot impute a cause for their change.

13.1.2. Sector-level data on prices, margins and trade flows

Sectoral data can provide further evidence that market integration has progressed and has had pro-competitive effects. In particular it allows the examination of trends in selected industries which were most heavily protected by non-tariff barriers, showed less trade flows or which exhibited persistent price differentials across Member States. The strong message from looking at sectoral data is that price-cost margins have indeed fallen relative to the trend observed in other sectors. Trade flows, however, do not show a stronger pattern in these so-called Buigues sectors against the trends observed in a larger sample of sectors.

We also undertook an analysis of price-cost margins by type of industry, similar to the analysis undertaken in other studies in *The Single Market Review*, using a classification of industries in terms of advertising and R&D intensity. This revealed only one sectoral effect: advertising intensive industry appears to exhibit increasing margins relative to other industries.

13.1.3. Theoretical analysis of potential anti-competitive responses

Although theory suggests potential benefits from integration in terms of increased competition, it also suggests that there are many ways in which firms may try to limit such beneficial effects. The next step is to enumerate the types of anti-competitive behaviour which could hinder integration. In our 'competition issues' chapters we have considered how the incentives for various types of anti-competitive behaviour have been changed by market integration. We consider that this theoretical analysis is a vital step on the route to obtaining generalizable conclusions relevant to policy formulation. It provides us with a list of types of behaviour which we can look for in actual examples.

13.1.4. Case study analysis

We have analysed a number of markets in detail (cars, beer, soda ash, airlines). These case studies are useful for a number of reasons.

(a)   They show that the effects of market integration may be very different in different markets. Typically, market integration may have a small effect on firms' conduct which may be masked by simultaneous changes in other environmental variables.

(b)   They illustrate some examples of what we have called 'anti-competitive responses' to integration. This confirms our general conclusion that achievement of the full potential benefits of integration is being hampered by the strategic behaviour of firms in some cases, despite on average there being pro-competitive benefits from integration.

13.1.5. Review of case law

Looking at recent competition law provides further examples of anti-competitive responses to market integration. In addition, it provides some evidence of the relative prevalence of different types of anti-competitive behaviour. However, looking at individual cases demonstrates again that there are many factors influencing firm behaviour, of which market integration is just one. Thus, case law helps our understanding of the competition issues involved and provides examples of anti-competitive responses to integration, but does not by itself provide much in the way of general conclusions about how integration has affected firm behaviour.

Market integration has been claimed by many to have substantial effects on competition (e.g. the Cecchini report). However, market integration clearly has a small incremental effect on firms already facing substantial changes in domestic economies and in world trading conditions. Thus identification of the effects of integration with any precision is very difficult. We contend that it is only by looking at the effects of integration on firm behaviour and on competition from all of the perspectives listed above that any reasonable general conclusions can be drawn. We therefore consider each of these perspectives in turn in the following sections.

13.2. General trends in integration and competition

The 1985 White Paper raised a number of expectations about the impact of removing non-tariff barriers on competition in enlarged and more integrated markets. Entry of EU producers into other EU countries should be facilitated by a reduction in both the fixed and variable costs of trading across EU internal borders.

As a consequence of integration, incumbent firms were expected to improve their efficiency in order to see off the challenge from new entrants. Price-cost margins would come under pressure. Incumbent firms previously exploiting a dominant position in national markets would earn fewer rents. Similarly, more direct measures to open up markets that were previously regulated, or reserved to domestic firms, would dramatically change the manner in which firms behaved in a more competitive market environment. Some firms could be expected to exit, while more efficient firms would be able expand their sales exploiting economies of scale. Finally, entry of new firms and the enlargement of markets was thought to lead to a breakdown of collusion.

Has our study revealed any evidence that is consistent with these expectations? In our review of empirical evidence of markets and selected industrial sectors in Chapter 5 we have indeed found evidence of integration and changes in competition conditions. The findings for the period leading up to 1992 show that trade flows across Members States increased; post-tax prices converged; firm size generally increased; and industry concentration increased. Intra-EU trade flow increased, albeit at the expense of some trade diversion.

Of particular interest is the detailed study of price-cost margins undertaken in Chapter 5. This research provides strong econometric evidence of a significant impact of integration on price-cost margins. Moreover, the overall magnitude of the effect is large. We also find statistically significant evidence of a fall in cross-country differences in margins since 1987. It is of considerable significance that both the fall in margins and the reduction in cross-country differences in margins appear to have started in 1986, and to have accelerated from 1987 onwards. This timing is consistent with the single market programme having a slightly delayed impact.

Table 13.1. General trends in aggregate statistics

Trade creation	yes
Price convergence	yes
Exploitation of economies of scale/exit in response to increased competition	yes
Reductions in price-cost margins	yes
Fall in cross-country variance of mergers	yes

This picture of increased trade, decreasing price differentials, reduced price-cost margins and increasing firm size and concentration is consistent with the expectations associated with the single market programme. Price differentials should fall as a response to reduced costs of arbitrage across EU economies and economic fundamentals (driving costs and hence prices) becoming more similar. The increased possibility of substitution of domestically produced products by those produced in other EU countries should lead to falling price-cost margins in the absence of countervailing changes in market structure. Also, we would expect market structure itself to be affected by integration, with firms exiting as a response to tougher competition. As domestic markets are broken down and market size increased, at the EU level this should lead to fewer firms as an equilibrium response.

However, we need to be careful to relate these trends causally to the effect of the removal of non-tariff trade barriers in the single market. There are other significant forces that may have been responsible for the observed effects. The main reason is that trade liberalization at the Community level cannot easily be distinguished from the impact of external trade liberalization, industry deregulation or industry-specific technological developments. We agree with Neven and Röller [1990] and other commentators (Silberston and Raymond [1996]) that these effects are difficult to disentangle. Clearly, there are industries where reform and direct liberalization have made a significant impact on the development of competition. In other cases it is arguable that technological developments are the principal drivers of change.

For example, the liberalization of telecommunication services and equipment procurement has had a widespread impact. But at the same time this industry experienced the development of digital switching technology. This technological development has radically altered the production and R&D conditions under which firms supplying telecommunications switching equipment operate, leading to major changes in market structure.

Despite the EU's procurement initiative, the procurement patterns have not changed much. The reason is transaction-specific instruments. Thus, multiple sourcing is still limited. But the option to switch has had a big effect on prices (plus 'digitalization'). For both airlines and telecommunication equipment, EU measures have only limited effects because of global, extra-EU competition forces.

The airline sector, or rather more precisely the markets for scheduled air travel, are similarly characterized by a combination of trade liberalization between Member States, and between Member States and third countries. Intra-EU and domestic travel are only slowly being opened up to competition. This is in contrast to the market for charter travel where competition has historically been much tougher.

13.3. Changes in competition conditions: sectoral trends in trade flows and price-cost margins

It is appropriate to consider a cross-sectoral view, and to try to identify integration in the differential response to those sectors expected to be strongly affected by integration relative to the average of all sectors. Looking at the differential effects on those sectors we strongly expect to be affected by integration also filters out some of the common influences on firm behaviour which might otherwise mask any integration effects. However, a problem will always remain that it is very difficult to disentangle the effects of intra-EU and extra-EU trade liberalization, since the same sectors will tend to be most strongly influenced by both these factors. In fact our analysis of trade flows shows an increasing degree of correlation between intra- and extra-EU trade.

At the sectoral level our analysis centred around two types of industry classifications: (a) the so-called Buigues sectors and (b) the Davies/Lyons sectoral classification.

Buigues et al. [1990] identified 40 industrial sectors as being particularly exposed to single market measures.

(a)   High technology public procurement sectors, where non-tariff trade barriers were considered to be high (Group 1).

(b)   Traditional public procurement or regulated markets, where non-tariff trade barriers were also high (Groups 2 and 3).

(c)   Sectors with moderate trade barriers, covering various consumer, capital and intermediate goods (Group 4).

The evidence from the analysis of trade flows and price-cost margins is partly consistent with these expectations.

The analysis of price-cost margins, wholly original research which to our knowledge has not so far been undertaken, revealed a significant policy impact on the non-Buigues sectors and a significantly lower impact on Group 4. We summarize the results in Table 13.2.

Table 13.2.   Impact on price-cost margins

	Average level of margin across EU in sample period	Policy impact on non-Buigues sectors	Policy impact on group 4
Margin definition M1	44.1%	-0.7% per annum	-0.9% per annum
Margin definition M2	15.2%	-0.2% per annum	-0.2% per annum

These are large effects. Over a decade, a 0.2% per annum reduction in margins with an average level of 15% amounts to a fall of 2%.

Sectors 2 and 3 show a significant lack of impact on integration. (There was significantly less impact than for the non-Buigues sectors.) Thus the public procurement sectors appear to have been affected by integration, despite expectations. We could not determine the nature of the effect of integration on Group 1 from the available data.

Those sectors characterized by an *ex ante* high degree of single market sensitivity have not, in fact, shown marked trends towards integration. Indeed, for these sectors, integration between the EU and the rest of the world economy appears to be happening at a faster rate than integration within the EU. This result could be interpreted to mean that competition from outside the EU had a major impact.

Nevertheless, we would point to the evidence provided by the coincidence of the fall in margins with the onset of the single market programme to suggest that in fact the single market programme is likely to be the cause of these changes. However, it is methodologically impossible ever to prove this conclusively.

We also looked at sectors according to whether they were advertising intensive, R&D intensive or both. We found that advertising intensive sectors had a significantly smaller impact of integration than other sectors. Possible interpretations of this finding are that advertising intensive sectors produce differential goods that are less affected by integration, or possibly even that product differentiation through advertising has been a response to the potential increase in competition caused by market integration. This is consistent with the finding by EAG of rising firm size for this group.

However, care is needed when generalizing from statistical indicators in this way. We have assessed the degree to which the statistical picture is consistent with expectations about the single market programme. What we have not assessed is whether the single market programme has caused changes in our statistical indicators. For example, we have observed an increasing degree of correlation of internal EU trade and external EU trade. This observation is consistent with expectations of external trade liberalization in the wake of the GATT and those created through the single market programme.

13.4. Interaction of competition and integration in selected markets

Our findings suggest that it is misleading to make generalized and unconditional statements about the impact of market integration. Firstly, integration impacts on different sectors to quite different degrees. Secondly, where integration has a significant potential effect, that effect may be mitigated by anti-competitive responses. To the extent that these anti-competitive responses are of different magnitudes, yet further heterogeneity is introduced in the observed pattern of firm behaviour. Our selected market studies exemplify this aspect of the interaction of integration and competition. These market studies, summarized in Chapter 6, provide examples of the differences between those sectors where major progress in integration could have been realistically expected and those where markets do not offer any scope for integration. Moreover, they indicate the importance of drivers other than market integration on firm behaviour.

Table 13.3.   Drivers of competition and integration

	Soda ash	Beer	Cars	Air travel	Washing machines
Single market programme	no	little	yes	yes	little
External trade	yes	no	yes	yes	yes
Technological change	no	yes	yes	maybe	yes
Industry reforms	no	no	no	yes	no
Competition policy	yes	yes	yes	yes	no

Soda ash is a market for which expectations for major changes in firm behaviour following market integration are not realistic, given the nature of the product. Soda ash is a homogeneous raw material and its markets are chiefly determined by transport costs. With high transport costs soda ash will never be sold across a single European market. Rather local markets will be determined by plant location and transport costs. The scope of these local markets was in large measure independent of national borders before and after market integration. Changes in competition conditions in this market were induced by two types of government measures outside the single market programme. First, the lifting of anti-dumping duties in 1990 made importation of soda ash from the US attractive for those markets that could be accessed in sufficiently large volumes by sea transport. Second, the imposition of tough penalties on the major European companies, in the antitrust decisions of late 1990, signalled the end of the stand-off agreements that had characterized this industry for a century. As a consequence the major customers of this key raw material, the European glass industry, were able to source more competitively.

We would conclude that by far the most important determinant in the soda ash market has been external rather than internal EU trade policy. In particular, the removing of external duties appeared to reduce price, and their later reimposition to raise it.

Major changes in competition conditions were observed in the market for washing machines, and white goods more generally. Having already shown decreasing price dispersion across Member States in the early 1980s, this sector saw major technological changes that facilitated large-scale production whilst maintaining product variety. This in turn drove progressive integration with fewer production locations and increased trade. In parallel, there were major attempts by leading manufacturers to establish European brands and adopt a common approach to advertising and distribution, while at the same time meeting national differences in preferences. At best the single market programme can be considered to have contributed to this development by easing this restructuring process, and reducing the costs of pan-European production and distribution strategies. The wave of mergers that helped to create major players such as Electrolux, the Swedish company that took over Zanussi and many other domestic appliance companies in the 1980s, and Phillips who took over Whirlpool in 1986, did not raise major competition concerns. Nevertheless, as a consequence industry concentration increased significantly. Although market integration is likely to have had some effect, it would seem that at most it reinforced underlying technological changes, rather than being instrumental in changes in firm behaviour.

In the case of cars expectations of progress in integration were relatively high given that national price differentials were high, and national registration and approval systems provided domestic manufacturers with a considerable degree of protection. In addition, most national markets were subject to import restrictions for non-EU manufacturers. What we observe today is the continued organization of distribution at the national level that is supported by a recently renewed block exemption of the Commission. Other non-tariff barriers have been largely abolished and external trade restrictions are progressively weakened. At the level of production and development there appears to be evidence of (a) more cooperation between manufacturers and (b) an organization of production across Europe that seeks to exploit locational cost advantages. This case study concludes that the trends are toward more competition rather than less, but that full liberalization and further integration is a prospect rather than a reality. Price differentials have not been eliminated. However, this is interesting for policy, since we argue that it is not necessarily welfare-improving to eliminate them.

The airline sector, for intra-EU and domestic travel, is only slowly being opened up to competition. Overall, European air transport markets are still dominated by national flag carriers who benefit from many incumbent advantages. Fuller liberalization can be expected with the implementation of the third package in 1997, which grants increased access to international and domestic routes and introduces the concept of Community ownership, instead of national ownership and control of carriers. In response to this liberalization programme, this sector has seen significant changes in market structure and firms' behaviour. Against a background of increased traffic since 1992, several national carriers have reduced their capacity (Air France, Aer Lingus, Iberia and Air Portugal). Others have embarked on a number of collaborative agreements ranging from code-sharing to more extensive joint ventures. Several mergers have taken place, leading to a consolidation of the position of major carriers such as British Airways and Air France. Evidence on changes in competition (fare levels and entry) is thin. The limited degree of entry highlights the problem that in this industry there are many city pair routes where the number of carriers that can viably compete is relatively small. Not many routes allow more than two carriers, to offer the minimum scale of operation of three to four flights a day. The proportion of round trip flights with two or more competitors on scheduled routes has increased, but is still only 36% for domestic routes and 25% for international routes (CAA [1995]). Our conclusion on airlines is that there are large potential effects of integration, but only limited progress in realizing them.

For beer, the single market programme had a special significance: German purity laws and Danish packaging laws were seen to be typical non-tariff barriers that prevented integration and inhibited entry into national markets by other European brewers. While there is evidence of increased trade and entry of brewers from smaller Member States into larger markets, Europe is still best considered as a set of intersecting beer markets that are based on local tastes and traditions and the scope for integration may well be limited. Our case study reveals that there are a number of responses by national incumbents that appear to continue to support national market segmentation. The Commission has taken a permissive stance towards selective distribution agreements that include tying of retail outlets to brewers and to the increasing use of cross-licensing agreements whereby major national brewers market and distribute foreign brands under licence. In conclusion, we find that a complex interaction of traditions and firm behaviour limit the degree of integration, even if full integration is not possible due to cost conditions and local preferences.

13.5. The scope for further progress in integration

Case study evidence suggests that in a number of cases the single market measures provide – unless accompanied by sector-specific measures and additional policy interventions – a mainly facilitating function, rather then being instrumental in change. Observed heterogeneity in the cross-sectoral pattern of responses to integration is consistent with the hypothesis that there are 'laggard' sectors where the full potential benefits of integration have not been achieved. For example, public procurement sectors have not demonstrated a positive impact from integration, despite the expectation by Buigues et al. that they would. Also, as we will see in the following section, there are numerous instances where the general positive impact of single market measures meets with anti-competitive responses that may hinder the achievement of the full potential benefits of integration. These responses, if they remain unchecked, operate against the aims of the single market, and prevent the realization of the expected benefits of integration. Competition policy plays an important role in bringing about the gains from increased competition in integrated markets. It is therefore necessary to review carefully what the obstacles to further integration are, and how competition policy can assist in progressing the positive developments of competition.

Having observed the heterogeneous pattern of progress in integration across sectors, there are, nevertheless, some tentative conclusions that we would like to draw regarding the remaining obstacles to integration.

Except in some well-defined areas where single market measures and other liberalization still need to be implemented (e.g. airlines and certain procurement markets), there are no longer major non-tariff barriers of the kind that the single market programme tried to tackle (administrative, fiscal and technical barriers). Any real obstacles that we observe are of a more behavioural nature. If further progress is to be achieved then it is through measures that have a direct impact on behaviour of firms and governments. The behavioural obstacles that we have in mind here are firstly those that we analysed in our review of competition issues in Part II. Then there are those obstacles that derive from historical traditions and purchasing habits. In combination they may have the effect of maintaining segmentation of markets along national borders. We can use our case studies to illustrate this point.

Tacit collusion, market-sharing agreements and entry deterrence. The case of soda ash demonstrated a type of behaviour where stand-off agreements between suppliers in the UK and other parts of the EU helped to support national pricing policies that prevented customers from obtaining competitive supplies from alternative sources. In the case of airlines city pair markets in the EU have been traditionally serviced by flag carriers with little entry from other countries. Even with increased liberalization there are few routes where more then two carriers operate in a competitive environment, not least because of major barriers to entry that can be exploited by incumbents. In the case of beer the observation of fairly extensive licensing across national markets can be contrasted with the more competitive effect of direct entry by foreign brands.

Purchasing habits. For a number of reasons European countries exhibit different purchasing habits. Some have a wholly objective justification in terms of climate, or geography. Cinema going in southern countries such as Italy or Greece is highly seasonal given that cinemas are generally not air-conditioned. Purchasing habits for clothes and footwear will differ with the climate. Tumble dryers, for example, are not needed in warmer countries. Other purchasing habits are not so easily justifiable on an objective basis. Many patterns of consumption are based on national preferences. Cultural differences contribute to these patterns of consumption and are themselves often the product of habit if nothing else. National preferences for domestically produced cars, for example, may have some justification in superior domestic distribution and servicing systems, but are often the product of historical and political attachments to national brands. Culture supported by language barriers will always contribute to national purchasing habits that differ from Member State to Member State. These reasons for national market segmentation are not intrinsically bad or against the spirit of the EU. Nevertheless, to ignore the reality of them is to overlook their role as a potential obstacle to fuller integration.

National distribution organization. Many goods are distributed through a system of national distributors. Such national distribution systems will tend to support national market segmentation and can in some circumstances give rise to serious obstacles to competition and integration. The national organization of distribution can become an obstacle to integration if the two factors discussed above are present. Purchasing habits may be national, either because they are objectively justified or because they are based on more subjective or cultural systems of preferences. It may then be easy to support national market segmentation through agreements or types of behaviour that may be considered anti-competitive because of their entry deterrent effects. For example, both the car and beer industries exhibit strong patterns of national purchasing habits and are characterized by an organization of distribution in form of agreements that require an exemption from the competition articles of the Treaty of Rome. These block exemptions have been renewed by the Commission in the last few years (beer 1991 and cars 1995) and in both cases were subject to extensive debate and lobbying by the respective industries. Without judging here the merits of the case for or against, it is fair to say that these agreements may have as their object or effect the organization of distribution along national lines. The Commission, in its interpretation of the Treaty of Rome, has focused on the scope for market segmentation and has insisted on limiting the parallel import restrictions.

In the next sections, we proceed to summarize our conclusions on the analysis of competition issues in Part II of our report. We present our conclusion of how integration interacts with firm behaviour and try, where possible, to generalize our findings with respect to the case studies and case law that have been reviewed as part of the analysis.

The discussion of competition issues was guided by the assumption that changes in some types of behaviour are related to the integration process. We deliberately avoided the headings under which competition policy is usually discussed, and focused on behaviour that can be seen as a response to single market measures. Not surprisingly, therefore, we discussed types of behaviour at the beginning of Part II that are particularly closely related to the single market programme:

> Chapter 7: geographical price discrimination and arbitrage restrictions;
> Chapter 8: entry barriers and access restrictions.

We followed this discussion with an examination of:

> Chapters 9 and 10: cooperative behaviour (collusion, joint ventures (JV) and other cooperative agreements);
> Chapter 11: mergers;
> Chapter 12: state aids.

The remainder of this chapter follows the same order.

13.6. Measures preventing arbitrage

The existence of price differentials across Member States is one of the main indicators of market segmentation. The single market was expected to lead to a reduction in price differentials through a process whereby price differentials are competed away by firms or by consumers who arbitrage between markets. Reducing cross-border transaction costs reduces the costs of arbitrage and makes arbitrage more effective. The removal of arbitrage restrictions can have a pro-competitive effect (though we also see cases in which this is not true).

Our study analysed the economics of price discrimination in Chapter 7 and recognized that price discrimination may well be a symptom of market power. Dominant firms faced with an opportunity to exploit differences in preferences and income across Member States may want to use parallel import restrictions that prevent or restrict arbitrage. In other circumstances, however, there may also be incentives to engage in price discrimination that have beneficial effects in terms of allowing firms to compete for marginal customers and to access new markets. Firms that can vary their prices depending on location have a richer set of instruments with which to compete. This effect has, for example, been applied to the case of mill pricing versus discriminatory pricing. It could be shown that uniform mill pricing by a manufacturer of a product such as cement is likely to lessen price competition compared to a situation where manufacturers price differentially by location of consumers. Price discrimination provides an interesting example of an issue where pursuing integration objectives exclusively (e.g. prohibiting price discrimination generally) is not competition- or indeed welfare-enhancing. We discuss this point in the second part of the conclusion.

It has been the policy of the Commission to clamp down severely on any 'agreements which have the effect of resealing borders that have been opened up by the single market programme'.[229] The sample of cases that we listed in Section 7.4 is only illustrative of the cases in this area. They include:

(a)   pharmaceutical products (Sandoz Italia case 1987);
(b)   machinery (combine harvesters in Sperry New Holland 1985);
(c)   cars (block exemption Regulation (EC) No 1475/95 and Ecosystem v. Peugeot 1990);
(d)   consumer products (tennis balls in Tretorn 1994 and Newitt/Dunlop/Slazenger
        International 1992); writing instruments (Parker Pens 1992, Tipp-Ex 1987);
        photographic films (Konica 1987); toys (Fisher Price 1987) and drinks (Gosme/Martell
        1991).

This illustrative list is not necessarily representative of the type of industries where parallel import restrictions are prevalent. A wide variety of industries are likely to be affected. What is apparent, though, is that there are quite a few well-known brand names in our list of cases. If we refer back to the motivation to price discriminate discussed in Chapter 7, then differences in price elasticities are a reason for price discrimination. Branded goods may well face differing preferences in different Member States, and certainly face different average income levels. If for certain goods price elasticities vary with income, then this may lead to different market positioning of brands and provide a strong incentive for engaging in price discrimination between national markets.

Chapter 7 also assesses the welfare implications of measures to support price discrimination. We consider that in a number of instances measures facilitating price discrimination can be pro-competitive rather then anti-competitive, particularly where market concentration is low and interbrand competition strong. In unconcentrated markets with many competitors, arbitrage restrictions cannot have any major negative welfare effects, given that we would expect sufficient competitive pressure to prevent the occurrence of major price differentials.

13.7. Access restrictions and other exclusionary practices

To the extent that the single market programme succeeds in removing barriers to trade, entry into foreign markets presents a direct threat to incumbents. Their incentive to try and re-erect barriers to entry or deny new competitors access to essential infrastructure must be obvious. Chapter 8 discusses ways in which firms may respond to this threat in some detail. In general, we identify two ways in which exclusionary behaviour is likely to prevent entry and therefore inhibit the realization of the aim of integration:

(a)   the first type of behaviour relates to restrictions of access to a complementary asset;
(b)   the second relates to exclusionary pricing on markets.

In addition our analysis identifies how institutional entry barriers can be exploited to prevent entry of new competitors.

13.7.1. Restrictions of access to complementary assets

Chapter 8 lists many cases where new entrants were denied access to essential facilities and other complementary assets. Typically these cases occur where major infrastructure facilities

---

[229]   *XXIVth Report on Competition Policy 1994*, p. 11.

are necessary for the provision of a downstream service, and are difficult or wasteful to replicate for a new entrant. In a similar manner, operators of essential facilities may price access to these complementary assets excessively, which again has the effect of deterring entry. Such issues are likely to be a significant reason why the full potential benefits of integration are not being achieved in some markets.

There are many examples of access restrictions, particularly in utilities where often – but not always – entrants need to rely on infrastructure networks to access another market. These include electricity distribution and transmission networks, gas pipelines and telecommunication and broadcasting networks.

Similarly, transport services rely on access to sea and air ports, including a number of related services, such as baggage and ground handling, and computer reservation systems. In all of these industries there is considerable scope for undermining progress in integration by deterring the entry of new competitors who require access to essential facilities.

Also, vertical restraints between suppliers and retailers can raise access issues in situations where there is foreclosure of outlets to new entrants. In Chapter 8 we dealt with the ice cream case, where freezer exclusivity in contracts between retailers and suppliers of single-wrapped ice cream were found to foreclose entry to these mainly small retail outlets. Generally though, vertical restraints, including tying practices, rarely have foreclosure effects. If they do not, then it is difficult to see how they inhibit integration and the development of effective competition in the single market. While integration may well provide an incentive to use vertical restraints to maintain national distribution systems, there are not that many instances where these restrictions can prevent entry.

An unusual but interesting example of a complementary asset is intellectual property rights. In a small number of cases the Commission has established that IPRs were being used to exploit a dominant position and to leverage market power from one market to other markets. Copyright over TV listings is one such example, where the broadcaster tried to extend his market power in the broadcasting market by claiming copyright over his programme schedule in order to dominate the market for weekly publications with TV listings.

13.7.2. Foreclosure through exclusionary pricing

It is extremely difficult to asses the extent to which predatory pricing strategies are a prevalent anti-competitive response to integration since it is rarely the subject of competition authority action. On the one hand, predation is one of the responses that an incumbent, faced with entry, may want to use. On the other, there are probably fewer reasons why incumbent firms, faced with more competition in enlarged markets, can credibly use predatory behaviour. In markets with an increased number of competitors the ability to raise prices after the exit of one competitor is less then before. Hence the benefit of predation, which involves foregoing current profits for the benefit of higher profits in the future, is reduced.

There is not much evidence of predatory behaviour in the single market. The classic predation case in the Community is AKZO, but this case dates from 1982. One of the problems is the detectability of predatory behaviour. It is generally very difficult to distinguish between predatory behaviour and the vigorous pricing that is the sign of healthy competition in a market.

Non-linear pricing is the other type of pricing behaviour that can have exclusionary effects. This form of pricing behaviour includes offering discounts to customers who buy large quantities, and amounts to a penalty for buying from a competitor. It is not obvious how non-linear pricing behaviour relates to integration. In enlarged markets with more competitors, firms may have to offer larger discounts to have the effect of deterring competitors. The negative effect of such pricing behaviour heavily depends on the existence of dominant firms in concentrated industries.

13.7.3. Institutional entry barriers

Institutional features of a market, such as rules and regulation imposed by governments, can be exploited by firms to create institutional barriers to entry. While the scope for erecting these barriers to entry will be reduced with harmonization of regulation throughout the EU, there may still be some room for firms to behave in an anti-competitive manner. Examples of this type of behaviour have been found in our study on airlines. Regulation of airports, including traffic management and airport slots, may be combined with other strategic behaviour to establish institutional barriers to entry that affects the nature of competition in air travel. National flag carriers are usually in a privileged position at their domestic airport. Given that airport facilities in the EU are heavily congested – in contrast to the US where airport congestion is the exception rather than the rule – there is considerable scope for preventing entrants from establishing themselves as serious competitors unless government or competition authorities intervene.

Environmental regulations such as those that governed the bottling of German mineral water, are another example in our study that shows how domestic incumbents are able to foreclose entry. In this case German mineral water manufacturers exploited packaging rules that are unique to the manufacture of recyclable bottles by a cooperative of German mineral water manufacturers. Combined with a refusal to supply that affected foreign firms, these arrangements worked to the disadvantage of other European mineral water producers. The Commission rightly took an unkind view of this type of behaviour.

13.8. Collusion

Chapter 9 distinguishes between two types of collusive agreement that are affected by the single market programme: 'stand-off' agreements between potential competitors that segment markets along national borders, and national cartels that establish within-country collusion and are designed to keep entrants out.

The opportunities to enter into new within-country cartels and other collusive agreements are not substantially increased when markets become integrated and enlarged. Even if some firms may want to protect their previously protected position in a national market by entering into such agreements, then there is the potential disciplining effect of entry of other EU producers. In addition, market integration may cause problems in sustaining these agreements and stopping colluding partners cheating on the agreement; the incentives to cheat become larger when markets become integrated, as the gains from cheating increase. We therefore expect within-country collusion to become less of a competition issue in the single market.

In contrast, effects on cross-country collusion are unclear because both incentives to cheat and means to punish deviant cartel members become greater. Pan-European market-sharing agreements which operate along national borders may thus be expected to continue to be attractive in the single market. National borders form a focal point for market-sharing agreements. In some industries, though, conditions may change if national regulations which have helped to sustain or even actively support cartels (airlines, telecommunications, postal services, broadcasting) are replaced by pan-European regulation or liberalization.

There are a number of cases of price-fixing agreements that have been investigated by the Commission: Polypropylene (1986), milk market quotas in Meldoc (1986), roofing felt in Belasco (1986), flat glass in Italy (1988), thermoplastics (1988), welded steel mesh (1989), storage facilities in VOTOB (1992), the Dutch construction industry (1992), customs agents in Italy (1993), lifts in NVL (1993), steel beams (1994), Cement (1994), Cartonboard (1994).

What some of these industries have in common are features of their industry which predispose them towards entering into agreements that, among other things, help to stabilize prices:

(a)   they are relatively homogeneous goods which serve as intermediate goods for other manufacturing industries;
(b)   production is characterized by large sunk costs investment, into capacity that cannot be shed if demand is substantially reduced or excess capacity is built;
(c)   demand fluctuates with the macroeconomic cycle, leading either to excess levels of capacity or shortages of capacity, and hence to strong price fluctuations.

If some other conditions are present that facilitate the operation of a pricing agreement (such as the prevalence of list prices that can easily be monitored), we would expect collusion to occur more frequently in these industries rather than in other industries which do not exhibit the characteristics listed above.

What the soda ash case demonstrates is that competitive conditions in markets with collusion can be affected both by competition policy measures and by other measures such as trade liberalization. External trade barriers such as tariffs can affect the competitive pressures that imports can bring to bear on a market. In the case of soda ash, the defensive action of European producers, in bringing an anti-dumping action against US exporters, looks suspiciously like a collusive response to competitive pressures.

13.9. Efficiency defences for cooperative agreements

In Chapter 10 we address expectations that market integration was to lead to an increase in cross-border cooperative agreements between firms, thus allowing the realization of various types of efficiency gains. These include combining resources or assets in a way that is more efficient, entering a new market, and carrying out joint R&D.

An important frame of reference is the distinction between substitute and complementary assets. The efficiency gains are more obvious where cooperation brings under joint control assets with strong complementarities, such as is often the case with vertical integration of activities in one firm. Where the agreement joins firms with substitute assets, there is greater potential for horizontal concentration, making the market more concentrated. That is, cooperation between firms with substitute assets is more suspicious, because comparable benefits can often be realized through open market transactions, without restrictive effects on competition in the product market. Thus, for example, claims of cost reductions and rationalization of capacity should be treated with caution.

A more robust case can be produced in favour of joint R&D, though the distinction between substitute and complementary assets for inventing new products/services remains important – both for competition in the product market and competition in the dynamic process of innovation.

In our adopted framework, cooperation for achieving entry into a new geographical market is likely to be welfare-enhancing when it combines complementary assets (e.g. manufacturing and marketing skills), but the benefits of increased variety for the consumer may be outweighed if this type of entry effectively eliminates the competitive effects of entry. This may be the case, for example, when entry into a new geographical market is achieved through licensing of know-how and trademarks to a product-market competitor, which receives exclusive production and distribution rights. Where the licensee has substitute assets and is already supplying similar products, the licence may be an effective device for sharing markets between the parties, and avoiding the competitive effects of entry. We have given as an example the case of the European beer industry, where brewers have in some cases adopted the practice of licensing a dominant rival brewer in the destination market for the production, distribution and marketing of a brand. It is arguable that rivalry through direct entry would be more competitive, unless there are other barriers to entry that would deter direct entry.

We have considered in some depth the impact of market integration on firms' incentives to enter into cooperative agreements. To the extent that cooperation is motivated by firms' efforts to overcome certain artificial or institutional barriers to market access, we would expect market integration to weaken the incentive to cooperate. This is because in an integrated market there should be increased opportunities for direct entry – as suggested by the case of the US, an integrated market in which there are comparatively few joint ventures between domestic firms.

At the same time, there may also be stronger incentives to enter into cooperative agreements which reduce the intensity of competition from new rivals (for example, in order to avoid the competitive effects of entry). That is, as competitive pressures increase – both inside the EU and possibly from rivals in other trading blocs – the strategic motive for cooperation may become stronger.

Aggregate information on cooperation suggests some evidence of both these effects. Firstly, the proportion of all cross-border agreements which involved partners within the EU declined over the period 1986–93, relative to 1975–85 – which is consistent with the possibility that more direct entry might have occurred.

Secondly, however, the incidence of cooperation with rivals in the same product market remains very high, relative to cooperation with 'complementary' firms. There has also been some shift from agreements on R&D to agreements for joint production and joint marketing.

In Chapter 9 we consider in some detail a number of agreements for which firms have sought individual exemption from the EU competition authorities. These often concern the concession of a know-how licence of some sort, including exclusive distribution rights for the licensee over a given territory. A variety of cases concern agreements for the organization of production or marketing between competitors – for example using each other's products to fill gaps in their respective product lines – which is effectively equivalent to sharing geographical markets between them. In several cases there is a clear effort to share markets and reduce the intensity of competition.

These cases can be contrasted with some recent examples of agreements joining together telecoms/media/IT firms with complementary assets and skills, for the purposes of developing a new product. The emergence of cable operators, often with their independent infrastructure for the delivery of TV programmes to the home, has created the opportunity for new complementarities and synergies, for example with input providers (e.g. of programmes and movies). As new possibilities have arisen for combining complementary assets and developing new products, there has been an increase in joint ventures and strategic alliances for the provision of the new services created by convergence.

13.10. Mergers

The impact of market integration on firms' incentives to merge is discussed in Chapter 11. We focus in particular on two product-market incentives for merger (as opposed to those incentives linked to managerial labour markets, and financial markets): the incentive to enhance market power, and to achieve cost reductions and other efficiency gains.

We argue that in a wider integrated market, which should result from the elimination of various artificial barriers to entry, the private benefits of merger in terms of market power may or may not be greater for the merging parties (relative to what they would be in pre-integration segmented markets). This will depend on structural features such as the number of firms which effectively compete in the wider market. It may well be the case that the sum of firms in the pre-integration market is greater than in the larger post-integration market as some firms would exit in a tougher competitive environment. It is thus not clear a priori whether from the point of view of market power, integration should be expected to encourage or deter mergers.

A more clear-cut view can be taken, however, of the effects of integration on firms' incentives to merge for achieving cost reductions and efficiency gains. The enlargement of market size as a result of integration should enable firms to exploit certain economies of operation internally, through organic growth, without mergers. The efficiency rationale for mergers could thus be weakened by integration in a few cases. In addition, as artificial barriers to entry into other geographical markets are eliminated, the use of merger as an instrument for achieving new market entry may also be reduced. As a more general point, the distinction made in the previous chapter, between the benefits of common ownership for complementary and for substitute assets, also remains valid when assessing efficiency defences for mergers. Claims of large merger-induced efficiency gains should be viewed very cautiously in the case of most horizontal mergers.

13.11. State aids

Our review of the interaction of state aids and integration in Chapter 12 emphasized the danger that the efforts of firms to lobby national governments for subsidies may well increase as a consequence of the single market programme. If single market measures have the effect of increasing competitive pressures in previously protected national markets, then one of the possible responses is to seek continued protection, claiming that transitional support is necessary to facilitate the adjustment process. While there are circumstances where such support may indeed be justified, there must be serious concern that the system of state aids could be exploited. Furthermore, if firms lobby for state aids then this in itself may be a wasteful activity.

State aids have a distorting effect on competition and can change market structure in an undesirable way. If state aid supports a relatively inefficient firm in a market, then exit of more efficient rivals may be one of the consequences. Such an effect would adversely affect allocative efficiency. When several firms are simultaneously affected by major changes in their previousl markets, then a race between firms may ensue whereby firms seek support from their respective governments. In particular geographic areas, such state aid races can easily happen in industries with so-called 'national champions' and high concentration of employment. The result may be an unchanged market structure, and a transfer of government revenues to suppliers of plant and protected labour.

With integration all these negative effects of state aid are amplified:

(a)   the costs of granting protection in larger markets increase;
(b)   the number of firms affected by market structure distortions caused by state aids increases.

Nevertheless, there are justifiable reasons why governments may grant state aids. These have to do with market failures and negative externalities. Generally, if the social rate of return is higher than the private rate of return, a state subsidy for the undertaking is justified (e.g. R&D). The process of integration may affect these reasons in the following manner.

(a)   In the short run, state aid may be needed to smooth the adjustment process for immobile resources that become underemployed as a consequence of rapid change. This is particularly the case when these resources are concentrated in a geographical area, or in a very specific industrial sector.
(b)   Capital market imperfections may exacerbate the problem of adjustment, leading to a socially excessive number of bankruptcies.
(c)   In the long run, we would expect the economically justifiable reasons for granting state aids in integrated markets to weaken as the adjustment to an integrated market is achieved (as capital markets become more efficient).

Our review of trends in state aid in Chapter 12 shows that between 1988 and 1992 state aid to the manufacturing sector in the EU has decreased. The number of decisions has increased and with it the number of objections, which in 1994 had reached 83.5% of all decisions. Against that trend we need to set the marked increase in Community expenditure through regional and social funds that often substitutes for national aid.

One of our market studies offers an example of the impact of integration on state aid, namely the air travel sector. The impact of the three liberalization packages agreed at the Community level under the single market programme is difficult to gauge. The sector is in a process of transition and the full impact of the third package will only be felt in 1997. Nevertheless the amount of state aids to national flag carriers granted since 1991 is very substantial. An expenditure of ECU 9,433 million has been granted in nine cases, with Air France benefiting three times to the tune of ECU 4 billion. This massive amount of government aid has invariably been justified in terms of the need to restructure a carrier that was faced with major adjustment problems. Most state aid cases in the airline sector have been very controversial and were dealt with by the Commission in a highly political environment.

Without a more detailed study of state aid cases and other Community support programmes, it is difficult to generalize from this example. There appears to be some reason to believe that those sectors that were the target of the single market programme are also the sectors that most often seek protection from the effects of the measures. It is a difficult task for the Commission to sanction state aid in the knowledge that one of the effects of state aid will be that competition may be distorted as a consequence. Moreover, it is particularly difficult to accept the appropriateness of state aid, when there are doubts over the true transitional nature of the aid.

13.12. Summary conclusions

How can we summarize our conclusions on the evolution of competition in the single market and changes in firm behaviour caused by market integration?

There is strong evidence of positive trends in integration. Generally trade flows increased, price differentials across Member States have been reduced and price-cost margins show a significant decrease that can be related to the impact of the single market programme. These results present an encouraging picture but do not offer conclusive evidence of causality. Our findings are mainly consistent with the general expectation that integration had pro-competitive effects but could also have been the result of increased external trade liberalization. In fact, there is some evidence that shows the so-called Buigues sectors exhibiting a significant degree of external trade diversion.

Our more detailed analysis of case studies in selected markets shows that not all sectors expected to be affected by integration have seen corresponding changes in behaviour. Generally, if there is a patchy response, this is, we hypothesize, due to:

(a)   differential effects of integration in different markets;
(b)   anti-competitive responses hindering the achievement of the full potential benefits of integration;
(c)   a combination of historical distribution patterns and strategic behaviour.

There are some indicators that integration has been progressing more in markets where external trade has increased – relevant markets for some goods change over time with technological change or ongoing trade liberalization on a global scale. Therefore, relevant markets in some industries are not compatible with EU boundaries and become drivers of change beside any EU single market measures.

More generally, it becomes apparent that other drivers of competition have played a significant role. The chief drivers that appear to have been of major importance are:

(a)   external trade liberalization: examples are the airline sector, cars and to a more limited extent soda ash;
(b)   sector-specific reform; air travel is undergoing major liberalization, as is the telecommunications sector;
(c)   technological developments; telecommunication is the chief example, domestic appliance production another.

Against this complex picture of the interaction of integration and competition, we have focused our attention on the analysis of behavioural obstacles to further integration. We believe that in many industries the remaining obstacles to integration are based on a combination of factors that can reinforce each other. Purchasing habits that are based on national preferences or are due to environmental factors can be exploited in conjunction with anti-competitive behaviour. This behaviour then has the effect of maintaining the segmentation of markets along national borders.

Our analysis of the behaviour of firms in the single market has therefore focused on those responses that are most closely related to the single market programme. At the same time, we tried to make generalizations about the likelihood of such responses by type of industry. While extremely difficult, in a few instances we have been able to make some comments on the conditions that may favour certain strategic responses backed up by examples from our case studies and EU case law.

(a) Price discrimination and parallel import restrictions: the relatively high number of cases involving branded goods indicates a desire to segment markets that have different demand elasticities across the EU.
(b) Access restrictions: typically these apply to industries where infrastructure facilities and networks are essential for entering a new market.
(c) Collusion: homogeneous goods industries with high sunk costs that are exposed to demand fluctuations have been shown to have strong incentives to enter into collusive agreements.
(d) Joint ventures: a complex picture emerges of a general decline in the need to establish collaborative agreements to enter new markets. Against that trend there are concerns over the potential anti-competitive effects of agreements that avoid direct entry into new markets and combine substitutable activities of two potential competitors.
(e) Mergers: no obvious trend or generalizations can be made.
(f) State aids: industries that are subject to major restructuring under the single market programme may be particularly prone to state aid cases.

What remains to be discussed are the policy implications of our findings. The next and final chapter draws conclusions on the role of competition policy in dealing with these behavioural obstacles to integration and, more generally, with the function of competition policy in preventing and challenging distortions of competition, once markets have become integrated.

14. Policy conclusions

14.1. Introduction

The ultimate aim of this study is to assess the significance and the implications of European market integration for competition policy. In the previous chapter we have drawn our conclusions on the evolution of competition in the single market. Our specific focus there has been on how the integration process has affected the incentive of firms to adopt certain types of anti-competitive behaviour. We have shown that progress in integration across sectors has been patchy and incomplete. In particular we have demonstrated the scope for firms to frustrate the aims of integration through anti-competitive responses.

In this chapter we build on this body of work to make a variety of suggestions as to the role of EU competition policy in a more integrated market. Indeed integration makes this exercise necessary: as the market becomes more integrated, and there is more cross-border activity, the geographical limits of national competition policies to national boundaries will coincide less and less often with relevant geographical markets. This leads to overlaps of national jurisdictions, and therefore multiple competencies and a need for coordination. Given that, the social costs of bad rules and a poor decision-making structure at the EU level will become greater. In other words, the costs of bad decisions are higher, and therefore the benefits of improving rules are greater. For this reason market integration is an important point at which to consider critically the application of Community instruments of competition policy.

Through the Treaty of Rome, the Commission has considerable powers to investigate anti-competitive behaviour in the Common Market. In addition, the Merger Regulation of 1989 has given the Commission an effective instrument through which it can control larger-scale mergers with a Community dimension.

In the remainder of this chapter we present our conclusions on policy under the headings of the main competition policy instruments:

(a)   restrictive practices (Art. 85, Treaty of Rome);
(b)   monopolies (Art. 86 and 90, Treaty of Rome);
(c)   mergers (Regulation (EEC) No 4064/89);
(d)   state aids (Art. 92-95, Treaty of Rome).

As a preliminary step, the next section discusses the interaction between competition policy and trade policy. These two policy instruments are frequently seen as substitutes: a liberal trade policy regime is said to create the same or similar competitive pressures on firms in Europe as the instrument of competition policy. We disagree, and argue that in order to appreciate the interaction of competition policy and trade liberalization – whether external or between Member States – it is important to understand the extent to which these policy instruments differ in their impact on competition in markets.

14.2. Market integration, competition policy and trade policy

Over the last few years a considerable literature has emerged on the relationship between trade liberalization and competition policy (Smith and Venables [1988]; Emerson et al. [1988]; Levinsohn [1994]; Jacquemin and Sapir [1991a, 1991b]; Neven and Seabright [1995]; Gual [1995]). The general approach is to consider whether market integration and trade liberalization should be considered 'substitutes' or 'complements' to competition policy. Traditionally trade liberalization has been viewed as a 'substitute' for competition policy, because both policy instruments are thought to lead to more effective competition in markets – in the sense of prices reflecting more closely marginal costs (this is sometimes discussed in terms of a 'disciplining effect' of trade liberalization on domestic market power). The contrary view that these policy instruments have to be considered 'complements' reflects the notion that firms will respond to the elimination of trade barriers by erecting new barriers to competition in the absence of strong competition policy measures (e.g. Smith and Venables [1988]).

In this report we take the view that competition policy and trade liberalization differ in the way they impact competition in the market. We certainly disagree with the notion that the two policy instruments are 'substitutes'. Therefore we cannot agree with the corollary that there should be less competition policy intervention if there is trade liberalization, or that as a response to trade liberalization competition rules can and should be relaxed. To see this, let us consider the respective effects of competition policy and trade liberalization.

The conventional goal of competition policy is to restrict firms from exercising market power in a given market. Thus relative to a situation without intervention in the market, competition policy prevents for example external growth through merger in very concentrated markets, and imposes restrictions on firms that make collusive behaviour difficult. Other policies are aimed at eliminating artificially erected barriers to entry. Conceptually, virtually all competition policy instruments attempt to limit the degree to which firms can sustain raising prices above marginal costs for any significant length of time.

Trade liberalization achieves more competitive outcomes in a fundamentally different way from competition policy. Instead of aiming directly at firms' strategies to raise prices, the effect of trade liberalization works through augmenting the size of the market. Typically, doubling the size of the market will not double the number of firms present in the market in equilibrium. However, in a market half the size there will typically be less firms than in the larger market. Intuitively, more firms can make positive profits in a larger market for a given price-cost differential. Hence, more firms will tend to enter the market and drive price-cost margins down; therefore a closer relation between prices and marginal costs will typically be achieved in the long run in a larger market.[230]

Trade liberalization is therefore very different from competition policy in its effects. While competition policy attempts directly to limit market power for given market size, trade

---

[230]   Because of this effect, markets with horizontal product differentiation have equilibrium prices that converge to marginal costs as the market becomes arbitrarily large. This may not be the case in markets with vertical product differentiation (see Shaked and Sutton [1987] for limiting results as market size is increased). However, only with pure vertical product differentiation, a case that we do not expect in practice, does an increase in market size not increase the number of firms in the market and leave market prices unaffected.

liberalization increases market size and therefore allows a larger number of firms to survive in equilibrium. This only indirectly limits the market power of firms.

14.3. Restrictive practices

Art. 85 prohibits a large range of anti-competitive agreements and practices among firms. The policy aim is to prevent coordinated market behaviour.[231] Articles 85(1) and (2) cast a wide net by declaring all agreements or concerted practices void which have as their object or effect the prevention, restriction or distortion of competition in the Common Market. The list of practices in Art. 85(1) covers cartels, price-fixing market-sharing agreements as well as discriminatory agreements that disadvantage third parties. The former group of agreements are of a horizontal nature, whereas the second are vertical restrictions between parties at different levels of the market. Art. 85(3) allows for exemptions from this wide-ranging prohibition and narrows down the scope of Art. 85(1) in circumstances where agreements or concerted practices provide significant benefits in terms of improved production, distribution or innovation. The control of restrictive practices in European competition law is, therefore, at the same time both wide and narrow.

After careful analysis, we have come to the conclusion that the application of Art. 85 is sometime too tough and sometimes too lax. In particular, we find that for a broad class of horizontal cooperative agreements, a more careful assessment of their anti-competitive and anti-integration impact is required. On the other hand, the rather rigid attitude towards vertical restraints, such as parallel import restrictions, is too much influenced by the single market objective of the Treaty of Rome. Not enough attention is paid towards the pro-competitive effects of price discrimination and some other forms of vertical restraints.

The following sections deal with the policy implications of our analysis of integration and restrictive practices, covering:

(a)   collusion;
(b)   price discrimination and parallel import restrictions;
(c)   joint ventures and other cooperative agreements.

14.3.1. Collusion

Market-sharing agreements on a country by country basis are among the most notable obstacles to integration due to anti-competitive behaviour. The Commission has used its powers to challenge cartels and collusive behaviour, and in the last few years there have been some notable cases resulting in large fines (Steel beams (1994), Cement (1994) and Cartonboard (1994)).

In Chapter 9 we have argued that between-country collusion, which results in market-sharing, is affected through the incentive to replace non-tariff barriers. We have also argued that the effects of market integration on the sustainability of general EU-wide collusion are ambiguous. Within-country collusion, however, will we believe be undermined by the fact that entry is becoming easier and cartels more difficult to sustain.

---

[231]   Whish [1993, p.186].

From the integration point of view, the most important collusive agreements are therefore:

(a)   collusive agreements not to enter a market (mutual stand-offs);
(b)   joint threats to deploy predatory responses to market entry from another region.

Antitrust enforcement against such practices is generally extremely difficult. Evidence of explicit price-fixing or market-sharing is hard to obtain, even though the Commission has considerably more powers to investigate than competition authorities in other countries. Collusive pricing behaviour is often difficult to distinguish from the outcome of competition in markets with few competitors. Furthermore, the absence of market entry as a response to market integration cannot be seen as a sufficient evidence for market-sharing agreements or for predatory threats.

More generally we have made the following observations on policy.

(a)   In a relatively small market very strong enforcement of competition policy may in some senses be self-defeating. Technological considerations may limit the number of firms that can be in a market, for a given market size, and tougher competition policy enforcement may just reduce the number of firms in the same market. For example, consider a market in which two firms could cover their fixed costs if they raised prices moderately through collusive means. However, were they to refrain from collusion, prices would be so close to marginal costs that fixed costs could not be covered. In such a market very strong enforcement of rules against collusion may lead to exit (or lack of entry) of the second firm and the result would be a monopoly without price constraints from a competitor. However, if the market size is increased, the same degree of enforcement may still give enough profits to the second firm to enter the market, and lower prices become sustainable. In this sense we may think of market integration as a process which makes tougher competition policy enforcement feasible: market integration creates more room for effective competition policy enforcement.

(b)   Given that competition policy authorities find it hard to collect evidence on collusive agreements that documents the existence of negotiations about prices and production, the promise of reduced fines for firms that surrender evidence that helps convict others seems like a powerful incentive scheme to detect collusion. The recent proposals along these lines by the Commission certainly go in this direction. However, market integration will change nothing in the way this policy should be employed.

(c)   Agreements on market-sharing according to geographic boundaries rely on careful monitoring of entry and market shares by the firms and the use of national focal points. One of the most effective destabilization policies available to the EU Commission appears to be a liberal trade policy which opens up the market in the EU to competition from the rest of the world. A good example of the complementary nature of trade policy and competition policy is provided by the soda ash case study where protectionist measures such as anti-dumping actions can be seen as attempts to foster conditions that facilitate collusive behaviour.

(d)   Predatory threats that induce exit or preclude entry into the market appear to be effective only where the firms colluding on predatory action can assure each other that this action will not affect their relative position in the market. In these cases, extensive exchange of information is needed to coordinate predatory action credibly. Restrictions on individualized information exchanges could therefore be introduced to deal with this issue.

(e)   More generally, individualized information-sharing can be considered a crucial instrument for maintaining any collusive agreement. If competition authorities find it hard to obtain direct evidence of collusion then action against measures that greatly facilitate collusion need to be brought into consideration. Certain forms of information exchange, such as direct exchange of price and quantity information, could be considered a direct infringement of Art. 85(1).

14.3.2. Policy towards geographic price discrimination and parallel import restrictions

Competition policy in the EU has traditionally been very hostile to geographic price discrimination. Article 86 of the Treaty of Rome contains a *per se* prohibition of price discrimination by dominant firms, while agreements between firms that facilitate price discrimination are also *per se* illegal under Art. 85(1). As seen in Chapter 7, this treatment is not always justified in economic reasoning, and the approach appears motivated to a large extent by the integration goals of the Treaty of Rome.

Price discrimination

Our review in Chapter 7 suggests that a 'rule of reason' approach towards geographic price discrimination may be the most appropriate. This follows from the fact that geographic price discrimination can be welfare-enhancing even with a monopoly, and may lead to pro-competitive effects in oligopolies. In many cases, uniform prices are therefore not second-best optimal. Furthermore, when there is sufficient competition in the market, potential welfare losses from geographic price discrimination will tend to be small (i.e. welfare losses are second-order in price differentials).[232]

This suggests that the following rules may be appropriate from a theoretical point of view.

(a)   Where market concentration is low there should be a presumption that price discrimination is permissible. In such a situation, firms have little market power in each market and effective geographic price discrimination cannot be large. Any welfare losses from price discrimination will therefore be of small order, while the potential pro-competitive effects of price discrimination may still be significant. Hence a prohibition of price discrimination in markets that are not very concentrated is not economically justifiable.
(b)   Geographic price discrimination raises potential concerns when:
        (i)   there are few producers;
        (ii)   the price differentials across geographical markets are large.

However, this is in itself not sufficient to conclude that price discrimination leads to welfare losses. It is important to consider also whether a reduction in output in the low-price market will lead to exit from that market. The first point is that where price discrimination does not lead to an expansion of output relative to the situation where it is prohibited, then in reasonable circumstances price discrimination should be expected to produce a welfare loss.[233]

---

[232]   It is important to emphasize that the issue of whether price discrimination should be prohibited or not is treated here as a second-best problem, i.e. given the extent of market power. In other words, we consider whether price discrimination should be prohibited or not given the existing level of market power; it is therefore a second-best problem.

[233]   Unfortunately not even **this** simple conclusion is entirely robust, since certain specifications of demand can overturn it.

In addition, if the elimination of price discrimination gives the firm an incentive to exit the low-price market in order to sustain high prices in the high-price market, we would expect the welfare losses from an anti-discriminatory policy to be potentially high. (The test of whether a market would still be supplied if price discrimination was not allowed also applies to a market where price is high.)

Parallel import restrictions

In Chapter 7 we also discussed the role of various practices that may be used to facilitate price discrimination across borders. The ability to sustain such discrimination crucially depends on arbitrage (by intermediaries or final consumers) being restricted or ineffective. The most obvious way for firms to achieve this are clauses which restrict the ability of purchasers to resell, as are often attached to other vertical restraints. For example, exclusive distribution agreements often include an 'export ban' clause forbidding the distributor from selling to foreign customers or to arbitrageurs. The effect of these clauses is effectively to eliminate the arbitrage possibilities that arise when different prices are charged in different areas.

It can be argued that practices facilitating price discrimination should be assessed by the competition authorities on the same criteria as price discrimination. From an economic point of view, in circumstances where price discrimination cannot be considered welfare-reducing, the practices which make this possible should not be deemed illegal. For example, a policy of selective discounts which are conditional on location may be pro-competitive. And contractual restrictions which make price discrimination feasible should only be deemed illegal if the effect of such practices is welfare-reducing as well.

It is also important to emphasize that the welfare effects of price discrimination are separate from the efficiency effects of closed territory distribution in some instances. That is, there are cases where arbitrage is restricted with the sole purpose of achieving price discrimination, and others where the motivation is to achieve efficiency in distribution (it may be efficient for a particular product to be sold under conditions of territorial exclusivity, for example where there are significant pre-sale services or provision of information by retailers). In these cases, distribution agreements will also feature clauses which restrict the distributor's ability to resell, and price differentials will not be eroded by arbitrage. As in all cases concerning price discrimination, the welfare effects of prices being different in different countries should be assessed; and if these are not found to be welfare-reducing, then a fortiori there is no reason to be concerned about clauses restricting arbitrage (because these may have positive side effects in terms of allowing more efficient vertical contracts to be written).

In summary, a *per se* prohibition of all agreements restricting resale or parallel imports does not appear to be socially optimal. As we have already noted, this is one clear case where integration objectives are being pursued to the detriment of efficiency considerations. In fact, from a competition policy point of view parallel import restrictions should be treated like any other restriction on resale, and evaluated on the basis of the welfare effects of price discrimination. Given that we have argued that price discrimination is less likely to be a problem where it is practised by non-dominant firms, in practice restrictions on resale should not be prohibited when they involve firms that do not have a dominant (or joint-dominant) position in a market.

Unfortunately, the current wording of the Treaty of Rome implies a very inconsistent treatment of price discrimination, on the one hand, and practices that facilitate price discrimination on the other. A clear dominance criterion is applied to price discrimination as such, because it is dealt with under Article 86 (which makes a particular conduct 'abusive' only when practised by a 'dominant' firm). However practices such as parallel import restrictions, which facilitate geographic price discrimination, are dealt with under Article 85(1) (on agreements between firms which restrict competition); and are *per se* illegal according to the Commission's action record. There is no economic efficiency justification for this harsh treatment of parallel import restrictions. The only justification derives from the secondary objective of the competition articles of the Treaty of Rome to pursue integration in the single market. This objective appears to clash here with considerations of efficiency that support competition policy in most other jurisdictions. A solution to this tension would be to apply our proposed rule of reason under Art. 85(3) or to make the test of Art. 85(1) tougher, such that price discriminatory behaviour would not automatically be covered by the *per se* prohibition. This would mean focusing on the effect of price discrimination rather than on the form.

14.3.3. Joint ventures and other cooperative agreements

As discussed in Chapter 10, joint ventures imply cooperation between firms across any of a wide range of their activities. These can only be justified when there are significant efficiency defences for such behaviour. We take the position that such efficiency defences have much greater importance in areas in which R&D or new product introduction is involved, than when claimed efficiency gains are not related to such activities.

Joint ventures in production and sales

When considering joint ventures in production and sales, it is important to distinguish whether their effect is merely one of horizontal concentration, or includes elements of vertical integration.

(a) Cases with horizontal joint ventures on production and sales should simply be considered as collusive agreements under Art. 85(1), and should be treated as such.
(b) If production and sales joint ventures merely lead to selective vertical integration, they should generally be allowed. The main effect we should expect from this is, for example, that a producer gains access to a market by finding an established distributor – and thereby saves on distribution costs. Such agreements should only be impeded by the Commission if it finds strong evidence that the agreement has been reached to avoid the entry of a potential competitor. In particular, there should be scrutiny of such an agreement if there are exclusive dealing restrictions which have foreclosing effects.

As in other cases, there should be some kind of market structure test: action should be taken only in very concentrated markets.

As a general rule, in line with our general recommendation to separate competition policy from other issues, we believe that the mere fact that cooperation goes across national boundaries should not affect the decision on whether to allow a joint venture or not. As far as the Commission has accepted such arguments in the past (Whish [1993, p. 441]), we believe that given the degree of integration reached in some markets it is undesirable generally to sacrifice competition policy goals.

Joint ventures involving R&D or product introduction

We do not find the general 'financial restrictions' argument for joint R&D very convincing, particularly in the case of large, established firms which tend to have large cash flows and the opportunity to diversify their R&D portfolio. There should therefore be obvious firm size criteria.

Similarly the argument that an R&D joint venture allows 'completion of a product line' is not compelling.

Most importantly, the crucial question is whether the joint venture integrates activities that are complements or substitutes for either inventing new products/services, or launching new products into a market. That is, competition policy should discriminate between cases in which firms participating in the joint ventures contribute complementary skills and assets to these activities, and those in which these are substitutes (concrete examples: joint ventures of telecoms and publishing companies vs. joint ventures between telecom operators).

As a general rule, we would think that joint ventures in which assets that are substitutes are combined would be primarily competition-reducing, unless the parties to the joint venture can demonstrate that there are substantial economies of scale in the R&D activity. In contrast, we would expect substantial efficiency gains from combining complementary assets, for the speed of R&D both in new products and processes.[234] However, even when firms have substitute assets, joint ventures avoid the duplication of costs.

We would also recommend a distinction between product development (i.e. producing new varieties of existing products) and technological development (i.e. new production processes combining assets that had not been combined before). All large firms have ongoing in-house product development, and therefore their product development divisions are very much substitutable assets. But also in the case of technological development we can see reasons for exempting fewer agreements, because we are concerned with competition in the product market – in that context, even an agreement that combines complementary assets has to be evaluated according to the existence of other horizontal agreements which tie together substitute assets in the market. We therefore would argue in favour of:

(a)   preference for agreements between firms with complementary assets, relative to substitute assets;

(b)   assessing the overall concentration in the notional market for these new products; i.e. concentration of firms who hold assets that are relevant to that market.

---

[234]   However the competition authority should apply a caveat to this simple rule, if the joint venture between firms with complementary assets includes one firm already involved in joint ventures with other partners with similar complementary assets. This would essentially imply concentration of control over relevant assets that are in fact substitutes, and could significantly reduce competition in the market (case: Optical fibres (1986): joint ventures were set up between Corning Glass Works (US), world leader in the production and distribution of optical fibres, and BICC in the UK and Siemens in Germany. Although the Commission found that the individual joint venture agreements did not restrict competition between Corning and its partners, it found that there was a distortion of competition in the relationship between the joint ventures, and the existence of other similar joint ventures in which Corning participated actively. The network of joint ventures was considered likely to lead to market sharing between them. However, after amendments, the Commission granted an Art. 85(3) exemption since it enabled several European companies to manufacture a high-technology product, thereby promoting technical progress and benefiting consumers).

More generally, as discussed in the chapter on cooperative agreements (Chapter 10), the social benefits of cooperative agreements in R&D depend very much on the dynamic process of innovation, and retaining competition in innovation may be an important objective. For this reason, the exemption of R&D activity from competition policy rules – which is implied by the block exemption on R&D agreements – may be going too far in withdrawing competition policy control from this dimension of competition. As is well known, the firm competing in research may have excessive or not enough incentives to join R&D from a welfare point of view. Current policy takes for granted that cooperation enhances welfare because it allows firms to internalize the effect of each firm's research on the profits of rivals.

Overall, the effects of cooperation in R&D and product introduction should be evaluated with reference to the effects of this cooperation on the elimination of potential competitors in developing markets. For this reason, it would be appropriate to condition policy on the degree of complementarity/substitutability between assets, and on the extent to which cooperation removes from the market assets which could give rise to competition in R&D (as well as in the product market). The current treatment of R&D cooperation under the block exemption appears not to satisfy this criterion, because it ignores the effects of cooperation on competition in R&D, and therefore on potential competition in future product markets. An important advantage of cooperative agreements, however, is that they save on research costs by avoiding duplication and this can yield social benefits even when cooperating firms have substitute assets. This may be particularly important when the lack of cooperation results in excessive investments in research.

Licensing agreements

One of the most effective entry-avoidance strategies, which has similar effects on prices as tacit market-sharing according to geographical area, is to grant manufacturing licences and trademark licences to a competitor, with or without exclusivity.

Such licensing agreements usually involve the delegation of pricing and marketing decisions to the licensee and may be seen as a commitment of the licensor to the licensee not to enter the market. This is obvious in the case of exclusive dealing; however, even licensing agreements without exclusive dealing imply a strong commitment not to enter the market. The reason is that by entering, the licensor and the licensee would compete with each other. In the context of a homogeneous product, this may lead to such strong price competition that entry would not be as attractive as licensing. Thus one could think of licensing agreements as an indication that the licensor does not intend to enter the market.

From a social welfare point of view, the strategy of avoiding competitive entry through licensing is not as detrimental to consumers as tacit market-sharing at a collusive price, because consumers gain through the increase in variety. However, the 'increased variety' argument should not necessarily be deemed to be a sufficient defence to allow licensing agreements, if the licensor would have entered the market anyway. These agreements are therefore only beneficial if firms could not enter the market at minimum efficient scale. In economic terms, these agreements can be interpreted as selective mergers in geographical sub-markets.

An argument frequently made by firms for defending licensing agreements is that they serve as a foothold to achieve brand recognition in a market in which firms plan to compete in the future. This does not appear to be a credible argument on economic grounds. If this argument were true, it is hard to see why licensees would accept licence contracts in the prospect of promoting future competition to themselves unless they considered the effect of future competition to be insignificant. Furthermore, the promised benefits from future competition should be deemed small, if contracts have such long terms that the effect of competition lies so far in the future that it can be neglected in current decisions. Overall, this argument does not alter our view that the appropriate test to be applied is that of the failure of 'entry at minimum efficient scale'.

We would suggest the adoption of a procedure whereby cases are preselected on the basis of market structure. As in all competition policy issues, we do not believe that cooperation of small firms in the market has enough effects on outcomes to justify competition policy intervention. Thus in markets that are concentrated, licensing agreements with dominant firms that avoid the competitive effect of entry should be deemed an infringement of Art. 85(1), unless firms can credibly demonstrate that entry at minimum efficient scale is not profitable. Furthermore, in markets that are fairly concentrated we may have an a priori presumption that entry at the margin would be more profitable (on average). Hence in concentrated markets it is likely both that entry would occur in the absence of licensing agreements, and that entry avoidance through licensing agreements has large welfare-reducing effects.

The case evidence suggests that the policy of the Commission does generally go in this direction. However, there are also cases where the Commission has been convinced that licensing should be allowed because direct entry is hampered by peculiar arrangements. For example, in the case of beer, contractual barriers to entry (ties between brewers and publicans) were seen as sufficient reason for allowing licensing agreements (Moosehead/Whitbread, 1990). In Carlsberg/Courage (1992), a less favourable stance was taken, as the agreement included exclusive distribution rights for Courage in the UK.

14.4. Monopolies

Article 86 of the Treaty of Rome deals with the exploitation of market power at the expense of customers or suppliers, as well as anti-competitive practices which have the effect of damaging competitors or restricting competition.[235] It is aimed primarily at the conduct of a single dominant company. A dominant position was defined by the European Court of Justice as the power to behave to an appreciable extent independently of one's competitors, customers and ultimately of one's consumers. Like Art. 85, Art. 86 lists examples of behaviour that constitute abuse: these examples cover excessive pricing, discriminatory pricing or other trading conditions, and tying. Another instrument that it is relevant to consider in this study of competition issues in the single market is Art. 90. Art. 90 is not addressed at anti-competitive behaviour of firms. Rather, it obliges Member States not to enact or maintain in force any measure contrary to the Treaty and, in particular, one which would contravene Articles 7, 85 or 86.[236] As government regulation is a major source of monopoly power, this instrument of the Commission to challenge monopolies protected by Member States is worth considering. In

---

[235]   Department of Trade and Industry, *Abuse of market power, a consultative document on possible legislative options*, HMSO, London, 1992, p. 9.

[236]   Whish [1993, p. 333].

fact, some of our case studies deal with competition issues that have at their source regulatory restrictions (airlines).

In the remainder of this section we present our conclusions on four types of anti-competitive behaviour in the single market that are associated with monopoly or market dominance:[237]

(a)   price discrimination;
(b)   access restrictions and foreclosure;
(c)   tying;
(d)   exclusionary pricing.

14.4.1. Price discrimination

In principle, we believe that Art. 86 is appropriate in making the concern over price discrimination contingent on dominance; however, given the ambiguous effects of price discrimination discussed in Chapter 7, and summarized in section 14.3.1 above, even in the context of this Article the *per se* prohibition of price discrimination is questionable. A 'rule of reason' approach that takes into account the degree of price discrimination (i.e. the size of price differentials), and the potential entry/exit effects from geographical markets, may be more appropriate. However, such a rule may be difficult to implement. A general prohibition, in cases where significant price differentials have been established, may have to be followed.

In terms of policy relevance, it appears to be more important to spend resources on the prosecution of competition policy cases with potentially larger efficiency effects than those of price discrimination, particularly as the degree of integration achieved through the single market programme increases. Given the ambiguities in the welfare effects of price discrimination, which do not easily allow one to reach clear-cut conclusions, we would expect more important issues for competition policy than the issue of price discrimination.

In our view, therefore, two further questions should be considered:

(a)   whether prohibiting price discrimination is going to cause exit of the firm from one or more markets;
(b)   whether price discrimination is being used as a pro-competitive device to compete for marginal consumers (and therefore prohibition of price discrimination would reduce competition).

The grounds on which cases are brought should be more selective, with the focus being on the abuse which brings the largest welfare damage. This is clearly illustrated by cases such as Tetra Pak-II or AKZO, where the welfare effect of price discrimination was second-order relative to that of exclusion resulting from tying.

14.4.2. Access restrictions to essential facilities: refusal to supply

There are an increasing number of sectors in which access problems arise, and which have not at any point been subject to regulation. The classic case – as seen in Chapter 10 – is ports, but there are various other possibilities: one of many examples is local telephone access to the

---

[237]   We do not, however, review the policy implications for Art. 90 actions.

Internet, which is achieved by modem users through a facility offered by the telephone companies. As this facility is very costly to duplicate, others cannot set up a rival service. The question is whether, as these access issues arise, we should take these sectors into regulation; or, given the unpredictability of how these issues arise, they should be taken under the control of Article 86, and an appropriate procedure should be set up for determining access pricing. Here we make a suggestion as to how the problem of dealing with these new access issues in deregulated sectors could be addressed through Article 86. In particular, given that in a wider market access prices become more and more important, this is a suggestion on how to use competition policy to avoid permanent regulation of sectors with access problems.

The first point to make is on the correct definition of an essential facility: an asset should not be defined as an essential facility if there are other services outside those using the essential facility that are in the same market. The simplest example is that of a ferry service between Calais and Dover; here the extent to which the port of Dover may be defined as an essential facility is reduced, if we consider that there is also the Channel Tunnel, and to some extent the ferry and the train are in the same market. That is, an asset should not be defined an essential facility if the firm that owns or controls it would not have a dominant position in the market if it completely refused access to the essential facility.

Two general principles must be established for a correct approach to access restriction issues.

Firstly, a simple prohibition of refusal to supply is not a sufficient remedy to achieve access in such markets, and induce competition. This is because a firm can duplicate the effects of refusal to supply by charging high access pricing. The competition policy authority is therefore faced with the problem of determining how access should be priced in the difficult situation where the firm controlling the essential input has private information about the cost of access.

Secondly, ordering non-discriminatory access is also not a sufficient remedy, i.e. the imposition of a non-discrimination condition, whereby the owner/controller of the essential input must set the same terms for a competitor as it sets to its own subsidiary, is not in itself sufficient to solve the access problem (thus the 'essential facilities doctrine' as defined in Holyhead II does not appear satisfactory). This would simply create the incentive for the incumbent to charge a high access price, and thus recover any losses made by its downstream subsidiary through the high access charges paid by rivals.

Solving the access problem when an essential facility is involved always requires an element of price regulation of access. However it is clearly desirable to avoid full-scale, systematic regulation of all sectors whenever access issues arise. Competition policy offers an attractive model, because it relies on the element of complaint on the part of the competitor which is 'hurt'. The competition authorities tend to intervene selectively upon complaint; similarly with access pricing, selective regulatory intervention upon complaint becomes feasible when there is someone who will complain.

For these reasons, we suggest a two-step procedure for dealing with access problems.

(a)   Establish whether an input may be defined as an essential facility in the sense defined above. This involves a careful market structure analysis of the relevant market. For access to be a problem, the duplication of the essential facility must be very costly relative to the value of the product, while the shadow cost of access is low. Secondly, there must be a lack of substitutes for the essential facility in question. Only if it is deemed that neither duplication of the facility is feasible, nor that substitutes are accessible to the firm, should the competition authorities consider taking action to order access.

(b) If subsequently there is a complaint about the price of access, there is a second step which consists of regulating the conditions of access. That is: if, because of limited substitution possibilities, the facility is deemed to be essential for the firm that has brought the complaint, then the conditions of access (access price) should be regulated. An advantage of regulation on complaint is that it implicitly makes use of the entrant's information on costs (which is likely to be higher that the regulator's).

From an institutional point of view, it may be appropriate to delegate this step to a separate body within DG IV. This body should be considered a regulatory agency for access issues, and should be vested with the power of eliciting the necessary data on costs and demand in order to estimate appropriate access prices. This body should be conceived as a residual authority, in the sense that it would only deal with those sectors which are not permanently regulated (see below).

The agency would collect cost data, and calculate the appropriate access charges according to generally accepted best-practice regulatory rules for access pricing, such as the Baumol-Willig rule which is based on the opportunity cost of access. A good regulatory formula is one with the smallest information requirement (a cost-based formula) and which is simple enough to apply to generate security about competition policy in the market. This means generating a generally accepted benchmark for an acceptable price of access, which is consistent with accepted practices.

Obviously this procedure will only produce good results on the following conditions.

(a) The regulatory rule is simple. Simplicity is advisable because it may save more on regulatory costs than that which is gained through setting the 'right' access charges. Also formulae which are demand-based are undesirable because they are often too complicated.

(b) There is full transparency.

(c) The firm owning the essential facility is given certainties on the rules applied by the authorities, which should be clearly known *ex ante*. Giving the firm greater certainty in this way should minimize regulatory intervention, because it should enable it, at any point in time, to capitalize costs and set appropriate access prices on the basis of its own data – and thus avoid complaints.

There may be, however, some sectors in which permanent regulation may be needed. In these cases it makes sense to maintain and enforce access prices, as part of the overall regulatory regime. Hence our recommendations are really about residual regulation in all those areas where it is not desirable to have permanent regulatory oversight.

While our suggested procedure minimizes regulatory intervention, it also takes care of the dual problem that – as seen above – simply 'ordering access' is not sufficient to ensure access at the right price; while at the same time setting access prices is a regulatory problem, which requires detailed cost information. Secondly, this procedure allows for complete flexibility of access prices to adjust to changing cost conditions.

To summarize: a general decision has to be taken whether to submit specific sectors to regulation of access prices (with specific bodies), or to transfer the whole access issue to the area of Article 86. In the latter case, a procedure like the one we have just suggested is necessary to solve the access pricing problem. The most detrimental way of dealing with the access pricing problem is in our view the combination of both the explicit regulation and case-by-case competition policy intervention, which would lead to a high degree of uncertainty on the part of firms on the regulatory regime and a duplication of administrative cost.

In other words: Article 86 should be used for sectors which are not regulated, and not for those which are regulated.

14.4.3. Vertical restraints as an access restriction

As seen in Chapter 9, foreclosure of competitors by restricting access to an essential complementary input can in fact take various forms, from vertical restraints which tie up the downstream retail function, such as exclusive dealing, to long-term contracts which impose high penalties for exiting, and so on.

The conceptual approach to these practices should be the same as that to any other restriction of access to a complementary input controlled by the incumbent, and without which the competitor cannot supply the final market. That is, the 'access' framework can be applied to all types of vertical contracts which may lead to foreclosure effects. In this way the threshold for vertical restraints to be considered anti-competitive is raised considerably.

In particular, a complaint that the incumbent has 'tied up' the distribution sector through a network of exclusive purchasing agreements, and made entry at minimum efficient scale unfeasible, is essentially a complaint of 'refusal to supply'. In these cases, what must be verified is whether:

(a)   the distribution channel has the characteristics of an essential facility: here, as in the above definition, a distribution chain can be considered an essential facility for a manufacturer if his good has low value relative to the cost of setting up an alternative distribution channel, and exclusivity imposed by a competitor forecloses access to the downstream market;

(b)   there are any efficiency defences for restricting access.

When it has been ascertained that there are essential facility characteristics, and no efficiency defences, access should be essentially 'ordered' by disallowing the vertical (exclusive purchasing) agreement. Whether this solves the problem will depend on who is actually imposing the exclusive agreement (the manufacturer or the retailer).

The distributor is then in principle free to charge manufacturers a fee for 'access' to its facility (e.g. for retail space, for stocking products lines, etc.), and in the case of a complaint about the fee, this should be dealt with in the same way as access pricing. That is, the 'access price' for retailing would be a fee set by the retailer to accept business from various manufacturers; and if there is a complaint about the level of such a fee, this should be looked at by the competition authorities.

Notice, however, that exclusive purchasing agreements – i.e. contractual clauses imposing the obligation not to purchase from a third party – may also be in some cases instances of **refusal** to buy on the part of the retailer. This case is much more problematic than refusal to supply, because in order to establish whether this practice is restrictive, it is necessary to obtain information about demand. Purchase may have been refused because the retailer deemed the cost of supplying the good too high, but generally in order to see whether refusal to buy was 'unreasonable' and a restriction of competition, what is needed is an evaluation of demand. This is not feasible, which suggests that competition policy should not intervene in these cases. In addition, there may be the usual efficiency reasons for the vertical restraint, which reinforces the position that action should not be pursued.

14.4.4. Tying of products for sale to consumers

Tying occurs when the producer makes the sale of a particular product conditional on the purchaser also acquiring another good (or service).

Following from the analysis in Chapter 9, tying is not a concern where the firm does not have market power. This suggests that a very clear dominance criterion should also apply in this case. Tying should be permitted where the firm does not have large market shares in either the tying or the tied product. The argument is that under such circumstances, the firm has a small market share in the market for the 'bundle' (the 'system' of the tying and the tied product); hence competition on the bundle 'parts' will tend to reduce effective mark-ups in both markets.

Conversely, tying raises concerns where the firm has achieved monopoly power over a (durable) good – often obtained through the patent system – and is able to tie sales of a complementary product in which there are potential rival suppliers. In other words, monopoly power can be extended to goods which are complements to the good in which the firm has its monopoly power. In these cases it is appropriate that such tying arrangements should be illegal, and the prohibition of tying by dominant firms under Article 86 appears quite satisfactory.

In addition, there are various ways in which firms may seek to justify tying agreements for efficiency reasons, and some of these efficiency defences may be appropriate for tying even in concentrated markets. Here the competition authorities will have the task of trading off claims of efficiency defences, against the loss from the exclusion of competition on the market for the tied product. The main criterion here is that tying should not be allowed if there exist substitute arrangements that can achieve the same efficiency gains.

Beer may be a good example, and may serve to illustrate the point that in the area of tie-ins, competition policy should consider the interaction of different restraints on competition. In the British pubs system, typically finance and beer sales are bundled together. While there are claimed efficiency reasons for such 'bundling', the effect may be a barrier to entry for new brewers (as there is, supposedly, a 'fixed' stock of pubs). Indeed, European brewers have claimed that the tying system for British pubs has not allowed them entry into the UK market at minimum efficient scale, and has required them to adopt production licensing arrangements instead. This case illustrates the need to re-evaluate the trade-offs between efficiency defences for ties, and potential losses from restriction of competition.

An interesting variety of the tying problem arises with aftermarkets, i.e. markets for complementary products which are bought subsequent to an original durable purchase. Suppliers of a durable good often face little competition in the supply of subsequent complementary products. As seen in Chapter 9, observing that manufacturers have large market shares in aftermarkets related to their primary products should not necessarily lead to the conclusion that aggressive competition intervention is warranted.

In particular, even if there is little competition in an aftermarket, this may not affect consumers too greatly if there is competition in the primary *ex ante* market for the supply of the durable good. Consumers may be protected by primary market competition. If competition in the primary market is vigorous, then any profits that manufacturers expect to make through high prices in their aftermarkets might be competed away in the primary market, with prices in this market being set below costs. Thus, markets cannot be investigated in isolation, but their interaction should be taken into account.

We have also argued that the problem of firms taking advantage of consumers' bounded rationality may be reduced if firms offer contracts which bundle the purchase of a durable good with aftermarket services for a single price, in which case manufacturers of the primary good essentially engage in competition in the contracts which they offer. Provided the *ex ante* market is competitive, interbrand competition in the primary market is sufficient to protect consumers: contracts bind the actions of equipment suppliers and commit them not to engage in installed-base opportunism. Thus, contracts which fix the terms of future aftermarket services in advance, and so remove this informational burden on consumers, should be encouraged. For example, laser printers are often advertised stating the low price of the toner cartridges. However, a policy concern must be the situation where firms can unilaterally change the terms of the implicit contracts once consumers are locked in, i.e., the price of the toner can be changed as soon as the advertising campaign is over.

If primary market competition is strong, and if firms offer contracts of the type discussed above, then the observation that each manufacturer has a high share of its own aftermarket should not worry competition authorities. However, action may be needed to ensure that contracts for aftermarket services are sufficiently transparent to ensure that primary market competition alone is sufficient to protect consumers. For example, the Office of Fair Trading has recently investigated the practice of photocopier manufacturers in the UK purposefully putting hidden charges into the small print of their leasing arrangements. The encouragement of active competition in transparent contracts is to be encouraged by competition authorities, since it effectively removes the need to worry about aftermarket power whether or not consumers are rational and forward-looking.

If there is market power in the primary market, it is no longer obvious that profits earned in aftermarkets will be dissipated by primary market competition, and direct competition action against the primary market power will tend to be most desirable. However, there may be a limit to how much primary market concentration can be reduced, in which case reduction of aftermarket power may be beneficial.

In all cases, a clear conclusion is that competition in transparent contracts – which specify at the time of the initial purchase the terms on which aftermarket services will be available – is to be encouraged as a relatively simple way of protecting consumers without requiring direct intervention in the conduct of aftermarkets. Competition authorities should be concerned only when firms can change unilaterally the terms of the contracts.

14.4.5. Exclusionary pricing

We have considered two forms of exclusionary pricing which are relevant in the context of integration: predatory pricing to force the exit of a competitor; and non-linear pricing which is aimed at increasing the customers' cost of dealing with a competitor, and was thereby argued to have similar effects to exclusive dealing (see Chapter 8).

Predatory pricing is a very difficult area in any case, because of the detection problems which make policy intervention based just on pricing a particularly delicate exercise. The most important conclusion is that market structure must be considered first: this is important, because if this is not sufficiently concentrated, it will not be possible for the predator to raise prices after the exit of the rival – and therefore predation will not be a rational strategy. More generally, we recommend considering the overall pattern of market structure, the financial strength of the firm, and the path of prices over time, in order to create 'safe haven' situations where the competition authorities should not intervene.

On non-linear pricing, we have made a clear distinction between quantity discounting over a single purchase, which is pro-competitive, and discounts on aggregate purchases over time, which effectively amount to penalties for purchasing from a rival supplier, and in this sense have a certain analogy with exclusivity requirements. The reason is that in this way the downstream sector is 'tied' to the incumbent offering the discounts, and the rival may not be able to enter at the minimum efficient scale.

14.5. Mergers

Unlike joint ventures, mergers are a complete and permanent combination of assets and control of the merging parties. The Commission controls mergers of firms with a minimum turnover and a Community dimension by virtue of Regulation (EEC) No 4064/89. Since its establishment, the Commission's Merger Task Force has dealt with a large number of merger proposals and in a minority of cases has subjected them to more close scrutiny. Very few mergers have been blocked outright (four).

Our conclusions on policy dealing with mergers are twofold: first, there are those considerations that are similar to the conclusions on policy towards joint ventures and other cooperative agreements. In particular, we expressed our doubts as to the strength of efficiency defences except in a well-defined set of circumstances. Second, there are considerations of a more institutional nature. More integrated markets raise issues of allocation of jurisdiction and coordination of national merger control.

14.5.1. Efficiency defences

Our analysis of the impact of market integration on firms' incentives to merge is that the effect on the market power incentive is ambiguous, while economies of scale, scope and selection effects may be achieved in a wider market organically, rather than through mergers. We have generally argued therefore that no more weight should be given as a result of integration to firms' efficiency defences for merger. Indeed we wish to recommend against more emphasis being placed on efficiency defences: these are always hard to evaluate, and policy-making based on them is not practical. The only notable exception should be those defences which are based on arguments of complementarities in R&D. This position finds support in the fact that the empirical literature on mergers (see Chapter 10) fails to demonstrate substantial efficiency gains. Indeed, it may be argued that by allowing mergers at all when there is not much increase in concentration, we are already implicitly allowing for some efficiency defence. The case is different for R&D because in that case the potential efficiency gains are of a different order of magnitude.

The current distinction between cooperative and concentrative joint ventures[238] makes little sense from the point of view of economic analysis. We believe that the main difference from an economic point of view has to be seen in a concentrative joint venture being a cooperative agreement with a permanent institutional structure, i.e. not limited in time. In contrast, cooperative joint ventures are institutionally less durable, and in R&D they are explicitly limited in their duration by the protection conferred by IPRs.

This leads to several conclusions.

(a)   Concentrative joint ventures should be defined only by the characteristic that they give rise to a separate legal entity. For that reason, they should be treated under the Merger Regulation. All other cooperative agreements should be dealt with under Art. 85.

(b)   The standards of efficiency defences for cooperation should be stricter for concentrative joint ventures than for cooperative joint ventures in R&D, where these involve cooperation on production and sales. This is because one regime essentially gives a permanent allowance, while the other is only over the lifetime of the patent.

14.5.2. Institutional implications

In general, there is no reason for merger policy at the EU level to slacken as a response to integration; if anything, there is an argument for tightening such policy, because – as argued in Chapter 11 – firms in a larger market can achieve greater economies of scale internally, and therefore do not need mergers to exploit volume effects, for example. On the other hand, we believe that national merger policy needs to be refocused. National merger control in markets that have a wider geographic dimension must take the competition effect of integration into account, or leave it to supranational authorities to deal with mergers that have a transnational dimension.

The overall recommendation is therefore that there should be tighter EU policies and policy coordination with delegation of implementation to the national authorities.

It is thus crucial that EU competition policy rules dealing with mergers are improved to reflect this enhanced role. A wider market resulting from integration also implies that, at the margin, the decisions of the competition authority tend to affect a larger population. Hence the marginal benefits of correct and rigorous application of competition rules become greater, and so do the marginal costs of bad decisions. This strongly suggests that (unlike national rules) the criteria for the evaluation of mergers at the EU level should not be slackened as a result of integration. Furthermore, there is a case for more resources being allocated to deciding cases in an integrated market.

---

[238]   Cooperative joint ventures are dealt with under Art. 85, concentrative joint ventures under the Merger Regulation. As seen in Chapter 7, this implies important jurisdictional and procedural differences.

The most important issues arising from integration in the case of mergers are therefore institutional. As a response to more cases occurring at the EU level, procedures have to be adapted. This means in particular an increase in transparency, and the separation of competition policy concerns from other concerns. This particular recommendation could be embodied institutionally into the formation of an independent competition authority, with clear mechanisms whereby decisions of the authority can be explicitly overruled by the Commission only on grounds other than competition. That is, the Commission should not be able to overrule decisions on mergers on competition grounds, but only explicitly for example on the basis of industrial policy considerations (separation of merger policy from other policy areas).

14.6. State aids

State aid control in the EU constitutes a policy model without precedent, with the aim of separating economically justified subsidies from unjustified ones. The aim is to avoid distortions of competition and trade between Member States, although some objectives will take precedence, such as making aid compatible with the common market, even if it has distorting effects.

While this policy orientation can be regarded as economically reasonable, our analysis suggests that in the application of state aid control some problems remain unsolved. As suggested in Chapter 11, using the so-called market economy investor principle for determining the presence and the amount of aid suffers from inherent inconsistencies given the economic rationale for government subsidies.

One precondition for the application of European state aid control is an effect of the aid measure on competition and trade between Member States. Although the Commission and the European Court of Justice operate what is nearly a *per se* rule on the basis of which the conclusion of distortive effects follows almost automatically from the detection of aid, the Commission must at least give reasons why aid will distort trade and competition.

Given that in order to have any real effects subsidies have to affect firms' behaviour and, therefore, trade and competition, this rule does not seem very reasonable. If it is accepted that government subsidies are likely to have effects on competition and trade which may be justified by correcting market failures or addressing specific policy objectives (such as cohesion), then an effective approach to state aid control should require governments to prove that any financial transfer in whatever form:

(a)   is an attempt to address a specific market failure or pursue a specific policy objective;
(b)   is suitable to correct the specific market failure or promote the policy objective;
(c)   will not have adverse effects which could more than compensate for the gains from correcting the market failure. Where state aid is intended to achieve other policy objectives, the potential trade-off between efficiency and a more equal distribution should be made clear.

We therefore believe that the MEIP as a guiding principle should be revoked, that the burden of proof should lie entirely on the subsidizing governments, and that in order to receive approval these governments should have to prove the suitability and effectiveness of the measure in the pursuit of acknowledged policy objectives.

14.7. Summary

Our review of policy recommendations suggests both a tougher approach and a more relaxed stance compared to our perception of current practice. The Commission has considerable powers to deal with anti-competitive behaviour that frustrates the achievement of integration and prevents the reaping of the expected benefits of intensified competition. Those powers to support the integration objective of the single market programme are predominantly applied to restrictive practices, which may take the effect of sharing markets along national borders and, thus, inhibit integration. We conclude that the enforcement of competition policy in this area remains as important as ever, and that there are no grounds to believe that collusive behaviour, except maybe for the case of within-country collusion, is any less of a problem in the single market. We have suggested that for a broad class of cooperative agreements the scope for exemption under Art. 85(3) is perhaps too wide, given that some types of agreements are prima facie likely to frustrate integration with negative effects on the competitive process.

We further suggested that the emphasis on prohibiting price discrimination and measures facilitating price discrimination is too tough, given that price discrimination can often be justified as pro-competitive behaviour. It is in this area that the objective to achieve integration clashes with the efficiency objective underlying competition policy. Certainly for markets where integration has substantially been achieved, and where market structure does not give rise to major concerns, strict enforcement of price discrimination is counterproductive to the ultimate aim of achieving effective competition in the single market.

Similarly, we reviewed the scope for anti-competitive practices for monopolies and provided conclusions for policy. One major policy issue here for the Commission is to establish clear rules and an efficient allocation of responsibilities on access restrictions and access pricing. We suggest that DG IV, the Competition Policy Directorate of the Commission, play the role of a residual regulatory authority in areas which are not subject to Community regulation or national regulatory control. Other types of anti-competitive behaviour in monopoly situations have been reviewed and recommendations made.

One general recommendation that relates to the application of both Art. 85 and Art. 86 is that action by the competition authorities should be contingent on market structure/analysis. It is worth mentioning that our work has found that documentation on trends in concentration and price-cost margins is very difficult to obtain and is generally much worse at the EU level than at the national level. We would thus recommend to the competition authority to make it a duty to track these indicators of market structure in a systematic way.

Another important issue relates to rules that govern the implementation policy and whether they should be adjusted to the change in market size induced by market integration. The first point here is that if there should be any adjustment, this should only be towards tougher competition policy rules. In small markets the dead-weight losses are relatively small for a given exercise of market power. In larger markets these costs are larger, so that it becomes more worthwhile to spend resources on limiting the market power of firms. In this sense, for example, the market share criteria for mergers (at the EU level) should not be relaxed (i.e. raised) when the market grows.[239] Since it seems very difficult to fine-tune rules to market

---

[239]   On the other hand, it makes sense to raise indicators of financial strength to take account of the larger market size.

size, this suggests that otherwise the basic principles and rules on which competition policy rests should not be affected by market integration.

Finally, a general issue arises as to the appropriate level of resources that should be spent on the enforcement of competition policy in integrated markets. At the margin, individual competition policy decisions in integrated markets will affect a larger population. This implies that the marginal benefits of competition policy enforcement are increased, and also the marginal costs of bad decisions will be larger. Hence for every case that does raise competition policy concerns, the effort spent by the competition policy authorities should increase. This is in contrast to some commentators who argue that market integration, or trade liberalization more generally, may be a 'substitute' for the enforcement of competition policy in integrated markets. In other words competition policy in larger integrated markets becomes less important given the impact of trade liberalization. In our view, however, competition policy enforcement efforts are crucial for the achievement of the single market and have to be seen as a complement rather than a substitute.

APPENDIX A

NACE sectors included in the analysis of trade flows

NACE sectors included in the analysis of trade flows

1400	Mineral oil refining
2210	Iron and steel industry excluding integrated coke ovens
2220	Manufacture of steel tubes
2230	Drawing, cold rolling and cold folding of steel
2240	NF-Metals (Prod., Prel. Proc.)
2300	Extraction of minerals other than metalliferous and energy-producing; peat extraction
2400	Manufacture of non-metallic mineral products
2500	Chemical industry
2600	Man-made fibres industry
3110	Foundries
3120	Forging; closed die-forging, pressing, stamping
3130	Sec. transf., treatment and coating of metal
3140	Manufacture of structural metal products
3150	Boilermaking, manufacture of reservoirs, tanks and other sheet-metal containers
3160	Manufacture of tools & finished metal goods, except electrical equipment
3210	Manufacture of agricultural machinery & tractors
3220	Manufacture of machine-tools for working metal, and of other tools and equipment for use with machines
3230	Manufacture of textile mach. and accessories; manufacture of sewing mach.
3240	Manufacture of machinery for food, chem. and related ind.
3250	Manufacture of plant for mines, the iron and steel industry and foundries, civil engineering and the building trade; manufacture of mechanic handling equipment
3270	Manufacture of other machinery and equipment for use in specific branches of industry
3300	Manufacture of office machinery and data processing machinery, office and DP machinery
3440	Manufacture of telecoms equipment, electrical and electronic measuring and recording equipment and electro-medical equipment
3450	Manufacture of radios & TV receiving sets, sound reproducing and recording equipment and apparatus, manufacture of gramophone records and pre-recorded magnetic tapes
3460	Manufacture of domestic type elec. appl.
3470	Manuf. electric lamps & other electric lightening equipment
3500	Manufacture of motor vehicles and motor vehicle parts and accessories
3600	Manufacture of other means of transp.
3700	Instrument engineering
4100	Food, drink, tobacco industry
4200	Sugar manuf. and refining
4400	Leather and leather goods
4510	Manufacture of mass-produced footwear
4530	Manuf. of ready-made clothing and accessories
4610	Sawing and process of wood
4620	Manufacture of semi-finished wood products
4630	Manufacture of carpentry & joinery compon.
4640	Manufacture of wooden containers
4650	Other wood manuf. (excl. furn.)

NACE sectors included in the analysis of trade flows

4660	Manufacture of articles of cork and articles of straw and other plaiting materials; manufacture of brushes and brooms
4670	Manuf. of wooden furn.
4710	Manuf. of pulp, paper, board
4740	Publishing
4820	Retreading and repairing of rubber tyres
4940	Manufacture of toys and sports goods
5100	Building and civil engineering without specialization

APPENDIX B

NACE sectors included in the analysis of price-cost margins

NACE sectors included in the analysis of price-cost margins

2100	Extraction and preparation of metalliferous ores
2110	Extraction and preparation of iron ores
2120	Extraction and preparation of non-ferrous metal ores
2200	Production and preliminary processing of metals
2210	Iron and steel industry excluding integrated coke ovens
2220	Manufacture of steel tubes
2230	Drawing, cold rolling and cold folding of steel
2240	NF-Metals (Prod., Prel. Proc.)
2300	Extraction of minerals other than metalliferous and energy-producing; peat extraction
2310	Extraction of building materials and refractory clays
2320	Mining of potassium salt and natural phosphates
2400	Manufacture of non-metallic mineral products
2410	Manufacture of clay products for constructional purposes
2420	Manufacture of cement, lime and plaster
2430	Manufacture of concrete, cement of plaster products for constructional purposes
2440	Manufacture of articles of asbestos
2450	Working of stone and of non-metallic mineral products
2460	Production of grindstones and other abrasive products
2470	Manufacture of glass and glassware
2480	Manufacture of ceramic goods
2500	Chemical industry
2510	Manufacture of basic industrial chemicals and manufacture followed by further processing of such products
2550	Manufacture of paint, painters' fillings, varnish and printing ink
2560	Manufacture of other chemical products, mainly for industrial and agricultural purposes
2570	Manufacture of pharmaceutical products
2580	Manufacture of soap, synthetic detergents, perfume and toilet preparation
2590	Manufacture of other chemical products, chiefly for household and office use
2600	Man-made fibres industry
3100	Manufacture of metal articles (except for mechanical, electrical and instrument engineering and vehicles)
3110	Foundries
3120	Forging; closed die-forging, pressing, stamping
3130	Sec. transf., treatment and coating of metal
3140	Manufacture of structural metal products

NACE sectors included in the analysis of price-cost margins (cont'd)

3150	Boilermaking, manufacture of reservoirs, tanks and other sheet-metal containers
3160	Manufacture of tools & finished metal goods, except electrical equipment
3190	Other metal workshops not elsewhere specified
3200	Mechanical engineering
3210	Manufacture of agricultural machinery & tractors
3220	Manufacture of machine-tools for working metal, and of other tools and equipment for use with machines
3230	Manufacture of textile mach. and accessories; manufacture of sewing mach.
3240	Manufacture of machinery for food, chem. and related ind.
3250	Manufacture of plant for mines, the iron and steel industry and foundries, civil engineering and the building trade; manufacture of mechanic handling equipment
3260	Manufacture of transmission equipment for motive power
3270	Manufacture of other machinery and equipment for use in specific branches of industry
3280	Manufacture of other machinery and equipment
3300	Manufacture of office machinery and data processing machinery, office and DP machinery
3400	Electrical engineering
3410	Manufacture of insulated wires and cables
3420	Manufacture of electrical machinery
3430	Manufacture of electrical apparatus and appliances for industrial use; manufacture of batteries and accumulators
3440	Manufacture of telecoms equipment, electrical and electronic measuring and recording equipment and electro-medical equipment
3450	Manufacture of radios & TV receiving sets, sound reproducing and recording equipment and apparatus, manufacture of gramophone records and pre-recorded magnetic tapes
3460	Manufacture of domestic type elec. appl.
3470	Manuf. electric lamps & other electric lightening equipment
3480	Assembly and installation of electrical equipment and apparatus
3500	Manufacture of motor vehicles and motor vehicle parts and accessories
3510	Manufacture and assembly of motor vehicles and manufacture of motor vehicle engines
3520	Manufacture of bodies for motor vehicles and of motor-drawn trailers and caravans
3530	Manufacture of parts and accessories for motor vehicles
3600	Manufacture of other means of transp.
3610	Shipbuilding
3620	Manufacture of standard and narrow-gauge railway and tramway rolling stock
3630	Manufacture of cycles, motorcycles and parts and accessories thereof
3640	Aerospace equipment manufacturing and repairing
3650	Manufacture of transport equipment not elsewhere specified
3700	Instrument engineering
3710	Manufacture of measuring, checking and precision instruments and apparatus
3720	Manufacture of medical and surgical equipment and orthopaedic appliances

NACE sectors included in the analysis of price-cost margins (cont'd)

3430	Manufacture of optical instruments and photographic equipment
3740	Manufacture of clocks and watches and parts thereof
4100	Food, drink, tobacco industry
4110	Manufacture of vegetable and animal oils and fats
4120	Slaughtering, preparing and preserving of meat
4130	Manufacture of dairy products
4140	Processing and preserving of fruit and vegetables
4150	Processing and preserving of fish and other sea food fit for human consumption
4160	Grain milling
4170	Manufacture of spaghetti, macaroni, etc.
4180	Manufacture of starch and starch products
4190	Bread and flour confectioning
4200	Sugar manuf. and refining
4210	Manufacture of cocoa, chocolate and sugar confection
4220	Manufacture of animal and poultry foods
4230	Manufacture of other food products
4240	Manufacture of ethyl alcohol from fermented materials; spirit distilling and compounding
4250	Manufacture of wine of fresh grapes and of beverages based thereon
4270	Brewing and malting
4280	Manufacture of soft drinks, including the bottling of natural spa waters
4290	Manufacture of tobacco products
4300	Textile industry
4310	Wool industry
4320	Cotton industry
4330	Silk industry
4340	Preparation, spinning and weaving of flax, hemp and ramie
4350	Jute industry
4360	Knitting industry
4370	Textile finishing
4380	Manufacture of carpets, linoleum and other floor coverings, including leather cloth and similar supported synthetic sheetings
4390	Miscellaneous textile industries
4600	Timber and wooden furniture industries
4610	Sawing and process of wood
4620	Manufacture of semi-finished wood products
4630	Manufacture of carpentry & joinery compon.
4640	Manufacture of wooden containers
4650	Other wood manuf. (excl. furn.)

NACE sectors included in the analysis of price-cost margins (cont'd)

4660	Manufacture of articles of cork and articles of straw and other plaiting materials; manufacture of brushes and brooms
4670	Manuf. of wooden furn.
4700	Manuf. of paper and paper products; printing and publishing
4710	Manuf. of pulp, paper, board
4720	Processing of paper and board
4730	Printing and allied industries
4740	Publishing
4800	Processing of rubber and plastic
4810	Manufacture of rubber products
4820	Retreading and repairing of rubber tyres
4830	Processing of plastic
4900	Other manufacturing industries
4910	Manufacture of articles of jewellery and goldsmiths' and silversmiths' wares
4920	Manuf. of musical instruments
4930	Photographic and cinematographic laboratories
4940	Manufacture of toys and sports goods
4950	Miscellaneous manufacturing industries
5100	Building and civil engineering without specialization
5000	Building and civil engineering
5010	Construction of flats, office blocks, hospitals and other buildings, both residential and not residential
5020	Civil engineering: construction of roads, bridges, railways
5030	Installation
5040	Building completion work

APPENDIX C

Analysis of price-cost margins

C.1. Data

The data was drawn from the Survey of Industrial Production for 1980–92 compiled by Eurostat. This consists of data on a number of variables at a finely disaggregated sector level (3-digit NACE sectors) for the EUR-12 countries. This is the most recent data available from Eurostat.

Price-cost margins were calculated from this data set using two alternative definitions:

M1 = (value added - labour costs) / value added

M2 = (value added - labour costs) / sales

Both of these definitions have been used in previous empirical studies. The first (M1) has been widely used in studies assessing the relationship between profitability and concentration. The second definition (M2) has been used less widely, but does in theory conform more closely to the true definition of margin as (price - average cost)/price. The justification is as follows. Under the assumption of constant returns to scale:

(price - unit cost)/price = (sales - total cost)/ sales = profit / sales

We use (value added - labour costs) to measure profit, giving the definition M2.

Throughout we report results using both definitions of margin. The results are generally not too sensitive to which definition is used.

The original data set had a number of missing observations of variables required to calculate margins. In particular, a very large number of observations for Spain and Portugal were missing. In addition, there are a small number of sectors for which value added is less than labour cost, giving a negative margin. The approach taken was to drop those observations for which:

(a)   either M1 or M2 was not defined due to missing data;
(b)   or M1 and M2 are negative.

Thus on remaining observations, both M1 and M2 are defined. This procedure required the dropping of Spain and Portugal from the data set as there were insufficient observations left for these countries. This left an unbalanced panel with 7,917 observations.

C.2. Summary statistics

The following tables give means for the margin definition M1 across time and countries.

Table C.1.   Margin definition M1 across time and countries

	Germany	France	Italy	Netherl.	Belgium	Luxem.	UK	Ireland	Denmark	Greece	Total
80	0.354	0.470	0.515	0.432	0.495		0.406		0.250		0.422
81	0.336	0.471	0.508	0.393	0.487		0.394		0.267		0.414
82	0.346	0.464	0.513	0.398	0.513	0.337	0.403		0.280		0.420
83	0.354	0.464	0.517	0.434	0.522		0.436		0.310		0.437
84	0.358	0.443	0.539	0.448	0.510		0.443		0.317		0.438
85	0.357	0.452	0.547	0.454	0.543	0.372	0.438		0.301		0.441
86	0.361	0.464	0.560	0.469	0.555	0.402	0.436		0.301		0.451
87	0.366	0.475	0.570	0.468	0.554	0.400	0.455		0.302	0.371	0.448
88	0.377	0.499	0.578	0.462	0.584	0.397	0.467	0.475	0.369	0.360	0.466
89	0.379	0.498	0.553	0.488	0.563	0.375		0.495	0.374	0.341	0.463
90	0.388	0.494	0.540	0.458		0.423	0.435	0.486	0.376	0.361	0.446
91	0.383	0.483	0.527	0.441			0.408		0.393	0.353	0.434
92		0.456							0.401		0.432
Ttl	0.363	0.472	0.539	0.449	0.533	0.386	0.429	0.485	0.325	0.358	0.441

The average row at the bottom of this table gives an indication of the relative sizes of margins in different countries. Germany, Denmark and Greece have relatively low margins, whereas Italy and Belgium have relatively high margins. For the measure M1, the overall average level of margins was 41.1%.

The following table gives the means of M1 by group and by year.

Table C.2.   M1 by group and year

	Non-Buigues	Group 1	Group 2	Group 3	Group 4	Total
80	0.427	0.431	0.489	0.407	0.396	0.422
81	0.415	0.441	0.483	0.395	0.398	0.414
82	0.421	0.459	0.499	0.393	0.401	0.420
83	0.440	0.467	0.501	0.412	0.414	0.437
84	0.442	0.480	0.471	0.414	0.422	0.438
85	0.446	0.459	0.484	0.407	0.424	0.441
86	0.458	0.462	0.490	0.418	0.425	0.451
87	0.455	0.463	0.482	0.398	0.428	0.448
88	0.472	0.512	0.518	0.422	0.441	0.466
89	0.468	0.523	0.478	0.459	0.438	0.463
90	0.452	0.484	0.514	0.440	0.413	0.446
91	0.441	0.447	0.488	0.441	0.399	0.434
92	0.443	0.435	0.473	0.448	0.401	0.432
Total	0.446	0.470	0.492	0.419	0.417	0.441

The corresponding tables for M2 are given below.

Table C.3.   M2 by group and year

	Germany	France	Italy	Neth.	Belgium	Luxem.	UK	Ireland	Denmk	Greece	Total
80	0.129	0.173	0.176	0.142	0.181		0.151		0.087		0.151
81	0.121	0.173	0.176	0.118	0.172		0.146		0.091		0.147
82	0.123	0.168	0.176	0.124	0.182	0.145	0.146		0.096		0.149
83	0.124	0.166	0.174	0.127	0.177		0.159		0.108		0.151
84	0.124	0.155	0.176	0.140	0.174		0.159		0.108		0.149
85	0.123	0.155	0.178	0.140	0.184	0.146	0.155		0.099		0.149
86	0.127	0.161	0.187	0.153	0.191	0.163	0.155		0.100		0.155
87	0.130	0.163	0.199	0.155	0.200	0.166	0.166		0.105	0.106	0.156
88	0.134	0.169	0.190	0.157	0.204	0.161	0.171	0.175	0.149	0.103	0.162
89	0.132	0.162	0.163	0.161	0.193	0.156		0.183	0.150	0.098	0.155
90	0.134	0.159	0.161	0.151		0.172	0.154	0.179	0.148	0.099	0.149
91	0.133	0.154	0.157	0.146			0.143		0.158	0.097	0.143
92		0.155							0.163		0.159
Total	0.128	0.163	0.176	0.144	0.186	0.158	0.155	0.179	0.119	0.101	0.152

	Non-Buigues	Group 1	Group 2	Group 3	Group 4	Total
80	0.147	0.212	0.176	0.140	0.153	0.151
81	0.141	0.211	0.172	0.138	0.151	0.147
82	0.144	0.220	0.176	0.132	0.151	0.149
83	0.147	0.216	0.175	0.134	0.152	0.151
84	0.145	0.215	0.161	0.135	0.152	0.149
85	0.146	0.198	0.164	0.122	0.151	0.149
86	0.155	0.201	0.165	0.125	0.154	0.155
87	0.156	0.196	0.157	0.124	0.156	0.156
88	0.161	0.217	0.179	0.131	0.162	0.162
89	0.153	0.228	0.163	0.135	0.155	0.155
90	0.147	0.203	0.173	0.134	0.147	0.149
91	0.142	0.183	0.154	0.130	0.140	0.143
92	0.160	0.195	0.199	0.159	0.147	0.159
Total	0.149	0.208	0.168	0.132	0.152	0.152

On average, M2 is considerably less than M1 (15% compared with 44%) since the value added (the denominator of M2) is usually considerably less than sales (the denominator of M1). The pattern of cross-country and cross-group variation is similar for both measures.

C.3. Cross-country differences in margins

The following table gives the cross-country variance in average margins year by year.

Table C.4.   Cross-country variance in average margins by year

	Cross-country variance		No of
	M1	M2	countries
80	0.00725	0.00096	7
81	0.00649	0.00096	7
82	0.00633	0.00078	8
83	0.00536	0.00066	7
84	0.00524	0.00055	7
85	0.00662	0.00067	8
86	0.00697	0.00077	8
87	0.00701	0.00109	9
88	0.00603	0.00074	10
89	0.00639	0.00070	9
90	0.00320	0.00049	9
91	0.00318	0.00039	7
92	0.00076	0.00565	2

There is some evidence here of decline in the differences between margins across countries since 1987. The results for 1992 are unreliable due to lack of data.

A quick but unsophisticated test of whether this drop has been statistically significant can be achieved by testing:

H_0:   variance the same in every year

against

H_1:   variance different for the periods 1980–89 and 1990–92

using an F-test. The p-values of the F-test are 7.7% for M1 and 5.3% for M2. Thus there is a significant change in the variance during the sample period at the 10% level, though not at the 5% level.

However, this method of testing does not properly capture the cumulative impact of the single market programme from 1986 to 1992, proxying it crudely by a step change in 1990. Thus, although the test (just) fails to be significant at the 5% level, more realistic modelling of the policy impact might well produce more significant results.

C.4. Policy impact

The aim of the analysis was to identify any potential impact of the single market programme on price-cost margins. We can seek to identify this impact by looking at differences in margins:

(a)   between time periods when the single market programme was active and when it was not;

(b)   between sectors expected to be more affected by integration and those not.

There is clearly some difficulty in deciding how the single market programme impacted over time. The programme started in 1986 and concluded in 1992, with measures being introduced incrementally throughout this period. In addition, different sectors are likely to have been affected by measures at different times. Given this difficulty in modelling the impact of the programme over time, a simple ramped policy variable was created with a linear trend between 1986 and 1992. The possibility of a delayed impact of the programme was also investigated, with a trend starting in 1987.

Given the uncertainty about the timing of the impact of the programme, and consequently the appropriate definition of the policy variable, a preliminary analysis of the data using dummy variables for each year is reported.

Cross-sectoral variation in the impact of the programme was captured using the Buigues sector classification scheme.

C.5. Evolution of margins

Given the difficulty in determining the appropriate form for the policy variable, as discussed above, a preliminary analysis using time dummies was conducted. This allows the average behaviour of margins over time to be investigated without requiring a particular functional form to be specified for the policy intervention.

Margins are known to be strongly affected by the economic cycle. Thus a cycle variable was created to take account of this effect. Real GDP figures (source: OECD) were regressed on a trend, country-specific effects and country-specific trends. The residual of this regression was taken as the cycle variable.

The results of this analysis are recorded on the following pages. For each of the two definitions of margins, a random effects regression was carried out using as explanatory variables: the cycle variable; country dummies; time dummies; group dummies; group and time interaction dummies. Dummies were omitted for: Germany; the year 1980 and the non-Buigues sectors, so the reported dummies measure effects relative to these cases. The NACE sectors were modelled as having a random effect on margins, thus allowing the systematic effects of the Buigues Groups 1 to 4 to be determined. This approach was found to be an acceptable specification using the diagnostic statistics reported below (in particular passing the Hausman test which checks the validity of the random NACE effects assumption).

On the basis of these regressions, a table was drawn up of the effects of each Buigues group in each successive year. The results have been plotted in the graphs in Chapter 5 (Figures 5.4 to 5.7) for ease of comprehension. A warning must be made that the standard errors associated with the time dummies are rather large, so not too much should be inferred from the graphs in the main text; individual points on the graphs have a large measure of uncertainty associated with them. This technique is of value in understanding the data, but we claim no more; precise statistical tests are formulated in the following section.

C.6. Preliminary analysis of margin definition M1

Table C.5.   M1 by group and year

		Random-effects GLS regression
sd(u_nace)	= .0542045	Number of obs = 7917
sd(e_nace_t)	= .0821763	n = 115
sd(e_nace_t + u_nace)	= .0984432	T-bar = 60.6245
corr(u_nace, X)	= 0 (assumed)	R-sq within = 0.4772
		between = 0.0593
		overall = 0.3729

```
------------------- theta -------------------
```

min	5%	median	95%	max	chi2(74) = 7027.93
0.5490	0.7696	0.8264	0.8405	0.8479	Prob > chi2 = 0.0000

m1	Coef.	Std. Err.	z	P>|z|	[95% Conf. Interval]	
Cycle	.0198245	.0626033	0.317	0.751	-.1028756	.1425246
France	.1065755	.0032686	32.605	0.000	.1001691	.1129819
Italy	.1754828	.0032478	54.032	0.000	.1691172	.1818483
Netherl.	.0827653	.0045817	18.064	0.000	.0737853	.0917453
Belgium	.167044	.003851	43.377	0.000	.1594963	.1745918
Luxemb'rg	.0277796	.0082439	3.370	0.001	.0116217	.0439374
UK	.0665284	.0034401	19.339	0.000	.059786	.0732708
Ireland	.0863351	.0069254	12.466	0.000	.0727616	.0999086
Denmark	-.0449652	.0036298	-12.388	0.000	-.0520795	-.0378508
Greece	-.0389366	.0051849	-7.510	0.000	-.0490987	-.0287745
Group 1	.016468	.0395525	0.416	0.677	-.0610535	.0939894

Group 2	|	.0584538	.0275998	2.118	0.034	.0043592	.1125484
Group 3	|	-.0156215	.030732	-0.508	0.611	-.0758552	.0446122
Group 4	|	-.0239987	.0147471	-1.627	0.104	-.0529024	.004905
81	|	-.0103652	.006095	-1.701	0.089	-.0223111	.0015807
82	|	-.0010668	.0062924	-0.170	0.865	-.0133997	.0112661
83	|	.0132272	.0064864	2.039	0.041	.000514	.0259403
84	|	.0178346	.0063967	2.788	0.005	.0052974	.0303718
85	|	.0229607	.0063262	3.629	0.000	.0105615	.0353599
86	|	.0347906	.0062185	5.595	0.000	.0226026	.0469785
87	|	.0435777	.0061196	7.121	0.000	.0315836	.0555718
88	|	.0576942	.0057992	9.949	0.000	.0463279	.0690605
89	|	.0516419	.0059232	8.719	0.000	.0400326	.0632512
90	|	.0461861	.0059462	7.767	0.000	.0345318	.0578403
91	|	.0373321	.0062564	5.967	0.000	.0250698	.0495944
92	|	.0626626	.0099476	6.299	0.000	.0431656	.0821596
81 * Grp1	|	.0065693	.0317809	0.207	0.836	-.0557202	.0688588
82 * Grp1	|	.0162052	.031774	0.510	0.610	-.0460708	.0784811
83 * Grp1	|	.0136935	.0313361	0.437	0.662	-.0477241	.0751111
84 * Grp1	|	.0188095	.0309452	0.608	0.543	-.0418419	.079461
85 * Grp1	|	-.003359	.0313259	-0.107	0.915	-.0647566	.0580385
86 * Grp1	|	-.0123669	.031322	-0.395	0.693	-.0737568	.049023
87 * Grp1	|	-.0149349	.0312918	-0.477	0.633	-.0762658	.0463959
88 * Grp1	|	.0200188	.0302041	0.663	0.507	-.0391802	.0792177
89 * Grp1	|	.0310516	.0309317	1.004	0.315	-.0295735	.0916767
90 * Grp1	|	.0188243	.031329	0.601	0.548	-.0425794	.080228
91 * Grp1	|	-.0074882	.0318037	-0.235	0.814	-.0698224	.054846
92 * Grp1	|	-.0351333	.0444016	-0.791	0.429	-.1221588	.0518923
81 * Grp2	|	.0130262	.0212758	0.612	0.540	-.0286737	.054726
82 * Grp2	|	.0175006	.0212675	0.823	0.411	-.024183	.0591842
83 * Grp2	|	.0079468	.0212679	0.374	0.709	-.0337376	.0496312
84 * Grp2	|	-.0269727	.0212608	-1.269	0.205	-.0686431	.0146977
85 * Grp2	|	-.0191799	.0209794	-0.914	0.361	-.0602988	.0219391

86 * Grp2|	-.0282497	.0207218	-1.363	0.173	-.0688636	.0123642
87 * Grp2|	-.0360166	.0203698	-1.768	0.077	-.0759407	.0039075
88 * Grp2|	-.0144186	.020054	-0.719	0.472	-.0537237	.0248866
89 * Grp2|	-.037707	.0206102	-1.830	0.067	-.0781022	.0026882
90 * Grp2|	.0107285	.0206181	0.520	0.603	-.0296822	.0511392
91 * Grp2|	-.0031332	.0211733	-0.148	0.882	-.0446322	.0383658
92 * Grp2|	.0214261	.037978	0.564	0.573	-.0530094	.0958617
81 * Grp3|	.0104513	.0247563	0.422	0.673	-.0380702	.0589729
82 * Grp3|	-.000335	.0247484	-0.014	0.989	-.048841	.048171
83 * Grp3|	.0004629	.0245214	0.019	0.985	-.0475981	.0485239
84 * Grp3|	-.0015669	.0245153	-0.064	0.949	-.049616	.0464821
85 * Grp3|	-.0170289	.0242958	-0.701	0.483	-.0646478	.0305899
86 * Grp3|	-.0241827	.0245073	-0.987	0.324	-.0722161	.0238508
87 * Grp3|	-.023122	.0240689	-0.961	0.337	-.0702963	.0240523
88 * Grp3|	-.0257228	.0233683	-1.101	0.271	-.0715237	.0200782
89 * Grp3|	-.0051559	.0235959	-0.219	0.827	-.051403	.0410912
90 * Grp3|	-.0005949	.0237531	-0.025	0.980	-.04715	.0459603
91 * Grp3|	.0153603	.0243606	0.631	0.528	-.0323857	.0631062
92 * Grp3|	.060695	.0417924	1.452	0.146	-.0212166	.1426066
81 * Grp4|	.0119319	.0113301	1.053	0.292	-.0102746	.0341384
82 * Grp4|	.0080385	.0112259	0.716	0.474	-.0139639	.0300408
83 * Grp4|	.0046719	.0113011	0.413	0.679	-.0174779	.0268217
84 * Grp4|	.0088812	.0111551	0.796	0.426	-.0129823	.0307447
85 * Grp4|	.0080569	.0111885	0.720	0.471	-.0138722	.029986
86 * Grp4|	-.0024522	.0111029	-0.221	0.825	-.0242134	.0193091
87 * Grp4|	.0031822	.0109382	0.291	0.771	-.0182562	.0246207
88 * Grp4|	-.0012355	.0107702	-0.115	0.909	-.0223448	.0198737
89 * Grp4|	-.0021228	.0111669	-0.190	0.849	-.0240096	.0197639
90 * Grp4|	-.0068306	.0111219	-0.614	0.539	-.0286291	.0149679
91 * Grp4|	-.0097044	.0114458	-0.848	0.397	-.0321378	.012729
92 * Grp4|	-.016309	.0169352	-0.963	0.336	-.0495014	.0168833
Constant		.3397922	.0080418	42.253	0.000	.3240305	.3555538

```
-----------------------------------------------------------------------

Hausman specification test
Test:  Ho: NACE effects not systematic

            chi2( 70) = (b-B)'[S^(-1)](b-B), S = (S_fe - S_re)

                    =        0.00

        Prob>chi2 =      1.0000



        Accept Ho.
```

Table C.6.   Group and year effects for margin definition M1

Year	Overall	Group 1	Group 2	Group 3	Group 4
80	0.0000	0.0165	0.0585	-0.0156	-0.0240
81	-0.0104	0.0127	0.0611	-0.0155	-0.0224
82	-0.0011	0.0316	0.0749	-0.0170	-0.0170
83	0.0132	0.0434	0.0796	-0.0019	-0.0061
84	0.0178	0.0531	0.0493	0.0006	0.0027
85	0.0230	0.0361	0.0622	-0.0097	0.0070
86	0.0348	0.0389	0.0650	-0.0050	0.0083
87	0.0436	0.0451	0.0660	0.0048	0.0228
88	0.0577	0.0942	0.1017	0.0163	0.0325
89	0.0516	0.0992	0.0724	0.0309	0.0255
90	0.0462	0.0815	0.1154	0.0300	0.0154
91	0.0373	0.0463	0.0927	0.0371	0.0036
92	0.0627	0.0440	0.1425	0.1077	0.0224

C.7. Preliminary analysis of margin definition M2

Table C.7.   Fit of margin M2 to time dummies

```
Random-effects GLS regression

sd(u_nace)                    = .0350403          Number of obs =     7917

sd(e_nace_t)                  = .0468162                      n =      115

sd(e_nace_t + u_nace)         = .0584771                  T-bar = 60.6245


corr(u_nace, X)               = 0 (assumed)        R-sq within   =  0.2079

                                                       between   =  0.1264

                                                       overall   =  0.1785

------------------ theta -------------------

  min      5%      median       95%       max      chi2( 74)    = 2042.55

0.5932   0.7957    0.8465     0.8590    0.8656      Prob > chi2  =  0.0000



-------------------------------------------------------------------------
      m2 |      Coef.    Std. Err.       z      P>|z|     [95% Conf. Interval]
---------+---------------------------------------------------------------
   cycle |  -.0538359   .0356138    -1.512    0.131    -.1236377    .0159658

  France |   .0318594   .0018597    17.131    0.000     .0282144    .0355044

   Italy |   .0464884   .0018477    25.160    0.000     .0428669    .0501098

Netherl. |   .0196744   .0026069     7.547    0.000      .014565    .0247837

 Belgium |   .0568335   .0021911    25.939    0.000     .0525391    .0611279

Luxemb'rg|   .0291404   .0046909     6.212    0.000     .0199465    .0383343

      UK |   .0274216   .0019572    14.011    0.000     .0235856    .0312575

 Ireland |   .0489922     .00394    12.434    0.000     .0412699    .0567145

 Denmark |  -.0064897   .0020653    -3.142    0.002    -.0105376   -.0024418

  Greece |  -.0298796   .0029498   -10.129    0.000    -.0356611    -.024098

 Group 1 |   .0647337   .0245269     2.639    0.008     .0166619    .1128054

 Group 2 |   .0217971   .0172046     1.267    0.205    -.0119233    .0555175

 Group 3 |  -.0107194   .0190865    -0.562    0.574    -.0481282    .0266894

 Group 4 |   .0034982   .0091989     0.380    0.704    -.0145312    .0215277
```

81		-.007032	.0034673	-2.028	0.043	-.0138277	-.0002362
82		-.0059074	.0035796	-1.650	0.099	-.0129233	.0011086
83		-.0012513	.00369	-0.339	0.735	-.0084836	.0059809
84		-.0025591	.0036389	-0.703	0.482	-.0096913	.0045731
85		-.0019364	.0035989	-0.538	0.591	-.00899	.0051173
86		.0058847	.0035376	1.663	0.096	-.0010488	.0128182
87		.0127878	.0034813	3.673	0.000	.0059645	.0196111
88		.01698	.0032991	5.147	0.000	.0105139	.0234461
89		.0094281	.0033696	2.798	0.005	.0028237	.0160325
90		.007209	.0033827	2.131	0.033	.000579	.013839
91		.0055328	.0035592	1.555	0.120	-.0014431	.0125087
92		.0171293	.0056591	3.027	0.002	.0060378	.0282209
81 * Grp1|	-.0003538	.0180795	-0.020	0.984	-.0357889	.0350813
82 * Grp1|	.0065268	.0180755	0.361	0.718	-.0289006	.0419542
83 * Grp1|	-.0008392	.0178265	-0.047	0.962	-.0357784	.0341
84 * Grp1|	-.0013257	.0176041	-0.075	0.940	-.0358292	.0331778
85 * Grp1|	-.018422	.0178206	-1.034	0.301	-.0533498	.0165058
86 * Grp1|	-.0232069	.0178184	-1.302	0.193	-.0581304	.0117165
87 * Grp1|	-.0321061	.0178012	-1.804	0.071	-.0669958	.0027837
88 * Grp1|	-.0155308	.0171825	-0.904	0.366	-.0492079	.0181462
89 * Grp1|	.001316	.0175965	0.075	0.940	-.0331724	.0358045
90 * Grp1|	-.0147343	.0178224	-0.827	0.408	-.0496656	.020197
91 * Grp1|	-.0311171	.0180925	-1.720	0.085	-.0665776	.0043435
92 * Grp1|	-.031495	.0252592	-1.247	0.212	-.0810021	.0180121
81 * Grp2|	.0030069	.0121033	0.248	0.804	-.0207152	.026729
82 * Grp2|	.004117	.0120986	0.340	0.734	-.0195959	.0278299
83 * Grp2|	-.0007007	.0120989	-0.058	0.954	-.024414	.0230126
84 * Grp2|	-.0128249	.0120948	-1.060	0.289	-.0365303	.0108805
85 * Grp2|	-.0126446	.0119348	-1.059	0.289	-.0360363	.0107471
86 * Grp2|	-.0188353	.0117882	-1.598	0.110	-.0419397	.0042691
87 * Grp2|	-.0257033	.011588	-2.218	0.027	-.0484154	-.0029913
88 * Grp2|	-.0104781	.0114083	-0.918	0.358	-.032838	.0118818

89 * Grp2|	-.0155383	.0117247	-1.325	0.185	-.0385183	.0074418
90 * Grp2|	.0003878	.0117292	0.033	0.974	-.0226011	.0233767
91 * Grp2|	-.0132467	.0120451	-1.100	0.271	-.0368546	.0103613
92 * Grp2|	.0106734	.0216054	0.494	0.621	-.0316723	.0530191
81 * Grp3|	.0066871	.0140833	0.475	0.635	-.0209157	.03429
82 * Grp3|	-.0015965	.0140788	-0.113	0.910	-.0291905	.0259975
83 * Grp3|	-.0043445	.0139497	-0.311	0.755	-.0316853	.0229964
84 * Grp3|	-.0027265	.0139462	-0.195	0.845	-.0300605	.0246076
85 * Grp3|	-.0149369	.0138213	-1.081	0.280	-.0420262	.0121525
86 * Grp3|	-.0208452	.0139417	-1.495	0.135	-.0481704	.0064801
87 * Grp3|	-.0203146	.0136923	-1.484	0.138	-.0471511	.0065218
88 * Grp3|	-.0224601	.0132937	-1.690	0.091	-.0485153	.0035951
89 * Grp3|	-.0139414	.0134233	-1.039	0.299	-.0402507	.0123679
90 * Grp3|	-.0082431	.0135127	-0.610	0.542	-.0347275	.0182413
91 * Grp3|	-.0057393	.0138583	-0.414	0.679	-.0329012	.0214225
92 * Grp3|	.0117664	.023775	0.495	0.621	-.0348318	.0583646
81 * Grp4|	.0040797	.0064454	0.633	0.527	-.0085531	.0167125
82 * Grp4|	.0021227	.0063862	0.332	0.740	-.010394	.0146393
83 * Grp4|	-.0020866	.006429	-0.325	0.746	-.0146871	.010514
84 * Grp4|	-.0006844	.0063459	-0.108	0.914	-.0131221	.0117533
85 * Grp4|	-.0022689	.0063649	-0.356	0.721	-.0147439	.0102061
86 * Grp4|	-.0060937	.0063162	-0.965	0.335	-.0184732	.0062858
87 * Grp4|	-.0049286	.0062225	-0.792	0.428	-.0171245	.0072674
88 * Grp4|	-.0053543	.006127	-0.874	0.382	-.017363	.0066543
89 * Grp4|	-.0047539	.0063527	-0.748	0.454	-.0172048	.0076971
90 * Grp4|	-.0062371	.0063271	-0.986	0.324	-.0186379	.0061637
91 * Grp4|	-.0095476	.0065113	-1.466	0.143	-.0223096	.0032144
92 * Grp4|	-.014241	.0096341	-1.478	0.139	-.0331235	.0046414
Constant |	.1256303	.0049594	25.332	0.000	.1159101	.1353506

```
Hausman specification test:
    Test:  Ho: NACE effects not systematic
```

```
chi2( 70) = (b-B)'[S^(-1)](b-B), S = (S_fe - S_re)

          =        0.00

Prob>chi2 =      1.0000
```

Accept Ho.

Table C.8.   Group and year effects for margin definition M2

Year	Other	Group 1	Group 2	Group 3	Group 4
80	0.0000	0.0647	0.0218	-0.0107	0.0035
81	-0.0070	0.0573	0.0178	-0.0111	0.0005
82	-0.0059	0.0654	0.0200	-0.0182	-0.0003
83	-0.0013	0.0626	0.0198	-0.0163	0.0002
84	-0.0026	0.0608	0.0064	-0.0160	0.0003
85	-0.0019	0.0444	0.0072	-0.0276	-0.0007
86	0.0059	0.0474	0.0088	-0.0257	0.0033.
87	0.0128	0.0454	0.0089	-0.0182	0.0114
88	0.0170	0.0662	0.0283	-0.0162	0.0151
89	0.0094	0.0755	0.0157	-0.0152	0.0082
90	0.0072	0.0572	0.0294	-0.0118	0.0045
91	0.0055	0.0391	0.0141	-0.0109	-0.0005
92	0.0171	0.0504	0.0496	0.0182	0.0064

C.8. Assessing policy impact

It is difficult to assess the impact of integration from the previous tables. In particular, the estimates for 1992 are subject to considerable uncertainty due to lack of data. We now consider a more careful investigate of the impact of integration.

We include a policy variable of the type discussed earlier into the regression analysis and consider whether there are any significant effects. The following two tables report a variety of different model specifications (numbered 1 to 16). These models vary in a number of respects.

(a)   The definition of margin used (M1 or M2).
(b)   The date from which the policy was assumed to impact (1986 or 1987).
(c)   The modelling of the effect of the NACE sectors (either as random or fixed effects). Where NACE sectors are modelled as having fixed effects, it is not possible to identify group-specific effects so group dummies are omitted from the model.
(d)   Whether a trend which differs across groups was included or not.

The preferred models are shown in bold, which are numbers 5 and 13. These are both random effects models which pass the Hausman test. The reported t-statistics have all been corrected to be robust to heteroskedasticity.

The coefficients reported for the interaction of the policy variable and the time trend with the Buigues sectors should be interpreted as measuring (respectively) the total impact of the trend or the policy on that group. The coefficients show the impact per annum on margins for that group. For example, the coefficient of -0.002 on 'Trend * Group 1' reported for model 1 should be interpreted as saying that for Group 1 there was trend of -0.2% per annum in margins controlling for other variables.

Table C.9. Coefficient estimates for alternative models of margins

	1 M2 Random 1986	2 M2 Fixed 1986	3 M2 Random 1986	4 M2 Fixed 1986	5 **M2** **Random** **1986**	6 M2 Fixed 1987	7 M2 Random 1987	8 M2 Fixed 1987
Cycle	0.0124	0.0122	0.0132	0.0130	**0.0262**	0.0260	0.0269	0.0267
	(0.41)	(0.41)	(0.44)	(0.44)	**(0.90)**	(0.91)	(0.93)	(0.93)
France	0.0321	0.0320	0.0321	0.0320	**0.0322**	0.0321	0.0322	0.0321
	(17.37)	(27.36)	(17.35)	(27.35)	**(17.44)**	(27.48)	(17.42)	(27.47)
Italy	0.0465	0.0464	0.0465	0.0464	**0.0465**	0.0464	0.0465	0.0464
	(25.13)	(35.94)	(25.10)	(35.98)	**(25.14)**	(36.01)	(25.11)	(36.04)
Netherlands	0.0193	0.0193	0.0192	0.0193	**0.0191**	0.0192	0.0190	0.0190
	(7.40)	(9.82)	(7.36)	(9.74)	**(7.34)**	(9.76)	(7.28)	(9.65)
Belgium	0.0577	0.0577	0.0576	0.0576	**0.0575**	0.0575	0.0575	0.0574
	(26.38)	(22.75)	(26.33)	(22.62)	**(26.31)**	(22.70)	(26.25)	(22.55)
Luxembourg	0.0300	0.0300	0.0302	0.0303	**0.0296**	0.0296	0.0299	0.0300
	(6.41)	(5.43)	(6.45)	(5.52)	**(6.32)**	(5.35)	(6.39)	(5.46)
UK	0.0273	0.0274	0.0273	0.0274	**0.0273**	0.0273	0.0273	0.0273
	(13.99)	(17.29)	(13.98)	(17.27)	**(13.98)**	(17.29)	(13.96)	(17.25)
Ireland	0.0521	0.0522	0.0521	0.0522	**0.0523**	0.0524	0.0522	0.0523
	(13.54)	(7.11)	(13.52)	(7.11)	**(13.59)**	(7.13)	(13.56)	(7.13)
Denmark	-0.0061	-0.0060	-0.0062	-0.0061	**-0.0060**	-0.0059	-0.0061	-0.0060
	(-2.99)	(-3.27)	(-3.01)	(-3.29)	**(-2.92)**	(-3.19)	(-2.95)	(-3.21)
Greece	-0.0280	-0.0280	-0.0280	-0.0281	**-0.0279**	-0.0279	-0.0280	-0.0280
	(-9.58)	(-9.22)	(-9.57)	(-9.22)	**(-9.55)**	(-9.19)	(-9.55)	(-9.21)
Group 1	0.0715		0.0588		**0.0717**		0.0574	
	(2.99)		(2.64)		**(3.02)**		(2.57)	
Group 2	0.0288		0.0145		**0.0285**		0.0135	
	(1.69)		(0.90)		**(1.68)**		(0.84)	
Group 3	-0.0034		-0.0184		**-0.0033**		-0.0195	
	(-0.18)		(-1.05)		**(-0.18)**		(-1.12)	
Group 4	0.0060		0.0030		**0.0062**		0.0024	
	(0.66)		(0.34)		**(0.68)**		(0.28)	
Trend			0.0013	0.0013			0.0017	0.0017
			(3.19)	(3.28)			(5.24)	(5.32)
Trend * Group 1	-0.0020	-0.0020			**-0.0016**	-0.0016		
	(-0.81)	(-0.80)			**(-0.79)**	(-0.80)		
Trend * Group 2	-0.0027	-0.0027			**-0.0018**	-0.0018		
	(-1.61)	(-1.48)			**(-1.36)**	(-1.22)		
Trend * Group 3	-0.0029	-0.0029			**-0.0022**	-0.0022		
	(-1.46)	(-1.93)			**(-1.38)**	(-1.83)		
Trend * Group 4	0.0011	0.0011			**0.0014**	0.0014		
	(1.37)	(1.46)			**(2.18)**	(2.31)		
Trend * Non-Buigues	0.0021	0.0021			**0.0025**	0.0025		
	(4.20)	(4.45)			**(6.20)**	(6.41)		
Policy * Group 1	0.0021	0.0021	-0.0027		**0.0017**	0.0017	-0.0037	-0.0037
	(0.54)	(0.51)	(-1.67)	(-1.64)	**(0.45)**	(0.45)	(-1.97)	(-2.01)
Policy * Group 2	0.0053	0.0053	-0.0005	-0.0005	**0.0049**	0.0049	-0.0010	-0.0010
	(2.02)	(1.65)	(-0.42)	(-0.32)	**(1.91)**	(1.49)	(-0.74)	(-0.53)
Policy * Group 3	0.0054	0.0054	-0.0007	-0.0007	**0.0054**	0.0054	-0.0011	-0.0012
	(1.76)	(2.28)	(-0.49)	(-0.60)	**(1.79)**	(2.33)	(-0.73)	(-0.90)
Policy * Group 4	-0.0009	-0.0009	-0.0012	-0.0012	**-0.0018**	-0.0018	-0.0023	-0.0023
	(-0.70)	(-0.76)	(-1.55)	(-1.66)	**(-1.46)**	(-1.60)	(-2.86)	(-3.08)
Policy * Non-Buigues	-0.0009	-0.0009	0.0002	0.0002	**-0.0020**	-0.0020	-0.0007	-0.0007
	(-1.12)	(-1.17)	(0.34)	(0.36)	**(-2.55)**	(-2.61)	(-1.03)	(-1.02)
Constant	0.1188	Not	0.1212	Not	**0.1177**	Not	0.1204	Not
	(24.61)	Reported	(25.78)	Reported	**(24.53)**	Reported	(25.74)	Reported
115 NACE dummies	N/A	Not Reported	N/A	Not Reported	**N/A**	Not Reported	N/A	Not Reported
R-squared:	0.172	0.482	0.171	0.481	**0.172**	0.482	0.171	0.481
Hausman p-value	0	N/A	0.0467	N/A	**0.1338**	N/A	0.1529	N/A

	9 M1 Random 1986	10 M1 Fixed 1986	11 M1 Random 1986	12 M1 Fixed 1986	13 **M1 Random 1987**	14 M1 Fixed 1987	15 M1 Random 1987	16 M1 Fixed 1987
Cycle	0.1524	0.1520	0.1551	0.1548	**0.1459**	0.1456	0.1483	0.1480
	(2.89)	(2.71)	(2.94)	(2.76)	**(2.86)**	(2.73)	(2.91)	(2.77)
France	0.1071	0.1071	0.1071	0.1071	**0.1073**	0.1073	0.1073	0.1073
	(32.99)	(52.11)	(32.97)	(52.02)	**(33.06)**	(52.20)	(33.04)	(52.12)
Italy	0.1755	0.1756	0.1755	0.1756	**0.1755**	0.1756	0.1755	0.1756
	(54.01)	(77.80)	(53.99)	(77.90)	**(54.04)**	(77.95)	(54.02)	(78.04)
Netherlands	0.0821	0.0819	0.0819	0.0817	**0.0820**	0.0818	0.0817	0.0815
	(17.92)	(21.91)	(17.87)	(21.86)	**(17.93)**	(21.96)	(17.86)	(21.88)
Belgium	0.1686	0.1684	0.1685	0.1683	**0.1683**	0.1681	0.1683	0.1681
	(43.89)	(41.08)	(43.85)	(40.88)	**(43.83)**	(41.06)	(43.80)	(40.84)
Luxembourg	0.0294	0.0298	0.0295	0.0300	**0.0288**	0.0292	0.0290	0.0294
	(3.58)	(3.16)	(3.59)	(3.19)	**(3.50)**	(3.09)	(3.53)	(3.13)
UK	0.0660	0.0659	0.0660	0.0659	**0.0659**	0.0658	0.0660	0.0659
	(19.22)	(21.53)	(19.22)	(21.51)	**(19.23)**	(21.54)	(19.23)	(21.51)
Ireland	0.0939	0.0935	0.0939	0.0935	**0.0937**	0.0933	0.0936	0.0933
	(13.88)	(8.79)	(13.88)	(8.79)	**(13.86)**	(8.76)	(13.85)	(8.77)
Denmark	-0.0443	-0.0445	-0.0444	-0.0446	**-0.0441**	-0.0443	-0.0441	-0.0444
	(-12.30)	(-12.78)	(-12.31)	(-12.79)	**(-12.24)**	(-12.69)	(-12.26)	(-12.69)
Greece	-0.0362	-0.0365	-0.0362	-0.0366	**-0.0365**	-0.0369	-0.0366	-0.0370
	(-7.04)	(-4.83)	(-7.04)	(-4.84)	**(-7.11)**	(-4.88)	(-7.13)	(-4.90)
Group 1	0.0257		0.0238		**0.0266**		0.0234	
	(0.66)		(0.64)		**(0.70)**		(0.63)	
Group 2	0.0772		0.0494		**0.0764**		0.0477	
	(2.76)		(1.85)		**(2.79)**		(1.79)	
Group 3	-0.0037		-0.0245		**-0.0034**		-0.0255	
	(-0.12)		(-0.84)		**(-0.11)**		(-0.88)	
Group 4	-0.0183		-0.0175		**-0.0170**		-0.0183	
	(-1.22)		(-1.23)		**(-1.16)**		(-1.28)	
Trend			0.0083	0.0083			0.0079	0.0079
			(11.26)	(11.13)			(13.72)	(13.79)
Trend * Group 1	0.0083	0.0083			**0.0078**	0.0078		
	(1.90)	(2.14)			**(2.19)**	(2.41)		
Trend * Group 2	-0.0003	-0.0003			**0.0005**	0.0005		
	(-0.10)	(-0.10)			**(0.21)**	(0.20)		
Trend * Group 3	0.0021	0.0020			**0.0024**	0.0023		
	(0.60)	(0.75)			**(0.85)**	(1.02)		
Trend * Group 4	0.0092	0.0093			**0.0083**	0.0083		
	(6.60)	(7.73)			**(7.40)**	(8.56)		
Trend * Non-Buigues	0.0090	0.0090			**0.0087**	0.0087		
	(10.09)	(9.94)			**(12.34)**	(12.30)		
Policy * Group 1	-0.0052	-0.0051	-0.0051	-0.0051	**-0.0054**	-0.0053	-0.0056	-0.0056
	(-0.76)	(-0.78)	(-1.78)	(-1.69)	**(-0.80)**	(-0.82)	(-1.68)	(-1.61)
Policy * Group 2	0.0072	0.0072	-0.0053	-0.0053	**0.0074**	0.0075	-0.0050	-0.0050
	(1.56)	(1.36)	(-2.48)	(-2.03)	**(1.65)**	(1.42)	(-2.06)	(-1.65)
Policy * Group 3	0.0060	0.0059	-0.0031	-0.0031	**0.0069**	0.0069	-0.0024	-0.0025
	(1.10)	(1.37)	(-1.30)	(-1.48)	**(1.30)**	(1.53)	(-0.88)	(-1.02)
Policy * Group 4	-0.0088	-0.0088	-0.0074	-0.0074	**-0.0092**	-0.0092	-0.0085	-0.0085
	(-3.97)	(-4.58)	(-5.32)	(-5.41)	**(-4.28)**	(-4.85)	(-5.97)	(-6.19)
Policy * Non-Buigues	-0.0058	-0.0058	-0.0048	-0.0048	**-0.0068**	-0.0068	-0.0055	-0.0055
	(-4.06)	(-3.91)	(-3.88)	(-3.73)	**(-4.96)**	(-4.79)	(-4.60)	(-4.42)
Constant	0.3266	Not	0.3288	Not	**0.3264**	Not	0.3292	Not
	(40.99)	Reported	(41.76)	Reported	**(41.89)**	Reported	(42.08)	Reported
115 NACE dummies	N/A	Not Reported	N/A	Not Reported	**N/A**	Not Reported	N/A	Not Reported
R-squared:	0.3688	0.6073	0.3682	0.6066	**0.3693**	0.6079	0.3687	0.6071
Hausman p-value	0.9893	N/A	0.0068	N/A	**1**	N/A	0.0422	N/A

C.8.1.   Relative effects on Buigues and non-Buigues sectors

The following tables report the same models, but measure now the differences of the Buigues sectors relative to the non-Buigues sectors. Notice the dummies variables used here are different but the overall model is still equivalent to that used in the table above. The trend and policy variables in the tables below measure the average impact for the non-Buigues sectors. The 'trend * group x' and 'policy * group x' now measure the additional impact for group x above and beyond the impact of the trend or policy for the non-Buigues sectors.

Table C.10.   Estimated coefficients of relative impacts on Buigues sectors

Model number	1	2	3	4	5	6	7	8
Definition of margin	M2	M2	M2	M2	**M2**	M2	M2	M2
NACE effects:	Random	Fixed	Random	Fixed	**Random**	Fixed	Random	Fixed
Policy impact from:	1986	1986	1986	1986	**1987**	1987	1987	1987
Trend	0.0021	0.0021	0.0013	0.0013	**0.0025**	0.0025	0.0017	0.0017
	(4.198)	(4.447)	(3.187)	(3.276)	**(6.204)**	(6.406)	(5.237)	(5.321)
Trend * Group 1	-0.0042	-0.0042			**-0.0041**	-0.0041		
	(-1.639)	(-1.615)			**(-1.985)**	(-2.012)		
Trend * Group 2	-0.0048	-0.0048			**-0.0043**	-0.0043		
	(-2.793)	(-2.604)			**(-3.114)**	(-2.807)		
Trend * Group 3	-0.0050	-0.0050			**-0.0047**	-0.0047		
	(-2.49)	(-3.277)			**(-2.878)**	(-3.784)		
Trend * Group 4	-0.0010	-0.0010			**-0.0011**	-0.0011		
	(-1.131)	(-1.24)			**(-1.481)**	(-1.593)		
Policy	-0.0009	-0.0009	0.0002	0.0002	**-0.0020**	-0.0020	-0.0007	-0.0007
	(-1.124)	(-1.174)	(0.337)	(0.359)	**(-2.547)**	(-2.609)	(-1.029)	(-1.024)
Policy * Group 1	0.0030	0.0030	-0.0030	-0.0030	**0.0037**	0.0037	-0.0030	-0.0031
	(0.767)	(0.721)	(-1.923)	(-1.907)	**(0.962)**	(0.959)	(-1.642)	(-1.688)
Policy * Group 2	0.0062	0.0062	-0.0007	-0.0008	**0.0069**	0.0069	-0.0003	-0.0003
	(2.291)	(1.91)	(-0.69)	(-0.509)	**(2.594)**	(2.057)	(-0.245)	(-0.183)
Policy * Group 3	0.0063	0.0063	-0.0009	-0.0009	**0.0074**	0.0074	-0.0004	-0.0005
	(2.006)	(2.598)	(-0.733)	(-0.951)	**(2.386)**	(3.083)	(-0.29)	(-0.39)
Policy * Group 4	0.0000	0.0000	-0.0015	-0.0015	**0.0002**	0.0002	-0.0016	-0.0016
	(0.026)	(0.033)	(-2.559)	(-2.832)	**(0.145)**	(0.162)	(-2.357)	(-2.619)

Model number:	9	10	11	12	13	14	15	16
Definition of margin	M1	M1	M1	M1	**M1**	M1	M1	M1
NACE effects:	Random	Fixed	Random	Fixed	**Random**	Fixed	Random	Fixed
Policy impact from:	1986	1986	1986	1986	**1987**	1987	1987	1987
Trend	0.0090	0.0090	0.0083	0.0083	**0.0087**	0.0087	0.0079	0.0079
	(10.092)	(9.941)	(11.259)	(11.13)	**(12.335)**	(12.303)	(13.721)	(13.785)
Trend * Group 1	-0.0007	-0.0007			**-0.0009**	-0.0010		
	(-0.149)	(-0.175)			**(-0.26)**	(-0.291)		
Trend * Group 2	-0.0093	-0.0093			**-0.0082**	-0.0082		
	(-3.081)	(-2.997)			**(-3.375)**	(-3.269)		
Trend * Group 3	-0.0069	-0.0070			**-0.0064**	-0.0064		
	(-1.975)	(-2.5)			**(-2.227)**	(-2.706)		
Trend * Group 4	0.0002	0.0003			**-0.0004**	-0.0004		
	(0.155)	(0.186)			**(-0.299)**	(-0.33)		
Policy	-0.0058	-0.0058	-0.0048	-0.0048	**-0.0068**	-0.0068	-0.0055	-0.0055
	(-4.056)	(-3.909)	(-3.883)	(-3.726)	**(-4.963)**	(-4.792)	(-4.602)	(-4.417)
Policy * Group 1	0.0007	0.0007	-0.0003	-0.0003	**0.0015**	0.0015	-0.0001	-0.0001
	(0.096)	(0.109)	(-0.111)	(-0.101)	**(0.216)**	(0.23)	(-0.032)	(-0.025)
Policy * Group 2	0.0130	0.0130	-0.0005	-0.0005	**0.0143**	0.0143	0.0005	0.0005
	(2.724)	(2.408)	(-0.262)	(-0.207)	**(3.051)**	(2.657)	(0.222)	(0.182)
Policy * Group 3	0.0118	0.0118	0.0017	0.0017	**0.0137**	0.0137	0.0031	0.0030
	(2.129)	(2.628)	(0.794)	(0.911)	**(2.522)**	(2.952)	(1.182)	(1.355)
Policy * Group 4	-0.0030	-0.0030	-0.0026	-0.0026	**-0.0024**	-0.0024	-0.0030	-0.0030
	(-1.176)	(-1.35)	(-2.615)	(-2.823)	**(-0.957)**	(-1.074)	(-2.501)	(-2.692)

Table C.11.   Regression results using A/R classification (random NACE effects and 1987 start of policy impact)

Margin	M1	M2
Cycle	0.150672	0.027548
	(2.959)	(0.95)
France	0.107369	0.032263
	(33.094)	(17.45)
Italy	0.175536	0.046456
	(54.059)	(25.107)
Netherlands	0.081535	0.018812
	(17.82)	(7.215)
Belgium	0.168317	0.0575
	(43.838)	(26.279)
Luxembourg	0.029473	0.029938
	(3.585)	(6.39)
UK	0.065909	0.027281
	(19.226)	(13.965)
Ireland	0.093479	0.051992
	(13.837)	(13.506)
Denmark	-0.0443	-0.00613
	(-12.307)	(-2.987)
Greece	-0.03682	-0.02822
	(-7.176)	(-9.653)
A	0.093249	-0.02125
	(4.739)	(-1.677)
R	-0.01497	0.009829
	(-1.019)	(1.043)
AR	-0.07253	0.006879
	(-2.303)	(0.34)
Trend	0.007735	0.001768

Margin	M1	M2
	(10.739)	(4.309)
A * Trend	-0.00139	-0.00074
	(-0.783)	(-0.728)
R * Trend	0.001773	0.000166
	(1.252)	(0.206)
AR * Trend	-0.00015	0.000731
	(-0.051)	(0.435)
Policy	-0.0063	-0.0015
	(-4.513)	(-1.886)
A * Policy	0.006631	0.004522
	(1.933)	(2.314)
R * Policy	-0.00375	-0.00136
	(-1.387)	(-0.883)
AR * Policy	-0.00044	-0.00248
	(-0.079)	(-0.776)
Constant	0.320073	0.122683
	(40.221)	(24.166)
R-squared	0.407	0.1594
Hausman p-	0.7448	0.3613

Bibliography

Abbott, K. and Thompson, D. 'De-regulating European aviation: the impact of bilateral liberalisation', *International Journal of Industrial Organization*, Vol. 9, No 1, 1991, pp. 125–40.

Abreu, D., Pearce, D. and Stacchetti, E. 'Optimal Cartel Equilibria with Imperfect Monitoring', *Journal of Economic Theory*, Vol. 39, 1986, pp. 251–69.

Adams, W.J. *Singular Europe – Economy and Policy of the European Community After 1992*, University of Michigan Press, 1992.

Aghion, P. and Bolton, P. 'Contracts as a Barrier to Entry', *The American Economic Review*, Vol. 77, No 3, 1987, pp. 389–401.

Allen, C. 'An Empirical Model of Pricing, Market Share and Market Conduct: An Application to Import Competition in US Manufacturing', *Discussion Papers in Economics*, No 10/94, University of Sussex, 1994.

Allen, C., Stephen, A. and Bove, S. *Electrolux Group*, ECCH, Cranfield Ltd, 1991.

Anderson, S.P., Schmitt, N. and Thisse, J.F. 'Who Benefits from Antidumping Legislation?', *CEPR Discussion Paper Series*, No 731, 1992.

Anderson, S.P., de Palma, A. and Thisse, J.F. 'Spatial Price Policies Reconsidered', *Journal of Industrial Economics*, Vol. 38, 1989, pp. 1–18.

Anderson, S.P. and Thisse, J.F. 'Price Discrimination in Spatial Competitive Markets', *European Economic Review*, Vol. 32, 1988, pp. 578–90.

Armstrong, M. and Vickers, J. 'Price Discrimination, Competition, and Regulation', *Journal of Industrial Economics*, Vol. 41, 1993, pp. 335–60.

Armstrong, M. and Vickers, J. 'The Access Pricing Problem', *Discussion Papers in Economics and Econometrics*, No 9506, University of Southampton, 1995.

Armstrong, M. and Doyle, C. 'Access Pricing, Entry and the Baumol-Willig Rule', Discussion Paper No 9422, Department of Economics, University of Southampton, 1994.

Arrow, K.J. 'Economic Welfare and the Allocation of Resources for Invention', in *The Rate and Direction of Inventive Activity: Economic and Social Factors*, Princeton University Press, NBER, 1962, pp. 609–25.

Ashworth, M.H.; Kay, J.A. and Sharpe, T.A.E. 'Differentials between car prices in the United Kingdom and Belgium,' *IFS Report Series*, No 2, The Institute for Fiscal Studies, 1982.

Audretsch, D.B., Sleuwaegen, L. and Yamawaki, H. (eds.). 'The Convergence of International and Domestic Markets', *Contributions to Economic Analysis*, North Holland, 1989.

Baily, M.N. 'Competition, Regulation, and Efficiency in Service Industries', *Brookings Papers in Microeconomics*, Vol. 2, 1993, pp. 71–159.

Baldwin, R. 'The Growth Effects of 1992', *Economic Policy*, October 1989, pp. 248–79.

Barile, L. 'Opel e Ford criticano il progetto del diesel "tedesco" per il 2000', Article on Il Sole-24 Ore, 15 August 1995.

Barro, R.J. and Sala-i-Martin, X. 'Convergence', *Journal of Political Economy*, April 1992.

Baumol, W.J. 'Quasi-permanence of price reductions: a policy for preventing predatory pricing', *Yale Law Journal*, Vol. 89, 1979, pp. 1–26.

Baumol, W.J. and Gomory, R. 'International Trade and Scale Economies – A New Analysis', Discussion Paper No 205, Centre for Economic Performance, London School of Economics, 1994.

Baumol, W.J. and Sidak, J.G. 'The Pricing of Inputs sold to Competitors: Rejoinder and Epilogue', *Yale Journal on Regulation*, 1995.

Baumol, W.J. and Sidak, J.G. 'The Pricing of Inputs sold to Competitors', *Yale Journal on Regulation*, Vol. 11, 1994, pp. 171–202.

Baxter, M. 'International Trade and Business Cycles', *Working Paper Series*, No 5025, NBER, 1995.

Bean, C.R. 'Economic and Monetary Union in Europe', *Journal of Economic Perspectives*, Vol. 6, 1992, pp. 31–52.

Begg, I. 'Factor Mobility and Regional Disparities in the European Union', *Oxford Review of Economic Policy*, Vol. 11, pp. 96–112.

Bensaid, B., Encaoua, D. and Winckler, A. 'Competition , Co-operation and Mergers: Economic and Policy Issues', *European Economic Review*, Vol. 38. 1994, pp. 637–50.

Berg, A. and Sachs, J. 'Structural Adjustment and International Trade in Eastern Europe: the Case of Poland', *Economic Policy,* April 1992, pp. 118–73.

Bernheim, B.D. and Whinston, M.D. 'Multimarket Contact and Collusive Behavior', *Rand Journal of Economics*, Vol. 21, No 1, 1990, pp. 1–26.

Bernheim, B.D., 'Common Marketing Agency as a Device for Facilitating Collusion', *Rand Journal of Economics*, Vol. 16, 1985, pp. 269–81.

Besanko, D. and Perry, M.K. 'Exclusive Dealing in a Spatial Model of Retail Competition', *International Journal of Industrial Organization*, Vol. 12, 1994, pp. 646–67.

Bhattacharya, S. 'Corporate Finance and the Legacy of Miller and Modigliani', *Journal of Economic Perspectives*, Vol. 2, No 4, 1988, pp. 135–48.

Bishop, M. and Kay, J. *European mergers and merger policy*, Oxford University Press, 1993.

Blundell, Richard et al. 'Dynamic count data models of technological innovation', *Economic Journal*, March 1995.

Boehnlein, B. 'The Soda-ash Market in Europe: Collusive and Competitive Equilibria with and without Foreign Entry', *Discussion Paper*, European University Institute, 1994.

Bolton, P. and Scharfstein, D. 'A Theory of Predation Based on Agency Problems in Financial Contracting', *American Economic Review*, Vol. 80, 1990, pp. 93–106.

Bonanno, G. and Vickers, J. 'Vertical Separation', *Journal of Industrial Economics*, Vol. 36, 1988, pp. 257–65.

Borenstein, S. 'The dominant-firm advantage in multiproduct industries: evidence from US airlines', *Quarterly Journal of Economics*, November 1991, pp. 1237–66.

Borenstein, S. 'Hubs and high fares: dominance and market power in the US airline industry', *Rand Journal of Economics*, Autumn 1989, pp. 344–65.

Borenstein, S. 'Price discrimination in free-entry markets', *Rand Journal of Economics*, No 16, 1985, pp. 380–97.

Bork, R. *The Antitrust Paradox*, New York, Basic Books, 1978.

Brander, J.A. 'Strategic Trade Policy', *Working Paper Series*, No 5020, NBER, 1995.

Brander, J.A. and Spencer, B. 'Tacit Collusion, Free Entry and Welfare', *Journal of Industrial Economics*, Vol. 33, No 3, 1985, pp. 277–94.

Brander, J.A. and Spencer, B. 'International R&D Rivalry and Industrial Strategy', *Review of Economic Studies*, Vol. 50, No 4, 1983, pp. 707–22.

Brander, J.A. and Spencer, B. 'Tariffs and the Extraction of Foreign Monopoly Rents under Potential Entry', *Canadian Journal of Economics*, Vol. 14, No 3, 1981, pp. 371–89.

Braxton Associates, Horack Adler and Associates, and Prof. Morris, D. *A European Approach to Strategic Alliances*, 1995.

Bresnahan, T.F. 'Competition and Collusion in the American Automobile Industry: The 1955 Price War', *Journal of Industrial Economics*, Vol. 35, 1987, pp. 457–81.

Bresnahan, T.F. and Salop, S.C. 'Quantifying the Competitive Effects of Production Joint Ventures', *International Journal of Industrial Organization*, Vol. 4, 1986, pp. 155–75.

Brueckner, J.K. and Spiller, P.T. 'Competition and mergers in airline networks', *International Journal of Industrial Organization*, Vol. 9, No 3, 1991, pp. 323–42.

British Airways. Global Scenarios 1995–2005.

Brittan, Leon. 'European competition policy: keeping the playing field level', CEPS, 1992.

Buigues, P., Ilzkovitz, F., Lebrun, J.-F. and Sapir, A. (eds.). *Market Services and European Integration – The Challenges for the 1990s,* 1995.

Buigues, P., Ilzkovitz, F. and Lebrun, J.-F. 'The impact of the internal market by industrial sector: the challenge for the Member States', *European Economy, Social Europe*, special edition, 1990.

Buigues, P. and Jacquemin, A. 'Strategies of Firms and Structural Environments in the Large Internal Market', *Journal of Common Market Studies*, Vol. 28, 1989, pp. 53–67.

Bureau Européen des Unions de Consommateurs (BEUC). 'EEC study on car prices and progress towards 1992', BEUC/10/89, 15 October 1989.

Caballero, R.J. and Lyons, R.K. 'External Effects and Europe's Integration', in Winters, L.A., and Venables, A.J., (eds.), *European Integration: Trade and Industry*, Cambridge University Press, 1990a.

Caballero, R.J. and Lyons, R.K. 'Internal versus External Economies in European Manufacturing', *European Economic Review*, Vol. 34, 1990b, pp. 805–30.

Caminal, R. and Matutes, C. 'Endogenous Switching Costs in a Duopoly Model', *International Journal of Industrial Organization*, Vol. 8 No 3, 1990, pp. 353–73.

Caves, R. et al. 'Productivity dynamics in manufacturing plants: comments and discussion', *Brookings Papers on Economic Activity*, 1992, pp. 187–267.

Caves, R. and Barton, D.R. *Efficiency in US Manufacturing Industries*, Cambridge (Mass.), MIT Press, 1990.

Caves, R. 'Industrial organization, corporate strategy and structure', *Journal of Economic Literature*, March 1980, pp. 64-92.

Cecchini, P. et al. *The European Challenge – 1992 – The Benefits of a Single Market*, Wildwood House, 1988.

Chamley, C. and Gale, D. 'Information Revelation and Strategic Delay in a Model of Investment', *Econometrica*, Vol. 9, No 3, September, 1994, pp. 1065–85.

Civil Aviation Authority. *The Single European Aviation Market: Progress So Far*, London, 1995.

Civil Aviation Authority. *Airline Competition in the Single European Market*, London, 1993.

Cohen, W. and Levinthal, D.A. 'Innovation and learning: The two faces of R&D', *Economic Journal*, September 1989, pp. 569–96.

Comanor, W.S. and Frech, H.E. 'The Competitive Effects of Vertical Agreements?', *American Economic Review*, Vol. 75, No 3, 1985, pp. 539–45.

Comment, R. and Schwert, G.W. 'Poison or placebo? Evidence on the deterrence and wealth effects of modern anti-takeover measures', *Journal of Financial Economics*, September 1995, pp. 3–43.

Coopers and Lybrand. 'The application and possible modification of Council Regulation 95/93 on common rules for the allocation of slots at Community airports', final report, 1995.

Davidson, R., Dewatripont, M., Gisburgh, V. and Labbé, M. 'On the Welfare Effects of Anti-discrimination Regulations in the EC Car Market', *International Journal of Industrial Organization*, Vol. 7, 1989, pp. 205–30.

Davies, S. and Geroski, P.A. 'Changes in Concentration and the Dynamics of Market Shares', *Discussion Paper*, No 9415, The Economics Research Centre, University of East Anglia, 1994.

Davies, S. and Lyons, B. (eds.). *Industrial Organisation of the European Community*, Oxford University Press, 1996 (forthcoming).

Department of Trade and Industry. *Abuse of market power, a consultative document on possible legislative options*, London, HMSO, 1992.

Dixit, A.K. and Kyle, A.S. 'The Use of Protection or Subsidies for Entry Promotion and Deterrence', *American Economic Review*, Vol. 75, No 1, March, 1985, pp. 139–52.

Dobson, P.W. and Waterson, M. 'The Effects of Exclusive Purchasing on Interbrand and Intrabrand Rivalry', *Warwick Economics Working Paper*, No 94-15, University of Warwick, 1994a.

Dobson, P.W. and Waterson, M. 'Exclusivity Agreements between Manufacturers and Retailers', mimeo, University of Nottingham, 1994b.

Dowrick, S. 'Wage pressure, bargaining and price-cost margins in UK manufacturing', *Journal of Industrial Economics*, Vol. 38, No 3, March 1990, pp. 239–67.

DRI, de Ghellinck, E., Horack, Adler & Associates. *Study on the Emergence of panEuropean Markets*, final draft report, February 1996.

Eckbo, B.A. 'Horizontal mergers, industry structure and the market concentration doctrine', University of Rochester Managerial Economics Research Center Working Papers: 84-08, March 1984.

Eckbo, B.A. 'Horizontal mergers, collusion and stockholder wealth', *Journal of Financial Economics*, April 1983, pp. 241–73.

The Economist. 'Slug or Caterpillars?', 2 September 1995.

Economists Advisory Group Ltd. 'Study on oligopolistic structures in industrial markets', prepared for Commission of the European Communities, DG III, 1995.

Ehlermann, C.D. 'State Aid Control: Failure or Success?', mimeo, European Commission, 1995.

Ehlermann, C.D. 'State Aids under European Community Competition Law', *Fordham International Law Journal*, Vol. 18, 1994, pp. 410–36.

Ellison, G. 'Theories of Cartel Stability and the Joint Executive Committee', *Rand Journal of Economics*, Vol. 25, No 1, 1994, pp. 37–57.

Emerson, M. et al. 'The Economics of 1992', *European Economy*, No 35, March 1988.

Encaoua, David. 'Liberalizing European airlines: cost and factor productivity, evidence', *International Journal of Industrial Organization*, Vol. 9, No 1, 1991, pp. 109–24.

Eswaran, M. 'Cross-Licensing of Competing Patents as a Facilitating Device', *Canadian Journal of Economics*, Vol. 27, 1994, pp. 689–708.

Euromotor Reports. 'Year 2000 and beyond – the car marketing challenge in Europe', 1991.

European Commission. *Single Market Review* Volume V:4, Economies of scale, Luxembourg, Office for Official Publications of the EC and London, Kogan Page, 1997a.

European Commission. *Single Market Review* Volume II:2, Air transport, Luxembourg, Office for Official Publications of the EC and London, Kogan Page, 1997b.

European Commission. 'Competition Policy in the New Trade Order: Strengthening International Cooperation and Rules', Report of the Groups of Experts (DG IV), 1995.

European Commission. 'Competition Policy, an essential instrument for establishing the Internal Market', XXIV Report on Competition Policy, 1995, pp. 4–18.

European Commission. 'Car price differentials in the European Union on 1 May 1995', IP/95/768, Brussels, 24 July 1995.

European Commission. 'State of Community law concerning the internal market', XV/530/95/EN, 1995.

European Commission. 'Competition and Integration – Community Merger Control Policy', *European Economy*, No 57, 1994.

European Commission. 'Assessment of the implementation of Community Law regarding the internal market', *European Economy*, No 55, 1993, pp. 79–92.

European Commission. *Annual Report of the Commission on Competition Policy*, various issues.

European Commission. 'The Economics of 1992', *European Economy*, No 35, March 1988.

European Commission. 'Assessment of the implementation of Community law regarding the internal market', *European Economy*, No 55, 1993, pp. 79–92.

European Commission. *Completing the internal market: White Paper from the Commission to the Council*, COM(85) 310 final (Brussels, June 1985).

European Research Associates and Prognos. 'Obstacles to Trans-border Business Activity', in *Research on the Costs of non-Europe – Basic Findings*, Vol. 7, 1988.

Evans, A. and Martin, S. 'Socially Acceptable Distortions of Competition: Community Policy on State Aid', *European Law Review*, Vol. 16, 1991, pp. 79–111.

Evans, W.N. and Kessides, I.N. 'Localized market power in the US airline industry', *Review of Economics and Statistics*, February 1993, pp. 66–75.

Farrell, J. and Shapiro, C. 'Asset ownership and market structure in oligopoly', *Rand Journal of Economics*, Summer 1990, pp. 275–92.

Faull, J. 'Some of the questions you always wanted to ask about state aid', *EC Competition Policy Newsletter*, 1(2), 1994, pp. 48–49.

Feinberg, R.M. 'Imports as a Threat to Cartel Stability', *International Journal of Industrial Organization*, Vol. 7, 1989, pp. 281–288.

Fershtman, C. and Gandal, N. 'Disadvantageous semicollusion', *International Journal of Industrial Organization*, Vol. 12, 1994, pp. 141–54.

Fershtman, C. and Judd, K.L. 'Equilibrium Incentives in Oligopoly', *American Economic Review* Vol. 77, 1987, pp. 927–40.

Flam, H. 'Product Markets and 1992: Full Integration, Large Gains?', *Journal of Economic Perspectives*, Vol. 6, 1992, pp. 7–30.

Flam, H. and Nordstrom, H. 'Why do pre-tax car prices differ so much across European countries?', *CEPR Discussion Paper Series*, No 1181, May 1995.

Franks, J. and Mayer, C. 'Capital requirements and investor protection: An international perspective', *National Westminster Bank Quarterly Review*, August 1990, pp. 69–86.

Frazer, T. and Waterson, M. *Competition Law and Policy: Cases, Materials and Commentary*, Harvester Wheatsheaf, 1994.

Friedman, J.W. and Thisse J.F. 'Sustainable Collusion in Oligopoly with Free Entry', *European Economic Review*, Vol. 38, 1994, pp. 271–83.

Fudenberg, D. and Tirole, J. ' A "Signalling Jamming" Theory of Predation', *Rand Journal of Economics*, Vol. 17, 1986, pp. 366–76.

General Accounting Office (GAO). 'International Aviation, Airline Alliances Produce Benefits but Effect on Competition is Uncertain', report to Congressional Requesters, Washington, 1995.

Garcia Peñalosa, C. 'Small is beautiful: intentional R&D and the role of firm size', Universitat Autònoma de Barcelona, 1996.

Gasiorek, M., Smith, A. and Venables, A.J. '1992: Trade and Welfare; A General Equilibrium Model', *Discussion Paper Series*, No 672, London, CEPR, 1992.

Gasiorek, M., Smith, A. and Venables, A.J. 'Completing the Internal Market in the EC: Factor Demands and Comparative Advantage', in *European Integration: Trade and Industry*, L.A. Winters and A.J. Venables (eds.), Cambridge University Press, 1991.

Gatsios, K. and Karp, L. 'The Welfare Effects of Imperfect Harmonisation of Trade and Industrial Policy', *The Economic Journal*, Vol. 102, 1992, pp. 107–16.

George, K. and Jacquemin, A. 'Competition Policy in the European Community', in *Competition Policy in Europe and North America: Economic Issues and Institutions*, A. Jacquemin (ed.), Harwood Academic Publishers, 1990, pp. 206–45.

Geroski, P.A. and Jacquemin, A. 'Industrial change, barriers to mobility, and European industrial policy', in Geroski, P.A., and Jacquemin, A. (eds.), *The European Internal Market: Trade and Competition – Selected Readings*, Oxford University Press, 1989, pp. 298–333.

Geroski, P.A. 'Antitrust Policy towards Co-operative R&D Ventures', *Oxford Review of Economic Policy*, Vol. 9, 1993, pp. 58–71.

de Ghellinck, E., Geroski, P.A. and Jacquemin, A. 'Inter-industry Variations in the Effect of Trade on Industry Performance', *Journal of Industrial Economics*, Vol. 37, 1988, pp. 1–19.

Gilbert, R.J. and Newbery, D.M. 'Alternative entry paths, the build or buy decision', *Journal of Economics and Management Strategy*, Spring 1992, pp. 129–50.

Gilbert, R.J. and Vives, X. 'Entry deterrence and the free rider problem', *Review of Economic Studies*, No 53, 1986, pp. 71–83.

Glaister, K.W. and Buckley, P.J. 'UK International Joint Ventures: An Analysis of Patterns of Activity and Distribution', *British Journal of Management*, Vol. 5, 1994, pp. 33–51.

Goyder, J. *EC Distribution Law*, European Practice Library, London, Chancery Law Publishing, 1992.

Green, N. *Commercial Agreements and Competition Law: Practice and Procedure in the UK and EEC*, London, Graham and Trotman, 1986.

Green, N. and Porter, R.H. 'Non-cooperative Collusion under Imperfect Price Information', *Econometrica*, Vol. 52, 1984, pp. 87–100.

Grossman, G.M. 'Book Reviews', *Journal of International Economics*, Vol. 28, North Holland, 1990, pp. 385–88.

Grossman, G.M. and Hart, O. 'The costs and benefits of ownership: a theory of lateral and vertical integration', *Journal of Political Economy*, No 94, 1986, pp. 691–719.

Grossman, G.M. and Shapiro, C. 'Optimal dynamic R&D programs', *Rand Journal of Economics*, No 17, 1986, pp. 581–93.

Gual, Jordi. 'An econometric analysis of price differentials in the EEC automobile market', *Applied Economics*, Vol. 25, No 5, May 1993, pp. 599–607.

Haaland, J.I. and Norman, V.D. 'Global Production Effects of European Integration', *Discussion Paper Series*, No 669, London, CEPR, 1992.

Haaland, J.I. 'Trade effects of European integration', *Discussion Paper*, 8/94, Norwegian School of Economics, July 1994.

Hackner, J. 'Collusive Pricing in Markets for Perfectly Differentiated Products', *International Journal of Industrial Organization*, Vol. 12, 1994, pp. 155–77.

Hancher, L.T., Ottervanger, T. and Slot P.J. *EC State Aids,* Chancery Law Publishing, 1994.

Hancher, L.T. 'State aids and judicial control in the European Community', *ECLR* 3, 1994, pp.134–50.

Harbord, D. and Hoehn, T. 'Barriers to Entry and Exit in European Competition Policy', *International Review of Law and Economics*, Vol. 14, 1994, pp. 411–35.

Harriman Chemsult Ltd. Monthly reports, various issues, 1995.

Harrington, J.E. 'Collusion and Predation under (almost) Free Entry', *International Journal of Industrial Organization*, Vol. 7, 1989, pp. 381–401.

Harris, C. and Vickers, J. 'Patent Races and the Persistence of Monopoly', *Journal of Industrial Economics*, Volume 33, 1985, pp. 461–77.

Harris, C. and Vickers, J. 'Racing with Uncertainty', *Review of Economic Studies*, Vol. 54, No 1, 1987, pp.1–21.

Harstad, R.M. and Phlips, L. 'Informational Requirements of Collusion Detection: Simple Seasonal Markets', mimeo, European University Institute, 1994.

Hart, O.L. 'The Market Mechanism as an Incentive Scheme', *Bell Journal of Economics*, Vol. 1, 1983.

Hart, O.L. and Moore, J. 'Property Rights and the Nature of the Firm', *Journal of Political Economy*, Vol. 98, 1990, pp. 1119–58.

Hart, O. 'Corporate governance: Some theory and implications', *Economic Journal*, Vol. 105, No 430, May 1995, pp. 678–89.

Hausman, J.A. and MacKie-Mason, J.K. 'Price Discrimination and Patent Policy', *Rand Journal of Economics*, Vol. 19, 1988, pp. 253–65.

Hausman, J.A., Leonard, G. and Zona, J.D. 'Competitive analysis with differentiated products', *Annales d'économie et de statistique*, April-June 1994, pp. 159–80.

Hay, D. 'The Assessment: Competition Policy', *Oxford Review of Economic Policy*, Vol. 9, No 2, Oxford University Press, 1993, pp. 1–26.

Hay, D. and Morris, D.J. *Industrial Economics and Organization*, Oxford University Press, 1991.

Helpman, E. and Krugman, P. *Trade Policy and Market Structure*, Cambridge (Mass.), MIT Press, 1989.

Hergert, M. and Morris, D. 'Trends in international collaborative agreements', in *Cooperative strategies in international business*, Heath, Lexington, 1988, pp. 99–109.

Hoekman, B.B. and Mavroidis, P.C. 'Competition, Competition Policy and the GATT', *Discussion Paper Series*, No 876, London, CEPR, 1994.

Hoekman, B.B. 'The WTO's Agreement on Government Procurement: Expanding Disciplines, Declining Membership', Discussion Paper No 1112, CEPR, January 1995.

Holmström, B. 'Moral Hazard in Teams', *Bell Journal of Economics*, Vol. 13, 1982, pp. 324–40.

Holmström, B. and Milgrom, P. 'Aggregation and Linearity in the Provision of Intertemporal Incentives', *Econometrica*, Vol. 55, 1987, pp. 303–28.

Horn, H., Lang, H. and Lundgren, S. 'Managerial Effort Incentives, X-inefficiency and International Trade', *European Economic Review*, Vol. 39, 1995, pp. 117–38.

Huston, J.H. and Butler, R.V. 'Airline hubs in the single European market', *Review of Industrial Organization*, August 1993, pp. 407–17.

Jacquemin, A. (ed.). *Competition Policy in Europe and North America: Economic Issues and Institutions*, Harwood Academic Publishers, 1990.

Jacquemin, A. 'Co-operative Agreements in R&D and European Antitrust Policy', *European Economic Review*, Vol. 32, 1988, pp. 551–60.

Jacquemin, A. and Sapir, A. 'The discipline of imports in the European markets', in *European Trade and Industry: The Impact of 1992,* A.J. Venables and L.A. Winters (eds.), Cambridge University Press, 1991.

Jacquemin, A. and Sapir, A. 'Competition and Imports in the European Market', in Winters, L.A., and Venables, A.J., (eds.), *European Integration: Trade and Industry*, Cambridge University Press, 1991.

Jacquemin, A. and Sapir, A. 'International Trade and Integration of the European Community', *European Economic Review*, Vol. 32, 1988.

Jacquemin, A. and Wright, D. 'Corporate Strategies and European Challenges Post-1992', *Journal of Common Market Studies*, Vol. 31, 1993, pp. 525–37.

Jaffee, D. and Russell, T. 'Imperfect Information, Uncertainty and Credit Rationing', *Quarterly Journal of Economics*, Vol. 90, No 4, 1976, pp. 651–66.

Kamien, M.I., and Schwartz, N.L. 'Cournot oligopoly with uncertain entry', *Review of Economic Studies*, January 1975, pp. 125–31.

Katics, M.M., and Petersen, B.C. 'The Effect of Rising Import Competition on Market Power: A Panel Data Study of USA Manufacturing', *Journal of Industrial Economics*, Vol. 42, 1994, pp. 277–86.

Katz, M.L. 'The Welfare Effects of Third-Degree Price Discrimination in Intermediate Goods Markets', *American Economic Review*, Vol. 77, 1987.

Katz, M.L. 'Vertical contractual relations', in *Handbook of Industrial Organization*, Vol. 1, Schmalensee, R. and Willig R.D. (eds.), New York, Elsevier Science, 1989.

Kay, J.A. 'Myths and Realities' in *1992 – Myths and Realities*, Centre for Business Strategy, London Business School, 1989.

Kay, N. 'Industrial Collaborative Activity and the Completion of the Internal Market', *Journal of Common Market Studies*, Vol. 29, 1991, pp. 347–62.

Keeler, J.P. and Formby, J.P. 'Cost economies and consolidation in the US airline industry', *International Journal of Transport Economics*, February 1994, pp. 21–45.

Kim, E. Han and Singal, V. 'Mergers and market power: evidence from the airline industry', *American Economic Review*, June 1993, pp. 549–69.

Klemperer, P.D. 'Competition when Consumers have Switching Costs: An Overview', Review of Economic Studies Lecture, presented at the Royal Economic Society Annual Conference, 1990.

Klemperer, P.D 'The competitiveness of markets with switching costs', *Rand Journal of Economics*, Spring 1987, pp. 137–50.

Korah, V. and Rothnie, W.A. *Exclusive Distribution and the EEC Competition Rules* (second edition), European Competition Law Monographs, London, Sweet and Maxwell, 1993.

Kreps, D. and Wilson, R. 'Reputation and Imperfect Information', *Journal of Economic Theory*, Vol. 27, 1982, pp. 253–79.

Krishna, K. 'Trade Restrictions as Facilitating Practices', *Journal of International Economics*, Vol. 26, 1989, pp. 251–70.

Krugman, P.R. *The age of diminished expectations: US economic policy in the 1990s*, MIT Press, 1994.

Krugman, P.R. *Rethinking International Trade*, Cambridge (Mass.), MIT Press, 1990.

Krugman, P.R. 'Macroeconomic Adjustment and Entry into the EC: a note', in Winters, L.A., and Venables, A.J. (eds.), *European Integration: Trade and Industry*, Cambridge University Press, 1990.

Krugman, P.R. 'Scale Economies, Product Differentiation, and the Pattern of Trade', *American Economic Review*, 1980, pp. 950–59.

Krugman, P.R. and Venables, A.J. 'Integration, Specialization and Adjustment', *Discussion Paper Series*, No 886, London, CEPR, December 1993.

Kühn, K.-U. 'Labour contracts, product market oligopoly and involuntary unemployment', *Oxford Economic Papers*, Vol. 46, No 3, July 1994, pp. 366–84.

Kühn, K.-U., Seabright, P. and Smith, A. 'Competition Policy Research: Where do we stand?', Occasional Paper No 8, CEPR, 1992.

Kühn, K.-U. and Vives, X. *Information Exchanges among Firms and their Impact on Competition,* Commission of the European Communities, 1995.

Kühn, K.J. and Vives, X. 'Excess Entry, Vertical Integration, and Welfare', Working Paper, Barcelona, 1994.

Kühn, K.J. 'On the Role of Economic Theory in Competition Policy', *Cuadernos Economicos*, Vol. 57, 1994, pp. 9–29.

Laffont, J.J. and Tirole, J. 'Access Pricing and Competition', *European Economic Review*, Vol. 38, 1994, pp. 1673–1710.

Layson, S.K. 'Market Opening under Third-degree Price Discrimination', *Journal of Industrial Economics*, Vol. 42, 1994, pp. 335–40.

Lehner, S. and Meiklejohn, R. 'Fair Competition in the Internal Market: Community State Aid Policy', *European Economy*, Vol. 48, 1991, pp. 7–114.

Levenstein, M. 'Price Wars and the Stability of Collusion: A Study of the Pre-World War I Bromine Industry', *Working Paper Series on Historical Factors in the Long Run Growth*, No 50, 1993, NBER.

Levinsohn, J. 'Competition Policy and International Trade', Discussion Paper No 362, Institute of Public Policy Studies, The University of Michigan, 1994.

Lichtenberg, F.R. 'Industrial de-diversification and its consequences for productivity', *Journal of Economic Behavior and Organization*, August 1992, pp. 427–38.

Logan, J.W. and Lutter, R. W. 'Guaranteed Lowest Prices: Do They Facilitate Collusion?', *Economic Letters*, Vol. 31, 1989, pp. 189–92.

Lyons, B.R. and Matraves, C. 'Industrial Concentration and Endogenous Sunk Costs in the European Union', Discussion Paper No 9505, Norwich, UEA, 1995.

MacDonald, J.M. 'Does Import Competition Force Efficient Production?' *Review of Economics and Statistics*, 1994, pp. 721–27.

MacLeod, W.B., Norman, G. and Thisse, J.F. 'Competition, Tacit Collusion and Free Entry', *The Economic Journal*, Vol. 97, 1987, pp. 189–98.

MacLeod, W.B. 'A Theory of Conscious Parallelism', *European Economic Review*, Vol. 27, 1985, pp. 25–44.

Malueg, D.A. and Schwartz, M. 'Parallel Imports, Demand Dispersion, and International Price Discrimination', *Journal of International Economics*, Vol. 37, No 3–4, 1994, pp. 167–95.

Mankiw, N.G. and Whinston, M.D. 'Free entry and social inefficiency', *Rand Journal of Economics*, Vol. 17, 1986, pp. 48–58.

Marin, P. 'The Remains of Regulation: Airlines' Profits After Liberalization', *Working Paper, The Economics of Industry Group*, London, London School of Economics, 1995.

Martin, S. 'Private and Social Incentives to Form R&D Joint Ventures', *Review of Industrial Organisation*, Vol. 9, 1994, pp. 157–171.

Martin, S. and Hartley, K. 'European Collaboration in Civil Aerospace: Success or Failure ?', *Journal of Common Market Studies*, Vol. 32, 1995, pp. 275–91.

Marvel, H.P. 'Exclusive Dealing', *Journal of Law and Economics*, Vol. 25, 1982, pp. 1–25.

Mathewson, G.F. and Winter, R.A. 'The Competitive Effect of Vertical Agreements: Comment', *American Economic Review*, Vol. 77, No 5, 1987, pp. 1057–62.

Mathewson, G.F. and Winter, R.A. 'The Economics of Franchise Contracts', *Journal of Law and Economics*, Vol. 28, 1985, pp. 503–26.

Mathewson, G.F. and Winter, R.A. 'An Economic Theory of Vertical Restraints', *Rand Journal of Economics*, Vol. 15, No 1, 1984, pp. 27–38.

Matutes, C. and Regibeau, P. 'Standardization across Markets and Entry', *Journal of Industrial Economics*, Vol. 37, No 4, 1989, pp. 359–71.

McAfee, R.P. and Williams, M.A. 'Can event studies detect anti-competitive mergers?', *Economics Letters*, Vol. 28, No 2, 1988, pp. 199–203.

McGuckin, R.H. and Nguyen, S.V. 'On productivity and plant ownership change: New evidence from the Longitudinal Research Database', *Rand Journal of Economics*, Summer 1995, pp. 257–76.

de Melo, J. and Urata, S. 'The Influence of Increased Foreign Competition on Industrial Concentration and Profitability', *International Journal of Industrial Organization*, Vol. 4, 1986, pp. 287–304.

Mertens, Y. and Ginsburgh, V. 'Product differentiation and price discrimination in the European Community. The case of automobiles', *Journal of Industrial Economics*, Vol. 34, December 1985.

Meyer, M.A. and Vickers, J. 'Performance Comparisons and Dynamic Incentives', Discussion Paper No 1107, Centre for Economic Policy Research, 1995.

Milgrom, P. and Roberts, J. 'Limit Pricing and Entry under Incomplete Information and Equilibrium Analysis', *Econometrica*, Vol. 50, 1982, pp. 443–59.

Miller, M. 'The Modigliani-Miller Proposition After Thirty Years', *Journal of Economic Perspectives*, Vol. 2, No 4, 1988, pp. 99–120.

Millington, A.I. and Bayliss, B.T. 'Trans-national Joint Ventures between UK and EU Manufacturing Companies and the Structure of Competition', *Journal of International Business Studies*, Vol. 26, No 2, 1995, pp. 239–54.

MMC. 'New motor cars: a report on the supply of new motor cars within the United Kingdom', 1992.

Modigliani, F. 'MM – Past, Present, Future', *Journal of Economic Perspectives* 2, 1988, pp.149–58.

Modigliani, F. and Miller, M. 'The Cost of Capital, Corporate Finance, and the Theory of Investment', *American Economic Review*, Vol. 48, 1958, pp. 261–97.

Molyneux, P. 'European Links', *Banking World*, September 1991, pp. 25–27.

Montagnon, P. 'The Trade Policy Connection', in *European Competition Policy*, P. Montagnon (ed.), London, Royal Institute for International Affairs, 1991, pp. 76–98.

Mookherjee, D. 'Optimal incentive schemes with many agents', *Review of Economic Studies*, No 51, 1984, pp. 433–46.

Moore, J. 'The Firm as a Collection of Assets', *European Economic Review*, Vol. 36, 1992, pp. 493–507.

Morris, D. and Hegert, M. 'Trends in International Collaborative Agreements', *Columbia Journal of World Business*, 1987, pp. 15–21.

Mytelka, L.K. and Delapierre, M. 'The Alliance Strategies of European Firms in the Information Technology Industry and the Role of Esprit', *Journal of Common Market Studies*, Vol. 2, 1987, pp. 231–53.

Nalebuff, B. and Stiglitz, J. 'Information, Competition and Markets', *American Economic Review*, Vol. 73, 1983, pp. 278–83.

Nerb, G. 'A Survey of European Industry's Perceptions of the Likely Effects', in *Research on the Costs of non-Europe – Basic Findings*, Vol. 3, 1988.

Neven, D.J. 'The Political Economy of State Aids in the European Community: Some Econometric Evidence', *Discussion Paper Series*, No 945, Centre for Economic Policy Research, April 1994.

Neven, D.J. 'EEC Integration towards 1992: Some Distributional Aspects', *Economic Policy*, April 1992, pp. 14–62.

Neven, D.J. 'EC Integration towards 1992: Some Distributional Aspects', *European Policy*, Vol. 10, 1990, pp. 13–63.

Neven, D.J., Norman, G., and Thisse, J.F. 'Attitudes towards Foreign Products and International Price Competition', *Canadian Journal of Economics*, Vol. 24, 1991, pp. 1–11.

Neven, D.J., Nuttall, R., and Seabright, P. *Mergers in Daylight: The Economics and Politics of European Merger Control*, Centre for Economic and Policy Research, London, 1993.

Neven, D.J. and Phlips, L. 'Discriminating Oligopolists and Common Markets', *Journal of Industrial Economics*, Vol. 34, 1985, pp. 133–49.

Neven, D.J., and Röller, L.H. 'European integration and trade flows', *European Economic Review*, Vol. 35, No 6, 1991, pp. 1295–1309.

Neven, D.J. and Röller, L.H. 'European Integration and Trade Flows', *Discussion Paper Series*, No 367, Centre for Economic Policy Research, 1990.

Neven, D.J. and Seabright, P. 'Trade Liberalisation and the Co-ordination of Competition Policy', *Cahiers de Recherche Économiques*, No 9503, 1995, Université de Lausanne.

Nickell, S.J. 'Competition and Corporate Performance', *Journal of Political Economy*, Vol. 104, No 4, 1996, pp. 724–46.

Nickell, S.J., Wadhwani, S. and Wall, M. 'Productivity Growth in UK Companies, 1975–86', *European Economic Review*, Vol. 36, 1992, pp. 1055–91.

Norman, V. 'EFTA and the Internal European Market', *Economic Policy*, 1989, pp. 424–65.

Nye, W. 'Can a joint venture lessen competition more than a merger ?', *Economics Letters*, Vol. 40, pp. 487–89.

OECD. 'The EC's Internal Market: Implementation, Economic Consequences, Unfinished Business', Vol. II, OECD Working Papers No 52, 1994, Paris.

OECD. *Competition Policy and Vertical Restraints: Franchising Agreements*, Paris, 1994.

Onida, F. 'Structural Change and International Integration of the European Single Market', in Barfield, C.E. and Perlman, M. (eds.), *Industry, Services, and Agriculture. The United States Faces a United Europe*, Washington D.C., The AEI Press, 1992.

Ordover, J.A. and Willig, R.D. 'Antitrust for high-technology industries: Assessing research joint ventures and mergers', *Journal of Law and Economics*, May 1985, pp. 311–33.

Ornstein, S.I. 'Exclusive Dealing and Antitrust', *Antitrust Bulletin*, Vol. 34, 1989, pp. 65–98.

Phlips, L. *Competition Policy: A Game-theoretic Perspective*, Cambridge University Press, 1995.

Phlips, L. 'On the Detection of Collusion and Predation', mimeo, European University Institute, 1995a.

Phlips, L. *The Economics of Price Discrimination*, Cambridge University Press, 1983.

Phlips, L. and Moras, I.M. 'The AKZO decision: a case of predatory pricing?', *Journal of Industrial Economics*, Vol. 41, No 3, 1993, pp. 315–21.

Porter, R.H. 'Recent developments in empirical industrial organization', *Journal of Economic Education*, Spring 1994, pp. 149–61.

Porter, R.H. 'On the Incidence and Duration of Price Wars', *Journal of Industrial Economics*, Vol. 33, No 4, 1985, pp. 415–26.

Porter, R.H. 'A Study of Cartel Stability: The Joint Executive Committee, 1880–1886', *Bell Journal of Economics*, Vol. 14, 1983, pp. 301–14.

Posner, R.A. 'The Next Step in the Antitrust Treatment of Restricted Distribution: Per Se Legality', *University of Chicago Law Review*, Vol. 48, No 1, 1981, pp. 6–26.

Prager, R.A. 'The effects of horizontal mergers on competition: The case of the Northen Securities Company', *Rand Journal of Economics*, Spring 1992, pp. 123–33.

Rasmusen, E.B., Ramseyer, J.M. and Wiley, J.S. 'Naked Exclusion', *The American Economic Review*, 1991, pp. 1137–45.

Rees, R. 'Tacit Collusion', *Oxford Review of Economic Policy*, Vol. 9, Oxford University Press, 1993a, pp. 27–40.

Rees, R. 'Collusive Equilibrium in the Great Salt Duopoly', *The Economic Journal*, Vol. 103, 1993b, pp. 833–48.

Rey, P. and Stiglitz, J.E. 'Vertical restraints and producers' competition,' Working Paper 2601, National Bureau of Economic Research, March 1988.

Rey, P. and Tirole, J. 'The Logic of Vertical Restraints', *American Economic Review*, Vol. 76, No 5, 1986, pp. 921–39.

Rey, P. et al. 'The role of exclusive territories in producers' competition', *Rand Journal of Economics*, Autumn 1995, pp. 431–51.

Roberts, J. 'A Signalling Model of Predatory Pricing', *Oxford Economic Papers*, Vol. 38, Supp., 1986, pp. 75–93.

Romer, P.M. 'Increasing returns, specialization and external economies: Growth as described by Allyn Young', working paper, University of Rochester Center for Economic Research, December 1986.

Ross, T.W. 'Cartel Stability and Product Differentiation', *International Journal of Industrial Organization*, Vol. 10, 1992, pp. 1–13.

Rotemberg, J. and Saloner, G. 'A Supergame-Theoretic Model of Price Wars During Booms', *American Economic Review*, Vol. 76, 1986, pp. 390–407.

Rotemberg, J. 'Collusive Price Leadership', *Journal of Industrial Economics*, Vol. 39, 1990, pp. 93–111.

Rotemberg, J. 'The Cyclical Behavior of Strategic Inventories', *Quarterly Journal of Economics*, Vol. 104, 1989, pp. 73–97.

Salop, S.C. and Scheffman, D.T. 'Raising Rivals Costs', *American Economic Review*, Vol. 73, 1983, pp. 267–71.

Salop, S.C. and Scheffman, D.T. 'Cost-raising strategies', working paper, Federal Trade Commission Bureau of Economics, July 1986.

Sapir, A., Buigues, P. and Jacquemin, A. 'European Competition Policy in Manufacturing and Services: A Two-speed Approach?', *Oxford Review of Economic Policy*, Vol. 9, No 2, 1993, pp. 113–32.

Scharfstein, D. 'Product-Market Competition and Managerial Slack', *Rand Journal of Economics*, Vol. 19, 1988, pp. 147–55.

Scherer, F. and Ross, T. *Industrial market structure and economic performance*, Chicago, Rand McNally, revised 1990.

Scherer, F. 'Research and development resource allocation under rivalry', *Quarterly Journal of Economics*, No 131, 1967, pp. 359–94.

Scherer, F.M. et al. *The economics of multi-plant operation: An international comparisons study*, Harvard University Press, 1975.

Schmalensee, R. 'Ease of entry: Has the concept been applied too readily?', 1981, pp. 41–51.

Schmidt, P. 'Frontier production functions', *Econometric Reviews*, Vol. 4, No 2, 1985, pp. 289–328.

Schnitzer, M. 'Dynamic Duopoly with Best Price Clauses', *Rand Journal of Economics*, Vol. 25, 1994, pp. 186–196.

Selten, R. 'A Simple Model of Imperfect Competition Where Four are Few and Six are Many', *International Journal of Game Theory*, Vol. 2, 1973, pp. 141–201.

Seth, R. 'Leverage and cyclicality', Federal Reserve Bank of New York Research Paper, September 1990.

Shaked, A. and Sutton, J. 'Product differentiation and industrial structure', *Journal of Industrial Economics*, Vol. 36, No 2, December 1987, pp. 131-46.

Shama, A. 'Entry Strategies of US Firms to the Newly Independent States, Baltic States, and Eastern European Countries', *California Management Review*, Vol. 37, 1995, pp. 90–109.

Shapiro, C. 'Aftermarkets and Consumer Welfare: Making Sense of Kodak', *Antitrust Law Joural*, Vol. 63, No 2, 1995, pp. 483–513.

Shapiro, C. and Willig, R.D. 'On Antitrust Treatment of Production Joint Ventures', *Journal of Economic Perspectives*, Vol. 4, 1990, pp. 113–29.

Silberston, A. and Raymond, C.P. *The changing industrial map of Europe*, Macmillan Press, 1996.

Slade, M.E. 'Interfirm Rivalry in a Repeated Game: An Empirical Test of Tacit Collusion', *Journal of Industrial Economics*, Vol. 35, 1987, pp. 499–516.

Sleuwaegen, L. and Yamawaki, H. 'The Formation of the European Common Market and Changes in Market Structure and Performance', *European Economic Review*, Vol. 32, 1988, pp. 1451–75.

Smith, A. 'The market for cars in the enlarged European Community', Discussion Paper No 360, London, Centre for Economic Policy Research (CEPR), 1989.

Smith, A. and Venables, A.J. 'Economic Integration and Market Access', *European Economic Review*, Vol. 35, 1991, pp. 388–95.

Smith, A. and Venables, A.J. 'Completing the Internal Market in the European Community', *European Economic Review*, Vol. 32, 1988, pp. 1501–25.

Staiger, R.W. and Wolak, F.A. 'Collusive Pricing with Capacity Constraints in the Presence of Demand Uncertainty', *Rand Journal of Economics*, Vol. 23, 1992, pp. 203–20.

Stålhammar, N.O. 'Domestic Market Power and Foreign Trade', *International Journal of Industrial Organization*, Vol. 9, 1991, pp. 407–24.

Steuer, R.M. 'Exclusive Dealing in Distribution', *Cornell Law Review*, Vol. 69, 1983, pp. 101–34.

Stigler, G.J. *The Organization of Industry*, Homewood, Richard D. Irwin Inc., 1968.

Stigler, G.J. 'A Theory of Oligopoly', *Journal of Political Economy*, Vol. 72, 1964, pp. 44–61.

Stigler, G.J. 'Monopoly and oligopoly by merger', *American Economic Review*, May 1950, pp. 23–34.

Stiglitz, J. 'Why Financial Structure Matters', *Journal of Economic Perspectives*, Vol. 2, No 4, 1988, pp. 121–26.

Stiglitz, J. and Weiss, A. 'Credit Rationing in Markets with Imperfect Information', *American Economic Review*, Vol. 71, 1981, pp.393–410.

Stillman, R. 'Examining antitrust policy towards horizontal mergers', *Journal of Financial Economics*, April 1983, pp. 225–40.

Sutton, J. *Sunk Costs, and Market Structure: Price Competition, Advertising and the Evolution of Concentration*, London, MIT Press, 1991.

Telser, L. 'Cutthroat Competition and the Long Purse', *Journal of Law and Economics*, Vol. 9, 1966, pp. 259–77.

Telser, L. 'Why Should Manufacturers Want Fair Trade?', *Journal of Law and Economics*, 1960.

Thisse, J.F. and Vives, X. 'On Strategic Choice of Spatial Price Policy', *The American Economic Review*, Vol. 78, 1988, pp. 122–37.

Town, R.J. 'Merger waves and the structure of merger and acquisition time-series', *Journal of Applied Econometrics*, December 1992, pp. S83–S100.

UK Department of Trade and Industry. *The Single Market – Progress on Commission White Paper*, Business in Europe, May 1993.

Varian, H. 'Sequential provision of public goods', University of Michigan Center for Research on Economic and Social Theory Working Paper, July 1989.

Varian, H. 'Price discrimination and social welfare', *American Economic Review*, No 75, 1985 pp. 870–75.

Vickers, J. *Concepts of Competition*, Oxford, Clarendon Press, 1994.

Vickers, J. 'Delegation and the Theory of the Firm', *Economic Journal Supplement* (Conference Papers), 1985, pp. 138–47.

Vickers, J. and Hay, D. (eds.). *The Economics of Market Dominance*, Oxford, Blackwell, 1987.

Vickers, J. and Yarrow, G. *Privatization – An Economic Analysis*, MIT Press, 1988.

Vives, X. 'Banking competition and European integration', in *European Financial Integration*, A. Giovannini and C. Mayer (eds.), Cambridge, Cambridge University Press, 1991.

Waterson, M. 'Vertical Integration and Vertical Restraints', *Oxford Review of Economic Policy*, Vol. 9, No 2, Oxford University Press, 1993, pp. 41–57.

Waterson, M. 'On Vertical Restraint and the Law', Discussion Paper No 87-13, Department of Economics, University of Newcastle Upon Tyne, 1987.

van Wegberg, M. et al. 'Multimarket and Multiproject Collusion: Why European Integration May Reduce Intra-Community Competition', *De-Economist*, Vol. 142, 1994, pp. 253–85.

von Weizsäcker, C.C. 'A Welfare Analysis of Barriers to Entry', *Bell Journal of Economics*, Vol. 11, 1980, pp. 399–420.

Werden, G.J., Joskow, A.S. and Johnson, R.L. 'The effects of mergers on price and output: two case studies from the airline industry', *Managerial and Decision Economics*, Vol. 12, No 5, 1991, pp. 1–12.

Whinston, M.D. 'Tying, Foreclosure and Exclusion', *The American Economic Review*, Vol. 80, No 4, 1990, pp. 837–59.

Whish, Richard. *Competition Law*, third edition, Butterworths, 1993.

Whitelock, J., and Rees, M. 'Trends in Mergers, Acquisitions, and Joint Ventures in the Single European Market', *European Business Review*, Vol. 4, 1993, pp. 26–32.

Winston, C. 'Economic Deregulation: Days of Reckoning for Microeconomists', *Journal of Economic Literature*, Vol. XXXI, 1993, pp. 1263–89.

Winters, L.A. 'International Trade and "1992"', *European Economic Review*, Vol. 35, 1991, pp. 367–77.

Winters, L.A. and Venables, A.J. 'Europen integration trade and industry', in Winters, L.A. and Venables, A.J. (eds.), *European Integration: Trade and Industry*, Cambridge University Press, 1991.

Wright, D.J. 'Price Discrimination with Transportation Costs and Arbitrage', *Economics Letters*, Vol. 41, 1993, pp. 441–45.

Yamawaki, H., Sleuwaegen, L. and Weiss, L.W. 'Industry Competition and the Formation of the European Common Market', *Concentration and Price*, MIT Press, 1989, pp. 112–43.